BRITAIN'S SECOND EMBASSY TO CHINA

LORD AMHERST'S 'SPECIAL MISSION'
TO THE JIAQING EMPEROR IN 1816

BRITAIN'S SECOND EMBASSY TO CHINA

LORD AMHERST'S 'SPECIAL MISSION'
TO THE JIAQING EMPEROR IN 1816

CAROLINE M. STEVENSON

PRESS

For Rex

Published by ANU Press
The Australian National University
Acton ACT 2601, Australia
Email: anupress@anu.edu.au

Available to download for free at press.anu.edu.au

ISBN (print): 9781760464080
ISBN (online): 9781760464097

WorldCat (print): 1232217390
WorldCat (online): 1232217587

DOI: 10.22459/BSEC.2020

This title is published under a Creative Commons Attribution-NonCommercial-NoDerivatives 4.0 International (CC BY-NC-ND 4.0).

The full licence terms are available at
creativecommons.org/licenses/by-nc-nd/4.0/legalcode

Cover design and layout by ANU Press

Cover image: William Havell, *Sunrise on the Grand Canal*. Image courtesy of Bonhams, Sydney, and with acknowledgment of Sphinx Fine Art, London, original owners of the copyright.

This edition © 2021 ANU Press

Contents

Acknowledgements ix
Note on Terminology and Romanisation and Monetary Values xi
1. Introduction 1
2. The Political Setting of the Amherst Embassy 15
3. Origins of the Amherst Embassy: Canton and Sir George
    Thomas Staunton. 33
4. The View from London: John Barrow and Lord William
    Pitt Amherst 63
5. Amherst's Preparations for the Embassy 91
6. The Voyage from Portsmouth to 'Hong Kong' 123
7. Up the Coast of China and Arrival at Tianjin 143
8. The Imperial Banquet of 13 August 1816 and Progress
    to Tongzhou. 173
9. To Yuanmingyuan, Reception and Dismissal. 215
10. Overland to Canton: The British Cultural Encounter
    with China 245
11. Aftermath: Britain's Reaction to the Failure of the
    Amherst Embassy 285
12. Retrospect: Reflections on the Amherst Embassy 299
Bibliography 317
Appendix A: List of Persons and Their Salaries. 341
Appendix B: Presents and Cost of the Amherst Embassy. 345
Appendix C: The Total Cost of the Amherst Embassy 349
Appendix D: Ball's Secret Report (Commissioner of Teas
at Canton) 351

Appendix E: List of Chinese Officials Responsible for the
Conduct of the Amherst Embassy 355

Appendix F: Imperial Edict: 'Ceremonies to Be Observed
at the Audience of Leave' 359

Appendix G: Substance of an Edict Seen on the Walls of a Building
in the 8th Moon of the 21st Year of Kia King .361

Appendix H: Itinerary of the Amherst Embassy 363

Appendix I: Morrison's Letters to Amherst (1821) 377

Index 381

Acknowledgements

My interest in Chinese maritime trade was sparked in 1970 when my husband, who was posted to the Australian High Commission in Kuala Lumpur, returned home from a trip to Sarawak with a small parcel wrapped in newspaper and tied with pink plastic string. Inside was a small celadon saucer decorated with two raised fish at its centre that, according to the shopkeeper of the antique shop in Sibu, had 'come from China hundreds of years ago'. Further research revealed that it did indeed date from the thirteenth or fourteenth century and was one of the thousands of Chinese 'Song fish plates' exported throughout maritime Southeast Asia at this time. Thanks to this plate, my interest expanded to include later categories of Chinese export porcelains, culminating with a fascination for those wares brought to Britain during the eighteenth century at the height of the *chinoiserie* period. A further interest in the Canton trade, the British East India Company and British society during the Georgian and Regency period was a natural progression.

The opportunity to formally pursue my interest opened up with a return to academic study after a lapse of over 40 years through the Master of Studies program at The Australian National University (ANU) in 2009. I wish to thank my daughter Alex for bringing this course to my attention, and to its academic advisor, Anna Robinson, for her guidance and friendship during the four years of the degree.

The most stimulating course at this time concerned Western views of China conducted by Benjamin Penny at China in the World (CIW). Ben's invitation to study for a doctorate at CIW and his suggestion that the Amherst Embassy required serious research struck a responsive chord. I had come across references to the embassy in my readings, but its details remained unrecorded due to the predisposition of scholars to gloss over its importance as a significant event in Anglo–Chinese relations in the early nineteenth century. I was delighted to be given the opportunity to research the embassy in depth and this book is the result.

I wish to thank Ben, Gillian Russell and Richard Rigby for their time and support. Gillian's deep knowledge and enthusiasm for Georgian and Regency Britain was invaluable for assisting me in understanding the cultural context of British values and sensibilities of the period. Richard's vast knowledge of China and Chinese diplomacy derived from personal experience in an earlier foreign service career similarly revealed insight into the diplomatic response of the British at the time of the Amherst Embassy.

Research for this study was conducted at the National Library of Australia, Canberra and, in 2015, at the British Library and the National Archives, Kew. I am grateful for the financial assistance from CIW at this time and also for assistance in 2016 when I attended a conference at the University of Manchester to deliver a paper on the British selection of presents for the Jiaqing emperor. While in London, I stayed with my friends Elizabeth and Allan Kelly, and I cannot thank them enough for their wonderful hospitality and stimulating company.

Friends in Canberra have been very generous with their time and offers to read and comment on my work. I especially wish to thank Louis Magee and Ian Hancock for their enthusiastic and helpful comments on the first draft of this study. Particular thanks to Joan Ritchie, whose proofreading skills at an early stage were of considerable assistance.

The staff at CIW provided a most conducive atmosphere for study. Sharon Strange's patience with formatting and help solving numerous computer problems is most appreciated. I also wish to thank Karina Pelling at CartoGIS, College of Asia and the Pacific, ANU, for drawing the maps included in this book.

My final thanks, as always, go to my family. My son Bill and daughters Victoria and Alex remained a constant source of encouragement throughout the process of researching and writing this book. Special thanks go to my husband Rex, whose insights were invaluable and whose support made this possible.

Note on Terminology and Romanisation and Monetary Values

Note on Terminology and Romanisation

In general, Chinese place names, personal names and terms are rendered into *pinyin* unless they are domesticated into English or are so common in the English-language historical literature of the Canton trade system that it would be confusing to do otherwise. Thus, Beijing is referred to as 'Peking', although 'Pekin' was used by the British at the time. Guangzhou is referred to as 'Canton', and its port, Huangpu, 12 miles downstream, as 'Whampoa'. The Zhujiang River is called the 'Pearl River', and the 'Bogue' or 'Bocca Tigris' refers to the Humen Strait situated at the start of the Pearl River. Chinese Government officials are referred to as 'mandarins'; these include the Hoppo, the chief superintendent of customs at Canton, who oversaw the activities of officially appointed Chinese merchants, referred to as the Hong merchants. The names of Chinese merchants of Canton and Macao have been left in their romanised form. Identifications, as far as they are possible, follow Van Dyke (2011). Chinese and Manchu officials have been identified where possible. The names of the senior mandarins who greeted the British in northern China have been rendered into *pinyin* based on Fu (1966, vol. II, pp. 627–681). Their anglicised names are given in Appendix E.

Original spellings such as 'Embassador' and British spellings of Chinese names have been retained in direct quotations.

Note on Present-Day Values of Money in the Period of the Amherst Embassy

This study bases the value of the British Pound on the index agreed on in 2003 by the House of Commons Library, Bank of England and Office of National Statistics, where £10,000 in 1778 was approximately equivalent to £1 million in 2003 (Hague, 2004, p. 42).

Figure 1: Lord Amherst in his peer's robes.
Note: Engraving by S. Freeman, published in 1846, after painting by Sir Thomas Lawrence in 1821.
Source: National Library of Australia.

1

Introduction

In early August 1816, Lord William Pitt Amherst, designated British Ambassador of the Special Mission to the Chinese Empire, arrived off the coast of northern China on board the man-of-war, HMS *Alceste*. Disembarking from the embassy ships with his suite on 11 August, Amherst, then 43 years of age, travelled in a procession of Chinese junks to the port of Dagu where he stepped onto Chinese soil. His primary mission, in his capacity as the second British ambassador to arrive in China, was to proceed to the imperial court at Peking to seek the assistance of the Jiaqing emperor with placing British trade at Canton on a reliable basis. Recent disputes between provincial Chinese Government officials and members of the Select Committee of the British East India Company had stopped the important tea trade, risking the supply of tea to Britain and threatening a substantial loss of revenue for both Company coffers and the British Treasury.[1] The personal intervention of the emperor was considered necessary to check the capricious and vexatious actions of the Canton Government and the Chinese Hong merchants who facilitated the trade. The embassy also sought to secure the means of a direct and official communication with the imperial court at Peking to facilitate negotiation and conciliation of any future disputes. Amherst's mission was an abysmal failure. He never appeared before the Jiaqing emperor and his embassy was expelled on the day it reached Peking.

---

1   Sales of tea in Britain in 1815 amounted to 22,758,155 lbs worth £4,058,092 (Tuck, 2000, p. x, fn. 9). For the British at this time, tea is described by historians as an 'indispensable necessity of daily life' (Porter, 2001, p. 193).

Two earlier British embassies had been dispatched to China under the auspices of the British East India Company and authorised by the British Government. The first, led by Lt Col. Cathcart in 1788, was aborted on his death on the outward voyage.[2] The second was the famous Macartney Embassy to the Qianlong emperor (r. 1735–1796) that arrived in China in 1793. Armed with impressive gifts showcasing the latest cutting-edge advances in British science and technology to impress the emperor of British 'excellence', Macartney hoped to open the door to expanded trade with China. Despite Macartney being received with politeness and hospitality, his attempts to engage the emperor or his court in any negotiation were comprehensively rebuffed. Nevertheless, the Macartney Embassy has been the subject of extensive historical research and is a major topic in Anglo–Chinese history (see Bickers, 1993; Fairbank, 1942; Hevia, 1995; Peyrefitte, 1992; Pritchard, 1936). This is in contrast to the Amherst Embassy, which has received little scholarly attention, generally being relegated (at best) to a historical footnote as a follow-up to Macartney. Accordingly, the aim of this study is to present the first comprehensive and detailed account of the Amherst Embassy from its conception to its conclusion, and to reassess its historical importance for Anglo–Chinese relations and British perceptions of China in the period leading to the First Opium War.

In approaching an in-depth study of the Amherst Embassy and its aftermath, initial attempts to structure it around an overriding theme or themes started to distort or complicate the setting out of what actually happened. In the end, a detailed, largely narrative treatment proved critical in being able to make more reliable judgements about the roles played by its key members, especially its leader, Lord Amherst.

A central research question addresses why the British believed that the Amherst Embassy would succeed in its objectives at the Qing court[3] where the earlier and better-prepared Macartney Embassy had failed. The importance of the precedent established by the Macartney Embassy during its diplomatic encounter with the Qianlong emperor becomes clear, as does its critical role in governing the Amherst Embassy's reception

---

2   Charles Cathcart died of tuberculosis at Java. Amherst visited his tomb at the Anjere Roads on his outward voyage to China (*Journal of Jeffrey Amherst, son of Lord Amherst, on his father's mission to China* (n.d., n.p.) in British Library (BL) India Office Records (IOR) MSS EUR F 140/37).
3   This study refers to the Chinese court of 1644–1911 as the 'Qing court'. The Amherst Embassy is often referred to as being sent to the Jiaqing court, which refers to the Jiaqing emperor (r. February 1796 – September 1820) who was the seventh emperor of the Qing dynasty.

at the Qing court. The British belief that the Macartney Embassy had established a new basis for the conduct of Anglo–Chinese relations is a central argument of this study.

The carriage of the embassy is examined through Amherst's leadership role and the embassy's encounter with Qing officialdom. It seeks to reappraise Amherst's performance, judged by historians to be inept and indecisive due to his decision to follow the advice of Sir George Thomas Staunton, the second commissioner in the embassy, not to kowtow before the Jiaqing emperor, thereby resulting in the premature dismissal of the embassy.

A full understanding of the Amherst Embassy is possible only within the commercial context of the Canton trade system whose rules governed all Western trade in China and the traditional tributary system that governed Chinese foreign relations. These are major scholarly themes in Anglo–Chinese historiography, outlined briefly in Chapter 2. This chapter also includes a short summary of the Westphalian principles of diplomacy that governed British diplomatic practice. Also included is a brief outline of the political instability of the Pearl River Delta—the maritime approach to Canton—resulting, in part, from international tensions at the time of the Napoleonic Wars.

The decision in 1815 to send another embassy is traced from the origin of the idea in 1800 through to its immediate causes resulting from events at Canton and Macao in 1814. These are discussed in Chapter 3, primarily through the activities of Staunton, an active advocate of a second embassy throughout his long service at Canton.[4] Staunton had gained widespread fame in England as the 12-year-old boy who had held a brief conversation in Mandarin with the Qianlong emperor at the time of the Macartney Embassy. He had kept up his Mandarin studies on return to England and was the first Chinese linguist posted to Canton with the East India Company.[5] He was also acknowledged as Britain's leading sinologist.

The fourth chapter shifts attention to London. The response of both the British Government and the Secret Board of Directors of the East India Company to the dispatch of an embassy to the Qing court is

---

4   George Thomas Staunton is not to be confused with his father Sir George Leonard Staunton who was the Secretary in Lord George Macartney's Embassy to the Qianlong court in 1793. References to 'Staunton' in this study always refer to the younger Staunton, while his father is referred to as G. L. Staunton.

5   G. L. Staunton returned to England from China with a Chinese servant engaged specifically to enable his son to practice his Chinese (De Gray, 1860, p. cxxiv).

examined, making clear John Barrow's key role as the instigator of the Amherst Embassy.[6] Barrow, an influential senior official in the Admiralty, was not only a veteran of the Macartney Embassy, but was also an active commentator on China through his reviews in the *Quarterly Review* journal as well as a close friend and correspondent of Staunton. Of critical importance was his reliance on outdated intelligence, resulting from the 12-month turnaround in mail between London and Canton, for shaping both his arguments for another embassy in 1815 and for his assessment that it would be received positively by the Qing court and, thus, promise favourable outcomes.

Amherst's appointment as ambassador is examined in Chapters 4 and 5. This section is set within the framework of his personal life and professional experience, as well as his research and preparation for his mission. While the body of knowledge on European missions to China available to the British in 1815 appears meagre by modern standards, Amherst nevertheless assiduously set about the task of learning as much as he could from the experience of previous missions before his departure for China. Chapter 5 also describes the choice of presents for the emperor and his officials,[7] as well as the fitting out of the HMS *Alceste* for its long journey to China.

The journey to China via Madeira, Rio de Janeiro, Cape Town and Batavia outlined briefly in Chapter 6 also includes reference to initial British reactions to scenes at Brazil, providing an interesting contrast with their later reactions to China. Additionally, it looks at the manner in which the members of the embassy 'as Englishmen abroad' reacted to their mission and conducted themselves on the outward voyage in 1816.

The inclusion of several East India Company representatives based at Canton in the ambassadorial suite marked a major difference between the Amherst Embassy and the earlier Macartney Embassy. These men included Staunton, the Reverend Doctor Robert Morrison, John Francis Davis and Thomas Manning, who spoke Mandarin and had considerable local experience in dealing with the Cantonese authorities. They joined the *Alceste* and the other ships of the embassy squadron in the waters off Macao, out of sight of local Chinese officials, as a result of a prearranged

---

6   For an excellent short biography of Barrow, see Osborne's introduction to the reprint of John Barrow's *A voyage to Cochinchina* (1806/1975), pp. v–xvii.
7   A full list of the presents and their cost is provided in Appendix B.

secret rendezvous. The ships commenced their voyage northwards to Dagu on 13 July 1816, which is the subject of Chapter 7. Their arrival in the north of China marked a brief period of cordial and spontaneous encounters with local Chinese, revealing a relaxed social atmosphere in marked contrast to later official occasions.

Amherst was met by mandarins sent by the Jiaqing emperor to organise his reception at Peking within days of arrival in northern China, and their negotiations comprise Chapter 8. These are discussed in detail, which is essential to fully appreciate the stress and strain generated by the negotiations, not only for Amherst and his commissioners but also for the Qing envoys, over a period of several intense weeks. Such an understanding of the daily trials and tribulations of the diplomatic encounter reveal new insights and information on the progress of the embassy that challenges the accepted narrative that Amherst was inept and dependent on Staunton for its conduct. Attention is focused on two major diplomatic receptions arranged for Amherst. The first, examined in Chapter 8, is an imperial banquet held at Tianjin on 13 August 1816 within three days of his arrival in China that was critical for the outcome of the embassy. The second event was Amherst's arrival at the Yuanmingyuan Summer Palace on the outskirts of Peking in the early morning of 29 August 1816 from where he was expelled on the same day. The trauma of his treatment at Yuanmingyuan and his expulsion from Peking, as well as the unfolding repercussions from this event, are described in Chapter 9.

The only worthwhile activity remaining for the British after their premature dismissal from the Qing court was the opportunity to acquire new information about China as the embassy proceeded down the canals and waterways from Peking to Canton. Their impressions of Chinese culture, society and the environment gathered over a four-month period served to confirm and consolidate earlier British knowledge of China collected by the Macartney Embassy and are examined in Chapter 10. This analysis is followed in Chapter 11 by a discussion of the public reaction in Britain, including the media, to the treatment of the Amherst Embassy, while the concluding Chapter 12 provides a retrospective evaluation of Amherst and his embassy.

Secondary Sources on the Amherst Embassy

Scholars, it has been noted, have paid scant attention to the Amherst Embassy. Alain Peyrefitte's (1992) study of the Macartney Embassy has a brief chapter on the Amherst Embassy, while James Hevia's (1995) postcolonial anthropological analysis *Cherishing men from afar* devoted only a couple of pages to the mission. Hevia concentrated on the importance of the precedent of the earlier reception of the Macartney Embassy for the response of the Qing court to Amherst and blamed the failure of the latter embassy on British behaviour in the former embassy. Hevia argued that their misinterpretation of correct Qing ceremonial procedure signified by Macartney's refusal to kowtow ensured the impossibility of the British being incorporated into the 'centering process' of Qing guest ritual, which functioned to place foreign envoys into a hierarchy of desirable or inferior relations (p. 123). He concluded, correctly, that Amherst was received within the framework of stricter ceremonial protocols than those imposed on Macartney.

Staunton's career at Canton and on his return to England in 1817 is the subject of an unpublished PhD dissertation by Jodi Eastberg (2009).[8] Her analysis of Staunton at Canton and his role in the Amherst Embassy is detailed and comprehensive, but failed to place the Anglo–Chinese diplomatic encounter within the wider context of the Chinese tribute system. Shunhong Zhang's (2013) book, *British views on China at a special time (1790–1820)*, presented a thorough coverage of extracts from contemporary British publications on the nature of British views on China formed in response to the Macartney and Amherst embassies, but provided no analysis of their failure.

Some recent publications have discussed aspects of the Amherst Embassy. Stephen Platt's (2018) wideranging account of the events leading to the First Opium War provided a colourful account of the personalities and events leading to the British decision to send an embassy in 1816. Platt covered the major issues surrounding the background and progress of the embassy but, like Peyrefitte (1992), dismissed Amherst by flippantly describing him as an intellectual lightweight and arrogant fool for 'fussing pointlessly over the kowtow' (p. 181). This assessment, due perhaps to

---

8   I thank Shih-Wen Chen for bringing this thesis to my attention.

the sweeping and general nature of his book, short-changes Amherst. Platt neither focused on the important context of the failure of earlier Western missions to the Qing court nor consulted Amherst's personal papers held in the British Library; these reveal Amherst's research and clearly indicate that he had a strong grasp of the complex issues involved. Platt also failed to place the diplomatic encounter within the crucial context of the Chinese tributary system and ignored the fact that, had Amherst kowtowed and placed himself and his monarch in the position of a tributary vassal, the Qing court would never have deigned to negotiate terms on a basis of equality.

Peter Kitson, Professor of Romantic Literature and Culture at the University of East Anglia, made several references to the Amherst Embassy in his book, *Forging Romantic China* (2013). His aim was not to present a historical account of the embassy, but to examine the process whereby knowledge of China entered the British Romantic imagination through the literary works of Lamb, Byron, Shelly, Coleridge and others, as well as discussion on *chinoiserie* influence in the form of porcelains and gardens. Macartney's and Amherst's refusal to kowtow before the Qing emperor is explained within the framework of a narrow cultural context of the British asserting their values of firmness and rectitude, equality and reciprocity. Once again, the fundamental political significance of such an act functioning to denigrate the status of the British sovereign and his ambassador to a tributary vassal is overlooked.

Another book edited by Kitson and Robert Markley, published in 2016 to mark the 200th anniversary of the event, contains two essays on the embassy. Kitson makes a serious historical error by suggesting that Amherst was a 'former Governor of Bengal' before taking up his assignment to China, thereby insinuating that Amherst had prior firsthand 'Asian' experience (p. 60); in fact, Amherst had been an ambassador to the Two Sicilies from 1809 to 1811, and was not appointed governor of Bengal until 1823. Kitson further asserted that the embassy of 1816 was 'a mechanism disguising Britain's involvement in the opium trade', but then admits, accurately, that there is no historical evidence in the records of the British Government or the East India Company to substantiate such a claim (2016, pp. 56–82).⁹ The present study, which relies on extensive archival material, shows that the 'opium trade' was never raised specifically in any connection with the Amherst Embassy. Markley's (2016) essay suggested that the impoverished state of the Chinese countryside seen by the British in 1816, resulting in an inaccurate assessment of poverty and backwardness, was caused by the effects of a volcanic eruption on the Indonesian island of Sumbawa in April 1815 that critically degraded the environment in northern China. Such a claim overlooks the long-term economic recession experienced during the Jiaqing reign, which was characterised by rapid population growth, food shortages, extensive ecological degradation of waterways and soil fertility, and inadequate government maintenance of canals and rivers (Rowe, 2011).

Kitson also published an article in 2017 on the Amherst Embassy, focusing on the 'catastrophe' of its reception, which provides a useful short overview of the published material and draws heavily on Hevia's (1995) work in its concluding section on 'The Kowtow Controversy'. Gao Hao has written two articles specifically on the Amherst Embassy. Gao (2014) referred to British reactions to China on their return journey from Peking to Canton, and argued that the embassy enjoyed unprecedented freedom to explore the countryside and Chinese cities—a point accepted unconditionally by Kitson (2016). Gao's other article (2016, p. 610) claimed that the embassy was marked by a discordant 'inner kowtow' debate following a division of opinion on the kowtow among the senior members of the embassy. Both assertions are not supported by a detailed examination of the primary sources.

Eun Kyung Min's (2004) thought-provoking article examined British responses to China at the time of the Amherst Embassy in the context of British concepts of commercialism and civility. She made an important distinction between the members in the embassy who travelled directly from England, who read the kowtow as a mere formality to achieve their goals, and the reaction of East India Company men from Canton who

---

9   Kitson (2016) stated, 'Given the importance of the opium trade in funding the Company's trade in tea with China ... it is surprising to note that there is no obvious mention of the trade and British participation within it, in any of the documents, published or otherwise, relating to the Embassy' (p. 66). I have found a reference in the East India Company records dated 15 November 1815, where the Select Committee voiced its concern over the need for more money from the sale of opium 'to meet our demands', but this appears unconnected with both the initiative for, and the conduct of, the specific goals of the Amherst Embassy (Papers consultation with the President and Sir George Staunton, dated 15 November 1815, in BL IOR G/12/196 (Reel 1) F 2).

saw the kowtow in Chinese symbolic terms and interpreted it as a sign of servitude, unbecoming for a British ambassador to perform (Reverend Doctor Morrison, Chief Interpreter on the Amherst Embassy, as quoted in Min, 2004, p. 168). One of her themes, namely, Macartney's belief that a Chinese observance of the 'manners, tempers, and discipline' at the time of his embassy resulted in Chinese admiration for the British nation and a love for them as individuals, is developed in the present study as an important factor in shaping British perceptions of the likely reception of the Amherst Embassy.

Ulrike Hillemann presented a useful and insightful five-page summary of the Amherst Embassy in her book, *Asian empire and British knowledge* (2009, pp. 75–80). She concluded that, because of Amherst's treatment at the Qing court, British perceptions of the Chinese emperor changed from one of a dignified, rational and enlightened despot to an uncivilised Tartar (p. 80), but made no mention of the tribute system's significance in dictating Chinese terms during the diplomatic encounter.

Recent scholarship in English has resulted in several published historical accounts of both the Qianlong and Jiaqing reigns that draw extensively on Chinese archival sources. Matthew Mosca's (2013) examination of Qing foreign policy initiatives towards Tibet and British India at this time provided the background for the broader context of Anglo–Chinese international relations, including the decline of Qing military power noted during the Anglo–Nepal War (1814–1816) (p. 184). Similarly, Wengsheng Wang's (2014) examination of the internal turmoil confronting the reign of the Jiaqing emperor and his response to it in the immediate period before the Amherst Embassy was invaluable for illuminating the specific context in which the British were received at Peking.

Patrick Tuck's Introduction to the reprint of Sir George Thomas Staunton's *Notes of proceedings and occurrences, during the British embassy to Pekin, in 1816* (1824/2000, pp. vii–xlii) remains the most thorough and comprehensive examination of the political context of the Amherst Embassy. Tuck's detailed and focused analysis falls on Staunton's role as the second commissioner in the embassy whose advice to Amherst not to kowtow before the Jiaqing emperor, Tuck argued, resulted in the embassy's failure (p. vii). His conclusion that the embassy was a 'fiasco' denigrates Amherst's reputation and dismisses the embassy as incompetent and historically insignificant (p. viii).

Primary Sources

The author's lack of Chinese linguistic ability has resulted in this study being based on English-language sources only and needing to rely on English translations of Chinese documents and edicts published in Lo-Shu Fu (1996) and Dun Li (1969). Within this context, this study seeks to provide a detailed and comprehensive account of the Amherst Embassy from a British perspective that nonetheless highlights the profound cultural differences that separated the West and, in this case, Britain from China at this time. It also underlines the continued failure of European-style diplomacy to engage the Qing court in this period as it had during the Macartney Embassy some decades earlier. As a corollary, it needs to be noted that the British in the first decades of the nineteenth century had very limited access to information on the Qing Government and its thinking beyond the immediate and very different environment of Canton. The information that they did have at hand is documented and presented in the subsequent chapters of this study. It is this body of knowledge, taken from British primary sources, that highlights the limitations and inadequacies of the 'intelligence' available to the British in the task they had set themselves. It is important to note that the assessments and value judgements about China referred to in this study are those of the British observers and commentators writing at this time.

Members of the Amherst Embassy published several accounts of their experiences in China on their return to England. Well known to scholars and referred to extensively in this study, these include the journal of Henry Ellis, Third Commissioner in the embassy, published in 1817 and acknowledged as the 'official' account of the mission. Clarke Abel, the surgeon and naturalist with the embassy, published his account in 1818, while Robert Morrison's *Memoir* of the embassy was published in 1820. Staunton's *Notes of proceedings and occurrences, during the British embassy to Pekin, in 1816* was printed privately in 1824. John Francis Davis's account in his *Sketches of China*, published later in 1841, is also widely referenced. The ships of the embassy squadron departed for a survey of the Korean coast and the Ryukyu Islands after Amherst disembarked at Dagu, and their experiences were subsequently the subject of two published accounts. The first was by John M'Leod, the physician on board the *Alceste*, whose book the *Voyage of His Majesty's Ship Alceste* was published in 1818. Basil Hall, the captain of HMS *Lyra*, which accompanied the *Alceste*, wrote several versions of his experiences along the Korean coast and at the Ryukyu Islands, including *Narrative of a voyage to Java, China, and the Great Loo-Choo Island* published in 1840.[10] Reference to these are made in passing in this study, but no examination is made of either the surveys or British experiences at these places.

This study refers to three unpublished journals that have received little attention from historians of the Amherst Embassy. The first is by the Rt Hon. Jeffrey Amherst, Amherst's 14-year-old son who accompanied the embassy as a page to his father, found in the British Library.[11] Zhang (2013) listed this journal in his bibliography but made no reference to it in his text, although he does refer, in passing, to the second resource, namely, the 'Diaries' of Amherst's private secretary, Henry Hayne.[12] William Fanshawe Martin, who travelled with the embassy as a 'First Class Volunteer' and midshipman on the *Alceste*, also left an account of his experiences in China.[13] This is also a rarely referenced resource, although Gao (2016) cited it in relation to the kowtow question. A resource that appears to be unknown to historians of the embassy is a volume of private letters sent to Amherst from his sister, Elizabeth Hale, who lived in Canada. While these contain little coverage of his appointment as ambassador to China, they are nevertheless valuable for the insight they provide into Amherst's private life (Hall & Shelton, 2002).

The official records of the Amherst Embassy are found in the British Library. Historians of the embassy have focused exclusively on the India Office Records (IOR) of the East India Company for China 1815–17 (referred to as the G/12/196, G/12/197 and G/12/198 files),[14] which include the *Papers relating to the embassy to China in the year 1815/1816* and *Papers relating to the embassy to China in the year 1817/1818*. Further

---

10 Hall had previously published his *Account of a voyage of discovery to the west coast of Corea, and the Great Loo-choo Island* (1818). The present study refers to his *Narrative of a voyage to Java, China, and the Great Loo-Choo Island: With accounts of Sir Murray Maxwell's attack on the Chinese batteries, and of an interview with Napoleon Bonaparte, at St. Helena* (1840/1865).
11 *Journal of Jeffrey Amherst, son of Lord Amherst, on his father's mission to China* (n.d.) in BL IOR MSS EUR F 140/37. Only a few pages of the original journal have survived. It was transcribed by Constance Amherst in February 1870 and is found in the Amherst Papers, BL IOR MSS EUR F 140/37.
12 'Diaries of Henry Hayne' in *China through Western eyes: Manuscript records of traders, travellers, missionaries and diplomats, 1792-1842* (Vols. 1–4) (1996). Hereafter referred to as 'Hayne, n.d.'.
13 William Fanshawe Martin, 'Journal', *Martin Family Papers, 1793-1860*, BL ADD MSS 41346-41475.
14 *East India Company Factory Records Part 2. China: India Office Records* cited as BL IOR G/12/196 and BL IOR G/12/197 for April 1815–1817.

extracts of these files are found in H. B. Morse's *The chronicles of the East India Company trading to China, 1635-1834* (1926/1966, Vol. 3), covering the period 1805–1820.

The seminal reference for the historical context of the first Anglo–Chinese diplomatic encounter is Lord Macartney's *An embassy to China: Lord Macartney's journal 1793–1794*, first published in 1962.[15] This volume contains Macartney's account of his visit to the court of the Qianlong emperor as well as Cranmer-Byng's detailed notes on Chinese officials and the places visited by the embassy. Earlier extracts of Macartney's journal are found in the second volume of Barrow's (1807) biography of Lord Macartney. Barrow's account of his own impressions of China at the time of the Macartney Embassy, *Travels in China*, first published in 1804, was instrumental for influencing the views of China held by the members of the Amherst Embassy.

The major primary resources for this study are two other archives, one that has received little or no previous attention from historians of the Amherst Embassy, and one that is referred to only by Eastberg (2009) in her study of Staunton and Platt, *Imperial twilight* (2018). The first consists of the papers of William Pitt Amherst, 1st Earl of Amherst, found in the British Library under the filing code of the BL IOR MSS EUR F 140.[16] The collection includes official and private correspondence and official papers covering Amherst's appointment as envoy to Naples (1809–1811), ambassador to China (1815–1817) and his term as governor-general of Bengal (1823–1828).

The second archive is housed at Duke University and consists of Sir George Thomas Staunton's private letters sent to his parents from Canton during his stay in China in the period 1800–1817.[17] These letters provide valuable insight into conditions at Canton and are similarly referred to extensively in this study in Chapter 3 in the period leading to

---

15 Cranmer-Byng (1962, pp. xi, 332) records that the original journal remained with Lord Macartney's descendants until sold in 1854. The journal of three volumes remained in a private library in England until sold to a private collector in Peking in 1913. In 1917, the volumes were sold again and taken to Tokyo where they remained in the Oriental Library. Cranmer-Byng's (1962) transcription represents the first time the journal was published in its entirety.
16 Amherst Papers, BL IOR MSS EUR F 140.
17 Letters from the Papers of George Thomas Staunton to his mother during his time working for the East India Company in Canton, Rare Book, Manuscript and Special Collections Library, Duke University. Retrieved from www.china.amdigital.co.uk. Hereafter referred to as the '*Staunton Letters*' with the place and date of writing provided where known. I thank Shih-Wen Chen for bringing this archive to my attention.

the dispatch of the embassy. Staunton's memoirs, printed privately in 1856, are an invaluable resource for his reflective insights into his experiences at Canton and his subsequent life in England. His other book, on China's commercial relations with Britain, published in 1821, contains a number of useful essays on the state of British trade at Canton.

A slim but interesting primary source not previously cited by historians is referred to in this study, namely, Lord Amherst's 'Dinner Book' (in Kent History and Library Centre, Amherst Manuscripts: Family Papers, U1350-E16), which lists the dinner guests invited to his Mayfair residence in the immediate period before and after his mission.

Selected direct quotations from contemporary sources and accounts of the embassy written by its members have been used liberally throughout this study to convey an accurate sense of period and especially the English reaction to an alien environment. One of this study's objectives is to depict as vividly as possible what the ambassadorial party looked like on its progress through China and how its members reacted to the daily challenges facing them. Direct quotations best achieve this goal. Inevitably, as noted above, this study is told from a British perspective, providing their views and opinions of China and the Qing court formed at the time.

Some of the personalities associated with the Amherst Embassy are notable for several firsts. Staunton's translation of a pamphlet on inoculation into Mandarin in 1805 was the first information on the medical procedure available to the Chinese and was later distributed to Chinese officials at the time of the Amherst Embassy.[18] Morrison, the senior interpreter of the embassy who arrived at Canton in 1807, was the first Protestant missionary sent to China. He was also the author of *A dictionary of the Chinese language* as well as the translator of several biblical texts into Chinese.[19] Accounts of the embassy also contain the first reference to 'Hong Kong' island in British sources, as the embassy used Hong Kong to replenish its supply of fresh water before sailing to northern China.

---

18 In May 1805, the Company's surgeon, Dr Pearson, received some smallpox vaccine from a Portuguese ship recently arrived at Macao (Morse, 1926/1966, vol. 3, pp. 16–17). Abel (1818, pp. 218–219) wrote that Pearson's first attempts at inoculation were 'pertinaciously opposed' but were accepted eventually by the Cantonese Government and were strongly supported by the Hong merchants.

19 These works included *Hora Sinica: Translations from the popular literature of the Chinese* (1812); *A grammar of the Chinese language* (1815); *A dictionary of the Chinese language: Chinese and English arranged according to the radicals* (1815); and *A view of China for philological purposes, containing a sketch of Chinese chronology, geography, government, religion & customs* (1817).

Travelling on board the *Alceste* was the wife of the boatswain, Mrs Loy, arguably the first European woman to visit northern China (M'Leod, 1818/1820, pp. 133–134).

The members of the embassy subscribed to the earlier views of Macartney who made a distinction between the behaviour of 'the Chinese' and their Manchu or 'Tartar' overlords.[20] Staunton (1824), for example, complained of the 'puffed-up Tartar family on the throne' whose uncivil and rude conduct was assessed as contrary to every 'Chinese' principle of conduct (p. 125). Amherst referred to the Qing court as the 'Tartar court' and the kowtow as the 'Tartar ceremony' in his official reports of the embassy. Morrison (1839, pp. 8–9) also made this distinction in relation to the kowtow ceremony. Similarly, the British attributed the actions of Qing court officials or mandarins towards them as governed by a fear of incurring the suspicion or disapproval of their superiors who reported directly to the emperor (Ellis, 1817, p. 202).

This study examines the Amherst Embassy using a traditional historical approach addressing causes, responses and outcomes resulting from a brief but intensive encounter between the British and Chinese. Timothy Hampton's (2009) book, *Fictions of embassy*, is referenced extensively in this study for the practices of Westphalian diplomacy and the protocols of diplomatic action. Some aspects of the encounter, however, lend themselves to inter-disciplinary analysis. Accordingly, the imperial banquet given for Amherst on his arrival at Tianjin is examined within an anthropological context as this was an occasion rich in ceremony and ritual. Consideration is also given to British sensory experiences as the embassy travelled through China where alien sights, smells, sounds, tastes and touch had a profound impact on the visitors' sensibilities.[21] Reference to the work of sensory historians assisted in enabling a greater understanding of British reactions and perceptions of China at this time (e.g. Howes & Lalonde, 1991). Finally, Richard Sennett's (1994) book, *Flesh and stone*, explained the importance of bodily comfort as a major factor in the way people respond culturally to their environment. His theme that 'a stressed and unhappy experience of our bodies makes us more aware of the world in which we live' (pp. 24–25) is especially relevant, it will be seen, to the conduct of the Englishmen of the Amherst Embassy during their time in China.

---

20   Porter (2001, p. 234) referred to Macartney's view of the 'foreignness of the Qing Dynasty' whose rulers were not 'Chinese' but Manchu or 'Tartar'.
21   This study's main references for placing British reactions to the Chinese sensory environment are the essays found in Howes (2005).

2

The Political Setting of the Amherst Embassy

China's worldview had a major impact on the fortunes of the Amherst Embassy and it is important to understand this context for framing what was a significant diplomatic event in Anglo–Chinese relations in the opening decades of the nineteenth century. British interest in China at this time was based solely on trade and profit and not on territory or conquest, unlike its activities in India and elsewhere around the globe. The dispatch of the Amherst Embassy represented a genuine British endeavour to negotiate a better trade relationship at Canton and, in the event that these negotiations were successful, to secure further trade concessions from China.

The Amherst Embassy, like its predecessor the Macartney Embassy of 1793, was received at the Qing court within the context of the traditional tributary system that governed Chinese international relations. The specific problems at Canton that initiated the dispatch of both embassies were caused by the constraints of the 'Canton trade system' established by the Qing court by 1760 to both contain and govern expanding European trade with China. An understanding of this system, as well as the principles and practices enshrined in the Westphalian system of European diplomacy that governed British diplomatic actions, provides a vital context for the approach, activities and reactions of the Amherst Embassy in its efforts to negotiate with the Qing court. Brief outlines of the British East India Company (henceforth referred to as 'the Company'), the political–military environment of the Pearl River (on which Canton was situated) in the immediate period before the Amherst Embassy, as well as the importance of the growth of British nationalism at this time, are also included to provide a wider context for an understanding of the embassy.

The Tribute System

The 'tribute system' has been the subject of extensive scholarship and debate by Western historians.[1] General references define it as 'a system under which foreign states submitted to Chinese suzerainty by exchanging gifts for trading privileges in China', where the emperor, designated the Son of Heaven, demanded 'submission from those outside the empire who were considered barbarians' (Perkins, 1999, p. 533). Foreign countries wishing to trade with China sent missions to the Chinese capital to submit to the sovereignty of the Chinese emperor, acknowledged by performing the kowtow before him. In return, permission was granted for the right to trade at stipulated times and designated ports along the Chinese coast (Perkins, 1999, p. 533). The tribute system applied to all of China's external relations but for the purposes of this study of the Amherst Embassy, the focus is on maritime Southeast Asia, the direction from which early Western maritime traders approached China.

O. W. Wolters, in his seminal study of Sino-Malay relations in the fourteenth century, explained the manner in which the Chinese emperor was perceived as the Son of Heaven that situated him above all other earthly sovereigns (1970, pp. 24–25). The emperor's efficacy was due to his being the repository of *de* (moral power or 'superior virtue') that functioned to legitimise his authority as well as defining Chinese cultural superiority and positioning him above all other sovereigns, who by definition were considered inferior or barbarians. Chinese, as well as barbarians, were attracted to the concept of *de*.[2] Foreign rulers drawn to *de* sent periodic gifts or tribute brought by envoys in 'acknowledgment of their cultural homage'

---

1 References on the 'tribute system' are numerous and include Andornino (2006), Fairbank (1942), Fairbank and Teng (1941) and Hevia (1995). Wills (2009) argued that, by the time of the Qing dynasty, the tributary system applied only to a handful of vassal states such as 'Korea, Ryukyu, Vietnam, and Siam' (p. 182). Nevertheless, for the purposes of this brief summary, reference made to the longer historical tradition of the tribute system serves to illustrate its cultural context beyond its economic aspect and is useful for a deeper appreciation of its role in Chinese external relations.

2 Staunton's (1821) translation of the *Narrative of the Chinese embassy to the Khan of the Tourgouth Tartars, in the years 1712, 13, 14, & 15* refers to the Khan being attracted to China: 'I have admired from afar your heavenly court, and the most excellent and most resplendent virtues of your Emperor; the contemplation of such sublime perfection made me wish to draw near, so as actually to behold the heavenly countenance' (p. 204).

to the Chinese emperor, thus ensuring order and security built up through a system of alliances.³ The tribute system rested on an ideological platform that distinguished between civilisation and barbarism where compliance with correct ritual behaviour was essential for the tribute system's operation. The historian Simon Leys stressed the importance of rites in the Confucian order where 'the true cohesion of a society is secured not through legal rules but through ritual observances' (1997, p. xxv). Wolters (1970) quoted Confucius on the nature of *de* to explain its function in the context of ensuring order in international relations:

> If such a [well-ordered] state of affairs exists, yet the people of far-off lands still do not submit, then the ruler must attract them by enhancing the prestige [*de*] of his culture; and when they have been truly attracted, he contents them. And where there is contentment there will be no upheavals. (p. 25)

The concept of submission and being attracted to embrace Chinese culture was an anathema to the British and, it will be seen, the antithesis of Westphalian principles. But Wolters explains that the verification of the power of *de* and its efficacy to attract vassal princes made possible the formation of an extensive trade network founded on the maritime trade routes to China. Emperors who ruled 'all under heaven' showed compassion to the men who had 'travelled from afar' and bestowed protection and titles on vassal princes who returned to their homelands with their right to rule legitimised by the Chinese emperor and transformed due to their contact with Chinese civilisation (Cranmer-Byng, 1962, p. 6). In this way, peace resulting from the tribute system operated as an external network of control, whereby security and stability reigned in the distant western oceans as Chinese influence spread out in a series of concentric circles to embrace the outlying petty states of maritime Southeast Asia (Hamashita, 1997).

The tributary system has been described by Richard Smith (2013, pp. 79–81) as a highly sophisticated, remarkably flexible and perfectly rational system of managing the world. Its specific nature changed in response to different historical forces impacting on China at different times; for example, during the Yuan dynasty, the power of *de* was replaced by military force. The historian Anthony Reid (1996, p. 17) wrote that in keeping with the Mongol's view as 'world conquerors', submission to the emperor was enforced in Java in 1293 through the dispatch of 20,000 soldiers by Kublai Khan to punish

---

3   These are Alexander Woodside's (1971, p. 235) words used in the context of the Vietnamese tributary system, but are applicable to this context.

King Kertanegara for 'his insolence'. The tribute system was restructured at the time of the Ming dynasty by the Hongwu emperor (r. 1368–1398) who restricted foreign maritime trade to official tribute missions and prohibited all private overseas trade (Wang, 2003, p. 53).

The incoming Qing dynasty in the seventeenth century adopted the essential tenets of the Ming policy, but with the consolidation of Qing rule in the early 1680s the Kangxi emperor (r. 1661–1722) issued an important and innovative edict that separated trade from tribute.[4] A distinction was made between traditional tribute vassal states that were still bound by the conventions of the tributary system and other non-tributary commercial countries that were now permitted to trade with China without having to go through the formality of sending an embassy. The tribute system remained, however, and the imperial audience represented its core ceremony (Wills, 2009, p. 2) where visiting ambassadors or princes performed *sangui jiukou*, or 'three prostrations and nine knockings' (Rawski, 1998, p. 149) of the head (to the ground) before the emperor.[5] Trade with vassal states such as Siam, for example, continued to operate at the diplomatic level and was permitted only at times of periodic missions to the Qing court to pay tribute. General, non-tributary trade and maritime trade with Southeast Asia now fell entirely into the hands of Chinese native private traders who were allowed to travel and trade abroad (Wills, 2009, p. 2).[6]

A number of Chinese ports were now opened to European trade including Shanghai, Ningbo, Dinghai, Wenzhou, Quanzhou, Chaozhou and Xiamen (Zhao, 2013, p. 111). English ships started arriving in greater numbers by the late seventeenth and early eighteenth centuries seeking Chinese luxury goods for a growing English market, but their numbers were still very small as evidenced by the fact that in 1723, for example, only four British ships visited Canton (Howard, 1994, p. 24).[7] This number is in stark contrast with the growth of a massive Asian junk trade carried on throughout Chinese ports by native Chinese traders and sailors—a fact often lost sight of in Western historical accounts given their emphasis on European trade with China at this time.

---

4 Evelyn Rawski (1998, p. 198) pointed out that the Qing were quick to demonstrate they were prepared to carry on Ming state rituals.
5 The British referred to the kowtow ceremony as '*san-kwei-kew-kow*', referred to as 'thrice kneeling and nine times bowing the head to the ground' (Ellis, 1817, p. 124).
6 Thai traders of Chinese ethnicity soon learned how to circumvent the official rules and traded openly to China as 'Chinese natives' using Chinese-style junks (Cushman, 1993, p. 129).
7 The *Macclesfield*, an English ship, returned from Canton with a cargo of Chinese products in the 1699–1700 season that was responsible for creating a demand for Chinese luxury products (Howard, 1994, p. 22).

The Canton Trade System

Figure 2: Painting by an unknown Chinese artist of the foreign factories or 'hongs' on the Canton waterfront in 1805 showing the location of the British factory situated between the Swedish and Dutch factories.
Source: Wikipedia Commons.

The growth of the *chinoiserie* craze in Europe, and especially in Britain, in the first half of the eighteenth century saw a rapid increase in the number of European ships arriving annually at Chinese ports.[8] The Qianlong emperor responded and, by 1760, edicts had been issued aimed at containing, controlling and regulating Western trade with the Chinese empire, which remained in effect until the signing of the Treaty of Nanjing in 1842 at the settlement of the First Opium War. Referred to as the 'Canton trade system' by Western historians, the decree laid down several stipulations for Western trade.[9] Trade was confined to the port of Canton and permitted only between November and March, after which all Western traders had to retire to the Portuguese settlement of Macao or return to Europe. Western merchants, known as supercargoes, were restricted to a six-acre enclave, measuring 400 yards in length and 300 yards in width, on the riverfront

---

8   See Van Dyke (2007) for a comprehensive history of Chinese trade with Western nations.
9   For a full account of these regulations, see the Memorial dated 1759 written by the governor-general of the Liangguang provinces, Li Shiyao, on 'Five Rules to Regulate Foreigners' in Li (1969, pp. 29–34).

in the suburbs of southwest Canton where they lived and worked in their respective warehouses or national Factories.[10] They were forbidden to enter the walled city of Canton and foreign women were not allowed. Westerners were forbidden to learn or speak Chinese and all communication between them and the Chinese Government was conducted only through officially appointed Chinese linguists. The reliability and truthfulness of the linguists in translating Western concerns and grievances was often suspect, but European traders had no other mechanism for reporting these to the Chinese Government. A major grievance was the fact that Western traders were not protected by a formal treaty governed by rights and obligations, nor was there any certainty that guaranteed their continuing presence at Canton. Further, periodic transgressions of Chinese law by British sailors caused serious disputes between the provincial government and Company officials who were understandably opposed to Englishmen being judged and sentenced by Chinese law.

The relationship between the Select Committee of the Company, which held the British tea monopoly and formed the major British merchant institution in China, and local authorities was critical for the wellbeing of trade at Canton. The provincial government was in the charge of the governor-general or viceroy who presided over the provinces of Guangdong and neighbouring Guangxi, and who worked in association with the viceroy of Canton (Cranmer-Byng, 1962, p. 8). The most important figure from the Company's Select Committee's perspective was the Hoppo, or chief superintendent of customs, who worked independently of the viceroy and was the emperor's financial representative at Canton. The Hoppo was appointed for three years, having purchased his commission at the imperial court. Cranmer-Byng (1962) adds that:

> During his term of office [the Hoppo] would have to remit considerable sums of money to the Imperial Treasury, to say nothing of magnificent 'presents' to the highest officials at Court: yet during his short period of office as Hoppo he usually managed to amass a fortune for himself. (p. 8)

---

10 A 'Factory' refers to a trading establishment in a foreign port and were also known as 'Hongs' in Canton (Conner, 2009, pp. 4–5). Factory buildings were leased from Chinese Hong merchants and built in a European style. The ground floor held the offices, storerooms or *godowns*, counting rooms and facilities for the 'compradore' and the servants. The compradore was responsible for food and other supplies for the Factory. The public rooms and dining rooms were situated on the first floor, while the private and sleeping accommodation of the Company members occupied the second floor. Teas were weighed, packed and sealed in crates and sent to the Company ships waiting at Whampoa (Crossman, 1991).

2. THE POLITICAL SETTING OF THE AMHERST EMBASSY

The Hoppo oversaw the small group of licensed Hong merchants consisting of 12 members who formed themselves into an association known as the co-Hong (Cranmer-Byng, 1962, p. 12). All foreign trade at Canton was handled and controlled by co-Hong merchants whose members 'acted together under pressure from the local officials to ensure control over the foreign merchants' (Cranmer-Byng, 1962, p. 12).[11] As a result of their role as the intermediaries between foreign merchants and the provincial government, Hong merchants were often caught in the middle between the demands of government officials or mandarins and those of the Company. Cranmer-Byng (1962) concludes that the actions of the provincial officials were critical for both the supercargoes and Hong merchants:

> The Supercargoes were constantly afraid that the Co-Hong merchants would be used by the Canton officials as an even more efficient tool for 'squeezing' the foreign merchants. Its members were exposed to the greed and extortion of the local officials, especially the Hoppo and his crew, and bankruptcies were frequent. (p. 12)

Nevertheless, the historian Paul van Dyke has evaluated the Canton trade system as an extremely sophisticated and successful mechanism for controlling and regulating the great amount of Western trade conducted through Canton, where commerce flourished, foreign investment flowed into the port and foreigners 'were attracted to China in increasing numbers' (2011, p. 3). From the Company's perspective, however, the system became intolerable at times, specifically because the supercargoes were 'at the mercy of the whims of the local officials' and because they did not have any mechanism of appeal to the emperor (Cranmer-Byng, 1962, p. 13).[12]

---

11 Cushman (1993, p. 29) added that, in addition to the Hong merchants who were in charge of Western shipping, two other co-Hong merchants were delegated at this time; one was in charge of Siamese tribute and trade, and one was in charge of the native coastal trade from Fukien and Chaozhou arriving and departing at Canton.

12 This assessment applies to the period before the Macartney Embassy, but it will be seen that it was just as applicable at the time of the Amherst Embassy.

The Westphalian System of European Diplomacy

A diplomatic exchange at the Qing court at the time of the Amherst Embassy was fraught with difficulties due to the difference in British and Chinese values and the institutional practices governing their respective diplomatic processes. The British approach was governed by the principles of the Westphalian system of diplomacy established in 1648 by the Treaty of Westphalia, which ended the Thirty Years War in Europe (Hampton, 2009, p. 116).[13] Fundamental to its operation was the concept of all sovereign nation states, regardless of size or power, being treated equally under international law. The ambassador's main task was to uphold his sovereign's honour at a foreign court (Mattingly, 1995/2010, p. 211).

Westphalian diplomacy, according to the historian Tim Hampton, involves three forms of action governed by set customs, ritual and law. The first is negotiation, which is the chief function of the ambassador, where the role of language as the message transmitter is fundamental in cross-cultural exchanges in addition to the need to understand gestures and body language. Therefore, diplomacy is not only a cultural exchange, but also a site of 'linguistic negotiation' (Hampton, 2009, pp. 5–6). This process is the most fragile of political encounters. The British travelled to the Qing court in 1816 to appeal to the emperor and conduct negotiations that would place trade at Canton on a more reliable basis. Included in the ambassadorial party were a number of Mandarin-speaking Englishmen who it was hoped would facilitate this process.

The second form of action taking place within Westphalian diplomacy is mediation, which, in a Western context, refers to the axiom that the interests of one party affects the interests of all parties (Hampton, 2009, p. 8). Again, the British were hopeful that their goal of greater trade with China and subsequent economic gains would be recognised as beneficial to both parties.

---

13   This system saw 176 plenipotentiaries from 194 European rulers codify laws between sovereign states based on the principle of the law between nations (Hampton, 2009, p. 117).

The third form of action is representation, which refers to the complex question of who, precisely, the ambassador is representing (Hampton, 2009, p. 8). This was a fundamental issue in the context of the Amherst Embassy where instructions were received from both the British Government and the Company Directors.

Ultimately, Western diplomacy centred on the principle that the person of the ambassador stood for the persona of the sovereign they represented when visiting another prince. An ambassador was invested further with political authority to speak on behalf of their sovereign at another court where the status of both sovereigns, in theory, was equal (Hampton, 2009, p. 10). Diplomatic locations were important sites of action and agency where an ambassador, while an intruder, had the inviolable right 'to travel to and from his destination' without being molested (Hampton, 2009, p. 75). This space was extremely difficult for the ambassador who was situated outside the geographical and legal confines of their own country and was dependent on the goodwill of foreigners for safe passage. Their power was endowed by those whom they represented and their reception depended on their host's recognition of the status of those who sent them. Both their behaviour and demeanour were important. Bodily appearance and actions, such as gestures, movements and dress, together with language were prescribed by protocols of reception and underpinned diplomatic engagements. Ultimately, an ambassador was judged by their hosts through the manner in which they presented themselves while representing another (Hampton, 2009, p. 9). The notion of the inviolability of the personage of an ambassador is a basic principle of Western diplomatic protocol. Their special status and that of their retinue renders the personnel of the embassy 'untouchable' and 'sacred' and serves to separate and isolate them from their host society. Individual perceptions and interpretations of the host society and culture made at the time of a diplomatic reception are governed by emotions formed under the pressures and outcomes of diplomatic encounters. The nature of Amherst's reception at the Summer Palace of Yuanmingyuan, it will be seen, was instrumental in the British reappraising their ideas of the Qing court and China.

The British East India Company[14]

A distinction needs to be made between British trade with China conducted by private merchants, known as the Country Trade, and the members of the Company. Private merchants from India exported large quantities of textiles and brought opium into China. Silver received from these sales was, in turn, exchanged for bank notes issued by the Company and drawn on banks in India and London. In the absence of a Chinese demand for British goods, tea could only be procured with payment in silver. The principal business of the Company was its highly profitable monopoly of the tea trade, which was reaffirmed in 1813 at the time of the British Parliament renewing the Company's charter (Morse, 1926/1966, vol. 3, p. 204).[15] Taxes from the sale of tea paid an estimated £4 million into the coffers of the British Government at the time of the Amherst Embassy (Staunton, 1822, p. 167).

The British East India Company was an amalgamation of two companies formed in 1708, namely, the joint-stock 'Governor and Company of Merchants of London Trading to the East Indies' formed in 1600 and the 'The English Company Trading to the East Indies' founded in 1698. Known as 'The United Company of Merchants of England Trading into the East Indies', it henceforth controlled all direct trade between England and Asia. The Company was governed by a 24-member Court of Directors, elected by stockholders. Decisions were made at East India House, located in Leadenhall Street, London.

The *Regulating Act of 1783* and *India Act of 1784* placed the affairs of the Company under a Board of Control of six members appointed by the British Government in charge of overseeing the governance of India. The head of the board during discussion on the inception of the Amherst Embassy was Lord Buckinghamshire, who died of a heart attack two days before the mission departed Portsmouth for China.[16] His place was taken by George Canning, one of Amherst's closest friends. The Company's management at Canton was conducted by a three-

---

14   Specific references on the British East India Company at Canton include Bowen (2006), Greenberg (1969), Keay (1991), Philips (1940), Van Dyke (2007) and Wakeman Jr (1978). For an in-depth study of the Company in India, see Dalrymple (2019).
15   Trade between England and India was opened to free traders at this time.
16   Buckinghamshire had been in ill health and had taken the waters at Bath in the week preceding his death. He died while riding in Hyde Park (Charles Grant to Amherst, 13 April 1816, in BL IOR MSS EUR F 140/38 (a)).

member Select Committee headed by the president of the committee. Extraordinary matters concerning Company ships or decisions on the dispatch of an embassy were managed by a small Secret Committee of three or four members sitting in London. Their instructions to the Select Committee at Canton were relayed via the ships of the season, which took six months to reach their destination. Therefore, the turnaround for responses and reporting on the latest developments was 12 months.

The British Factory at Canton housed 22 members in 1812.[17] These included eight supercargoes and three writers. Supercargoes were responsible for the 'Indiamen' that anchored each trading season at the island of Whampoa, 12 miles downstream from Canton. In 1812, these numbered between 20 and 30 ships whose respective crews added up to thousands of British sailors who visited the European enclave of Canton on leave and were often involved in altercations with local people. The smooth operation of the trade was dependent on relationships 'either direct or indirect, verbal or by letter' between the members of the Company Select Committee and the provincial government (Staunton, 1822, p. 196). Many of the earlier restrictions imposed by the Canton system had been relaxed by 1815, but serious altercations arising from the Anglo–French war played out in the waters of the Pearl River, inevitably arousing Chinese mistrust and suspicion of British actions and motives in this trade-rich maritime environment.

The Pearl River Setting

Western ships coming to trade at Canton stopped outside Macao where captains were issued with a permit and allocated a Chinese pilot who navigated the ship to its up-river anchorage at Whampoa. The island of Lingding was the first notable landmark seen after leaving Macao and was important as the designated mooring place for foreign warships, which were prohibited by Chinese law from proceeding any further into the Pearl River Delta.

---

17 Apart from the three members who made up the Select Committee, others were in charge of weighing teas, keeping the books and copying Consultation Books. Also included was an inspector of teas, Samuel Ball, and his assistant; a surgeon and his assistant; and the Reverend Doctor Robert Morrison, translator and teacher of Chinese (Morse, 1926/1966, vol. 3, pp. 176–177).

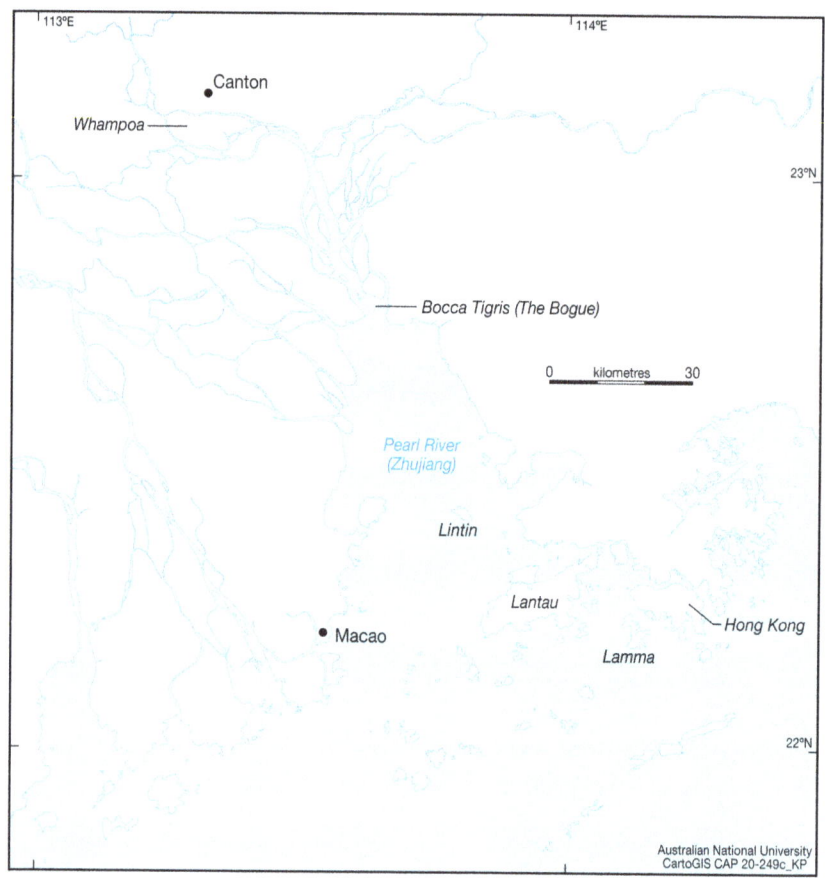

Figure 3: Map of the Pearl River estuary showing the locations of Macao, the Bocca Tigris and Whampoa island where Western ships anchored and loaded cargoes.
Source: CartoGIS, College of Asia and the Pacific, ANU.

The route to Canton commenced at the narrows of the Pearl River situated at the northern end of the estuary called the Bocca Tigris ('Tiger's Mouth') or the 'Bogue', which was guarded by three Chinese forts at its entrance.[18] The deterrent power of the forts for British warships was minimal. Commodore George Anson was suitably dismissive when visiting Canton during his voyage around the world in 1741–1742, and wrote of a 'motley band' from one of the forts who tried unsuccessfully to stop his illegal entry into the river (1790).

---

18 One fort was situated on two west-lying islands, while the other two sat at the foot of a larger island on the eastern side of the Bogue (Conner, 1997, p. 21).

Navigation on the Pearl River was difficult due to numerous sandbars, tidal patterns and thousands of junks housing Tanka families and others engaged in the vast domestic coastal trade that crowded the river. Arrival at Whampoa revealed the sight of Western ships at anchor surrounded by sampans engaged in the unloading and loading of cargoes, especially tea. A British naval officer, James Johnson, who visited Canton in 1804, described the scene in terms coloured by national pride:

> In viewing the various national flags flying on board their respective ships at Whampoa, it is highly gratifying to Englishmen's feelings, to observe the British, superior in numbers to all others collectively; while each individual ship, like a colossal emblem of the British commerce, appears to look down with contempt on the pigmy representatives of other nations that surround her. (1806, p. 63)

Johnson approached Canton at night and marvelled at the lights of the city and the number of boats surrounding the foreshore, as well as:

> The din of the Chinese language on every side; the clangour of their gongs, the shrill noise of their music, the glare of their fire works, all combine to form a scene so novel and striking, that the impression which it leaves on one's memory, can hardly ever be erased afterwards. (p. 65)

His arrival at the wharf outside the British Factory at Canton evoked a greater reaction. Johnson used italics to describe a scene where 'the *inhabitants, language, manners, customs,* even the *houses,* [and] *manufactures*' were 'so specifically *different*' from what he had seen before that he 'could almost fancy' himself 'transported into a new world' (p. 65).

Political–Military Factors: The Macao Expeditions of 1802 and 1808

A fundamental historical difference between the Macartney Embassy and Amherst Embassy was that the latter took place at the conclusion of a period of total war. International conflict arising from British wars with France and her ally Spain resulted in tensions being played out in Chinese territorial waters. An expedition of French and Spanish warships threatened Company ships in 1799, resulting in the introduction of a convoy system conducted by the Royal Navy that escorted British ships to St Helena (Wood, 1940, p. 139). A treaty signed between France and

Portugal, which henceforth closed all Portuguese ports to British ships, prompted the governor-general of Bengal in 1802 to send six British warships carrying an expeditionary force of Indian Sepoys to occupy Macao to prevent the settlement falling into French hands, which would have had disastrous effects for Company trade (Wood, 1940, p. 139).[19] The Portuguese authorities objected, fearing that Macao 'would be lost forever' if they accepted British assistance (Wang, 2014, p. 236).[20] British troops were denied permission to land and the Jiaqing emperor, understandably suspicious of British intentions, ordered the immediate departure of the troops from Chinese waters. The British refused, their ships remained anchored near Macao and trade was suspended. News of peace between Britain and France following the Treaty of Amiens (1802) reached Macao soon afterwards and the troops withdrew.[21] British actions, however, had sent a clear message to the emperor of their willingness to act decisively and use military force, if necessary, to safeguard the Canton trade. The Jiaqing emperor had been alarmed but, according to Wang (2014), was reassured by reports from Macao that 'no foreign countries, including Britain, could menace the dynasty' (p. 237).[22] The Portuguese at Macao also stepped up their campaign of spreading invidious reports of British intentions on the settlement at this time, alerting the Chinese Government to their 'captious and deceitful' intentions while masquerading as mere traders (Wood, 1940, p. 144).

A more serious dispute arose between the British and local Chinese authorities due to the British military occupation of Macao in 1808. Executed in response to a potential French threat as well as rampant local pirate activity in the Pearl River that threatened Company shipping and personnel, the governor-general of Bengal sent Admiral Drury with 300

---

19 The British had learned as early as 1778 that France and Portugal had held negotiations for the cession of Macao to France. For a full account of problems at Macao due to British military action in 1802 and 1808, see Wang (2014, pp. 236–244).
20 The Portuguese had been permitted to establish a trading base at Macao in 1557 and remained the only Europeans with a foothold in China until the Treaty of Nanking (1842) following the First Opium War ceded the island of Hong Kong to Britain.
21 Wood (1940) wrote that news of the treaty saved the Select Committee from making a 'catastrophic' decision as Wellesley, governor-general of Bengal, was about to send instructions to seize Macao by force. This would have placed the committee in an untenable position. Wood contended that Wellesley's order would not have been obeyed, as to do so would have confirmed Chinese suspicions of British intentions and placed the English in 'just as bad a light as the French' (p. 143).
22 The Jiaqing emperor's assessment is in stark contrast to his great grandfather, the Kangxi emperor, who stated with great foresight in 1716, 'Certainly ships from Western countries may sail to China if they wish, though I suspect that the countries in the Western Ocean will become a threat to China in one hundred years' (as quoted in Zhao, 2013, p. 153).

troops to occupy Macao.[23] Arriving on 11 September 1808 without prior notice to either the Chinese or Portuguese authorities, the troops were refused permission to land whereupon Drury took matters into his own hands and ordered their occupation of Macao on 21 September (Fu, 1966, vol. 2, p. 603). Following a series of complicated negotiations between the Select Committee and local government, trade at Canton was stopped on 8 October (Wood, 1940, p. 148). Drury endeavoured to arrange a meeting with the viceroy of Canton to resolve matters and to explain the British position, but his overtures were rejected. In response, Drury illegally entered the Pearl River in three heavily armed vessels, endeavouring to intimidate the Chinese to lift their embargo on trade. When this failed, he set off for Canton in an effort to meet the viceroy (Wang, 2014, p. 242). Nearing Canton, Drury found his passage blocked by Chinese war junks holding thousands of troops who fired on him and his military escort. A British soldier was injured, but Drury's order for his troops to return fire was not heard and he decided to withdraw at this time and retreated down river. He claimed later that he had held back deliberately, telling the president of the Select Committee:

> I never would consent to the slaughter of these defenceless multitudes [the people of Canton]; but if their commerce required to be supported by hostilities, and that if a single seaman of mine was killed, I would level Canton to the ground. (as quoted in Barrow, 1817b, p. 416)

Meanwhile, Chinese troops had massed around Canton and Macao with orders to set fire to British ships anchored at Whampoa and Macao. After further protracted negotiations, Drury decided to depart and withdrew his troops from Macao. Claiming a victory over the Royal Navy, the Chinese erected a pagoda to commemorate their success.

The Jiaqing emperor, angered by British actions, issued an edict condemning the occupation as an affront to Chinese sovereignty and dismissing British fears of a possible French invasion of Macao. Any aggressive French action, the emperor declared, would be met with Chinese military force where 'we would immediately send our mighty army to suppress and annihilate them in order to maintain our maritime

---

23 Wang (2014) wrote of the piracy threat, 'By the end of 1808, the pirate confederation even threatened to attack Canton after destroying almost half of the Qing fleet in Guangdong' (p. 240). Foreign merchants travelling between Macao and Canton were in constant danger of being attacked and had to be escorted by armed guards.

defence' (Imperial edict dated 14 November 1808 in Fu, 1966, vol. 1, p. 372). Regardless of the emperor's grandiose claims, Chinese concerns about British strategic intentions towards China had firmly registered. This fear, according to the British historian Herbert Wood (1940, p. 139), was the reason for the Jiaqing emperor's stand against Amherst.

British Nationalism and the Monarchy

The period between the Macartney and Amherst embassies (1793–1816) saw fundamental changes in Britain with the growth of nationalism centring on a veneration for the institution of the British monarchy. Historians have noted the construction of a patriotic identity that was inextricably connected with George III as the 'father' of the nation in which 'affection for the monarch' became a crucial test of British identity (Russell, 1995, p. 5). Explained largely as a response to the shock attack on the French monarchy during the French Revolution, Linda Colley (1984) wrote that celebrating the British monarch was 'a way of celebrating the nation's liberty as against the military despotism of France and the subservience of her satellite nations in Europe' (p. 121).

British victory over France in 1814 and, ultimately, in 1815, promoted Britain to the rank of the world's leading power. A shift in British values and concerns is reflected in the difference between the choice of personnel of the Macartney and Amherst embassies. The Macartney Embassy, which included scientists, mathematicians and other representatives of the sciences and technology, represented enlightenment concerns with the rational collating and measuring of cultural differences and artistic practices (Clingham, 2015). Eastberg (2009, pp. 39–46) argued that Staunton remained a man of the enlightenment due to his peculiar education in the classics and sciences. The other men of the Amherst Embassy, which included a large contingent of Company men from Canton, more closely reflected Regency values and were concerned primarily with pragmatic and material interests founded on commerce, signifying Britain's ascendency in manufacturing and trade, as well as a commitment to duty and respect for the institution of the British monarchy. Amherst, it will be seen, was above all a courtier of St James's; his paramount loyalty was to his sovereign whose honour had to be defended at all costs. Further, his time at St James's and earlier posting at the Italian court of the Two Sicilies (1809–1811) had given him firsthand experience of European courtly protocols and procedures. Amherst, unlike Macartney who had been governor of Madras, had no prior experience of eastern courts but came to the Qing court well versed in English and Continental court protocol, confident in the knowledge that he was the representative of the sovereign of the world's greatest power and would be received with honour. The importance of rank and honour for governing British behaviour in early nineteenth century aristocratic and military culture has been pointed out by historians (e.g. Bell, 2008, p. 36). Amherst, it will be seen, was not disposed to be relegated by his Chinese hosts to the inferior status of a tributary envoy from a vassal state.

Insight into British thinking on the connection between diplomacy and commerce at the time of the Amherst Embassy is found in Robert Morrison's (1820, p. 7) introductory remarks to his memoir of the Amherst Embassy. Morrison contended that improvement and progress for both individuals and independent nations was founded on an amiable intercourse with each other based on the principles of international law.[24] Governments who aspired to this goal while pursuing the good of their own country deserved the 'thanks of Mankind' (Morrison, 1820, p. 7). Commercial intercourse fostered the improvement of the 'temporal condition' of all, but only if it was conducted on the basis of equality and mutual reciprocity (Morrison, 1820, p. 8). Because the products of the earth were not evenly distributed between countries, it was the duty of governments to exert their influence on the leaders of other nations to alert them to the benefits of trade. Trade benefitted the farmers and manufacturers of all countries engaged in commerce, resulting in mutual improvement and progress.

Such beneficial results were possible only under conditions founded on equality and reciprocity, free of the control of slave owners or despotic lords: 'The idea that one owes and yields homage to the other is likely to be prejudicial to the fair commercial intercourse between the two nations' (Morrison, 1820, p. 8). The Chinese custom of the kowtow, if not mutually reciprocated, expressed in the strongest manner 'the submission and the homage of one person or state to another'. Morrison concluded that it should be carried out only by those European nations who 'consider themselves tributing and yielding homage to China'

---

24 Staunton (1821) wrote that because the Chinese were 'surrounded by barbarous tribes, and in great measure protected from their incursions by natural boundaries, they have neither had occasion for, nor the opportunity of learning, any of the principles of that inter-national law' (p. vi).

(Morrison, 1820, p. 8). The British Government, however, acted as every civilised government should act when endeavouring to cultivate a good understanding and liberal intercourse with China, and would never yield homage to China (Morrison, 1820, p. 8). British identity in this period was based on a strong belief in liberty, the institution of Parliament and the perceived rationality of the British people. David Armitage (2000) described the ideology of the British people at this time as one founded on Protestant values, the idea of progress and the freedom of maritime commerce. Porter similarly demonstrated that the British held the ideal of a healthy and unobstructed commerce, protected and encouraged by the state, leading to progress and economic wellbeing (Porter, 2001, p. 201). These categories, representing the British paradigm of the time, were the antithesis of Chinese values and attitudes and inevitably formed the context in which the British judged Qing control of society, commerce and trade (Porter, 2001, p. 201). British views of Chinese indifference to foreign trade, and their confinement of the British to the port of Canton, described by Staunton (1822, p. 192) as 'a frontier town, on the remotest verge of the Asiatic continent' where they lived under 'a highly jealous, despotic, and arbitrary' government, inevitably created severe tensions and cultural clashes between the British and Chinese. The part these tensions played in giving rise to proposals for the dispatch of another British embassy to China is outlined in the following chapter.

3
Origins of the Amherst Embassy: Canton and Sir George Thomas Staunton

Historians have traditionally assessed Sir George Thomas Staunton's importance in the Amherst Embassy within the narrow context of his advice to Amherst to not kowtow before the Jiaqing emperor. While this advice was critical to the outcome of the embassy, Staunton's very significant role in the 16-year period leading eventually to the decision to dispatch an embassy in 1816 has been largely overlooked. Reference to Staunton's private letters written to his parents during his time as a servant of the Company at Canton from 1800 to 1817 provides a firsthand account of the specific conditions at Canton under which trade was conducted, as well as his role in the British decision to dispatch an embassy to the Qing court in 1816. Staunton, it will be seen, was a highly motivated individual who was determined to live up to the high expectations of his parents and mentors, namely, Lord Macartney and John Barrow. His shyness, social ineptness and intense dislike of the boisterous drinking culture of the British Factory, notable at the time of his early years at Canton, resulted in his taking refuge in the study of Chinese law, literature and Mandarin. Staunton's importance for the Amherst Embassy is traced in this chapter on a number of levels, dating from the time of his arrival at Canton as a junior writer with the Company, until his final departure from Canton in January 1817 as president of the Select Committee following the conclusion of the Amherst Embassy.

Figure 4: Portrait of Sir George Thomas Staunton at 52 years of age.
Note: Engraving after painting by Sir George Hayer in 1833.
Source: LibraryThing (www.librarything.com/gallery/author/stauntonsirgeorge).

First and significantly, Staunton exerted a strong influence on the views of his friend and mentor John Barrow, the second secretary to the Admiralty, who was the man most responsible in 1815 for advocating the need for an embassy to the Qing court. Staunton corresponded regularly with Barrow on the desirability of a follow-up to Macartney's Embassy and provided him with both reports and assessments to support this view. Second, Barrow thought that Staunton's unique knowledge of China, command of the Chinese language and experience in dealing with local officials at Canton was the key to a successful mission to the Qing court where the Macartney Embassy had been lacking and consequently failed. Moreover, Staunton enjoyed a reputation as Britain's leading sinologist with the publication in 1810 of his translation of the Chinese penal code under the title *Ta Tsing Leu Lee*. Third, Staunton exploited his unique position at Canton to acquire information on the Qing court that was denied to other Westerners. His systematic intelligence collection came from several sources including high-ranking mandarins, Hong merchants and Catholic missionaries based at Peking, as well as official Chinese publications originating in Peking. Taken together, these uniquely informed Staunton, who in turn informed Barrow of an embassy's prospects at the Qing court and revealed the state of British knowledge of Chinese attitudes to foreigners in the period before the Amherst Embassy. Finally, Staunton's great personal ambition, apart from making a substantial fortune at Canton, was to return to Peking in some capacity with a British embassy, preferably as its leader. To expedite his chances, Staunton drew up plans for another embassy, namely, in 1800–1801 and 1809–1810. Both plans were dismissed by the Court of Directors of the Company, for reasons that will be discussed in the first part of this chapter, who preferred to let matters rest with the status quo. The second part of the chapter focuses on the disputes at Canton in the immediate period of 1812–1814, where Staunton played a pivotal role and the Court of Directors finally became convinced of the need to finance an embassy to Peking.

George Thomas Staunton (1781–1859)

George Thomas Staunton was born at Salisbury on 26 May 1781. His father, Sir George Leonard Staunton, had left England in January of that year accompanying Lord Macartney on his posting as governor of Madras and did not see his son until his return to England in 1784.[1] The boy's education and welfare, Staunton wrote later, became the 'the master purpose of my father's mind' (1856, p. 3). Staunton was educated at home in the classics and sciences and spoke to his father only in Latin.

---

1   Sir G. L. Staunton was appointed Macartney's secretary in 1780, proceeded to India at the time of Macartney's appointment as governor of Madras and, while there, negotiated a peace settlement with the Tipu Sultan of Mysore that ended the Second Anglo–Mysore War in India (see Cranmer-Byng, 1962, p. 307; Eastberg, 2009, pp. 26–37).

The Percy anecdotes (Vol. 3) referred in 1826 to the young Staunton at the time of the Macartney Embassy's return voyage from China to England in 1794 where the boy:

> was on the deck of the *Lion* with his father … who imagining that a French man of war was going to engage them, desired his son in Latin … to go down below deck. 'Mi Pater, nunquam te desseram'. 'My father, I will never forsake you', was the spirited and affectionate reply. (p. 112)

One of Staunton's tutors during the Macartney Embassy (1792–1794) was John Barrow, who had been appointed the comptroller in charge of the presents sent by George III to the Qianlong emperor, on the recommendation of Staunton's father (Staunton, 1856, p. 9).

Participation in the Macartney Embassy defined the careers of not only Barrow, but also of Sir George and his son.[2] Staunton senior had hoped to remain in Peking as the resident minister for England after the departure of the embassy, but had to return to England at the time of its premature dismissal from Peking. An opportunity to return to Peking as the minister plenipotentiary in a proposed embassy to China in 1796 following the Qianlong emperor's invitation for another British mission to visit Peking was shelved after Staunton senior suffered a 'paralytic seizure' (Staunton, 1856, p. 16). Similarly, as noted above, Staunton became a widely known celebrity as the boy who spoke to the Qianlong emperor in Mandarin and received a gift of a small golden silk purse from the emperor's own hands (G. L. Staunton, 1797b, p. 348).

Young George Staunton entered Trinity College, Cambridge, at age 16 to read 'Arts and Manufactures' under Professor Farish. He lived off campus with his parents and mixed socially with senior academics, rather than with students of his own age.[3] However, Staunton senior withdrew his son from the university after only two terms in protest when he was awarded with the second, and not the first prize, in the first-year examinations. The family, while moderately wealthy and possessing landed estates in Ireland, did not have the financial resources for young Staunton to pursue an independent lifestyle befitting his station. His father, Staunton wrote,

---

2 Sir G. L. Staunton's (1797a) book was acknowledged as the official account of the embassy.

3 Staunton spent his summer holidays with his cousins, the children of the Reverend and Mrs Brodie, near Salisbury, just before he entered Cambridge. He wrote that this was a most enjoyable time and represented the only occasion where his father 'allowed me of freely associating with young persons of about my own age' (Staunton, 1856, p. 19).

now thought that 'an appointment in the service of the Company might still enable me to follow up my early introduction to Chinese diplomacy, and to acquire honour and distinction in that career' (Staunton, 1856, p. 17). Staunton's great ambition to lead another British embassy to China, doubtless influenced by his father's ambitions for him, was formed at this time.

Staunton's application to join the Company ranks was not a straightforward process. His appointment as a junior writer was secured only after some intense lobbying by both Macartney and Sir George promoting his cause as the only Englishman who knew Mandarin. The appointment was very unpopular within the Company and drew criticisms of 'undue interference with private patronage' as the lucrative post of writer was reserved traditionally for the sons and relatives of Company Directors (Staunton, 1856, p. 17). The position paid £2,000 a year (equivalent to approximately £200,000 in today's values), yet Staunton found this barely enough to cover daily living expenses at Canton and Macao, and he sought extra funds from his parents to provide loans on high interest to Hong merchants.[4]

Staunton embarked on the Indiaman, *Hindostan*, for the six-month journey to China on 18 June 1799. His father wrote to him the next day:

> I still believe that I have fallen upon the best, or at least the most likely, means of providing for your future happiness, but it is not the most happy for me to be thus separated from you … but you will finally return [from China] I hope, with a competent fortune. (Staunton, 1856, p. 23)

Staunton arrived in China in January 1800 and discovered that his fame as the 12-year-old English boy who had held a brief conversation with the Qianlong emperor at the time of the Macartney Embassy had gone before him. He was visited immediately on landing at Macao by Father Marchini, the chief cleric in charge of the Roman Catholic Mission.[5] Marchini, recently returned from Peking, remembered speaking to Staunton in Mandarin in 1793 (*Staunton Letters*, Macao, 20 January 1800). Staunton

---

4   Staunton wrote in his memoirs (1856) of a salary increase from £2,000 as a writer to £10,000 on promotion to a supercargo in 1804 (pp. 32–33). See fn. 31 of this chapter for further information on Staunton's loans to Hong merchants.

5   Staunton (1822, p. 81) recorded that John Baptist Marchini, was a 'highly esteemed and venerated ecclesiastic' whose 'liberal conduct and conciliating manners have gained him the general esteem of the Europeans in China'.

was also visited by two leading Hong merchants, Puankhequa and Chung Qua, on arrival at Canton.[6] Such a visit to the most junior member of the British Factory was unprecedented but, as Staunton told his parents, they 'knew of my speaking Chinese and one of them [Chung Qua] conversed with me in Chinese for half an hour' (*Staunton Letters*, Canton, 25 January 1800). Another mandarin of 'considerable rank', whose name is not known, also invited Staunton and the Company doctor to visit him using the pretext of attaining a consultation for an eye complaint. The mandarin, Staunton wrote, received them with:

> great complacency and good nature and addressing himself to me in Chinese declared that he recollected very well to have seen me when the Embassy was at Pekin and eagerly asked in return whether I did not recollect him also, which from civility I could not absolutely deny though I did not retain any remembrance of him, or was it likely that I should. During dinner he enquired after the health of the first Embassador and of the Second Commissioner … and where they resided and what stations they now filled in their Native country. (*Staunton Letters*, Macao, 26 May 1800)

Staunton enjoyed few other social occasions at Canton. At just 19 he held not only the most junior position at the British Factory but was also the youngest member among his 13 compatriots. His singular upbringing and previous life in England ill-prepared him for the society of an all-male expatriate culture of heavy drinking sessions and boisterous behaviour and he recorded in his memoirs that his first two years at Canton were 'the most gloomy period of my life' (Staunton, 1856, p. 25). 'I was singularly unprepared', he wrote, 'for those collisions which must always tend a youth's first initiation in mixed society' (Staunton, 1856, p. 25). He told his parents at the time that '[I] felt the greatest stranger amongst them' and was 'pretty well guarded against the temptations of the Canton table' (*Staunton Letters*, Macao, 12 May 1800). Fortunately for British sinology, Staunton devoted his leisure time at the British Factory to studying Mandarin and Chinese literature.

---

6   The former is likely to be, in Van Dyke's (2011) romanisation, Poankeequa II (Pan Youdu). The latter, likely to be Conqua in Van Dyke's (2011) romanisation, is more difficult to identify. For a discussion on possible people see Van Dyke (2011, pp. 325–362).

Propitiously, Staunton had arrived at Canton at the time of a major legal dispute between the Select Committee and local government. Known as the *Providence* affair, it concerned a Chinese boatman who had drowned while attempting to cut the cable and steal the anchor of a British ship moored at Whampoa. The subsequent demand by the Chinese authorities for the handover of the British sailor who had fired under orders over the head of the would-be thieves, thus causing the victim to jump overboard and drown, was rejected by the Select Committee. Staunton was engaged by the Company to interpret at the ensuing trial held before the senior mandarins, Hong merchants and Company Select Committee. His Mandarin skills, he modestly informed his parents, were 'wholly unequal' to the task. Nevertheless, the occasion provided an unprecedented opportunity for Staunton's involvement in composing personal and written communications in Mandarin to the Chinese Government (*Staunton Letters*, Macao, 25 September 1800).

Staunton's experience at the *Providence* trial revealed how a mastery in the language could gain access to high-ranking government officials. The viceroy, Staunton informed his parents, took the singular opportunity of visiting the British Factory without the Hong merchants, as 'he was sufficiently familiar with my foreign pronunciation' and did not need the aid of a Hong linguist (*Staunton Letters*, Macao, 27 March 1800). The president of the Select Committee, Richard Hall, informed Staunton that this was 'the only instance of direct communication with the Chinese government without the interference of the merchants' and, if continued, would prove 'a considerable check' on their behaviour, removing the need of 'exclusively confiding … in native linguists, who might be corrupted or intimidated' (*Staunton Letters*, Macao, 26 May 1800).[7] His participation at the trial, however, had a significant downside. Staunton wrote that it:

> in great measure indisposed the Hong Merchants towards me, who are sufficiently aware of the checks upon their conduct that my acquaintance with the language of the country, may hereafter become. (*Staunton Letters*, Canton, 27 March 1800)

---

7   The need for accurate communication between the Select Committee and Chinese authorities remained throughout this period. In 1805, the committee wrote on the matter of interpreting and translating communiques reliant on Chinese linguists who knew only 'pidgin' English: 'The difficulty in obtaining a faithful interpretation of a letter by means of the Merchants is almost insurmountable, it being only by general expressions that we can at any time render ourselves intelligible' (Morse, 1926/1966, vol. 3, p. 7).

Staunton was certainly motivated to pursue his studies in Mandarin following Hall's praise, if only to enhance his Company career.[8] His main aim, however, was to prepare himself in the event of another British embassy being sent to the Qing court. This remained his burning ambition until he finally abandoned the idea around 1812. He told his parents in 1800 that 'the principal advantage [of knowing Mandarin] which I look to is what you so frequently foretold, that of the event of another Embassy to this country'. This, he added, was 'frequently in my thoughts' (*Staunton Letters*, Canton, 15 November 1800). The praise he received following his participation in the *Providence* affair suggested to him that:

> my acquaintance with the Chinese gives me some chance of being called upon to accompany such an expedition [and] I cannot help fancying some connection with it ... I have been so fortunate as to have met with opportunities of giving proof of my acquaintance with the Chinese language, and that the Chief [Hall] has been so good as to record them ... I do not give up the expectation that if an Embassy were appointed some mentions could be made of me in some shape or other. (*Staunton Letters*, Macao, 26 May 1800)

Staunton set out to collect information on the Qing court to prepare himself for future diplomatic service. He learned a vital piece of intelligence from Marchini, who informed him of a significant change in the imperial attitude towards Westerners: 'The new [Jiaqing] Emperor', Staunton was told, 'is said to be more favourably inclined to the Europeans than his predecessor' (*Staunton Letters*, Macao, 20 January 1800). This represented a promising change in the attitude of the Chinese Government exemplified locally at Canton by:

> The kindness and humanity of the present Viceroy ... frequently shown to foreigners, [which] makes it reasonable to express that he would in some degree co-operate in the wishes of an Embassador or at least not prove an obstacle to the success of his measures. (*Staunton Letters*, Macao, 26 May 1800)

Further consultations with 'some intelligent Chinese' confirmed Staunton's growing belief that another British embassy to China 'would be met with a favourable reception' (*Staunton Letters*, Macao, 18 August 1800).

---

8   Staunton hoped Hall would advance his case for a further increase in his salary based on his proficiency in Mandarin, but the directors in London did not approve any compensation, much to his dismay (*Staunton Letters*, Canton, 9 January 1801).

Staunton also sought to cultivate the views of foreign missionaries based in Peking. Commenting on a letter he had received from the Vincentian priest, Louis Lamiot, Staunton told his parents:

> Lamiot seems to be a man of information and I shall cultivate his acquaintance by letter and newspapers which I hope to send to him by means of Portuguese Missionaries who are now at Canton and waiting for the Emperor's orders for them to proceed to Peking. (*Staunton Letters*, Canton, 9 January 1801)[9]

Staunton's intention was clear, namely, to ascertain 'the present disposition of the Court towards foreigners and what alteration the death of the late Minister [Heshen] and the succession of the present Emperor had made in the Government' (*Staunton Letters*, Canton, 26 February 1801).[10] He had high hopes that the Portuguese missionaries waiting at Macao for permission to travel to Peking would prove useful informants and sought to ingratiate himself by presenting them with newspapers and books recently received from India, to 'incline them to make me that kind of return which circumstances may put in their power' (*Staunton Letters*, Canton, 26 February 1801). A meeting with the missionaries proved disappointing. Staunton found they had neither 'the talents or capacity' to carry much weight at Peking and possessed little ability to 'exert any pressure' on behalf of the British people at the Qing court (*Staunton Letters*, Canton, 5 March 1801).[11] Father Lamiot, on the other hand, continued to write letters to Staunton and his views informed the assessments that were later passed to Amherst during his preparations for the embassy.

Staunton's major source of intelligence on the Qing court was the weekly Chinese Government publication, referred to by the British as the *Peking Gazette*, which arrived at Canton every four or five days. The *Gazette*,

---

9   Lamiot arrived in China at the end of 1793 and later served in the Secretariat at the Qing court as an interpreter, translating Chinese documents into Latin and sending them to Russia. He left Peking in 1819 and died at Macao (Fu, 1966, vol. 1, p. 327; 1966, vol. 2, p. 583).
10 The reference to Minister Heshen reflects the British view that he had played an important role in disposing the Qianlong emperor to refuse a dialogue with Macartney on British goals. Heshen was arrested by the Jiaqing emperor and his assets seized, acquired it was thought, through corruption and the favouritism of his father. Heshen was 'given Imperial permission to commit suicide' (Cranmer-Byng, 1962, pp. 321, 322).
11 Fu (1966, vol. 2, p. 591, fn. 25–26) documented that three Western missionaries were granted permission to travel to Peking at this time; namely, a Portuguese Lazarist appointed to the Board of Astronomy in December in 1801 and who died in 1823; Joseph Nunez Ribeiro; and Gaetan Pires-Pireira, who was sick and remained in Canton.

written in the 'court style', contained 'very curious information' found in imperial edicts and petitions giving 'insight into the policy of the Government' (*Staunton Letters*, Macao, 5 August and 9 August 1801).[12] The Chinese press, Staunton complained, while free of government censorship, focused mainly on literary forms rather than current political issues (Staunton, 1810, p. xii). He wrote later that the *Gazette*'s prime function was to 'influence and conciliate public opinion upon all state questions, which under a government theoretically so despotic, would hardly have been expected' (Staunton, 1821, p. xxi).

The Select Committee, meanwhile, sent copies of Staunton's translations of the *Gazette* to India following the request of the editor of the *Bombay Courier*. These, in turn, were passed directly to Governor-General Lord Wellesley. Staunton's linguistic skills had made it possible to transmit hitherto unavailable intelligence on the Qing court to British recipients throughout the region.

A major consequence of Staunton's involvement at the *Providence* trial was his discovery of the printed penal laws of China, which the Company proceeded to purchase on his behalf.[13] Staunton began translating these into English in late 1800 to assist the Company's understanding of Chinese law and its application. Their publication in 1810, under the title *Ta Tsing Leu Lee*, represented the first direct English translation of a Chinese text and firmly established Staunton as Britain's leading sinologist.[14]

Staunton's First Plan for Another British Embassy, 1800

Staunton drew up his first plan for another embassy to the Qing court in 1800. He focused on the important role of royal letters in Qing diplomacy and advocated that George III send an annual letter with a British

---

12 Staunton learned of the serious rebellions taking place in northern China in 1801, but was sceptical of government claims of victory after witnessing the number of troops mobilising on the river at Canton. This proved, he wrote, 'how little effect these victories have had in the pacification of the Provinces'.
13 Copies of the Penal Code were provided by the viceroy. Staunton also acquired a 24-volume set and 144-volume set of the code between March and November 1800 (*Staunton Letters*, Canton, 27 March and 8 November, 1800).
14 Staunton thought that while China's penal laws were 'not the most just and equitable', they were 'the most comprehensive, uniform, and suited to the genius of the people for whom [they were] designed, perhaps of any that ever existed' (Staunton, 1810, p. xi).

ambassador to the Jiaqing emperor with the first ships of the season, followed by the emperor's reply carried by the last ships. He thought that, given the distance between Britain and China, there would be no objection to a 'perpetual residence' being established at Peking. Such a privilege, he was aware, was denied to all the 'petty surrounding states who sent annual Ambassadors to the Court of Pekin from time immemorial', and who were seen by the Chinese as 'barbarians', but he felt an exception would be made for the British based on the fact of:

> The grandeur and respectability with which the former [Macartney] Embassy appeared at the Court of Pekin would prevent any future Ambassador from being degraded to the rank of messengers from tributary and subordinate states though he should annually attend with them at the Emperor's court. (*Staunton Letters*, Canton, 26 February 1801)

A similar assessment is found in Macartney's account, which refers to the Jesuit Father Amiot's view. While acknowledging that the Chinese had been alarmed on learning of news of war in Europe, Amiot assured Macartney that '[His] Embassy had been so brilliant, and ha[d] made such an impression in the country, as must in the end be productive of very happy consequences'. Further, Amiot advised that 'the ground gained by sending an Embassy from the King to the Emperor should by no means be lost, but be followed up by an intercourse of letters between them' (Cranmer-Byng, 1962, p. 151).

This view echoed those of Staunton senior, who wrote of the exceptional circumstances of Macartney's reception at the Qing court:

> The dignified and splendid manner in which the Embassy was received, influenced the minds of the Chinese, and induced them to believe that the government was about to make a change of measures favourable to the English. Embassadors were not usually received by the Emperor upon his throne; nor were their credentials delivered into his hands, but ordinarily into those of his ministers. (G. L. Staunton, 1797b, vol. 2, p. 347).

Macartney's legacy, especially being permitted to hand his credentials and the king's letters into the emperor's own hands and performing the British ceremony of bowing on one knee rather than the kowtow, persisted as the major flaw in British assessments of their likely reception by the Jiaqing emperor and represented a fundamental misunderstanding of Qing court protocol that lies at the core of Amherst's failure. Staunton's unwavering belief in the impact of the Macartney Embassy's splendid appearance and civility of manners in contrast to those of China's traditional vassal states is understandable if misplaced. His opinion, accepted unconditionally by Barrow, that the Qing court would make an exception for a British embassy and would receive it outside the framework of the traditional tribute system, was both a major factor in favour of sending a second embassy in 1816 and a key reason for its failure. Macartney's dispensation of not having to perform the kowtow before the Qianlong emperor resulted in the Jiaqing emperor being resolute in insisting on its performance. It is ironic, therefore, that the prime legacy of the Macartney Embassy for the outcome of the Amherst mission was to make the emperor determined that Amherst comply fully with the court ceremony that lay at the core of the tribute system.

The Company Directors in London did not share Staunton's enthusiasm for another embassy. No arrangements were made for a letter from George III congratulating the Jiaqing emperor on his accession to the throne and a disappointed Staunton told his parents:

> I am sorry to find how little disposed the Minds of the Directors and of others in power are to the idea of a second Embassy … one of the Directors thought it best to 'Let the Government of China alone'. (*Staunton Letters*, Canton, 26 February 1801)

Nevertheless, Staunton persisted with the hope of returning to Peking and turned his attention to learning the 'Mantokoo Tartar' language spoken at the Qing court (*Staunton Letters*, Canton, 26 February 1801). Fluency in the Manchu language, Staunton thought, would be very useful at Peking as it would enable a direct dialogue with the emperor in his native tongue. His assumption that the Jiaqing emperor would be open to personal conversation and negotiation, most likely founded on his boyhood experience of conversing with the Qianlong emperor in 1793, may be read as understandable but misguided, as events later proved.

Staunton Back in England, 1803–1804

Staunton was on leave in London during 1803–1804, having returned to England upon learning of his father's death.[15] He spent his time staying with Lord Macartney and his family, as well as with John Barrow who had recently been appointed second secretary to the Admiralty.[16] Barrow, no doubt prompted by Staunton, raised the matter of another embassy to China with the Company Directors. Their response remained 'cold and indifferent', although they did agree to send a letter from George III and gifts valued at £2,176 to the Jiaqing emperor to placate him over British military actions at Macao in 1802 (Fu, 1966, vol. 2, p. 595, fn. 51).[17]

Staunton still harboured hopes of being involved in another embassy and appearances were important. He wrote to his mother from Portsmouth on the eve of sailing for China, 'I have just complied with your wishes in having my hair cut … and henceforth shall leave off the powder' (*Staunton Letters*, Portsmouth, 31 May 1804).[18] His decision may be read as representing a historic change from the men of Georgian England, who, like the men of the Macartney Embassy, dressed in powdered wigs, tight silk britches and stockings. Dress for gentlemen at the beginning of the nineteenth century consisted of a more casual attire of tailored trousers, jackets and top hats.[19] Staunton added:

---

15   Sir G. L. Staunton died on 14 January 1801. News of his death reached Staunton in late August 1801 and was referred to as a 'melancholy catastrophe' (*Staunton Letters*, Macao, 28 August 1801). Staunton started planning his return to England with the first fleet to sail from China. Leave approval in London was secured through the efforts of Lord Macartney who convinced the Company Directors to allow Staunton to return. Staunton planned to take two Chinese Christian missionaries with him at his own expense for 'the benefit of pursuing my Chinese studies' on the passage to England to show the directors that he was not neglecting his duty to the Company (*Staunton Letters*, Macao, 3 October 1801). Staunton inherited his father's estate, apart from a small legacy left to his mother. He also succeeded to the Baronetcy.

16   Macartney pledged to take 'the place' of his father in promoting Staunton's interests. He presented him at court before George III and Queen Charlotte in December 1802 and was instrumental in having him elected at the Literary Club as well as the Royal Society (Staunton, 1856, p. 31).

17   George III's letter was dated 22 May 1804.

18   British attitudes to the use of hair powder by men had changed by the beginning of the nineteenth century. Seen previously as a badge of gentlemanly respectability, hair powder was now perceived as effeminate and indicative of the corrupting effects of modern commercialism that had taken place in Britain in the eighteenth century. Its use, still prominent among French emigres, was considered representative of dandyism and 'the irresponsible frivolity of the ancient regime' (see Barrell, 2006).

19   The mode of dressing fashionable among the British supercargoes at Canton is revealed in the oil painting by a Chinese artist of the trial of the *Neptune*'s seamen in 1807 (reproduced in Conner, 2009, pp. 68–69).

> As improbable things sometimes happen, Mr. Barrow's expectations of an Embassy may one day be realised - upon such an event you must judge what clothes etc, etc, may be fit to send me out upon such an occasion. (*Staunton Letters*, Portsmouth, 31 May 1804)

Staunton sent his mother another letter on arrival at St Helena, illustrating his confidence in the opinions of his two patrons:

> The etc, etc, which I expressed a desire might be sent me in the event of an Embassy, did not imply anything in particular, but I only wished that under such circumstances, anything really new, curious or useful, which might be suggested by my uncle [Macartney] or Mr. Barrow should not be rejected in order to save a little expense. (*Staunton Letters*, St Helena, 9 June 1804)

Curiously, the route to China went via Norfolk Island. Staunton told his mother:

> We have taken an unusual and circuitous route. The name of the remote spot ... will be familiar to you, from the circumstance of its having been the former residence of Governor and Mrs. King, who are still I believe at Port Jackson which is in the neighbourhood. (*Staunton Letters*, Staunton to his mother, written near Norfolk Island, 9 November 1804 but sent from Canton, 18 January 1805)

General letters for England were deposited at the time with two Botany Bay ships on their way to England (*Staunton Letters*, Canton, 24 February 1805).[20]

Staunton Returns to China, 1805

Staunton was promoted to the rank of supercargo on his return to the British Factory at Canton and enjoyed a substantial increase in salary from £2,000 to £10,000 per annum (Staunton, 1856, p. 32). Immediately upon his return, he was called on to attend the viceroy's palace to witness the Company's formal acceptance of a letter and presents from the emperor to George III, which had been sent in response to the king's letter and presents received in 1805 (Fu, 1966, vol. 1, p. 349). The king had endeavoured to reassure the emperor that the presence of six British warships off Macao in 1802 did not constitute a military threat,

---

20 The ships were the *Experiment* and *Ocean*.

as rumoured by the Portuguese and French, but sought only to protect British trade. Similarly, an explanation was given also for the presence of other British warships in Chinese waters required to convoy the Indiamen to protect them from French attack.

Permission to enter the city of Canton and a formal call on the viceroy at this time represented a rare opportunity for the British. They made their 'bows in the viceroy's palace' and received presents for the king consisting of teas, silks and porcelains.[21] Morse (1926/1966, vol. 3, p. 29) records:

> It had been previously ascertained that the Mandarines were to deliver the Imperial Letter standing, and that on receiving it no more would be required from [the British] than an obeisance conformably to the usages of Europe.

The viceroy, however, informed the emperor that the British had kowtowed, which they read as an indication of his fear of incurring the emperor's displeasure on learning the truth. The emperor's letter confirmed that another British embassy would be received strictly within the context of the traditional tribute system. It contained language read by the British as condescending, which referred to them as 'Strangers' who being 'awed by Our power, Nobly … bring their tributes from remote distances and throng to do homage to Our Empire'. Further:

> Your kingdom is far distant and separated from Us by the seas, yet you respectfully observe the duties of a vassal state. From a remote region, you manifest your loyalty toward the Sun [the emperor]. (as quoted in Fu, 1966, vol. 1, p. 361)

George III was informed that if the British:

> Continue to offer amity and friendship as an ally, if you can lead all your subjects to present tribute and serve Us as our vassals, then you will fulfil Our sublime principle of loving strangers and extending our benevolence to them. (as quoted in Fu, 1966, vol. 1, p. 361)

---

21 The presents consisted of 'fourteen suitcases which contained six rolls of silk … four porcelain vases, four porcelain plates, eight porcelain bowls and eight porcelain dishes, four boxes of spring tea, and four rolls of the P'u-er tea' (Fu, 1966, vol. 1, p. 367).

Regardless of the compromise made at the time of Macartney over the kowtow, the Jiaqing emperor made it clear that a future British embassy would receive no such dispensation. Prospects for a successful negotiation of British goals remained as remote as ever.

Staunton's hitherto favourable impression of the local government changed further with the arrival at Canton of a new viceroy who was ill-disposed and unfriendly to the British. He wrote contemptuously of 'the many instances I have witnessed lately of the pride, weakness and corruption of the Chinese government' (*Staunton Letters*, Canton, 5 November 1805). Dispirited, Staunton concluded in 1805 that the chances of a successful British mission to Peking 'are fewer and those of failure more numerous than I had anticipated'. He added:

> I am satisfied indeed that the success of any Mission to the Court of Pekin, must be very limited and precarious, but it is much easier now to satisfy the expectations of ministers and the Public [in England] than it was at the time of the former Embassy, since the flattering but groundless calculation of success which then existed are at present totally relinquished and the World is sufficiently acquainted with the Pride, meanness and ignorance which characterizes the Court of Pekin, which must obstruct the views of a Negotiator, publish the disgrace of his failure, and enhance the Men of [any] success. (*Staunton Letters*, Canton, 30 December 1805)

Despite the belief that the Macartney Embassy had deeply impressed its hosts, Staunton suggests that the expectations of the British public were more realistic following the popularity of Barrow's scathing account of China published in 1804. News of a failed Russian embassy sent to the Jiaqing emperor in 1805–1806, where the ambassador Count Golovkin was expelled from China for refusing to kowtow, reached Staunton late in 1806. His faith in a more positive reception for any future British ambassador was restored. Staunton asked his mother:

> Please inform my good friend Mr. Barrow … [that] the Emperor of China has been more polite to his brother the King of England having written him a civil letter and transmitted some presents. (*Staunton Letters*, Canton, 16 December 1806)[22]

---

22   The significance of the Golovkin Embassy for the Amherst Embassy is discussed later in this study.

Staunton's Second Plan for a British Embassy to the Jiaqing Emperor, 1810

Staunton returned to England on leave in 1808 following a serious dispute at Canton where trade was stopped over a fracas between local Chinese and British sailors.[23] He was absent also from China at the time of the second British occupation of Macao but, on learning the news in London, he joined with Barrow to lobby the Company Directors for an embassy to the Jiaqing emperor to repair relations (Morse, 1926/1966, vol. 3, pp. 79–99).[24]

The directors received Staunton's plan for another British embassy on 20 November 1809 (*Staunton Letters*, London, 20 November 1809).[25] Staunton again emphasised the importance of a formal letter sent from George III to the emperor informing him specifically of his strong desire for amicable and beneficial relations, and notifying him that the occupation of Macao by British troops was not authorised nor approved by the British Government. The inclusion of Mandarin translations of British Government documents would serve to convince the emperor of British integrity, thereby disposing him to encourage the viceroy at Canton to remove all trade restrictions imposed on the Company.

In a reference to himself and representing a new proposal, Staunton argued that the British now had a person 'never as yet afforded of conversing unreservedly and without the aid of interpreters, with those who influence the emperor's councils' (*Staunton Letters*, London, 20 November 1809). This person, he continued, was familiar with 'the modes of acting and thinking peculiar to the Chinese' and would enable a British ambassador to 'enter into confidential communications on subjects of mutual interests of both empires … it will not be too much to expect the most important and beneficial results from his negotiations' (*Staunton Letters*, London, 20 November 1809).

---

23   Known as the 'Neptune Affair'. For a concise summary, see Conner (2009, pp. 69–70).
24   See Morse (1926/1966, vol. 3, pp. 76–99) and Wood (1940) for a detailed account of the British occupation of Macao.
25   This is a formal letter written by Staunton to Charles Grant, the chairman of the Secret Committee of the East India Company, sent from his mother's house in Devonshire Street, London. The plan is written in a fine copperplate hand, suggesting that Staunton hired a professional scribe to offer the best presentation.

Staunton's expectations of beneficial 'negotiations' at the Qing court represented an obvious misjudgement, if not ignorance, of Qing diplomacy and indicates strongly his belief that any future British embassy would be received outside the tribute system. This assumption, it will be seen, was accepted unquestionably by Barrow in his call for an embassy in 1815, based on his confidence in Staunton's ability to communicate directly in Mandarin to ensure success for British goals. Further, the Qing court, Staunton pointed out, favourably received foreign missions as 'Embassies bearing presents are not only gratifying to the personal vanity of the Sovereign, but [were] also useful politic exhibitions to the people' (*Staunton Letters*, London, 20 November 1809).

Staunton was confident that his plan would be approved and waited for confirmation that he would be appointed the next British ambassador to the Jiaqing emperor. Barrow sent a letter marked 'Most Secret' dated 10 November 1809, which read, 'We have done the deed: and I most heartily congratulate you on the almost certain prospect of your going to Pekin as the King's ambassador' (Staunton, 1856, p. 43). The Company Directors, however, approved the plan in theory, but thought it 'most advisable not to include any person who was actually in the service of the East India Company' (Staunton, 1856, p. 44). The appearance of Company men would indicate that this was a mission sent primarily for commercial purposes and not as a compliment from the British sovereign. Staunton was devastated. He wrote later in his memoirs:

> It is impossible to express the mortification and irritation of mind which I felt at this most unlooked for communication; and I must say that now, coolly reflecting upon it, after a lapse of six-and-thirty years, I still think I was extremely ill used. (1856, p. 44)

Plans for a new embassy were shelved by the Company by the end of 1810 and the idea was placed in abeyance.

Staunton's Second Period at Canton, 1811–1816

Staunton arrived back at Canton in January 1811 to resume his posting where he met the new viceroy, Sungyun, who was well known to the British, having escorted the Macartney Embassy from Peking to Canton in 1793.[26] Macartney had praised Sungyun both for his 'strain of liberality scarcely to be expected in a Tartar or a Chinese' and for his 'most friendly and gentleman-like manner' (Cranmer-Byng, 1962, p. 178). Sungyun, on learning of Staunton's presence with the Company at Canton, 'Expressed himself surprised and much pleased that a person whom he well recollected with his Father in the British Embassy, happened to be at this time in China'. He also emphasised that he was 'very much the friend' of the British nation (Morse, 1926/1966, vol. 3, p. 169).

Staunton was invited, in a private capacity, to the viceroy's palace where conversation turned to Macartney. Staunton reminded the viceroy that it was time for another British embassy to the imperial court, but was quickly disabused of any such prospect. He was told in the firmest terms:

> There is no occasion for you to send another Embassy to Pekin. The Emperor knows it is a long way, and does not wish you to trouble yourselves. Besides the Climate does not agree with you; you may catch infectious Distempers. No! Your Nation must not send an Embassy. I will not allow it. It is out of the Question and you must not think of it. (Morse, 1926/1966, vol. 3, p. 173)

Crucially, it appears that Staunton's letter to Barrow failed to pass on this critical piece of information but stressed instead the 'civilities that had passed between the Chinese and the British' and the gifts of silks, Chinaware and 'other small articles, of no great value in themselves, but considered as tokens of friendship' (*Staunton Letters*, Macao, 20 July 1811).

A further dinner at the viceroy's palace was held a week later. Staunton was accompanied by John Roberts, the president of the Select Committee. Several high-ranking mandarins were present, referred to as 'the Tsiangkun [Tartar-General] … and the Hoppo' (*Staunton Letters*, Macao, 20 July 1811).[27] Their intense scrutiny of the viceroy inhibited informality. Rather, the British were addressed on the importance of conforming to the laws and customs of China and with correct protocol. Staunton wrote:

> At the end of the first conversation the Viceroy said 'As I have a great regard for you, you must allow me to shew you our Chinese customs, one of them is to bend the knee to great Mandarines,

---

26 Referred to as Sun-yün by Fu (1966). Fu added that Sungyun was aware of the cost of the Macartney Embassy to the Chinese treasury and 'the tension' it had caused in China (1966, vol. 2, p. 607, fn. 141).
27 I have been unable to identify the Tartar-General concerned.

> pray let me see you perform that ceremony'. Though not a little surprised at such an address, I at first simply answered that I had the greatest respect for His Excellency, but was obliged to decline paying him the compliment he required, as our English customs forbab [sic] it. (Staunton as quoted in East India Records, BL IOR G/12/196 (Reel 1) F 171).

The British judged the viceroy's manner as a need to distance himself from them in front of the mandarins. He threatened an end of his personal friendship and insinuated also that he would close Company trade.

Viceroy Sungyun's emphasis on correct protocol offers some insight into the historical mystery associated with Macartney's reception before the Qianlong emperor; namely, did Macartney perform the kowtow as the Chinese claimed, or did he perform the British ceremony of bending one knee described by Sungyun?[28] Sungyun's reference to 'bending the knee' suggests he witnessed Macartney performing this ceremony at the Qianlong court and was demanding a repeat performance by Staunton as a matter of form required on such occasions. Staunton remained firm and displayed the tenacity shown subsequently during the Amherst Embassy. He reassured Sungyun that his actions represented no disrespect towards him, but were governed rather by English custom stipulating that the requested ceremony was reserved only for the king or foreign sovereigns (Staunton as quoted in East India Records, BL IOR G/12/196 (Reel 1) F 171). The British position on the ceremony was certainly clarified at this time and would have served to alert the Qing authorities that the kowtow would not be performed before the emperor. Whether such information was passed on to Peking resulting in forewarning the court is not known, but it certainly helps explain the mandarins' immediate focus on the kowtow after the arrival of the Amherst Embassy in Tianjin in 1816.

Despite these events, Staunton's unique and friendly relationship with Sungyun endured. Sungyun invited the British to nine conferences and entertainments during his tenure at Canton (Staunton, 1822, p. 135). Like the earlier visit of the viceroy to the British Factory in 1800, Sungyun made an unprecedented call on Staunton and the Select Committee at Macao and visited the British ships anchored at Whampoa where he was lavishly received by a 19-gun salute and enjoyed a 'splendid

---

28 For a full discussion on the kowtow question, see Pritchard (1943).

entertainment'.²⁹ His visit was read as 'an extraordinary compliment' to the British and one never seen before in China (*Staunton Letters*, Canton, 15 November 1811). The Hoppo was also very accommodating at this time leading to British hopes of a 'more favourable opening' for improved relations between the Company and the Chinese. Staunton told Barrow:

> These things are trifling in themselves, [but] are very unusual here, where the Mandarins are in general too proud and ignorant, to take any notice of foreigners except to give them trouble and inconvenience. (*Staunton Letters*, Macao, 20 July 1811)

Sungyun, unfortunately, was prematurely recalled by Peking after a period of only six months to take up a position as president of the Board of Civil Office (Eastberg, 2009, p. 164). Relations at Canton, Staunton commented disparagingly, 'immediately fell back into the old channel' (Staunton, 1856, p. 56). Staunton had received mixed messages regarding the propriety of sending another embassy. Sungyun's long-lasting friendship, forged at the time of Macartney, had ensured a thaw in the normal chilly relations between the Select Committee and the Chinese Government. But Staunton was warned in explicit and unofficial terms that sending another embassy would not be welcomed.

Staunton received permission to return to England in 1812 after a period of ill health.³⁰ His arrival coincided with debate on the renewal of the Company's charter in the face of growing opposition to its monopoly of the tea trade from British free traders wishing to open trade with China. In consultations with the British Government, Staunton convinced Lord Buckinghamshire, President of the Board of Control, that a Company monopoly of the China tea trade was essential given the 'special circumstances … arising out of the extraordinary system of the Chinese government' (Buckinghamshire to Staunton, 2 September 1812, as quoted in Staunton, 1856, p. 58). The renewal of the Company's charter in 1813 opened the India trade to private merchants, but the China tea monopoly, which henceforth became the Company's most lucrative and important asset, remained and had to be protected at all costs.

---

29 The British gave the viceroy clocks and watches, which he did not accept, as well as foreign tobacco, wine, perfume, and clothes. The viceroy gave away the wine to the interpreters and other servants in the escort. The viceroy's presents to the British were 'double the value' (Fu, 1966, vol. 1, p. 383).
30 Platt (2018, p. 156) mistakenly wrote that Staunton remained continuously in Canton from 1810 until the arrival of Amherst in 1816.

The Immediate Causes for the Calling of an Embassy to the Qing Court

Company relations at Canton with the Hoppo and the viceroy were especially strained in the period between and 1813 and 1814. The cause was the insolvency of several Hong merchants who had borrowed heavily on credit from American private traders. Bankruptcy was a serious offence in China and the Company was concerned that the co-Hong merchants would seek to raise funds to pay debts resulting in impositions on foreign trade (Sargent, 1907, p. 21). Further, the emperor issued an edict proposing the co-Hong merchants be disbanded and all Western trade be placed under more rigorous conditions and in the charge of its two richest merchants (Morse, 1926/1966, vol. 3, p. 194).[31] The prospect of only two men controlling prices for exports and imports drew vehement opposition from the Select Committee who read the edict as an attempt to destroy all the privileges the Company had so far acquired. Charles Grant, the chairman of the Company Board of Directors, later reported to the House of Lords on the state of the China trade in 1821, 'Slender those privileges certainly are, but without them [the] trade would soon sink into absolute insignificance' (Charles Grant, 5 March 1821 as quoted in *Report [relative to the trade with the East Indies and China] from the Select Committee of the House of Lords*, 11 April 1821, p. 172). Staunton agreed. In his view, the placing of the trade in the hands of only one or two merchants was the equivalent of 'shutting up the port' (Staunton, 1822, p. 297). The Select Committee succeeded in having the proposal quashed.

Matters were not improved with the arrival of a new Hoppo in 1813 whose character towards the British was described as 'boorish' and 'overbearing' (Morse, 1926/1966, vol. 3, p. 197). A stickler for correct procedure on

---

31 These were Howqua (Wu Bingjian) and Kowqua (unidentified). Fu (1966, vol. 2, p. 605, fn. 126) commented that the British preferred to trade with the less prosperous merchants because they could lend money to them at a very high rate of interest. Staunton, in fact, proposed to his father very early in his career at Canton that money be sent out in order to lend it to Chinese Hong merchants at a high rate of interest, namely, 18 per cent. This, Staunton suggested, was a way to make 'an honourable fortune'. He added that it was possible 'to take advantage of these schemes when you are junior in the Company'. At a senior level, he continued, 'you expose the merchant to suspicion of favouring support to the detriment of the Company's interest' (*Staunton Letters*, Macao, 20 April 1801). In September 1814, Staunton referenced that he remitted bills in 1813 'totalling £5087.10', adding, 'the Chinese merchants are paying off their debts at a good rate'. It is not clear if this statement refers to personal loans he may have made, or to the general state of affairs at Canton (*Staunton Letters*, Macao, 22 September 1814).

all trade matters, the Hoppo prohibited direct communication with the Company and ordered that all reports be directed through the linguists (Morse, 1926/1966, vol. 3, p. 197). The Select Committee was alarmed by his attitude and reported that 'we must expect every possible annoyance and disruption which must necessarily arise from his rapacious Disposition' (Morse, 1926/1966, vol. 3, p. 197).

A most serious dispute at this time followed the actions of a British man-of-war, HMS *Doris*, during the 1814 trading season at the time of the Anglo–American War (1812–1814). The *Doris* had engaged 'in a very active blockade' of American shipping in Chinese territorial waters and illegally brought a captured American ship into the Pearl River. The viceroy informed the President of Select Committee, John Elphinstone, that:

> When two small countries [Great Britain and the United States] have petty quarrels overseas, the Celestial Empire is not concerned with them. However, when their ships enter territorial waters of the Interior [the Pearl River], they must obey and respect the prohibitions of the Celestial Empire … If [Elphinstone] dares to disobey us, then not only shall we destroy their warships, but we shall also suspend their trade. (Fu, 1966, vol. 1, p. 394)

The Select Committee was instructed by the viceroy to order the departure of the *Doris* from China. On being informed that the Company held no authority over a ship of the Royal Navy, the viceroy threatened not only to use force against the *Doris*, but also proceeded to implement a series of raids on the British Factory. John Francis Davis wrote later:

> The Chinese … entered upon a course of aggressive measures not against the frigate, but against the Factory, which soon became intolerable. The local government first prohibited the employment of native servants; they then sent persons to enter the Factory, and seize upon such Chinese as they found there. The boats of the Indiamen were molested while peacefully proceeding on their business on the river; and every attempt was made to prevent communication with our men-of-war. (1836/1851, vol. 1, p. 72)[32]

---

32 John Francis Davis was the eldest son of Samuel Davis, a director of the Company. Following precedence given to the sons of notable members of the Company, Davis arrived at Canton in 1813 as a junior writer with the Company. He was appointed governor of Hong Kong from 1844 to 1848.

A Chinese linguist, Ayew (Li Huaiyuan), based at the Factory was arrested at this time and sent to 'Tartary' (Xinjiang) in retaliation for the actions of the *Doris*.[33] His treatment at the hands of the Chinese authorities as well as the unauthorised entry of the Chinese in the British Factory were the immediate catalysts for the decision to send the Amherst Embassy. Staunton wrote:

> It may be observed that intrusion [into the Factory] is a very light term for the entry without notice or cause assigned of a police officer with his retinue, into a residence immediately distinguished by the national flag, and hitherto considered by foreigners as an inviolable sanctuary. If the inviolability of the British Factory were not maintained—what would become of the security of other foreign residences of less distinction and pretensions? (Staunton, 1822, p. 298)

The consequences of a Chinese attempt to place further restrictions on the activities of the Select Committee, the actions of the *Doris*, the raid on the British Factory and the arrest of Ayew had serious repercussions for Anglo–Chinese relations. Staunton, who was returning to China from England, had little idea of the turmoil he would confront. He wrote to his mother from the Anjere Roads in the Sunda Straits:

> My thoughts are now chiefly directed towards China, where I am in *some degree, at home*, and shall not be long to arrive. I understand everything was quiet there when the last accounts came away, and that Mr. Elphinstone's management of the Company's affairs continue to give great satisfaction. (*Staunton Letters*, Anjere Roads, Straits of Sunda, 14 August 1814, italics in original)

His last term in China, however, proved to be 'by far the most active and anxious I passed in that country' (Staunton, 1856, p. 61).

---

33   Chinese treatment of Ayew, a Factory linguist, was a specific concern of the Select Committee. Ayew had been assigned with the task of carrying a letter and presents to Sungyun sent by the president of the Board of Control and the directors of the Company in 1812 to thank him for his assistance during the Macartney Embassy and more recently at Canton, but he was arrested at Peking and charged with illegally bringing gifts from Westerners to Chinese officials. He was allowed to return to Canton and resume work at the British Factory. An article on this question was published in 2014 in Chinese in *The Journal of Chinese Studies* by Lawrence Wang-chi Wong under the translated title 'The 1814 "Ayew incident": Linguists in Sino-British relations in the nineteenth century'.

Staunton was called on immediately after his arrival at Macao in 1814 as the committee's sole negotiator with the Chinese authorities in the *Doris* dispute.³⁴ He briefed Barrow in a private letter and informed his mother that he was 'up to his head and ears in Discussions with the Chinese government' (*Staunton Letters*, Macao, 14 October 1814). While welcoming the opportunity to renew his acquaintance with 'the language and customs of this people', he refused absolutely to submit to the viceroy's demands (*Staunton Letters*, Canton, 14 December 1814). After an anxious month of fruitless and tedious negotiations with 'Mandarins of rank at the Factory' over the actions of British warships in Chinese territorial waters, Staunton took the initiative. Declaring the Select Committee had no control over the actions of the Royal Navy, Staunton took the unprecedented and tough decision to suspend trade and ordered all British subjects and ships to leave Canton (Fu, 1966, vol. 2, p. 612). Staunton wrote:

> I was compelled to break off the negotiation, to strike the British flag, and to retire with the whole body of British subjects from Canton; and that it was only when our ships [those already at Whampoa] were upon the point of sailing through the Bocca Tigris, and thus finally quitting the port, that I was overtaken by such a conciliatory overture from the Viceroy as warranted me in returning to Canton and renewing the negotiation. (1856, p. 63)

His strategy worked. The viceroy backed down, the ships were loaded and trade resumed. Staunton's firm stand against Qing officialdom set a precedent for Amherst's actions during the Amherst Embassy's future negotiations with the mandarins. '[My] only weapon[s]', Staunton (1856) recalled, 'were those of argument and an appeal to the universal principles of justice, forcibly addressed to the Chinese in their native language, though in a spirit of British independence' (p. 64), which had won the day.

Staunton's actions, significantly, brought an immediate rebuke from the Jiaqing emperor who issued an edict dated 8 January 1815:

> There is an English barbarian, Ssu-tang-tung [Staunton], who previously came to the Imperial capital at the time his country presented tribute, was young and crafty, and throughout his return journey drew maps of all strategic spots of the mountains and rivers … he passed through. After he arrived at Canton he did not return

---

34   He was assisted at this time by Morrison and Davis.

> to his native country, but has lived in Macao for twenty years. He understands Chinese ... Barbarians who come to Kwang-tung [Canton] ask his advice and follow his suggestions. Probably in the long run he will make trouble. (Fu, 1966, vol. 1, p. 394).[35]

A further edict concerning the actions of British warships was issued a couple of days later:

> Recently, the escorting warships of England, disobeying the established regulations that foreign ships must anchor outside our territorial sea, sailed into the Boque Fortress. Such deceit is unimaginable ... Hereafter, the escorting warships of various nations should continue to obey the established regulations against entering our territorial waters ... If they dare to enter our defensive zone, we should consider firing our cannon to scare them away so that they may clearly understand that they will have to deal with us. (Fu, 1966, vol. 1, p. 395)

Staunton was not the only Englishman to come under imperial suspicion at this time. In 1807, the Reverend Doctor Robert Morrison of the London Missionary Society arrived at Canton.[36] Destined to be the senior interpreter for the Amherst Embassy, his proficiency in Mandarin ensured his appointment in the same capacity with the Company. Morrison also engaged in the illegal activities of teaching Mandarin to Company personal at the British Factory and compiling a Chinese–English dictionary sponsored by the Company.[37] His major pursuit involved the translation of Christian texts into Chinese, which he printed illegally at Macao. This was in defiance of the Jiaqing emperor's imperial edict of 1805 that specifically prohibited books printed in the 'Chinese and Tartar

---

35 The edict reveals the Qing court's misinformation about Staunton that had repercussions later during negotiations between the British and Chinese at the time of the Amherst Embassy.
36 Morrison was the first Protestant missionary to arrive in China. He landed at Canton in 1807 on an American ship (as Company ships were forbidden to carry missionaries) and hoped to spread the gospel in China. Morrison first stayed in two small rooms at the American Factory where he went 'native', 'adopting the habits and ... dress of the natives' and eating Chinese food (see Morrison, 1839, pp. 187–188). Staunton had received a letter of introduction about Morrison from Sir Joseph Banks and became his 'friend and advocate' at Canton (Staunton, 1856, p. 36). Staunton recommended Morrison to John Roberts, the president of the Select Committee, and he was hired as a translator with the Company in 1809 with a salary of £200. He set out to work on a Chinese translation of *A grammar of the Chinese language* (1815), *A dictionary of the Chinese language* (1815) and the Scriptures (Morrison, 1839, pp. 239–240).
37 Morrison's skill in Chinese was acknowledged by Staunton who wrote, 'I was certainly several years prior to him in [studying Mandarin] but I cultivated the Chinese language altogether for different purposes, and much less exclusively and assiduously than he did [and] I ... with pleasure, acknowledge that he attained ultimately to a much greater degree of proficiency' (1856, p. 37).

languages' as these were viewed as attempts to 'facilitate the propagation of [European] tenets' (Barrow, 1810, fn. 304). His actions brought him to the notice of the Chinese authorities who, in 1815, conducted a raid on his office, destroying his printing press and arresting a Chinese employee (Staunton, 1856, p. 37). Morrison acknowledged, 'The present state of China is such as renders printing, and several other labours very difficult; and even personal residence uncertain' (Morrison, 1839, p. 385). Thus, Morrison and Staunton, both men destined to play a major role in the Amherst Embassy, had aroused Chinese Government suspicion on the eve of the embassy's arrival.[38] Informing British assessments of the Jiaqing emperor was his recent escape from an assassination attempt in 1813 which, in Morrison's view, contributed to the emperor's suspicion of Staunton. Morrison informed Staunton in 1815 that the emperor was:

> Immured in his palace, distrustful of all around him; a large number of persons denounced as rebel leaders not yet taken; he supposes that plans against his life and throne are carrying on, and may burst forth suddenly, as the last convulsion did. In this state of mind some designing villain brings your name before him, says that you took maps of the country twenty years ago; that the encroachments of the English bringing ships of war, bringing troops, entering the river, and attacking the people of other countries, &c., were acts all committed by your instigation! What then must His Majesty have thought with his fears already so much excited? (Morrison to Staunton, 10 January 1815, in Morrison, 1839, p. 425)

The loss of mutual trust between the British and Peking also extended to the Select Committee and the Chinese Government at Canton. The British blamed this, in part, on the obstreperous behaviour of the viceroy. Davis, writing in 1836, explained:

> The conduct and disposition of the Chinese government for some time past had been such, as to prove that the commercial interests of [Great Britain] in China were exposed to the utmost hazard from the chance of perpetual interruption at the will of a capricious and despotic set of delegates, who kept the court of Peking in profound ignorance of their own oppressive and arbitrary conduct towards the Company's trade. (1836/1851, vol. 1, p. 73)

---

38 Morrison informed the Select Committee of the 'personal hazard' and 'feeling an apprehension that writing or translating a Letter to His Majesty the Emperor of China, which will of course contain an impeachment of the local Government of this Province, will subject me to personal suffering from the Chinese even long after the present difference shall be arranged' (Morse, 1926/1966, vol. 3, p. 211).

He added:

> To these circumstances are to be attributed the Embassy of Lord Amherst in 1816 … which object was to secure, if possible, the commerce of Great Britain upon a solid and equitable footing under the cognizance of the emperor, and with the advantage of a ready appeal to him in case of need. (1836/1851, vol. 1, p. 73)

The Jiaqing emperor, the British assumed, was kept in ignorance of the true state of affairs of trade at Canton. His intervention, it was thought, would follow a direct official approach on behalf of the British sovereign and would serve to place trade on a secure and stable basis. But the fact that Staunton and Morrison, both men destined to play a vital role in Lord Amherst's Embassy, were regarded with the utmost suspicion by the Chinese authorities, did not augur well for their reception at the Qing court. Further, British military intervention at Macao in 1808 as well as the 'agitated' state of affairs in Shandong province, where a rebellion had resulted in the death of 20 court eunuchs on orders of the emperor, hardly disposed the imperial court to welcome meddlesome foreigners (Morrison's journal entry, 7 November 1813, as quoted in Morrison, 1839, p. 373). Historians, principally Wengsheng Wang, note a hardening of the Qing attitude towards the British who were now regarded as the most troublesome 'of all Westerners' with a voracious appetite for trade (Wang, 2014, p. 248). This change, in Wang's view, partly explains the 'emperor's rejection of the Amherst Embassy in 1816' (2014, p. 248). Further, rumours circulating at Macao of the British occupation of Washington in 1814 during the Anglo–American War heightened local suspicion of the British. Staunton commented on a 'ridiculous report' that 'the British who had recently landed in America, and destroyed the city of Washington, were destined ultimately for the coast of China, upon some similar service' (1822, p. 138). He added:

> There is great reason to believe that [the act of the *Doris*], together with the frequent cruizing of our ships of war on their coasts, was considered by the Chinese, not merely as a national affront, but as actually connected with some ulterior schemes for a hostile invasion of their territory. (p. 138)

Staunton first learned that an embassy was being contemplated in a personal letter from Barrow, dated 10 April 1815, which he received in September 1815. His reaction was far from enthusiastic. Another embassy, in his personal view:

> Is … a measure about which I have for some time ceased to be at all anxious and am so much aware of the risk of bad management, that I rather wish upon the whole that it might be abandoned. If however it is otherwise determined, it will of course command my best exertions and services. Whenever anything is settled, I trust due notice will be given us here, that we may be prepared accordingly. (*Staunton Letters*, Macao, 21 September 1815)

He hoped that an embassy would not damage Britain's reputation or cause it to:

> Recede from that high and honourable position which our commercial representatives had taken at Canton, as well as our former diplomatic representative, Lord Macartney, had taken at Pekin. (Staunton, 1856, p. 66)

The possibility of another embassy to the Qing court and the prospect of playing a leading role in such a major diplomatic initiative in Anglo–Chinese relations had long sustained Staunton's ambitions for recognition and fame beyond the accumulation of wealth as a Company servant in Canton. It is ironic that, at a time when Staunton's enthusiasm for such an enterprise had largely evaporated, his friend and mentor in London, John Barrow, would seize the opportunity presented by events at Canton, based largely on Staunton's earlier reporting, to argue successfully for an embassy as the best means to address the parlous state of the Company's relations with the local authorities in China.

Barrow's strong advocacy of an embassy took place entirely in London without further reference to Company representatives in Canton. Focus falls next on the events in Whitehall and Company headquarters in Leadenhall Street in connection with the decision to dispatch a special mission led by Lord William Pitt Amherst to the Chinese empire.

4

The View from London: John Barrow and Lord William Pitt Amherst

William Pitt Amherst (1773–1857), like his embassy, has received little attention from historians who have focused either on Sir George Thomas Staunton and his role in advising Amherst against kowtowing, or on John Francis Davis's literary accounts of the British reaction to China.[1] This study seeks to redress the imbalance and argues that Amherst was conscientious in discharging his duties and ably led the mission in difficult circumstances. His conduct reflected his upbringing conditioned by deeply imbued aristocratic values of allegiance to the British Crown and, by extension, the nation. A recognition of Amherst's previous experience and career as well as his personal response to his appointment is important in gauging his suitability for the position of ambassador to the Chinese Empire and for establishing his frame of mind on the eve of departure for China. The reactions of Amherst's family and friends to his appointment, found in personal letters, reveal the views held of China by the cosmopolitan and educated elite of British society at the time and are examined later in this chapter. This chapter commences with an examination of British opinions and observations in response to the proposal for a second embassy to China.

---

1 Tuck's (2000) analysis of the embassy, it has been noted, concentrated on Staunton (pp. vii–xlii). Kitson focused largely on Davis's writings in his *Forging romantic China* (2013) and 'The dark gift' (2016).

The plan for an embassy to the Qing court in 1816 originated at Whitehall, rather than with the directors of the Company or the Select Committee at Canton.[2] Regardless of Staunton's previous lobbying on the subject, the call for another embassy to China in 1815 was exclusively Barrow's initiative. His position as second secretary to the Admiralty represented one of the most important and influential civil service offices in the British Government and gave him direct access to Cabinet ministers, politicians and members of government boards.[3] His reputation as the foremost British-based expert on China ensured his views carried weight at the highest levels of the government. The intelligence on which he based his argument for another embassy in 1815, however, was either outdated or had been overtaken by events. The disputes at Canton prompting the call for an embassy had been settled by the time Amherst arrived in China in June 1816. Even Staunton, it has been seen, had lost his enthusiasm for an embassy, but his more recent views were overlooked by Barrow who proceeded to promote the project with Lord Buckinghamshire, the president of the Board of Control.[4]

Barrow Calls for an Embassy

Napoleon's abdication in April 1814 and the restoration of Louis XVIII to the French throne ushered in a new world order with Britain as its greatest power. Both the Royal Navy and the British merchant navy reigned supreme. Britain's traditional trading rivals—the French, Spanish, Portuguese and Dutch—had been defeated and the China trade was firmly in British hands, leaving only the United States as Britain's main

---

2   Gao (2016, p. 598) is wrong in his assertion that 'the EIC's Court of Directors in London pleaded with the British government for [sic] sending a royal ambassador to the Qing court'.
3   Christopher Lloyd (1970, p. 75) described the Board of Admiralty. It was headed by the First Lord (Lord Melville 1812–1828) who was also a Cabinet minister. Seven members, mostly politicians, comprised the board. Two secretaries assisted the board. The first secretary dealt with the political aspects of naval affairs. The second secretary was 'responsible for running the Admiralty office and supervising the very extensive correspondence with naval officers all over the world, as well as with agents of other Boards'. Barrow was paid a salary of £2,000 in wartime and £1,000 in peacetime.
4   Lord Buckinghamshire, previously Lord Hobart, was governor of Madras from 1794 to 1798. He was reputed as being headstrong and quarrelsome (Philips, 1940, p. 183). George Canning, on the other hand, described Lord Hobart to Amherst in 1794 as possessing 'every quality in him, that can make him useful and respectable in the high situation, that he is to fill' (BL IOR MSS EUR F 140/13). Buckinghamshire had several meetings with Staunton at the time of the renewal of the Company's charter in 1812–1813; Staunton urged him to support the continuing monopoly of the China trade (Philips, 1940, p. 186).

competitor.⁵ Barrow was concerned that world peace posed a potential threat to British trade with China and informed Buckinghamshire in a letter dated 14 February 1815 that these countries may be 'expected to endeavour to renew their trade in China' (Barrow to Buckinghamshire, 14 February 1815, in BL IOR G/12/196 (Reel 1) F 2–6). The French were especially threatening. Barrow believed they would get 'a start' on the British due to the mischievous French missionaries at Peking who were in 'full activity; [and who] have got the ear of the present Emperor' (Barrow to Buckinghamshire, 14 February 1815, in BL IOR G/12/196 (Reel 1) F 2–6). Buckinghamshire was warned that the British 'need not be surprised [that within the year] a communication will be made personally from the Court of France to [the Court] of Pekin' (Barrow to Buckinghamshire, 14 February 1815, in BL IOR G/12/196 (Reel 1) F 2–6). Again Barrow's judgement on this occasion was based on obsolete intelligence. The only French missionary at the Qing court was Father Lamiot who, it was noted earlier, had been in regular correspondence with Staunton. Rather, Barrow's scare campaign was based on a specific hatred of the French, understandable given a century of intermittent wars with France and his own experience at the time of the Macartney Embassy. 'The French Jesuits', Barrow wrote, were 'the enemies of Protestant England … [and had] contributed to blast the hopes … for the success of the British Embassy'. He continued:

> That Embassy, in the general estimation of the board, failed in its object: it was indeed too soon discovered that it could not do otherwise; Demands were made, which had the Chinese character been duly appreciated, could not have been preferred. Those very demands were an admirable instrument in the hands of our Enemies who adroitly turned against us—We were … most completely in the hands of those enemies … Our interpreters too, were Chinese Catholics … discovered by their countrymen [arriving in China] to be … unworthy beings who had deserted the Tombs and the Religion of their Fathers, they had not the courage … to advance

---

5 American trade increased substantially in the first decade of the nineteenth century due to the demand for tea and manufactured silk. American private traders were also exporting tea and other products from Canton into Europe. In 1815–1816, the Americans exported 4.5 million pounds of tea for American consumption and almost three million pounds of tea for European consumption, amounting to over US$5 million. The value of Company imports and exports between Britain and China was valued at £4,285,799, with the value of exports and imports between India and China in the hands of private English traders valued at £2,379,064 (*Report [relative to the trade with the East Indies and China] from the Select Committee of the House of Lords*, 11 April 1821, p. 162).

the cause of the Heretics more especially when under the eye of their Catholic Brothers. (Barrow to Buckinghamshire, 14 February 1815, in BL IOR G/12/196 (Reel 1) F 2–6)

But prospects for the success of a new British embassy were at hand. Referring to Staunton, Barrow wrote, 'We [can] now appear at the Chinese court with an advantage which we never before possessed'. He explained:

> The EIC have in their employ a Gentleman who can both *speak* to the Chinese and *write* to them in their own language, without the usual recourse to the medium of any Interpreter; an advantage which can only be duly appreciated by those who have had the mortification of experiencing the intrigues and chicanery ... when communications are to be held with this jealous and corrupt government through the interventions of Catholic missionaries. (Barrow to Buckinghamshire, 14 February 1815, in BL IOR G/12/196 (Reel 1) F 2–6, emphasis in original)

Barrow, in his praise for Staunton, ignored the other English Mandarin speakers at Canton, namely, Morrison, Davis, Toone and Thomas Manning.[6] News of the Jiaqing emperor's opinion of Staunton as 'the young and crafty Englishman' had yet to reach him. Staunton, in Barrow's view, was the only candidate qualified to lead an embassy to the Qing court:

> It is almost needless to add that Sir George Staunton, who is now on the spot, is the gentleman to whom I allude. From a long and intimate acquaintance with him, I cannot have the smallest doubt ... that his knowledge of the [Chinese] people and their language, his zeal and integrity, joined to the solid good sense which he possesses, would at least ensure [an honourable result for the British nation]. (Barrow to Buckinghamshire, 14 February 1815, in BL IOR G/12/196 (Reel 1) F 2–6)

Opening up the Chinese domestic market for British manufacturers was also a powerful argument. Buckinghamshire was reminded of the gains to the manufacturers of Sheffield and Birmingham if 'a single Penknife

---

6   Thomas Manning also joined the embassy suite as a Chinese interpreter and proceeded to Peking, thus achieving his ambition of visiting the Chinese capital after earlier failed attempts to enter China through Tibet. While in Lhasa, Manning kowtowed before Tibetan mandarins and the grand lama (Markham, 1876, pp. 259, 265). A cache of Manning's papers was discovered in 2014 that have since been archived at the Royal Asiatic Society, London. A quick review of the papers in 2016 (due to time restraints) unfortunately revealed little of specific relevance to the Amherst Embassy. For a more detailed examination of Manning, see Platt (2018, pp. 140–151).

or a pair of scissors, [produced by] the manufacturers of England, could be introduced into every family in China' (Barrow to Buckinghamshire, 14 February 1815, in BL IOR G/12/196 (Reel 1) F 2–6).

Regardless of ulterior British motives, the Chinese were to be informed that the mission was being sent in a spirit of courtly civility from the British monarch to the emperor, congratulating him specifically on his escape from the assassination attempt in 1813. The Qing court was to be notified further of the British desire for peaceful relations between the Select Committee at Canton and the provincial government.

The Company's Secret Court of Directors met in London on 3 March 1815 and agreed that an embassy could result in potential benefits provided it was 'judiciously arranged and ably executed' (Chairman and Deputy Chairman to Buckinghamshire, 3 March 1815, in BL IOR G/12/196 (Reel 1) F 7). A commission of three members was proposed. The first commissioner, or ambassador, would be nominated by the Prince Regent and would be in charge of his letter to the Jiaqing emperor. The other two commissioners were to be chosen from the Select Committee at Canton. This was to ensure that trust was not placed in a single individual. The inclusion of a gentleman nominated by the Prince Regent signified the official status of the embassy, serving to inform the Qing court of its special authority above one constituted only by men of the Company.

The choice of ambassador was an early concern. Recent British military activity in Nepal, a Chinese tributary, required a man 'best adapted to the feeling and taste of the Chinese'.[7] Such a candidate should be a 'Man of high Rank, and of Military character, and also of a pre-possessing appearance' (Chairs to Buckinghamshire, 3 March 1815, in BL IOR G/12/196 (Reel 1) F 9). Any hope Staunton may have had of returning to Peking as the leader of a British embassy was extinguished immediately by these criteria.

---

7   British military action in Nepal was thought to be of 'no small importance' for British interests in China. Lord Moira wrote to the Select Committee in November 1814 of a considerable Chinese force assembled in Tibet in response to Nepalese soldiers gathering on the frontier. The British had no designs on Tibet, but nonetheless, there was a 'threat of Chinese invasion of Nepaul for the purpose of imposing on that kingdom the delegations of feudal or tributary dependence, or perhaps of actually reducing it to subjection' (Letters from Lord Moira, November 1814, and Edward Gardner, British Resident, Catmandhu, in BL MSS EUR F 140/46). For a discussion on Anglo–Chinese relations concerning Tibet, Nepal and British India at this time, see Mosca (2013).

Buckinghamshire and the Company's chairman and deputy chairman visited Prime Minister Lord Liverpool. His response to an embassy was, at best, lukewarm. Doubt was expressed whether he could justify the idea of another embassy to the British public after Macartney's failure. Liverpool added, however, that he would not be deterred from the pressure of public opinion if adequate reasons were put forward and would do his duty (Secret Court of Directors held Tuesday 2 May 1815, in BL IOR G/12/196 (Reel 1) F 11). The Company chairs decided to postpone any decision until news of the latest developments was received from Canton.

News from Canton dated 16 January 1815 arrived at the beginning of July. The Secret Court of Directors responded in a dispatch dated 7 July 1815. Conditions at Canton and the conduct of the 'local government of Canton to our representatives in 1814' had revealed:

> The hazard to property and commerce of the Company [which has] been exposed by the violence, injustice and despotism of the Government - and the very precarious situation in which our affairs and the British interests operating under the unprincipled rules of those Chinese authorities—we cannot avoid seeing that it maybe our duty ... to engage the interposition and influence of H.M. government with the Court of Pekin. (Secret Commercial Letter to China, 7 July 1815, in BL IOR G/12/196 (Reel 1) F 12)

Buckinghamshire responded to this intelligence in a letter dated 26 July 1815. Details received lately from China had convinced him that the security of both Company personnel and trade at Canton 'can only be expected by the appointment of a Mission from the Prince Regent to the Emperor of China' (Chairman and Deputy Chairman of the East India Company to Buckinghamshire, 28 July 1815 and forwarded to Amherst at the time of his appointment, in BL IOR MSS EUR F 140/36). The Company chairs sent a detailed letter to Buckinghamshire's office two days later setting out the altercations that had taken place at Canton in 1813 and 1814. Focus fell on two main concerns. The Cantonese authorities, they reported, aimed to place the British Factory under their direct control. It was evident these authorities had little sense of public or personal honour and acted solely within their own interests, evidenced by their insistence that all communication with the Select Committee be in English, thus leaving scope for distorted and incorrect Mandarin translations to be passed to the Chinese Government. This strategy proved their motives of 'conceal[ing] the truth from the Emperor' and their fear of the Court of Peking (Chairman and Deputy Chairman of the East India Company to Buckinghamshire, 28 July 1815 and forwarded to Amherst at the time of his appointment, in BL IOR MSS EUR F 140/36). An open channel for official communication with the supreme Government of China at Peking was vital to correctly address British grievances at the highest level. Perceptions of British exceptionalism governing its affairs with the Qing court remained. Britain was 'a country whose people and whose greatness [the Chinese] are unwillingly obliged to respect', and an embassy sent in the name of the British sovereign would serve 'To place the Chinese trade on a basis of steady and fixed principles which will guard it against the fatal effects of an arbitrary, capricious, or unjust exercise of power' (Chairman and Deputy Chairman of the East India Company to Buckinghamshire, 28 July 1815 and forwarded to Amherst at the time of his appointment, in BL IOR MSS EUR F 140/36).

No new demands, concessions, or privileges were to be insisted on by the ambassador as this would serve to 'excite jealousy and resistance'; rather, his aim was to 'secure the enjoyment of privileges long conceded by the Emperor, and protection against the vexatious insults and impositions of the local authorities' (Chairman and Deputy Chairman of the East India Company to Buckinghamshire, 28 July 1815 and forwarded to Amherst at the time of his appointment, in BL IOR MSS EUR F 140/36). British intentions to observe the prescribed laws and regulations of China were to be made clear and negotiation was to centre on the following goals:

1. For the privileges of the Company to be more accurately defined and detailed.
2. To ensure trade security against sudden and capricious interruptions.
3. Freedom from the interference of Chinese Government officers in the Factory. The freedom to hire Chinese servants and an exemption from abusive, contemptuous, or insolent treatment from Chinese functionaries.
4. To open a channel of communication between members of the Factory and some public tribunal at Peking, either a British resident or by written representations in the Chinese language. And the right to use the Chinese language in all addresses and representations to the local government.
5. To give an explanation of the 'Affair of the *Doris*' or any other subject of a political nature on which it may be expedient to touch.

Success in any of these was of the highest importance and the Company chairs thought it was 'worth the cost of the attempt, if that were not otherwise a matter of duty' to proceed. It was important, however, not to incur any unnecessary splendour or expense (Chairman and Deputy Chairman of the East India Company to Buckinghamshire, 28 July 1815 and forwarded to Amherst at the time of his appointment, in BL IOR MSS EUR F 140/36).

Official Approval of an Embassy

Lord Liverpool informed the Company chairs of government approval for an embassy to the Qing court on 10 August 1815. A commission made up of three commissioners was to be appointed. The second and third commissioners were named as the president of the Select Committee at Canton, John Elphinstone, and Sir George Staunton. Their contribution to the embassy would be considerable due to their local experience and knowledge of Mandarin, but it must be understood:

> That the person selected by his Royal Highness the Prince Regent to be placed at the head of the Commission, and to be the bearer of the letter addressed by HRH the Prince Regent to the Emperor of China, should, as in the Government of India, be authorized to act upon his own responsibility upon any points of difference between him and the other Commissioners. (Buckinghamshire to Chairman and Deputy Chairman, EIC, 10 August 1815, in BL IOR G/12/196 (Reel 1) F 30)

Buckinghamshire's next task was finding a suitable person of rank to fill the position of ambassador on such a delicate and difficult mission. The successful candidate, as noted earlier, would be a military man as this profession, in the view of the Company Directors, was held in the highest honour by the Chinese and a man of that description 'would prove acceptable' to them as the principal member (Chairs to Buckinghamshire, 28 July 1815, in BL IOR MSS EUR F 140/36). The ambassador would receive the same allowance as Macartney, namely, £20,000 for the mission (equivalent to approximately £2 million in today's values). The Select Committee at Canton was to be notified officially that an embassy to the Qing court was being planned.[8]

---

8   Barrow had raised the matter unofficially with Staunton in his private letters, as noted earlier in this study.

4. THE VIEW FROM LONDON

Choice of a British Ambassador

Buckinghamshire's first choice to fill the position of first commissioner or ambassador in the proposed embassy was his brother-in-law and close friend, the Rt Hon. John Sullivan, who was appointed as one of the paid assistant commissioners and had served under him when he was governor of Madras (Philips, 1940, p. 202). Sullivan had made a considerable fortune from sugar plantations in Trinidad, was a member of the Board of Control and was also a servant of the Company (Philips, 1940, p. 202).[9] He was keen to take the appointment and had received Lord Liverpool's approval, but his nomination was declined by the Company Court of Directors who thought his rank and position in the Company did not qualify him for the role. Sullivan wrote to Buckinghamshire in a letter dated 26 August 1815:

> Though I have a strong sense of the difficulties I should have had to encounter, with a Government so constituted as that of China … I should not have despaired of overcoming them, if I could have carried with me a full conviction that the Court of Directors has ceased to consider it essential to the success of the Mission that it should be placed in the hands of a Peer, or of a distinguished Military character. But knowing as I now do that they continue to attach great importance to that point, I should ill deserve the good opinion of Lord Liverpool and yourself … I decline the honour. (John Sullivan to Buckinghamshire, 26 August 1815, in BL IOR G/12/196 (Reel 1) F 36–37)

Buckinghamshire now approached Lord William Pitt Amherst and sent a letter marked 'Private and Confidential' inviting Amherst to dine with him at the Fitzroy Room to 'entertain a subject I have to mention'. He continued:

> It is intended to send a Commission of Embassy to China. The business is to be conducted upon a liberal scale, but not as extravagant as in the case of Lord Macartney.
>
> In the event of you embarking in this undertaking, I conceive you must look to an absence of two years and might expect to put twenty thousand pounds in your pocket.

---

9   Sullivan had resided in Madras where he 'took a keen interest in Indian affairs, personally conducting useful research at the Board into the civil and political government of India'.

The consent of the Court of Directors is necessary. I write in Lord Liverpool's name as well as my own. (Buckinghamshire to Amherst, marked 'Private and Confidential', 29 August 1815, in BL IOR MSS EUR F 140/35)

Amherst declined the offer and Buckinghamshire approached Lord Binning.[10] Binning took a couple of weeks to make up his mind. Amherst, in the meantime, had reconsidered the appointment and informed Buckinghamshire that he would accept the nomination of ambassador to China if Binning turned it down. He informed Buckinghamshire, 'I have made up my mind to a separation of two years from my family for the sake of procuring for my children a provision of £20,000' (Amherst to Buckinghamshire, 8 September 1815, in BL IOR MSS EUR F 140/35).

A series of secret correspondences between Amherst and Buckinghamshire followed where Buckinghamshire forwarded in 'strict confidence some extracts of my letters to Binning' (Buckinghamshire to Amherst, 9 September 1815, in BL IOR MSS EUR F 140/35). Amherst was informed on 9 September by Buckinghamshire that he was expecting Binning's answer and that 'if in the affirmative you must be aware that he must have the appointment' (Buckinghamshire to Amherst, 9 September 1815, in BL IOR MSS EUR F 140/35). Binning's answer arrived on 15 September. He had declined the appointment. Amherst was requested to meet with Buckinghamshire 'without delay' (Buckinghamshire to Amherst, 15 September 1815, in BL IOR MSS EUR F 140/35).

Amherst's Appointment

Amherst's appointment was announced to the British public on 27 September 1815. The Company's Secret Court of Directors wrote to the president of the Select Committee at Canton on the same day announcing that the Company was going ahead with an embassy to China to address the arbitrary and injurious proceedings of the local authorities towards Company representatives and interests at Canton (Draft Letter in the Secret Commercial Department to the President and Select Committee of Supra Cargoes at Canton, reference made to letters of 7 July, n.d., in

---

10   Thomas Hamilton, Lord Binning (1780–1858). Binning, like Amherst, was a close friend of George Canning and later served under him on the Board of Control from 1816. He was a MP for Rochester from 1818–1832. A friend described Binning as 'a thin under jawed fellow' and 'one of the pleasantest men I ever met' (see *The History of Parliament*, www.historyofparliamentonline.org).

BL IOR MSS EUR F 140/43 (a)). The embassy was to consist of a person of high rank, namely, Lord Amherst, as first commissioner. The two most senior members of the Select Committee, John Elphinstone and Sir George Staunton, were nominated as the second commissioner and third commissioner, respectively, but their rank and inclusion was to be decided by Amherst on arrival in China (Staunton, 1824, p. 4).

Henry Ellis, the illegitimate son of Lord Buckinghamshire, was appointed secretary of the embassy with dormant credentials of minister plenipotentiary in the event of the death or absence of the ambassador (Castlereagh to Lord Amherst, 1 January 1816, in Morse, 1926/1966, vol. 3, p. 283).[11] Ellis had returned recently from an important diplomatic mission to Persia where, acting as the deputy minister plenipotentiary at Tehran in the absence of the minister, James Morier, he had successfully engaged in negotiations with the Shah of Persia and acquired a ratification of the Anglo–Persian Definitive Treaty signed in 1814 (Sir Gore Ouseley, James Morier, Henry Ellis, in Public Records Office [PRO], Kew, UK, FO 60/9).[12] His diplomatic skill was noted by Morier, who praised his efforts in achieving success during 'negotiations of considerable difficulty at Tehran' (James Morier, 21 August 1814, in PRO FO 60/9). Ellis, Morier wrote, was 'fully acquainted with the peculiar nature of the public service in Persia' (James Morier, 21 August 1814, in PRO FO 60/9). His experience of eastern diplomacy, it may be assumed, was seen as providing Amherst with valuable insight and assistance during forthcoming negotiations with the Qing court.

Lord Buckinghamshire's letter addressed to the viceroy of Canton informing him officially that an embassy was being dispatched was left unsealed so that the Select Committee could read its contents and present it together with the original and a copy of a Chinese translation. The timing of the letter's delivery at Canton was considered critical. An immediate delivery might lead the local government, acting 'from suspicion or hostility', to turn the emperor's ministers against the embassy with a danger of their

---

11   A secretary's task in a diplomatic mission is assisting the ambassador in drafting papers, examining documents and giving legal advice and providing the ambassador with the fruits of their professional experience (Mattingly, 1955/2010, p. 103).
12   An earlier treaty had been signed in 1812 by Ouseley. The Anglo–Persian Definitive Treaty (signed in 1814) guaranteed British military assistance in the event of European powers hostile to England entering Persian territory. Company interests in India were concerned about potential French incursions in Persia and sought to contain Russian threats that had resulted in their victory over Persia in the period 1805–1813. British embassies had pressured Persia to comply with Russian terms given that Russia was a British ally against Napoleon.

refusing its reception. News of the embassy's impending arrival was to be kept secret and was to be announced by the presentation of the letter when the ships-of-war conveying Amherst and the embassy arrived off the coast of China. Such a strategy would leave little time for Peking to be notified and for orders to arrive at Canton forbidding the progress of the embassy (Secret Commercial Letter to China, 27 September 1815, in BL IOR G/12/196 (Reel 1) F 39–40). Short notice of the embassy's arrival, on the other hand, ran the risk of offending the Chinese as well as leaving insufficient time for the Qing court to prepare for the embassy's arrival. Accordingly, the Select Committee was instructed by the directors to use their own discretion for timing the delivery of Buckinghamshire's letter and to take the most expedient course of action 'according to the circumstances in which you find yourselves placed' (Secret Commercial Letter to China, 27 September 1815, in BL IOR G/12/196 (Reel 1) F 41).

The issues to be raised with the Chinese Government were also left to the discretion of the Select Committee. The Chinese were to be informed that Elphinstone and Staunton's inclusion in the embassy was on the orders of the Prince Regent and not the Company and the presence of several Mandarin speakers from the British Factory was necessary to relieve Staunton from translation duties. These were Robert Morrison, who had 'given so many proofs of his skill in translation from either of the two languages into the other', Robert Toone and John Francis Davis (Secret Commercial Letter to China, 27 September 1815, in BL IOR G/12/196 (Reel 1) F 41).

Amherst was scheduled to arrive in Chinese waters on 1 May 1816, at which time he was to be presented with a full report on the latest intelligence of Company affairs. The directors reminded the Select Committee that the dispatch of an embassy represented a potential hazard to British interests where trade could be stopped and it was acknowledged that this was 'a perilous expedition' (Secret Commercial Letter to China, 27 September 1815, in BL IOR G/12/196 (Reel 1) F 43).

Lord William Pitt Amherst (1773–1857)

William Pitt Amherst, referred to as 'Pitt' by his family and close friends, was born at Bath on 14 January 1773.[13] Named in honour of the statesman William Pitt the Elder, Amherst was the first of three children of Lieutenant-General William Amherst, aide-de-camp to the king, governor of Newfoundland and adjutant-general of the army, and his wife, Elizabeth Patterson.[14] On the death of their parents in 1781, Amherst and his younger sister, Elizabeth, went to live with their uncle, Jeffrey Amherst, first Baron Amherst and commander in chief of the British Army, on his estate at Sevenoaks in Kent.[15] Named 'Montreal' after his celebrated victory over the French during the Seven Years War in 1760, the estate offered rolling hills, horses and an ideal country life for children. Elizabeth wrote to her brother in 1800, 'Surely no two people were ever more fortunate after losing their parents, to find themselves in a better situation than if they had lived' (Hall & Shelton, 2002, p. 49).[16]

Amherst was educated at Westminster School where he 'profited by the mould and conscientious rule of Dr Samuel Smith' and, at the age of 16, went to Christ Church Oxford to study for a Bachelor of Arts during the 'Saturnian reign' of Doctor Cyril Jackson from where he graduated in 1792 ('A commemoration speech on Amherst's life', read at the Christ Church Gaudy, 21 June 1876, in BL IOR MSS EUR F 140/221). Historians have concluded that young men of Amherst's aristocratic class led a sheltered existence:

---

13   Viscount Mersey (1949, p. 47) described the Amherst family as 'old legal gentry'. The family motto was 'Victoria Concordia Crescit' ('Victory springs from Concord') (*Debrett's New Peerage for 1822*, 1822).
14   Amherst's father, Lieutenant-General William Amherst, was born in 1732 and died in 1781. His mother, Elizabeth Patterson, died in 1777. The family lived on the Isle of Wight, on land inherited by Elizabeth, in a house described as a 'seven bay' Palladian style overlooking the sea (Peers, n.d.).
15   Field Marshal Jeffrey Amherst (1717–1797), 1st Baron Amherst, was instrumental in British victories against the French in Canada during the Seven Years War, including the capture of Montreal in September 1760 which ended French rule in North America. He was appointed governor-general of British North America or Canada, a position he held until 1763. Made a baron in 1776, Amherst was promoted to commander in chief of the British Army in 1778 (Peers, n.d.).
16   Amherst's youngest sister died soon after birth in 1775. Elizabeth Frances (Amherst) Hale was born at Walcott, England, in 1774 and moved to Canada in 1799 where she died at Quebec City, Quebec, in 1826. She had married John Hale and had 12 children. John Hale was the deputy paymaster British Forces in Quebec in 1798, and later became a member of Legislative Council for Lower Canada in 1808 (Hall & Shelton, 2002, pp. 448–450).

> By their social intercourse, their classical studies, their mingling in the affairs of county society, and their travels, they could be said to have had an extensive knowledge of three things above all else, namely, ancient Rome, modern (non-industrial) England south of the Trent, and those foreign parts which customarily featured on the itinerary of the Grand Tour. (R. J. White as quoted in Plowright, 2002, p. 23)

Amherst was a quiet and inoffensive student whose 'academic performance was unexceptional' (Peers, n.d.). Nevertheless, his high birth, good looks and fine character ensured his popularity with a group of very close friends made at school and university, many of whom were destined to become the leading politicians of their generation.[17] His friends included George Canning, future foreign secretary (1807–1809, 1822–1827) and prime minister (1827); John Parker, 1st Earl of Morley, a prominent Whig politician and a member of the House of Lords; Lord Sidmouth, Prime Minister (1801–1804) and Home Secretary (1812–1822); Charles Abbot, Speaker of the House of Commons (1802–1817); and Charles Wynn, a future president of the Board of Control (1822–1828). Archives housed in the British Library contain several letters written to Amherst over the course of his life that provide insight into his character, career and the importance of connections and patronage in Georgian and Regency high society.

In 1794, at the age of 21, Amherst travelled to Austria at the start of a grand tour of Europe. Lady Elizabeth Holland, the English socialite, met Amherst and recorded in her journal that he was 'a quiet, sedate young man, full of proprieties and all sorts of good things' (Holland, 1909, p. 129).[18] She continued, 'Mr. A. fell in love with me and Mrs. W [Mrs. Wyndham]; he was most in love with the one he last saw. We went to balls and were very gay' (Holland, 1909, p. 129). Lady Holland's group of friends reached Italy two years later where they met Lord Macartney, recently returned from the court of the Qianlong emperor and currently on a 'confidential mission to Louis XVIII at Verona' (Holland, 1909,

---

17 Jennifer Hall-Witt (2007, p. 17) stated the importance of 'one's dress, manners, wit, and attractiveness, as well as one's network of friends and acquaintances, which could influence one's entrance into elite social circles'. Amherst's sister referred to his good looks in the context of a newly arrived portrait of Amherst hanging 'over the chimney-piece' in 1806, adding that 'all the young ladies have fallen in love with you' (Hall & Shelton, 2002, p. 207). Curiously, Platt (2018, p. 159) belittles Amherst as 'neither brilliant nor particularly handsome'.
18 Mrs Wyndham was the wife of the British Minister at Florence.

p. 136).¹⁹ Lady Sarah Plymouth, married to Lord Plymouth and the mother of three children, joined Lady Holland's group in Naples.²⁰ She and Amherst were immediately attracted to each other. Lady Holland related, 'I went with Lady Plymouth and Amherst to Tivoli; we stayed a couple of days. Lord Macartney came, and … I saw a good deal of him' (Holland, 1909, p. 142). Lord Macartney's 'remarkable [and] retentive memory' and love of 'playing tricks' made him good company (Holland, 1909, p. 229). Whether or not Amherst and Macartney discussed China at this time is not known, but it is reasonable to suggest that the subject of Macartney's reception at the Qianlong court was raised at some point in light of his unique appointment as the first British ambassador to arrive in China and his disappointment at the failure of his mission.²¹ If so, such a conversation would likely have left a negative perception of China in Amherst's mind.

Amherst returned to Oxford in 1797 where he received a Master of Arts. Later that year, he succeeded to the title of Baron on the death of his uncle and was handed 'Montreal' by his aunt, the Dowager Amherst. A reference to the estate appears in an 1879 publication:

> The father of the first Lord Amherst had acquired a small estate near Seven Oaks; the son extended its boundaries by the purchase of the third part of Otford and other lands. He also pulled down the old house and built himself a mansion, which he called Montreal, in commemoration of his chief victory. (Evans, 1879, p. 162)²²

Meanwhile, Amherst's and Lady Sarah Plymouth's relationship developed into a romantic affair that impacted not only on his private life but also on his career. The fact that Amherst was concerned to keep the relationship a secret from both his sister Elizabeth and the Dowager Amherst is indicated in a letter to Elizabeth written at the end of 1799, where

---

19   Barrow (1807, p. 356) wrote, 'in June 1795, [Macartney] was again called upon to undertake an important mission to Italy of a delicate and confidential nature, the particulars of which there are many reasons for not disclosing at present'.
20   Lady Sarah Plymouth was born Sarah Archer in 1762. She married the 5th Earl of Plymouth in 1778 when she was only 16. She had a son and two daughters by this marriage.
21   Macartney wrote, 'I cannot help feeling the disappointment most severely' (Cranmer-Byng, 1962, p. 152).
22   The Palladian style house built by Lord Jeffrey Amherst in 1769–1770 at Sevenoaks was sold in 1926 to a local businessman where after it fell into disrepair. The house was demolished in 1936. The original estate comprised 2,500 acres of which 60 acres were subdivided into a housing estate between 1952 and 1963 and named 'Montreal Park'. The remaining land is presently a nature reserve managed by the Kent Wildlife Trust (www.montrealpark.org.uk/history/history.htm).

Amherst informed her that he had turned down the position of governor of Jamaica due to some 'most weighty reasons of a private nature' (BL IOR MSS EUR F 140/7). She replied in a letter dated 1 February 1800:

> You say your objections to accepting the place offered you are insuperable, but do not mention them; whatever they may be I have not the least doubt of their being founded in good sense & am very glad you are not going to what I fear is a bad climate. (as quoted in Hall & Shelton, 2002, p. 28)

His sister turned her attention to Amherst's maiden speech before the House of Lords in late 1799:

> All my friends write good accounts of your Lordship's speech … so I hope as you have begun so prosperously you will continue to exert your abilities on behalf of your Country. I am certain it only requires a little exertion for you to become a good Speaker, as you are certainly amply provided with good sense, judgment and information … I only wish to give you a little hint to speak <u>loud</u> enough … your voice naturally is not a very loud one. (as quoted in Hall & Shelton, 2002, p. 31, emphasis in original)

Lord Plymouth, described as 'a fine Fat round English Lord', died in 1800 (Figgis & Rowney, 2001, p. 140). His death, Lady Holland wrote, was 'a great release to his wife, who will be rewarded by marrying Amherst within the year. <u>His</u> constancy is unparalleled' (Holland, 1909, p. 264, emphasis in original). Amherst and Sarah were married on 24 July 1800. Their marriage was a very strong and loving union that bore three sons and a daughter.[23] Amherst's sister Elizabeth was not pleased about the marriage, citing the age difference—Amherst was 27 and Sarah was 38—and the fact that Sarah had three children from her previous marriage. Advantages were noted, however, and her response provides clues to the nature of Amherst's lifestyle and occupation at this time:

> Your circumstances will be extremely comfortable … Lady Amherst having so generously given up Montreal to you is a very great advantage and the farm around will be an additional employment and amusement for you.[24]

---

23 Jeffrey was born on 29 August 1802 at 'Montreal', Seven Oaks, and died on 2 August 1826 at Barrackpore, India. Jeffrey had been aide-de-camp to his father in India (BL IOL MSS EUR F 140/168). His brother, William, was born on 3 September 1805 and succeeded as the 2nd Earl on the death of Amherst in 1857.
24 Prior to his marriage, Amherst lived at 41 Duke Street, St James's (Hall & Shelton, 2002, p. 67).

4. THE VIEW FROM LONDON

'Montreal' remained his family home until after Sarah's death in 1838.[25] Fond references to the estate appear in several letters from friends over the years and portray an ideal country life with social gatherings spent around the fireplace in the grand house. Amherst was also fortunate in acquiring a fine London residence at 66 Grosvenor Street, Mayfair, inherited by his wife on the death of her father, whose contents were described as consisting of 'uncommonly elegant furniture' (Hall & Shelton, 2002, p. 48).

Amherst showed little interest in domestic politics and hated public speaking (Hall & Shelton, 2002, p. 47). His main interests were foreign affairs and coin collecting, and he was very fond of children (Hall & Shelton, 2002, pp. 49–51). Amherst's chief occupation at this time was the management of 'Montreal' as well as activities and responsibilities connected with the very fashionable St James's Volunteers, which he joined on 31 May 1798 with the gazetted rank of colonel.[26] This position entitled him to wear a splendid uniform of:

> Scarlet jacket, dark blue or black facings and collar with gilt edging, gold epaulettes, gilt gorget and buttons, gilt sword-hilt, dark blue or black trousers, black helmet with plume white out of red, pink sash, silver spurs on high black boots. (Walker, 1985, Item no. 1546)[27]

Amherst enjoyed military service, which was hardly surprising given his family background and upbringing. He wrote to his wife from Dover in 1806 at the time of British fears of a French invasion:

> I am very glad you are in town, and shall rejoice if it [an invasion] has the effect of giving me a little more military duty ... If the war continues we may be treated with a military spectacle all along the

---

25 Amherst's first wife, Lady Sarah, died in 1838. Amherst married Lady Mary Sackville, the daughter of the 6th Earl of Plymouth and the widow of Amherst's stepson, on 25 May 1839 at the age of 66. The couple lived at 'Knole House', Sevenoaks, one of England's grandest houses.

26 The volunteer movement was formed for the purpose of defending Britain against a French invasion. Gillian Russell (1995, pp. 13–15) has pointed out its important role in galvanising domestic support for king and country among groups that might otherwise have gravitated towards radicalism. The Volunteers were disbanded in 1802 after the Peace of Amiens, but reformed in June 1803 as the St James's Westminster Volunteers with Amherst as colonel. Amherst's sister refers to an incident in 1804 reported in a newspaper where the 'timely arrival' of Lord Amherst at the head of the Grenadier Company of the St James's Volunteers put down a 'rowdy mob' of demonstrators in Tenterden Street, off Hanover Square (Hall & Shelton, 2002, p. 180).

27 This is a description of a portrait of Amherst in full Volunteer uniform painted in 1803 by Arthur William Devis. The portrait remained in the Amherst family until it was lent to the War Office in 1926. It was sold at Sotheby's (Amherst Sale) on 29 January 1964 and again at Christie's on 23 November 1973.

coast, as camps succeed each other the whole way to Eastbourne without any great intervals. (Amherst to Lady Amherst, 1806, in Letters from the Yale Collection of American Literature)

Amherst and the British Court

Undoubtedly, the highlight of Amherst's early career was his appointment as a Lord of the Bedchamber to George III, a position he first held from 1802 to 1804.[28] The appointment represented a mark of royal favour and also carried an annual salary of £1,000 (equivalent to approximately £100,000 in today's values). Amherst's sister agreed that this was an opportunity that her brother could not possibly refuse, although she told him, 'it is not quite the line [of occupation] we could have wished. However, I conclude it is no bar to your taking some more active situation in future' (Elizabeth Hale to Amherst, 12 August 1802, in Hall & Shelton, 2002, p. 117). The opportunity to serve the king as one of his courtiers in the inner sanctum of the Court of St James's served to familiarise Amherst with the daily intricacies of court life marked by the decorous sociability of morality and taste (Brewer, 1997, p. 38). Further, the experience served to establish the subsequent context for his judgement of the manners and conduct of the Qing court, perceived as heavily ceremonial and prescribed in contrast to Regency England. The historian John Ashton wrote:

> The only etiquette observed on the *Terrace* is, that when the King passes, the ladies and gentlemen withdraw on either side, the latter merely uncovering the head; bows and curtsies being dispensed with on the occasion [when the king stops to converse] … this is done with the greatest urbanity. (1890, p. 8)

The fact that Amherst felt some sense of underachievement in light of the careers of his more illustrious political friends was reflected in his need to assure them that his appointment to the king's bedchamber was achieved without 'any solicitation on my part in any Quarter' (Amherst to George Canning, 28 April 1802, in BL IOR MSS EUR F 140/13). Canning replied that he never 'entertained a doubt of [Amherst] having obtained it [but] in the most honorable manner' (Canning to Amherst, 3 May 1802, in BL IOR MSS EUR F 140/13). Amherst's position was suspended momentarily

---

28 Amherst had three other terms as Lord of the Bedchamber: 1804–1813, 1815–1823 and 1829–1833 (Hall & Shelton, 2002, p. 450).

in early 1804 due to new arrangements in the royal household, but his quick reinstatement, brought about by Canning's recommendation, was met with an effusive response showing his high personal regard for the British monarch. Amherst wrote, 'I bow, with the utmost submission to His Majesty's demands' (Amherst to Earl of Winchilsea, 18 May 1804, in BL IOR MSS EUR F 140/11).[29]

While Amherst displayed a personal disdain for the behaviour of the Prince Regent, his respect, if not reverence, for the institution of the British monarchy remained steadfast.[30] For men of Amherst's class and station in life, commitment to the British Crown still embodied and symbolised the highest virtues of patriotic duty and national honour at a time when British politics were increasingly becoming accountable to Parliament, the press and public opinion (Dickinson, 1999, pp. 35–42). Webster wrote in his Introduction to *The letters of George IV* of the importance of royal patronage for personal advancement among the closed circle of the British aristocratic elite (1938, p. lxiv). Amherst's steadfastness in upholding vigorously the sanctity of the office of the British sovereign in the face of extreme pressure from the mandarins of the Qing court during discussions with the Chinese Government is explained by such allegiance.

Amherst's owed his first diplomatic appointment in 1808 as ambassador extraordinary to the Court of the Two Sicilies to the recommendation of George Canning.[31] His fluency in Italian and love of Italian culture eminently qualified him for this position, in marked contrast to his later appointment as an ambassador to China. His sister enquired of the decor at 'Montreal', 'You intended ornamenting some room with the largest general view of Rome at a distance; have you yet done so?' (Elizabeth Hale to Amherst, Quebec, 9 December 1800, in Hall & Shelton, 2002, p. 68).

---

29 Canning wrote to Amherst that the Prince Regent said to him following his recommendation, 'You wish Lord Amherst restored—I shall have the greatest pleasure in restoring him' (Canning to Amherst, 6 August 1804, in BL IOR MSS EUR F 140/13).

30 Amherst referred to the 'absurd and scandalous behaviour of the Prince', which made him ashamed to visit the Prince Regent in the drawing room at Carlton House. He commented: 'and yet what can an individual do!' (Amherst to Lady Amherst, 31 May 1814, in Letters from the Yale Collection of American Literature).

31 Amherst wrote that the appointment had received the full approval of the king. He added that his interview with Canning was 'very short as he was in a hurry to prepare for the Levee, where indeed I shall have an opportunity of again seeing him. Eighteen months is the time agreed upon, but he expressed a wish that I shall not publickly [sic] name this stipulation, in order to save him the application which would already be made for the reversion. I must now dress for His Majesty' (Amherst to Lady Amherst, 14 December 1808, in Letters from the Yale Collection of American Literature).

Amherst's two-year term at the Sicilian court, however, was described as:

> Fruitless as [Amherst] tried, without sufficient support from London, to patch over the rift between Sicilian constitutionalists and nationalists and the island's nominal rulers, the exiled Bourbon king of Naples and his wife, Maria Carolina, who fought tenaciously to defend their authority. (Peers, n.d.)[32]

On his return to England in 1811, Amherst spent his time commuting between 'Montreal' and his town house in Grosvenor Street. His letters reflect a busy and carefree social life of engagements in the highest circles of aristocratic and court society. Their nature is discerned in a reference to a recital at the London residence of Lady Salisbury where a performance of 'Spanish airs' sung by a Monsieur and Madame La Font, appearing on the recommendation of the Prince Regent, was on the program.[33] Amherst, whose taste in the arts was rather pedestrian, enjoyed the occasion.[34] He wrote to Lady Sarah, 'The harmony between [Monsieur Lamont] and his wife is quite edifying. They say they are French, but I can hardly believe it, they sing with so much taste' (Amherst to Lady Amherst, 1815, in BL MSS EUR B 363).

Amherst attended another social function a couple of nights later. His sense of humour is revealed in a letter to Lady Sarah:

> I found a diamond earring … and went about looking for an unadorned ear. I presently discovered the lady, Mrs. Harbord, and restored her _trim_ before she was aware she was lop-sided. (Amherst to Lady Amherst, 13 June 1815, in BL MSS EUR B 363, emphasis in original)[35]

---

32   The Bourbons ruled in Sicily under the protection of the British navy.
33   Lady Salisbury invited the singers on the recommendation of the Prince Regent who had heard them at a recital at Carlton House a few nights prior.
34   Amherst's correspondence shows little appreciation of the arts. In 1822, he attended the Hay Market Theatre with his son Jeff to see 'a laughable play called Matchmaking, and my old delight Peeping Tom [of Coventry]. I suppose I am grown grave, for Liston did not make me laugh as Edwin used to do. Amongst other songs is "Your Lordship is welcoming among us"' (Amherst to Lady Amherst, 1 August 1822, in Letters from the Yale Collection of American Literature). 'Liston' and 'Edwin' were two famous comic actors of the time. John Liston is referred to as a 'caricaturist' and Edwin played character roles depicting the lower orders of society and died in 1805 (Davis, 2015, pp. 61, 136). Robert Morrison (2019, p. 67) described Liston as relying on 'hilarious facial contortions' and making fun of conceited Cockneys and affected provincialists.
35   Mr Harbord was an MP.

Amherst also described dinners held in Hanover Square with General Bligh.³⁶ He spent a 'very merry night' with Bligh and a small group of friends at the Freemason's Tavern where a walk home after the festivities 'prevented my having a <u>very</u> bad headache' (Amherst to Lady Amherst, 1815, in BL MSS EUR B 363, emphasis in original). The subject of most of his letters at this time concerned his love and affection for his wife and children. Recalling 20 years of marriage, Amherst wrote to Sarah:

> What a delightful retrospect it is! And what an Angel in woman's shape art thou, my dearest. How I dwell upon all your amiable and excellent qualities, and how has possession, instead of producing satiety, only sharpened and increased my love for you. (Amherst to Lady Amherst, 12 June 1815, in BL MSS EUR B 363)

And, finally, in a letter to Sarah, who was spending time in Dublin: 'I wonder what would induce me to consent to pass another five weeks away from you … From my breast you must never more depart' (Amherst to Lady Amherst, 7 July 1815, in BL MSS EUR B 363).

Amherst's Personal Reaction to the Appointment of Ambassador

From the earlier account of the selection process surrounding the position of ambassador to the Qing court, it is not difficult to appreciate that Binning's indecision and Buckinghamshire's concern to keep the appointment process a secret caused Amherst and his wife great anxiety. Hugh Hammersley, a prominent banker, MP and close friend of Amherst, wrote to him on 8 September 1815:³⁷

> I am anxious for an explanation of that to which you allude as a painful struggle. I conclude it is some public employ which may interrupt the fire-side happiness so dear to you. (Hammersley to Amherst, 8 September 1815, in BL IOR MSS EUR F 140/35)

---

36   Bligh (1769–1840) was a general in the 33rd Regiment of Foot, an MP in the Irish House of Commons (1800–1801) and a leading cricketer of the day.
37   Hugh Hammersley's father was the banker to the Prince of Wales. Hammersley (1767–1840) was MP for Helston. Known as a 'Cannonite', Hammersley, like Amherst, had been a captain in the St James's Westminster Volunteers: 'In 1826 he irritated Canning by pressing the claims of his friend Lord Amherst for an earldom' (Thorne, 1986).

Binning's eventual rejection of the position and Amherst's decision to accept the appointment was governed principally, as noted earlier, by the inducement of earning £20,000 for his sons' inheritance (Amherst to Canning, 25 September 1815, in BL IOR MSS EUR F 140/35). A further incentive, and an indication of the importance of rank in English aristocratic circles, was his expectation that the completion of a successful mission might be 'a step to the earldom' to which 'My attention has been more alive since Lady Amherst by marrying me descended from the rank of Countess to that which she at present holds' (Amherst to Canning, 25 September 1815, in BL IOR MSS EUR F 140/35).

Amherst's reduced financial circumstances at the time were well known in London high society. Charles Bagot, who was shortly appointed as the British ambassador to the United States, wrote to Binning on his decision not to accept the appointment of ambassador to the Qing court:

> [You had] no choice I think but very civily to say no to it … Amherst did right to take it. His private circumstances are very bad, without any prospect of mending it by his own exertions. (as quoted in Bagot, 1909, pp. 10–11)

Knowledge and gossip about the affairs of one's friends and acquaintances reflected in Bagot's letter are read by historians as typical of the nature of Regency high society where the exclusive circle of friends and acquaintances making up the aristocracy ensured that everyone knew all about each other's domestic situation and financial position (Webster, 1938, p. xiv). Webster wrote in his Introduction to *The letters of King George IV*:

> Everyone knew about the incomes and the domestic circumstances of the rest—marriage difficulties, less respectful alliances, pressures of debts and the possibilities of inheritances daily canvassed in frank and familiar conversations and letters. (1938, p. xiv)

Sarah's initial reaction to Buckinghamshire's proposal was ambiguous. She informed Amherst that she had rushed to the local library, presumably at Sevenoaks, to get 'a copy of Macartney' to immerse herself in the account of his embassy (Correspondence between Amherst's appointment and departure, Sarah Amherst to Amherst, n.d., in BL IOR MSS EUR F 140/35). Remaining behind at 'Montreal' while Amherst went to London to hold discussions with Lord Buckinghamshire, she worked through her emotions while on an energetic ride with Jeffrey, their 13-year-old son. She wrote to Amherst on her return:

> My mind as you may suppose has been intent on nothing but the business of this morning—the time being only <u>two years</u> makes the undertaking a less one—but it is a very great sacrifice and ought to have a <u>large temptation</u>—If the voyage and every expense is paid by Government, so that we could be enabled to lay up our own Income it would greatly enhance the temptation. (Lady Amherst to Amherst, n.d., in BL IOR MSS EUR F 140/35, emphasis in original)

Sarah, it appeared, had hoped to accompany her husband to China, for she wrote 'if I am permitted to be with you, it matters little to me where I am' (Lady Amherst to Amherst, n.d., in BL IOR MSS EUR F 140/35). An embassy to China, in her view, was not a desirable undertaking and she expected to learn that Amherst had refused the appointment:

> If not, I dare say you might merely make your own terms, for few, very few of your Rank, to say nothing of Abilities ... would consent to go and I dare say [the] Government [will] have difficulties in getting any one to accept <u>such</u> a Mission (Lady Amherst to Amherst, n.d., in BL IOR MSS EUR F 140/35, emphasis in original).

Sarah listed her concerns, namely, 'the <u>climate</u> is a matter to enquire into' (emphasis in original) as well as the length of time her husband would be away from his family. She ended her letter with a note of resignation that deferred to her husband's wisdom:

> My head is not as good as yours, & can devise nothing we have not talk'd over already ... God bless you My dearest Love - who can tell what is to happen to [us] between sun rise and sun set. (Lady Amherst to Amherst, n.d., in BL IOR MSS EUR F 140/35)

Amherst informed Canning that he was due to sail before the end of November. He added:

> I am told ... I am to be joined, I believe at Canton, by the Chief of the Factory there and by Sir George Staunton (the boy in Lord Macartney's Voyage) who are to be united with me in the Commission. My absence from England will be short of two years. I conclude I may consider my appointment as decided tho' it is yet to be approved by the Regent and the Court of Directors ... I have had no judgment but my own to direct me in the decision which I have taken. (Amherst to Canning, 25 September 1815, in BL IOR MSS EUR F 140/35)

The Reaction of Amherst's Friends

Amherst's appointment was approved formally by the Prince Regent on 2 October 1815. His family and friends were astonished at the news. The Dowager Amherst wrote that she was stunned and added:

> I hope in God that the Embassy to Pekin may contribute … much to your Happiness and Advantage as every other event in your life has hitherto done; but this is a severe trial of your good Fortune. (Dowager Amherst to Amherst, 27 September 1815, in BL IOR MSS EUR F 140/35)

Hugh Hammersley was initially quite startled when he heard the news, but thought Amherst had 'done right to make a sacrifice of two years to the future advantage' of his family, adding:

> It is an undertaking of a very serious kind to be shut up for so many months on board a Ship, and in all probability to be allowed to satisfy your curiosity in a very confined degree at the end of your Sail … The shake by the hand you gave me in the Vestry on Tuesday is not to be repeated for more than two years. I thank you much for not disclosing the Secret that day, for you would have lessened my joy and happiness most seriously. We have only to hope that if you do the E. India Company a real benefit by the Sacrifice, they will act liberally in their turn, & the reward will be worth having. (Hugh Hammersley to Amherst, 23 September 1815, in BL IOR MSS EUR F 140/35)

Lord Boringdon agreed with Hammersley of the benefits of adding £20,000 to the family fortune but warned Amherst:[38]

> To take care and have a most complete understanding as to the powers and situations of the two gentlemen appointed with you; so that they should not be able in case of success to reap all the credit and in the event of failure to impose the blame upon you. (Lord Boringdon to Amherst, 28 September 1815, in BL IOR MSS EUR F 140/35)

---

38 Lord Boringdon was Lord Morley, created in 1815 for John Parker, 2nd Baron Boringdon (*Debrett's New Peerage for 1822*, 1822, p. 379).

4. THE VIEW FROM LONDON

Boringdon recommended strongly that Amherst should take his son, Jeffrey Amherst, to China. Not only was the boy of an age and character to benefit from the expedition, but also his presence would provide a source of great comfort to his father. Canning congratulated Amherst on his appointment:

> I hope you continue to be well pleased with the nature of your Embassy and as hopeful of the result of it as you describe yourself at present. With every good will for your success, and your safe return, my dear Amherst. (George Canning to Amherst, 20 October 1815, in BL IOR MSS EUR F 140/13)

The prospect of a visit to China did not excite much envy among Amherst's friends. Lord Camden, who had read Macartney, wrote to Amherst, 'The country you are about to visit is rather curious than interesting but I hope you will be able to see more of it than your Predecessors have done' (Lord Camden to Amherst, 28 September 1815, in BL IOR MSS EUR F 140/35). A letter received from Doctor D. Jackson, the retired dean of Amherst's alma mater Christ Church College, Oxford, reflected a wider reading of European diplomatic overtures to China. His opinion of Amherst's coming encounter with China and its court, however, was hardly enthusiastic. He wrote:

> There is a monotony in every thing belonging to China, which always tired me even when I have been reading about it … As for the negotiations in which you are to be engaged, there is a monotony in these also. I have read I believe all the accounts of … negotiations with the Court of Pekin that have been published, but the history of one is the history of all … one knows I think how every negotiation was or will be begun, carried on, and [ended]—or I should rather say broken off. (Dr D. Jackson to Amherst, 2 October 1815, in BL IOR MSS EUR F 140/35)

Amherst complained later that the implementation of his embassy was marked by great haste.[39] The circumstances were hardly propitious. Lord Melville, First Lord of the Admiralty, warned Amherst on 28 September 1815 that the proposed departure of the embassy on 1 December left no time to spare for making the necessary naval preparations (Lord Melville to Amherst, 28 September 1815, in BL IOR MSS EUR F 140/35). Henry Ellis, newly appointed secretary of the embassy, acted quickly

---

39 Amherst complained in his letter to George Canning in 1817 of his embassy being marked by 'hurry and confusion' (Amherst to Canning, 8 March 1817, in BL IOR G/12/197 (Reel 2) F 285).

and informed Amherst four days later of his 'intention, to proceed to London on Sunday, that I may be in readiness to receive Your Lordship's commands, and attend to any business that may arise connected with the Embassy' (Henry Ellis to Amherst, 27 September 1815, in BL IOR MSS EUR F 140/35).

Amherst's Response to the Embassy

Amherst's appointment as the ambassador-elect to China saw him diligently research all available information on China and his choice of dinner guests at his Mayfair residence reflected the need to entertain people connected with the forthcoming embassy. Thus, on Sunday 15 October 1815, Amherst's guests were Miss Temple and her brother, Lord Palmerston, then 31 years of age and the secretary of war; Mr and Mrs Sullivan, presumably the Rt Hon. John Sullivan, who it has been seen was the initial choice to lead an embassy to China; John Barrow; Hugh Hammersley; and Captain Murray Maxwell of the HMS *Alceste*, the man-of-war delegated to carry the embassy to China (Lord Amherst's 'Dinner Book' in Kent History and Library Centre, Amherst Manuscripts: Family Papers, U1350-E16). Captain Maxwell was a close friend of Amherst and is referred to in a letter he wrote to Sarah from Dover as early as 1806 (Amherst to Lady Amherst, Dover, 1806, in Letters from the Yale Collection of American Literature). Amherst also held a working dinner in late November where the absence of ladies presumably ensured an appropriate occasion for a discussion on the logistics of the embassy. Guests on this occasion were the Earl of Buckinghamshire; Chairman and Deputy Chairman of the Board of Directors of the Company, Charles Grant and Thomas Reid; Henry Ellis, Secretary of the embassy; John Barrow; Captain Maxwell and Captain Basil Hall, commander of the ten-gun brig HMS *Lyra* commissioned to accompany the *Alceste* to China; and Henry Hayne, Private Secretary to Amherst.[40] Other guests were Hugh Hammersley and Home Secretary Henry Addington, later Lord Sidmouth (Lord Amherst's 'Dinner Book' in Kent History and Library Centre, Amherst Manuscripts: Family Papers, U1350-E16).

---

40   Henry Hayne had accompanied Amherst on his posting to the Two Sicilies in 1809 on the recommendation of Lord Boringdon (Hayne, n.d.).

4. THE VIEW FROM LONDON

The Composition of the Amherst Embassy

Apart from Amherst and Ellis, other personnel assigned to the embassy included a chaplain, the Reverend Mr Griffith; two surgeons, namely, Clarke Abel who was to be paid an annual salary of £500 and Doctor Lynn who proceeded without salary.[41] The embassy draftsman was William Havell, while Lieutenant Cooke was in command of the Marine Contingent. A band of 10 musicians was included who were provided with a 'packet of music' sent by the Duke of Kent, which he hoped would be 'a source of some little amusement during the voyage' (Duke of Kent to Amherst, Kensington Palace, 28 December 1815, in BL IOR MSS EUR F 140/36).[42]

Amherst took a personal interest in the various occupations represented in the embassy. Sir Joseph Banks called on him and requested that an intelligent Kew gardener be included to collect seeds and plants under the charge of Clarke Abel who, while attending the embassy in the capacity of a medical man, had a considerable knowledge of natural history.[43] Amherst also thought a shoe maker would be a useful addition to the embassy but the Company Directors replied that this was unnecessary as it was planned to provide a sufficient supply of 'Shoes and Boots'.

On 15 October 1815, Buckinghamshire formally asked Lord Melville for a ship-of-war to be held in readiness to transport the embassy to the north of China. Amherst had written to his old friend Captain Murray Maxwell with the request that his ship HMS *Alceste* be commissioned to take him to China (Henderson III, 1970, p. 168).[44] Maxwell responded:

> Your letter has filled me with pride and happiness … the obtaining what I so anxiously desired … and excites such a tumult of pleasurable sensations that I am really My Lord unable to say more. (Captain Murray Maxwell to Amherst, 10 October 1815, in BL IOR MSS EUR F 140/35)

---

41   Clarke Abel was appointed the naturalist to the embassy at the suggestion of Sir Joseph Banks. He later accompanied Amherst in the position of physician when Amherst was governor-general of Bengal. He died at Cawnpore India on 14 November 1826. See Appendix A for a full list of the Amherst Embassy personnel sent from England.
42   The Duke stressed that he had already held a performance of the music to 'prove it was faultless' and pointed out that the score was specially calculated for the number of instruments in the band (Duke of Kent to Amherst, Kensington Palace, 28 December 1815, in BL IOR MSS EUR F 140/35).
43   See Fan (2004, pp. 18–19) for British instructions to naturalists in China to gather information and collect seeds.
44   Henderson (1970) writes that Amherst asked 'for the frigate, *Alceste*, commanded by his friend Capt. Murray Maxwell' (p. 168).

Captain Maxwell was described by one historian as the ideal captain in charge of a happy ship whose crew hero-worshipped him, admired him for his seamanship and were loath to displease him (Henderson III, 1970, p. 169). The unique opportunity to sail to the north of China under the charge of Captain Maxwell attracted a request from Speaker of the House of Commons Charles Abbot for the inclusion of his 17-year-old son as a midshipman on the voyage.[45] Abbot told Amherst that his son Charles had always wished to go to China:

> He [has] set his heart upon it, I do not well know why, except from the desire of visiting those Seas which do not come within the ordinary chances of his Profession … [Please] persuade the Captain to take him for one of his midshipmen … he will [derive enviable advantages] in the company of so many persons of science. (Charles Abbot to Amherst, 11 December 1815, in BL IOR MSS EUR F 140/35)

Abbot's request was granted. He and his son paid an early call on Amherst at his Grosvenor Street residence to pay their respects before his arrival on 'the Quarter Deck of the Alceste' (Charles Abbot to Amherst, 19 December 1815, in BL IOR MSS EUR F 140/35).

China was viewed by Amherst's friends and relatives, representatives of the privileged upper class of British society, as a curious country on the far side of the world. Most of their comment was cautious, muted and dwelt heavily on the negatives: time, distance, climate and separation from family made tolerable only by the handsome financial reward attached to it. None viewed China with any enthusiasm as a destination, nor thought about its importance to Britain. Earlier reports from the Macartney Embassy portrayed China as a difficult and monotonous destination, in contrast to the exciting or exotic cultures and countries visited traditionally during the grand tour of Europe by young people of Amherst's rank. Nevertheless, Amherst approached his assignment with application and energy. How he researched China and the strategies he formed for his forthcoming coming reception at the Qing court are the subject of the next chapter.

---

45 Maxwell was an officer of high repute. Henderson (1970) wrote that the action of the HMS *Alceste* under Captain Maxwell in the wars in the Adriatic 'may have changed history' when the *Alceste* and two other ships intercepted a French squadron carrying 200 guns bound for Trieste on 28 November 1811. Napoleon heard the news and abandoned plans to attack Constantinople and turned instead to Moscow (p. 169).

5
Amherst's Preparations for the Embassy

An examination of Amherst's notes (Amherst, 'Notes on policy to be pursued by the British Embassy to China' in BL IOR MSS EUR F 140/36) prepared at the time of his appointment as ambassador to the Qing court is important for a number of reasons. First, it reveals the body of knowledge on Chinese diplomacy available to the British at the time. This appears meagre when compared to information accessible to modern scholars, yet it represented a significant increase on what was at hand for Macartney 23 years earlier. Second, while historians have focused on the issue of Amherst's struggle to resolve the question of whether or not to perform the kowtow after his arrival in China, they have provided no insight into what informed his decision beyond the role played by Staunton (Tuck, 2000; Gao, 2016). His notes reveal his thinking, as well as offering insights into the strategies adopted by Macartney during his embassy, which, in turn, strongly influenced Amherst. Finally, Amherst's research shows that he approached his assignment in a diligent and conscientious manner in an endeavour to learn in advance as much as he could about Chinese diplomatic practice in order to achieve a successful outcome. While he did not have the cultural knowledge or in-country experience of Staunton, he may be judged as initially having an open mind and as having considered practical strategies and approaches from a systematic review of the limited information available to him. This attitude was to equip him well when he was faced with weighing up the advice he received from his two commissioners, Staunton and Ellis.

Amherst drew on three main sources of information in his research. The first consisted of the published accounts of previous Western embassies to the Qing court. Amherst's chief reference in preparing for his mission was Macartney's journal, provided to him by Foreign Minister Lord Castlereagh, as well as other extracts published in the second volume of Barrow's (1807) biography of Macartney (Castlereagh to Amherst, 1 January 1816, in BL MSS EUR F 140/43 (a)). Barrow was also consulted for his views, presumably at an official level in his office, as well as unofficially during working dinners held at Amherst's Mayfair townhouse (Lord Amherst's 'Dinner Book' in Kent History and Library Centre, Amherst Manuscripts: Family Papers, U1350-E16).

A major source was the accounts of the reception of two Russian embassies sent to the Qing court, namely, the Ismailof Embassy of 1721 and the Golovkin Embassy that arrived at the Chinese border in 1806.[1] Historians have overlooked their significance in shaping Amherst's thinking, but their influence is readily apparent in the official dispatches he wrote to George Canning, President of the Board of Control, dated 12 February 1817, 8 April 1817 and 21 April 1817.

Amherst's second resource consisted of the letters and reports written by foreign missionaries at Peking containing their views on the failure of Macartney's mission and providing their advice on what might be required for a successful mission.

Amherst's third and final source of information were reports containing intelligence from Canton whose significance had been overtaken by events by the time they reached London.[2] Castlereagh sent Amherst two dispatches dated 1 January 1816 together with instructions for discharging his duties at the Qing court that were based on events that had occurred at Canton in late 1814. The state of Company trade at Canton featured in several pages of Amherst's notes and are evidence that he was aware of all the main British grievances responsible for precipitating this embassy to the Qing court. His mastery of the issues represents a substantial increase in his knowledge of China when compared with his first pencilled jottings

---

1   Amherst had access to John Bell's (1763) *A Journey from St. Petersburg in Russia to Pekin in China*, but the reference he used for the Golovkin Embassy is not recorded. Staunton (1821, p. xvii) wrote regarding this embassy, 'No official accounts of its proceedings have been published, or at least have reached [England]'.
2   The latest intelligence received in July 1815 referred to events that took place in Canton at the end of 1814.

written on a scrappy piece of paper where two queries are noted, namely, 'What European nations have residents at the Court of Peking?' and 'What was the name of the island [Taiwan] in the Yellow Sea in which the English had formerly an established hub from whence they were expelled (within the memory of man) for improper conduct?' (Amherst, 'Notes on policy to be pursued by the British Embassy to China' in BL IOR MSS EUR F 140/36).

Historical Background: Earlier Embassies

The British may have been late comers to the Qing court, but they nevertheless had considerable experience engaging with the Mughal courts of India where their diplomats were confronted with similar protocol issues as faced by Macartney in China, in particular, the ceremony of the kowtow. Sir Thomas Roe, the first English ambassador to the Jahangir emperor in 1615, 'refus[ed] the demand of touching the ground with his head' before the prince in contrast to the Persian ambassador 'who came to court splendidly attired, and prostrated himself many times, knocking his head against the ground' (as quoted in Murray, 1820, vol. 2, p. 148).[3] Roe's firm and resolute refusal to compromise English honour in the face of the degrading ceremonial demands made of him at this time may be seen as setting a precedent for the behaviour of British ambassadors at other eastern courts (Sir William Foster's comment on Roe in Roe, 1899, p. xxiii).

Barrow had read an account of the Dutch embassy sent by the Dutch East India Company (VOC) to the Shunzhi Emperor (r. 1644–1661) in 1655 and his views on this and other diplomatic events were no doubt discussed with Amherst (Nieuhof, 1669; Wilkinson, 2000, p. 759).[4] Received as vassals before the Shunzhi emperor, the Dutch were also confronted with troublesome Jesuit missionaries who 'searched after all means possible to hinder the Hollanders access to the Court' (Kops, 2002, p. 554). Although the Dutch ambassador performed the kowtow and the Dutch were granted permission to return to China every eight years to pay tribute, they were not permitted any other trade (p. 565). Evidence of other unsatisfactory outcomes and dismissals of European embassies from the Qing court were

---

3   See also Roe (1899, p. 295).
4   The reference to the great popularity of Nieuhof's (1669) book is quoted in Kops (2002, p. 545).

available to the British. The first Russian ambassador, Iskowitz Baikov, sent in 1656, refused to kowtow and was dismissed without an audience (see Baikov, 1732), as was a second Dutch embassy sent in 1667 for the same reason (see Wills, 2009, pp. 41–86).[5] The Kangxi court, however, showed its pragmatic side when it signed a formal treaty with the Russian Government in 1689. The Treaty of Nerchinsk secured Russian and Chinese borders and established set trade routes between the two countries that were further ratified with the Treaty of Kyakhta in 1727. 'This was the first time in modern history', the historian Harry Gelber pointed out, 'that there were serious negotiations between China and a major foreign power' (2007, p. 140). The precedent of Western-style treaties negotiated by the Qing court with the Russians, although a special case resulting from a common border, was read by Europeans as representing a formal recognition of mutual obligation and national sovereignty based on equal status, and was noted by Amherst, indicating at least an example of negotiation if mutual interests were involved (Amherst, 'Notes on policy to be pursued by the British Embassy to China' in BL IOR MSS EUR F 140/36).

As indicated above, Amherst's focus was drawn in historical sequence to three earlier embassies: the Russian Ismailof Embassy of 1719–1722, the Macartney Embassy of 1792–1794 and the Golovkin Embassy of 1805–1806. Amherst drew points from each embassy that were instrumental in shaping his strategies for approaching the Qing court in 1816.

An Important Precedent: The Russian Ismailof Embassy of 1719–1722

Amherst's notes reveal his interest in the Scotsman John Bell's (1763) account of the Ismailof Embassy sent by Peter the Great to the Kangxi court in 1720. Ismailof's goals were similar to those of Macartney, namely, to negotiate trade concessions and open diplomatic representation at Peking. Ismailof initially refused to kowtow and insisted on delivering the Tsar's letter directly into the hands of the emperor. Seven days of negotiation took place before a compromise was reached. Amherst noted:

---

5   This was the embassy led by Pieter van Hoorn. Wills (2009, p. 41) wrote that 'despite their very substantial investment in this Embassy, the people who sent it did not have very high hopes for it. And they were right'.

> The Russian embassador Ismailoff endeavours to avoid the ceremony of prostration, but at last conforms to it under a stipulation that any Chinese Embassador* who may be sent to St. Petersburg shall conform to all the ceremonies of that court. (Amherst, 'Notes on policy to be pursued by the British Embassy to China' in BL IOR MSS EUR F 140/36)[6]

Amherst's asterisk placed next to the words 'Chinese Embassador' in this passage is a rare suggestion in the literature of Western embassies to China of a potential Chinese envoy embarking on a mission to a European court. Macartney adopted a reversed variation of this idea when he advocated that any future Chinese ambassador at the Court of St James's kowtow before the British sovereign, which in turn was advocated by Amherst during his mission. Amherst was clearly attracted to Ismailof's compromise at this stage of his research. The Russian ambassador, Amherst noted, was subsequently 'well and honestly treated' and invited to a 'great entertainment on new year's day [and] when the Chinese prostrated themselves, the Russians were allowed to salute the Emperor after their own fashion' (Amherst, 'Notes on policy to be pursued by the British Embassy to China' in BL IOR MSS EUR F 140/36). Amherst noted further that Ismailof met the Kangxi emperor on 10 or 12 occasions and was permitted to remain in Peking for three months, which exceeded the usual period of 40 days allotted to a foreign embassy.[7] Such impressive access to the emperor enjoyed by Ismailof resulting from the performance of a solitary kowtow was in stark contrast to Macartney who only had two formal audiences with the Qianlong emperor.[8] Intelligence received by the British that the Jiaqing emperor was better disposed to Westerners than his father would have suggested to Amherst that he could expect a favourable reception if he followed Ismailof's precedent of making an initial kowtow, followed thereafter by performing the British ceremony of kneeling on one knee and bowing before the Jiaqing emperor.

---

6   Naquin and Rawski (1987, pp. 30–31) pointed out that the Qing court's relations with Russia were quite different from that of other Western countries by noting that a Qing ambassador was prepared to perform the kowtow before the Tsar in Moscow in 1731 and St Petersburg in 1732. Nevertheless, Amherst classified the Russians as 'Westerners' for the purposes of his research.
7   His first meeting with the emperor was on 28 November 1720 and his last on 23 February 1721 (Amherst, 'Notes on policy to be pursued by the British Embassy to China' in BL IOR MSS EUR F 140/36).
8   Macartney also met the Qianlong emperor at an 'entertainment' but no business took place despite Macartney's efforts to 'lead him towards the subject of my Embassy' (Cranmer-Byng, 1962, p. 137).

The Impact of Macartney's Journal on Amherst: The Importance of Rank

Amherst turned his attention to Macartney's journal. Barrow thought the inclusion of several extracts from Macartney in his second volume of Macartney's biography 'may not … be wholly uninteresting to those who shall be concerned in any future mission to the court of Pekin' (Barrow, 1807, vol. 1, p. 348). Amherst noted these and also took copious notes from Macartney's journal handed to him by Castlereagh.

Amherst quotes Macartney's remarks on his escorts in his notes: 'Van [Wang] and Chou [were] family names. Taqin annexed to their Rank & signifies great man. Blue button inferior red, white to blue' (in Cranmer-Byng, 1962, p. 71).[9] Cheng, the 'Tartar legate' who met Macartney at Tianjin, Amherst noted, was unfriendly and exhibited a 'settled prejudice against the Embassy' arising out of a dispute over the delivery of the British presents to Jehol.[10] Amherst highlighted Macartney's passage, 'I have taken great pains to conciliate him; but I suspect he is not of a conciliable [sic] nature' (Amherst quoting Macartney's journal, pp. 201–202 in 'Notes on policy to be pursued by the British Embassy to China' in BL IOR MSS EUR F 140/36). The mandarins Wang and Chou, despite their high rank, were portrayed as men with 'no great regard to Truth' for they had no scruples in asking 'for a present saying the Emperor's allowance was not sufficient' (Amherst quoting Macartney's journal, p. 220 in 'Notes on policy to be pursued by the British Embassy to China' in BL IOR MSS EUR F 140/36). Amherst made a special note that his embassy would be subject to constant surveillance where its 'appearance, deportment and conversation' and 'Every thing they say & do [is] minutely reported & remembered' and brought to the attention of the emperor (Amherst quoting Macartney's journal, p. 233 in 'Notes on policy to be pursued by the British Embassy to China' in BL IOR MSS EUR F 140/36).

---

9   Amherst also noted the various Chinese 'Courts' or Boards of Government, and listed government titles including the 'Keun-Min-Too–Magistrate resident near Macao; Foo-yuen or Sun-foo 2nd in authority to Viceroy: Fsong-too—The Viceroy: Quang-tchoo-foo—Governor of City of Canton: another interpretation calls him the Magistrate of the district of Macao' (See Amherst, 'Notes on policy to be pursued by the British Embassy to China' in BL IOR MSS EUR F 140/36).

10   In contrast to the Amherst Embassy, where early discussion with the mandarins arose over the performance of the kowtow, initial talks at the time of Macartney Embassy concerned his insistence that the delicate and bulky presents of the planetarium, the globes, the great lustres, clocks and other articles remain in Peking and not travel to Jehol for fear of damage (Barrow, 1807, vol. 2, p. 191).

Amherst's readings of Macartney's journal contributed to his awareness of the importance of ceremony in Qing diplomatic encounters and special note was made of Macartney's conclusion:

> [Ceremonial] is a very serious matter with [the Chinese] … they pressed me most seriously to comply with it; said [the prostration] was a mere trifle, knelt down on the floor and practised it of their own accord to shew me the manner of it, and begged me to try whether I could perform it. (Barrow, 1807, vol. 2, p. 209, referred to by Amherst in his 'Notes on policy to be pursued by the British Embassy to China' in BL IOR MSS EUR F 140/36)

Amherst also possessed a dispatch written by Macartney after he had left the Qianlong court that emphasised the Qing mandarins' insistence that a foreign ambassador practice in their presence 'the adorations as the Chinese term expresses, or prostrations, which are constantly made before the throne by subjects and vassals of this Empire' (Amherst quoting Macartney's journal in 'Notes on policy to be pursued by the British Embassy to China' in BL IOR MSS EUR F 140/36).

> [Macartney] was well aware of the tenaciousness of this Court to a ceremony of which the humiliation on the one part contributed perhaps to render most Embassies so grateful to the other. (Amherst quoting Macartney's journal in 'Notes on policy to be pursued by the British Embassy to China' in BL IOR MSS EUR F 140/36)

But Macartney admitted that he was unaware of the true meaning of the characters on the flags adorning the embassy boats that read 'The Embassador bearing Tribute from the Kingdom of England'. Even if he had known, he would not have made a formal complaint in case this caused 'an abrupt as well as [an] unsuccessful termination to my Mission' (Amherst quoting Macartney's journal in 'Notes on policy to be pursued by the British Embassy to China' in BL IOR MSS EUR F 140/36).

Amherst noted Macartney's views on the mandarins, which were far from complimentary. The 'Tartar Chiefs' were suspicious of British designs 'as if we came to pry into the situation of the country' and intended under the 'specious and innocent pretext to trade, to insinuate ourselves gradually into some share with them of the domination over China' (Amherst quoting Macartney's journal in 'Notes on policy to be pursued by the British Embassy to China' in BL IOR MSS EUR F 140/36). He emphasised the difference in a proposed compromise in which he would kowtow if a mandarin of equal rank performed the same ceremony before a portrait of George III. The emperor agreed to this proposal only if the mandarin performed the ceremony 'in a private room, without parade, and would scarcely be known or mentioned in the Empire' (Amherst quoting Macartney's journal in 'Notes on policy to be pursued by the British Embassy to China' in BL IOR MSS EUR F 140/36). Macartney, on the other hand, would be performing the ceremony in public on the occasion of a festival 'before all the tributary Princes, and great subjects of State, and would be described in the Gazette' (Amherst quoting Macartney's journal in 'Notes on policy to be pursued by the British Embassy to China' in BL IOR MSS EUR F 140/36). He refused not only on these grounds but also because of the risk that the news of a humiliating public kowtow was 'likely even to find their way to Europe' due to the presence of Western Jesuits at the Qianlong court (Amherst quoting Macartney's journal in 'Notes on policy to be pursued by the British Embassy to China' in BL IOR MSS EUR F 140/36). Macartney concluded his dispatch in the strongest terms that to kowtow was to 'give stronger testimonies of homage to a foreign Prince, however respectable and great, than to my own sovereign, who was not less so' (Amherst quoting Macartney's journal in 'Notes on policy to be pursued by the British Embassy to China' in BL IOR MSS EUR F 140/36). A compromise was at length agreed on when the Qianlong emperor agreed to Macartney performing the British ceremony of bending one knee to him 'with the profoundest reverence'. The emperor, Macartney concluded, was 'much less eager in his pretensions, than his Courtiers for him' (Amherst quoting Macartney's journal in 'Notes on policy to be pursued by the British Embassy to China' in BL IOR MSS EUR F 140/36). Macartney's successful compromise no doubt assured Amherst that a precedent had been established where a British ambassador was no longer required to perform the kowtow.

Missionary Views on Macartney's Failure

The inclusion of China experts in the Amherst Embassy was thought to ensure its success where Macartney had failed. Jesuit interpreters at the Qing court would not be required and it is noteworthy that Amherst makes no reference to the 'mischievous' activities of the Jesuits blamed by Barrow (1807) for Macartney's failure. His indifference is explained by the fact, of course, that there were only five foreign missionaries still at the Qing court, namely, Father Lamiot and four Portuguese missionaries. The Company's Secret Court of Directors, no doubt reflecting the views of Staunton, described Lamiot as 'a respectable French missionary attached to the English by a long course of kindness from our Supra-Cargoes at Canton' (Secret Commercial Committee to Lord Amherst, 17 January 1816, in BL IOR G/12/196 (Reel 1) F 86).

Amherst had in his possession a letter dated 1794 written by a French Jesuit, Father Louis de Poirot, with his views on the Macartney Embassy (A Jesuit at Peking to Mr Raper enclosing a letter written by the Missionary Louis de Poirot dated 18 May 1794 on the Ceremony at Macartney's Reception, in BL IOR MSS EUR F 140/36). De Poirot stressed that the missionaries at the Qianlong court had been disposed to do all in their power to assist the Macartney Embassy but that their intentions were thwarted by the Qing Government's sudden prohibition on all communication with the British (A Jesuit at Peking to Mr Raper enclosing a letter written by the Missionary Louis de Poirot dated 18 May 1794 on the Ceremony at Macartney's Reception, in BL IOR MSS EUR F 140/36). Nevertheless, he now presented his 'friendly remarks' on the outcome of Macartney's Embassy. He attributed the failure of the embassy to the British reliance on a young and inexperienced Chinese interpreter and their refusal to 'pay the customary obedience' to the court. Macartney's failure to consult the Jesuits was a mistake as he would have been informed that the kowtow represented a 'Homage [that] was only a mere ceremony' (A Jesuit at Peking to Mr Raper enclosing a letter written by the Missionary Louis de Poirot dated 18 May 1794 on the Ceremony at Macartney's Reception, in BL IOR MSS EUR F 140/36). He added, revealing a fundamental ignorance of the British, that Portuguese and Papal ambassadors had been only too happy to perform the prostration ceremony. Referring to the Ismailof Embassy, de Poirot continued:

> [It was] true that a Muscovite Embassador was proud and would not submit to it … [but] Kanghi [showed] him that it was not meant as a submission from one Sovereign to another, [and] ordered one of his Nobles to make the same submission before the signet of the Czar of Muscovy. (A Jesuit at Peking to Mr Raper enclosing a letter written by the Missionary Louis de Poirot dated 18 May 1794 on the Ceremony at Macartney's Reception, in BL IOR MSS EUR F 140/36)

This was a confusing reference implying that the Kangxi emperor ordered a mandarin to kowtow before a representation of the Tsar instead of committing to the practices of the Russian court as suggested in Bell's (1763) account noted earlier. The British, de Poirot continued, 'might have performed this ceremony' on these terms. Significantly, given Amherst's future thoughts on the kowtow at the time of his mission, Ismailof's precedent of 1721 was once more invoked as representing an expedient course of action at the Qing court.

De Poirot also stressed that the British choice of presents, consisting of 'expensive pieces of mechanism', were not suitable and a missionary should have been consulted over their selection. The 'plainness of dress' of the members of the Macartney Embassy drew specific criticism because it left a bad impression of the British. 'Plain clothes', while acceptable in Europe, were considered by the Chinese as a 'mark either of poverty or disrespect'. Heavily embroidered clothes, on the other hand, commanded respect and gave the Chinese a 'greater idea of the Europeans'. De Poirot advised that future European ambassadors to the Qing court must wear clothes richly laced with gold to impress and 'dazzle the Eye' (A Jesuit at Peking to Mr Raper enclosing a letter written by the Missionary Louis de Poirot dated 18 May 1794 on the Ceremony at Macartney's Reception, in BL IOR MSS EUR F 140/36).

The Importance of the Golovkin Embassy of 1805–1806

The precedents of two other embassies to the Qing court after Macartney would have served to confuse Amherst. The Dutch mission to the Qianlong court in 1795 resulted only in humiliation and a failure to accomplish any of its goals despite the performance of an estimated 30 kowtows during its stay in China. Amherst makes no reference to this embassy in his notes, but Van Braam's (1798) account received substantial coverage in the British media and was well known to the British public.[11] Barrow showed particular interest in the embassy in his autobiography, stating that many of the details of its reception were 'too disgusting to repeat'. He adds, 'Van Braam, a jolly fat fellow, who, from the luxurious

---

11   Estimates of the number of kowtows performed vary, but a general figure places it at between 30 and 50. The Dutch travelled in miserable conditions, were lodged in dilapidated buildings and Van Braam, the second secretary in the embassy, was humiliated when his hat fell off while kowtowing to the Qianlong Emperor. The Dutch were even required to kowtow before a gift of a sturgeon sent from the palace. Rockhill (1905, p. 32) wrote, 'the envoys received the gift in the courtyard, kneeling and knocking their heads on the ground'. It needs to be noted that the Dutch mission was sent by the Dutch East India Company at Batavia, and not on behalf of the Netherlands Government, which, in any event, was a republic whose head of state was not a monarch.

life of Batavia, underwent a state of starvation in China, writes to his friend that he had returned as thin as a shotten herring' (Barrow, 1847, p. 98).[12] Certainly Staunton and Henry Ellis, the third commissioner in the Amherst Embassy, were well aware of this ill-fated embassy and both referred to it in later correspondence in connection with the kowtow.

The Russian embassy led by Count Golovkin in 1805–1806, as noted earlier, was important as the only European embassy sent to the court of the Jiaqing emperor, and was of great interest to Amherst who made several pages of mainly descriptive notes on its progress (Amherst, 'Notes on the Golovkin Embassy, 1805-06' in BL IOR MSS EUR F 140/36). The Golovkin Embassy was a grand and elaborate delegation consisting of over 300 people including Cossacks, dragoons, several young noblemen, scientists and an interpreter fluent in Mandarin. Presents for the emperor included furs of the highest quality and the finest products of Russian decorative arts. Arriving at the small village of Kiahta on the Chinese border, Golovkin, Amherst noted, set himself up in 'great magnificence' and commenced negotiations with the mandarins regarding his entrance into China (Amherst, 'Notes on the Golovkin Embassy, 1805-06' in BL IOR MSS EUR F 140/36). Inevitably, the question of the 'ko-teu' arose (Amherst, 'Notes on the Golovkin Embassy, 1805-06' in BL IOR MSS EUR F 140/36). Golovkin informed the mandarins that he intended to follow the precedent of former Russian ambassadors and would not be performing the ceremony. The embassy proceeded to enter Chinese territory while news of Golovkin's refusal was being transmitted to Peking. On arriving at Urga, 140 miles from the capital, Golovkin was met by the senior Qing commander, referred to as 'the Wan' by the Russians, who was also the Jiaqing emperor's brother-in-law. Delays were caused at Urga due to some confusion over the wording of the Tsar's letter to the emperor. While waiting for confirmation from Peking to proceed, Golovkin was invited to a 'solemn breakfast' where he noticed a table covered with yellow silk (Amherst, 'Notes on the Golovkin Embassy, 1805-06' in BL IOR MSS EUR F 140/36).[13] Informed that the table represented the presence of the emperor, Golovkin was instructed to kowtow before it. He refused. He insisted that previous Russian ambassadors had never performed the ceremony at the border but had been allowed to proceed directly to Peking where due respect was paid to the emperor. Further,

---

12   The *Shorter Oxford English Dictionary* defines 'shotten' as 'In *herring*, applied to a person who is exhausted by sickness or destitute of strength or resources'.
13   The term 'solemn breakfast' is used by Amherst in his notes.

Golovkin informed 'the Wan' that Macartney had not kowtowed and the Russians would not perform a ceremony from which the British had been excused. 'The Wan' was astonished on learning this and called it a 'misrepresentation' (Amherst, 'Notes on the Golovkin Embassy, 1805–06' in BL IOR MSS EUR F 140/36).

Golovkin was expelled immediately by the Jiaqing emperor on learning of his refusal to kowtow. Presents were returned and Golovkin and his grand retinue departed on the long and arduous return journey to St Petersburg. Amherst noted the role played by the mandarins. Golovkin, he wrote, 'seems to throw a great deal of the blame on the Wan', thus heralding the need, in Amherst's mind, to placate obstreperous mandarins acting in their capacity as gatekeepers to the emperor (Amherst, 'Notes on the Golovkin Embassy, 1805–06' in BL IOR MSS EUR F 140/36).

Lamiot's Letters

Amherst now had examples of two other failed European embassies to the Qing court: the Dutch embassy of 1795, which was dismissed with no reward after the ambassador performed numerous kowtows; and the Golovkin Embassy, expelled for refusing a single kowtow. Any confusion, however, was clarified with the receipt of informed comment in a letter written by the French Vincentian priest resident at the Qing court, Father Lamiot, which came to the attention of the British at Canton. The letter, dated 1 October 1807, was addressed to a 'Spanish agent' at Manila and commented on the failure of both Macartney and Golovkin.

The refusal of both ambassadors to kowtow before the respective emperors, Lamiot thought, was the fundamental cause for their failure, but he also blamed the actions of the mandarins who had blocked access to the emperor. This judgement, in the light of what Amherst had just read about the Golovkin Embassy, no doubt made perfect sense. The mandarins, Lamiot explained, were united against any foreign embassy and 'will readily use every means of intrigue, deception, and bribery to circumvent' them (Amherst, 'Notes on a letter written by Lamiot, dated 1 October 1807' in BL IOR MSS EUR F 140/36). Their actions were dictated specifically by concerns that any interference in dealings with foreigners would result in their having to pay compensation, leaving them open to accusations 'of plunderings which have brought no advantage to the government' (Amherst, 'Notes on a letter written by Lamiot, dated 1 October 1807' in BL IOR MSS EUR F 140/36).

Lamiot, understandably, shifted the blame for the failure of the Macartney Embassy away from the Jesuits, identified by Barrow as the primary cause for the failure of the embassy, to the devious and self-centred actions of the mandarins or gatekeepers. Their behaviour, Lamiot pointed out, was ruled by a fear and dread of incurring the emperor's displeasure. Accordingly, the emperor, who had absolute power to demote, punish or fine his officials, was never told the truth, but the mandarins dared not initiate any independent actions or shape agreements in their own right.[14] Amherst, it will be seen, was confronted with frustrating and inconclusive negotiations on his way to Peking, due to the mandarins' inability to make decisions independent of the emperor.

Lamiot recommended further that embassies be sent in the name of the sovereign and to proceed secretly and directly to the northern port of Tianjin. Amherst wrote next to this passage:

> This appears to me to be hardly possible, as notice must be given to the Government of its arrival not only to obtain permission to proceed but to make all the necessary preparations and arrangements. (Amherst, 'Notes on a letter written by Lamiot, dated 1 October 1807' in BL IOR MSS EUR F 140/36)

Lamiot also included his thoughts on the Jiaqing emperor in a letter dated 10 October 1808. Amherst noted that Lamiot 'speaks of [the Jiaqing emperor] as anxious only to govern well, [as] indifferent to rare and curious objects and is an enemy to luxury and fetes' (Amherst, 'Notes on a letter written by Lamiot, dated 1 October 1807' in BL IOR MSS EUR F 140/36). This assessment of the Jiaqing emperor reminded Amherst of earlier Western impressions of the Kangxi court, described by Bell as one of 'order and decency, rather than grandeur and magnificence' (Bell, 1763, vol. 2, p. 12).

---

14 The fact that the mandarins were not permitted to take any decisions without the emperor's permission is noted in Staunton's (1821) translation of the *Narrative of the Chinese embassy to the Khan of the Tourgouth Tartars*. In this account, the Chinese ambassador informed a Russian officer during his travels through Russia, 'In our empire of China, none of the great officers of state are empowered to transact state affairs upon their own authority ... They must, on all occasions, be regularly submitted to his Majesty' (p. 102).

The prospect of dealing with a responsible and pragmatic emperor encouraged British expectations of a fruitful diplomatic encounter at the Qing court where direct communication would result in negotiation and mediation. While Lamiot had reported that the Jiaqing emperor was adverse to ostentatious displays, it was thought that a splendid audience before the emperor displaying the civility and courtly demeanour of a British diplomatic mission would secure the Jiaqing emperor's 'good graces' and sanction the commencement of negotiations with Qing court officials.[15] Amherst was fully aware of the minefield of conventions that governed the site of diplomatic dialogue with the Qing court where misunderstandings had the power to disrupt or even sever negotiation. His main concern centred on the fact that once a written submission had been delivered to the Chinese authorities, it effectively closed off further opportunities for mediation. He made a note that 'there is no longer any opportunity to negotiate ... the determination is taken, and the business cannot be again reverted to' (Amherst, 'Notes on policy to be pursued by the British Embassy to China' in BL IOR MSS EUR F 140/36). Lamiot had given the same advice and Amherst wrote elsewhere:

> Follow M. Lamiot's advice in delaying as long as possible to give in to demands in writing (which would be speedily and conclusively answered) and take every possible means to ensure their success before they are definitely proposed. (Amherst, pencil notes on 'The objects of the Embassy' in BL IOR MSS EUR F 140/36)

Amherst, no doubt drawing on his own diplomatic experience at the Court of Palermo, wrote the following, which although logical in British terms, displayed a naiveté about Chinese diplomacy and reveals that he thought his embassy would be received outside the traditional tribute system:

> Negotiation should be conducted in the spirit of cordiality and with the feeling of equality. No offence taken at trifles nor intentional indignity overlooked. Act first and apologise afterwards. Firmness, dignity, and patience essential requisites. Resist any attempt of persons interested to terminate abruptly the Embassy. Any such attempt on the part of the Government to be represented as unjust and unfriendly. (Amherst, pencil notes on 'The objects of the Embassy' in BL IOR MSS EUR F 140/36)

---

15   Hampton (2009, p. 19) noted that Ermolao Barbaro wrote in the 1490s that the importance of an ambassador was to attain 'the good graces of those to whom he is sent'.

While such strategies might appear reasonable to pursue in a European diplomatic encounter, they were not realistic in the context of the Qing court. The emphasis on reasonableness revealed a major misunderstanding and lack of awareness of the practicalities of dealing with the Qing court where there was no scope for dialogue of any kind and no channel for diplomatic communication, and certainly not with one imbued with the feeling of equality. Further, while Macartney's visit happened to coincide with the unique event of the Qianlong emperor's 80th birthday celebrations, Amherst was visiting the Qing court uninvited and at a less auspicious time. The historian John Wills has pointed out that the emperor considered tribute audiences a routine formality in which ambassadors from tributary states were able to relax and engaged in cordial relations with the court once the ceremonial formalities had taken place (2009, p. 28). The British, on the other hand, saw an embassy to China as a singular opportunity to engage, persuade and exert diplomatic pressure on the Qing court where the real business of diplomacy was entered into after the ceremonials had concluded. Indeed, Amherst had gone as far as to prepare for a meeting with Qing officials along specific lines. He wrote, 'Would it be possible to <u>announce</u> to the Chinese rather than to <u>ask</u> from them, [for] the appointment of a Minister at Pekin, or at least a Consul at Canton?' (emphasis in original). Amherst acknowledged that such diplomatic negotiations would be delicate:

> By a precipitate enforcement of our demands the Embassy may be abruptly terminated. By a protraction of them, it may come to a conclusion before they are brought forward. It will be difficult to steer between these two courses. (Amherst, 'Notes on policy to be pursued by the British Embassy to China' in BL IOR MSS EUR F 140/36)

His aim, however, was 'to be cautious' and 'not to make demands which [might] rather produce new misunderstandings than remove old grievances' (Amherst, 'Notes on policy to be pursued by the British Embassy to China' in BL IOR MSS EUR F 140/36). Amherst understood that the Qing mandarins had no power to negotiate on their own initiative. At the end of the day, Amherst noted optimistically, 'all these obstacles are perhaps not insurmountable as the success depends upon the will of one Man' (Amherst quoting Letter by Lamiot, 1 October 1807, 'Notes on a letter written by Lamiot, dated 1 October 1807' in BL IOR MSS EUR F 140/36). But the will of the emperor was contingent on his willingness to compromise and recognise British exceptionalism. Amherst hoped that a splendid display by a new British embassy—following in the footsteps of the earlier impressive Macartney Embassy that had done so much to instil a favourable notion of the British nation in China in contrast to the barbaric appearance of traditional vassal missions—would ensure an honourable reception at the Qing court.

Amherst was fully aware that his was a difficult mission requiring tact and caution (Amherst, 'Notes on policy to be pursued by the British Embassy to China' in BL IOR MSS EUR F 140/36). Nevertheless, he remained hopeful, especially as the Jesuits were no longer a problem and the inclusion of Mandarin speakers would assist him in a successful outcome where Macartney had failed. The British ability to now communicate directly with the mandarins would ensure access to the court and succeed in overcoming obstacles initially put in place by the gatekeepers. The ability to engage in direct communication, as well as Amherst's personal charm and past diplomatic experience, would succeed in impressing the emperor who would hopefully initiate a series of negotiations on the state of trade at Canton and open an official channel for direct communication between the court at Peking and the Company at Canton. Macartney's firm actions had dispensed with the need to kowtow and the embassy had left a favourable impression at the Qing court. Barrow's words summed up Macartney's legacy:

> By this Embassy the British character became better known to the Chinese, and protection and respect were obtained for the British subjects resident at Canton. At the request of Lord Macartney they have since been permitted to address their complaints personally or by letter to the viceroy … It opened an amicable correspondence between His Majesty and the Emperor of China. (1807, vol. 2, p. 354)

Amherst was reassured further by a letter from the Company's Secret Commercial Committee, dated 17 January 1816, on the expected outcome of the embassy. Citing the examples of Ismailof and Macartney, the letter stated:

> It has been said that the Chinese government expects nothing more from an Embassy than some complementary proceedings, accompanied with presents; but it seems plain in the cases of more than one Russian Ambassador, and of Lord Macartney himself, that the Chinese Ministers did not decline all negotiations. And if that Government were given seriously to understand, that an attempt to avoid taking due cognizance of an affair so important to our

National interest and honour, would be viewed as a denial of justice and of a most unfriendly character, they would perhaps not persist in it. (Secret Commercial Committee to Lord Amherst, 17 January 1816, in BL IOR G/12/196 (Reel 1) F 86)

Amherst's Conclusions

Amherst concluded that concern with ceremony was a very serious matter at the Qing court. He earmarked a passage in Macartney's journal on the 'First mention of mode of presentation to the Emperor' (Amherst quoting Macartney's journal, p. 200 in 'Notes on policy to be pursued by the British Embassy to China' in BL IOR MSS EUR F 140/36). This was the occasion where Macartney was first informed by the mandarins that the ceremony of kneeling down on 'both knees and making nine prostrations or inclinations of the head to the ground … had never been and never could be dispensed with' (Amherst quoting Macartney's journal, p. 200 in 'Notes on policy to be pursued by the British Embassy to China' in BL IOR MSS EUR F 140/36). Macartney, following Westphalian principles, reiterated that his first duty was to perform the ceremony that was agreeable to his king.

Amherst's notes on 'Ceremonial' referred specifically to Barrow's views presented in his first volume of Macartney's biography (1807) and reveal that he was greatly influenced by them. Barrow emphasised Macartney's successful negotiation as the first European ambassador to appear before a Chinese emperor without performing the humiliating kowtow, thereby saving both personal and national honour.[16] Barrow, buoyed by Macartney's success, advocated specific instructions to future British ambassadors to China. These should be ambiguous and left open, leaving an ambassador free to make appropriate decisions based on the conditions found at the time. Ambassadors were further advised not to enter into discussions with the mandarins on the subject as it was important 'to keep the agents of the court in good humour' (Amherst, 'Notes on policy to be pursued by the British Embassy to China' in BL IOR MSS EUR F 140/36).

---

16   This was not strictly accurate. An earlier Portuguese embassy and a Papal embassy had been admitted to the Qianlong emperor and the envoys did not kowtow. However, an important distinction is that these embassies did not come with requests for trade. Rather, they concerned religious matters and, therefore, arrived and were received in China outside of the tributary system (Peyrefitte, 1992, p. xxiv). Reference is made to the Papal envoy, the Cardinal of Tournon who arrived at the Qing court 80 years before Macartney and did not kowtow.

Amherst's notes reveal that he was not convinced by this advice. He marked a passage in Barrow's (1804) book, *Travels in China*, on the reactions at Peking to the news that Macartney had not kowtowed before the Qianlong emperor:

> Nobody would speak to me [Barrow] ... I asked [our friend Deodato a Neapolitan missionary] what was the matter? His answer was, We are all lost, ruined, and undone! ... Macartney had refused to comply with the ceremony of prostrating himself, like the Embassadors of tributary princes ... [and had performed] the same ceremony of respect to the Emperor as to his own sovereign. That although little was thought of this affair at Gehol, the great officers of state [in the] department of ceremonies in Peking were mortified, and perplexed, and alarmed; and that ... it was impossible to say what might be the consequence of an event unprecedented in the annals of the empire. (p. 117)

Such 'embarrassment may be avoided', Amherst wrote, 'if the King makes a specific reference in the ambassador's instructions to approach the throne of China with the same ceremonial respect as appears before himself' (Amherst, 'Notes on policy to be pursued by the British Embassy to China' in BL IOR MSS EUR F 140/36). Amherst still persisted in viewing his upcoming mission within the terms of Westphalian diplomatic principles of equality between nations.

The Importance of Appearances

Amherst's need to present himself in the most prestigious light befitting his status as a British ambassador claiming his authority from the Prince Regent, and as a member of the British aristocratic elite, is reflected in a letter he wrote to Lord Buckinghamshire concerning both the appearance of his table while in China as well as his official wardrobe. Submitting a bill for expenses incurred in ordering extra silverware, Amherst reminded Buckinghamshire that only the finest silver, crystal and linens were appropriate for ambassadorial appearances. Such were:

> Absolutely necessary for the Table, which I shall have to keep for the Embassy when on show, and which, as the Chinese will probably be spectators of it, I have ordered more becoming to my station by a large addition of my own [silver] Plate, which will amount to about a thousand pounds. The cost of my state wardrobe and various incidental expenses ... which arise from the

circumstances of my appointment (I do not mean my outfit only) will amount to at least as much more: Thus leaving me charged at the very outset with an expense of upwards of £2000. (Amherst to Buckinghamshire, 28 December 1815, in BL IOR G/12/196 (Reel 1) F 66)

Amherst's early expectations of the manner in which he would be received by the Qing court and the opportunities this provided for a display of British taste and refinement are revealed in this letter. His reference to his dinner table being 'on show' suggests that he also anticipated playing the gracious host entertaining the mandarins in a formal European manner complete with silver and fine tableware, multiple courses and the best wines, served to create an atmosphere conducive to amiable conversation followed by frank and productive discussion. An impressive display of silver was essential as a visual representation of both Amherst's rank and Great Britain's prosperity.[17] The importance of appearances was not confined to the ambassador alone but was also a concern for at least one member of the British public who, knowing of the Chinese preference for etiquette, enquired if it:

> might be judicious with reference to the success of the Embassy, that the King's ship, carrying Lord Amherst, should wear a Broad Pendant (like [Macartney's ship] the Lion). Is this compatible with the rules of the Admiralty? (Chairman and Deputy Chairman, EIC, to Viscount Melville, 1 February 1816, in BL IOR G/12/196 (Reel 1) F 127–128)

The writer was informed that the HMS *Lion* had not flown a pendant and in fact:

> It is not probable at any rate that the Government or people of China would be sufficiently conversant in the details of the various degrees of rank in the British Navy to render it a matter of any consequence. (Chairman and Deputy Chairman, EIC, to Viscount Melville, 1 February 1816, in BL IOR G/12/196 (Reel 1) F 128)

---

17 'Nothing can be more superb than the silversmith's shops' reflecting the richness of the nation' (Brewer, 1997, p. 29).

Choice of Presents for the Jiaqing Emperor

Barrow (1807, vol. 1, p. 348) commented that the British knew little of the customs and manners of the Qing court at the time of the Macartney Embassy and had been dependent on the 'voluminous writings of the French missionaries' for guidance in the choice of presents for the Qianlong emperor. The Qing court, according to these sources, was interested primarily in 'the sciences', specifically 'astronomy and experimental philosophy' (Pritchard, 1943, p. 163). Scientific gifts including a planetarium, glass lenses and air pumps were chosen to showcase British scientific progress to 'excite at Peking a taste for many articles of English workmanship' in the hope of generating markets for British goods.[18] These gifts, however, were famously dismissed by the Qianlong emperor who told George III that China did not 'value ingenious articles, nor do we have the slightest need of your country's manufactures' ('Edict from the Emperor Qianlong to King George the Third of England', 23 September 1793, as quoted in Cranmer-Byng, 1962, p. 340).[19] Barrow (1807, vol. 1, pp. 348–349) complained that the scientific gifts were 'all lost and thrown away by the ignorant Chinese' and that if Chinese interest in the sciences had ever existed this was 'now completely worn out'. The previous British perception of the Qing court as a site of scientific interest and progress had changed, following Macartney, to one of ignorance and stagnation whose members were adverse to 'the introduction of all novelties' and were ruled by ceremonial and 'idolatrous worship' (Barrow, 1807, vol. 1, p. 349).

Barrow believed he had learned from the Macartney experience and was confident that he understood that the nature of Chinese taste was founded on objects of 'intrinsic value' (Minute of a Conference between the Chairs and Mr Barrow Respecting the Presents for the Emperor, in BL IOR G/12/196 (Reel 1) F 45). This judgement appears to have been based

---

18   Macartney's prime objective was to secure a treaty of trade with the Chinese Government. His embassy was primarily 'a trade mission to popularize British inventions and manufacturers' (Cranmer-Byng & Levere, 1981, p. 505).
19   A similar declaration is found in Staunton's (1821) translation of *Narrative of the Chinese embassy to the Khan of the Tourgouth Tartars*. The Kangxi emperor instructed the Chinese ambassador that in the event of the 'vain and ostentatious' Russians displaying unusual items, he was not to 'express admiration nor contempt; and [is] merely to say, "whether our country possesses or not such things as these, it is quite out of our province to determine"' (p. 17).

on Macartney's discovery of 40 or 50 garden pavilions situated among the imperial gardens at Jehol that were furnished 'in the richest manner' of the best of European taste, including fine paintings, European sing-songs and toys, and Chinese porcelains and enamel ware (Cranmer-Byng, 1962, pp. 125–126). Macartney was astonished at the sight of objects 'of such exquisite workmanship, and in such profusion' and thought that the British presents 'must shrink from the comparison and hide their diminished heads' (Cranmer-Byng, 1962, p. 125). A major consideration in the choice of presents was that they not offend Chinese pride (Barrow, 1807, vol. 1, p. 350). Barrow cautioned that Chinese sensibilities had to be considered. Gifts of a high standard representative of 'the talent and ingenuity of foreigners' were likely to draw 'jealous comparisons' with their own manufacturers and Lamiot had stressed that the Jiaqing emperor was averse to luxury and curious objects.

Presents chosen by the Amherst Embassy for the emperor included gold items such as a cup with a cover and a salver of beautiful workmanship; several silver vessels; a 24-piece china dessert service decorated with a white and gold scroll border with paintings of British landscapes; several large floral decorated china vases; glassware, bottles and liqueurs including brandy and dried fruits valued at £400; engravings of the coast of England and Wales; a painting of the Doncaster races; and portraits of the Prince Regent and Princess Caroline. Other gifts included two superb, elegantly finished and richly ornamented sedan chairs; super fine furs; perfumes; two ornamental clocks for the Hall of Audience; and a selection of superfine cloths of soft Spanish wool. It was hoped that their inclusion would attract Chinese attention and open a market among the superior mandarins and the principal officers of the Chinese Government (Secret Court of Directors to Amherst, 26 January 1816, in BL IOR G/12/196 (Reel 1) F 116).

De Poirot had thought that the Macartney Embassy's omission of presents for the mandarins at the Qianlong court had contributed to the embassy's failure. Accordingly, the Amherst Embassy carried an extra range of gifts including crystal chandeliers and glassware, porcelains, fine linens, clocks and watches, perfumes and snuffs. A selection of paintings, 'chiefly of Buildings, Flowers and Animals', as well as a map of London and prints showcasing prominent buildings and landmarks, such as St Paul's, the Greenwich Hospital and views of the Thames, were also chosen, as well as maps of the British Isles, a Chart of Navigation from Europe to China, hand telescopes, a model of a ship-of-war, a fire engine, and pocket books containing razors, scissors and pen knives. The total cost of all the presents was £22,005.13.7 (equivalent to over £2 million in today's values).[20]

Barrow also drew up a list of presents that were unsuitable to send to the Qing court including a barouche or carriage. The splendid gilded carriage sent with Macartney had been found subsequently by the Dutch in 1795, evidently never used, and Barrow commented that it was impossible 'to make them to suit Chinese taste', referring to the fact that the driver sat in an elevated position to the emperor (Minute of Conference between the Chairs, & Mr Barrow respecting Presents for China, in BL IOR G/12/196 (Reel 1) F 47). Presents of a military character were also not appropriate.[21] Six small brass cannons brought by Macartney that fired several times a minute had 'excited the darkest suspicion in the mind of the legate' who observed them (Minute of Conference between the Chairs, & Mr Barrow respecting Presents for China, in BL IOR G/12/196 (Reel 1) F 47). Maps of China and India were thought to also incite 'jealousy' in China, given Britain's presence in India, while botanical drawings were excluded as it was thought that the Chinese excelled British skill in that branch of drawing.

'Kia-King's' Tea Pot

Historians have documented that British manufacturers were approached at the time of the Macartney Embassy for their suggestions and assistance in the selection of presents for the Qianlong emperor (see Berg, 2006). It appears that Barrow also wrote to selected British manufacturers in the context of the Amherst Embassy for their thoughts on how the mission might assist their businesses. One who replied was L. W. Dillwyn, Esq., of the Cambrian Company, porcelain manufacturers of Swansea, Wales. Dillwyn thanked Barrow for his letter and informed him that the intended embassy could certainly 'assist my endeavours to rival the Chinese Porcelain' (L. W. Dillwyn to John Barrow, 7 January 1816, in BL IOR MSS EUR F 140/38(a)). Complaining that his knowledge of the

---

20   A full list of the presents and their cost is provided in Appendix B.
21   The Kangxi emperor's instructions to the ambassador to the Tourgouth Tartars declared that all firearms and 'similar goods' were 'prohibited goods; their exportation beyond the frontier is never permitted'. Accordingly, these were not appropriate gifts to be carried by diplomatic envoys (Staunton, 1821, p. 17).

manufacture of Chinese porcelain was based solely on the Jesuit account found in Du Halde (1741) and from examples of the 'very inferior wares of Canton', he continued:

> It is said that all the articles of the very finest quality are appropriated for the Emperor's Court, and of these I should greatly like to procure a piece. Any broken Article would answer my purpose as well as a perfect one; for my object would be to subject it to a course of experiments. (L. W. Dillwyn to John Barrow, 7 January 1816, in BL IOR MSS EUR F 140/38(a))[22]

Barrow, displaying a rare sense of humour, forwarded Dillwyn's letter to Amherst with the accompanying note:

> My Dear Lord,
> If you should happen to break one of Kia King's old Teapots or saucers, perhaps Your Lordship would have the goodness to recollect the wish of the ingenious writer of the enclosed and preserve the fragments. (Barrow to Amherst, n.d., in BL MSS EUR F 140/38 (a))

Dillwyn's expert admission that British china had yet to reach the technical perfection of imperial porcelain was dismissed by Barrow who appears to have assumed that a piece of Wedgwood china would suitably impress the Jiaqing emperor and be judged favourably next to the imperial wares that graced his table. The list of British presents reveals that their choice was decided on the basis of cultural assumptions reflecting and epitomising the values of aesthetic taste held by the British aristocracy and court society. Good taste, it was assumed, transcended cultural borders and the luxury goods prized and valued at St James's would similarly appeal to the high-ranking mandarins at the Qing court. The choice of tableware for the emperor's table appears incongruous given the cultural protocols of Chinese cuisine and serve to suggest that Barrow, despite his brief residence at the Qianlong court in his capacity as the comptroller of Macartney's presents, never witnessed the Chinese at table in the palace at Peking.

---

22   Dillwyn's reference to the Jesuit account of porcelain manufacture refers to d'Entrecolles's letters from the kilns of Jingdezhen in Du Halde's *Encyclopaedia of China* first published in Paris in 1735, which revealed the secrets of Chinese porcelain manufacturing techniques to the West.

Preparations of the HMS *Alceste*

Reference to the nature of the provisions and stores brought on board the *Alceste* for the long voyage to China indicate the lifestyle of privileged guests on board an early nineteenth-century British man-of-war. Included among the wine and spirits were 120 dozen bottles of first growth Chateau Margaux Claret at a cost of £444, 132 dozen Chateau Lafitte at a cost of £488 and 126 dozen bottles of Chateau Latour at a cost of £466. Aperitifs and liqueurs consisted of 240 dozen bottles of Superior Port at a cost of £528, 240 dozen bottles of East India Madeira and 108 dozen bottles of Superior Sherry. White wines included 78 dozen bottles of Old Hock, 30 dozen bottles of Sparkling Champagne and other white wines. The wine bill alone cost the Company £5,163.17.00. Other stores included '120 Packages' of cognac, Jamaica rum, brandy, Scotch whisky, cider and 'Taunton Ale' adding up to £5,710.6.8. Jams, jellies, preserved fruits, brandy fruits, raspberry vinegar and sundry confectionaries totalled £340.12.00. Dried fruits, chocolates, 'Jordan' almonds and 66 lbs of the 'finest Louchong and Hyson Teas' were included as well as '12 Canisters of Oatmeal, Groats & Pease' (BL IOR MSS EUR F 140/36). Spices and herbs were also loaded on board, as well as oils, sugar, vinegars, anchovies, caviar, pickles, cheeses, hams, pickled tongues, 'truffles and morsels' and crates of beef (BL IOR MSS EUR F 140/36).

Extra funds deposited in two chests amounting to £20,000 (equivalent to approximately £2 million in today's values) were added to the *Alceste*'s inventory in case extra supplies had to be purchased at ports of call during the voyage, although the Company Directors did question whether there was a need to stop at Madeira to purchase more wine.[23] A major expense was the refitting of an apartment on board the *Alceste* commensurate with Amherst's status as ambassador, as well as extra furniture required during his stay in China. An inventory of the furnishings included '4 Trafalga chairs, carv'd and cane seats' costing £10; two large lounging chairs; two large handsome indulgent sofas at a cost of £74.10.00; two large knee hole wash stands and one handsome Grecian couch; one very large sofa table; one superb British carpet made up to fit the cabin, five allover cases

---

23 The directors pointed out that the expenses of the embassy already exceeded that of the Macartney Embassy. Over 1,665 dozen bottles of spirits, cider, beer and wines had been provided. The question, therefore, was asked, 'So is it really necessary to stop at Madeira for more wine?'

of Crimson Calico for sofas, couches and elbow chairs; an ornamented bronze inkstand; and '28 yards of the best Print, Lace, and calicoes' (BL IOR MSS EUR F 140/36).[24]

The Embassy on the Eve of its Departure for China

Amherst had in his possession a letter dated 6 January 1816 from a member of the public that displayed an interest in the need for the British to acquire an understanding of China because a knowledge of Chinese 'desires, wants, likes, dislikes, prejudices etc.' was essential if the British were to learn 'how to manage them'. The author added:

> I hope my Lord, you will be able to prevail upon the Emperor to permit 12 of the most competent Englishmen, who are well acquainted with the Chinese language, to travel over the whole Empire—and I hope you will prevail upon the Emperor to send 12 of his most competent Mandarins to England, so they might learn our language as they came over; who would bring the Emperor an account of our Real-State. (Anonymous letter in Amherst's possession, postmark 6 January 1816, in BL IOR MSS EUR F 140/35)

This letter reflects Porter's (2001, p. 205) insight of the British belief in the value of 'voyages of reciprocal discovery' where scientific and cultural knowledge was appreciated and transmitted between nations. The author's confidence in the ability of the embassy to 'increase wisdom and knowledge and understanding' between East and the West reflects an optimistic expectation of a fruitful outcome for the embassy that mirrored Amherst's faith. China and the mentality of its people, it was hoped, would be accessible to British investigation.

---

24 It would appear that the colour yellow featured prominently in Amherst's furnishings. Reference is made to the colour during the salvaging of furniture from the wreck of the *Alceste* in February 1817. This was hardly a judicious choice considering the colour yellow was reserved in China for the sole use of the emperor.

George Rose, a diplomat and leading Treasury bureaucrat, had a more realistic assessment of the chances of the embassy.[25] He wrote to Charles Abbot, Speaker of the House of Commons, congratulating him on securing a passage for his son as a midshipman on the *Alceste*:

> The voyage to China in the way it is made by an ambassador is beyond all comparison more interesting than to any other part of the world … your mentioning his accompanying Lord Amherst leads me to mention a circumstance I should not otherwise have done. (Colchester, 1861, vol. 2, p. 562)[26]

Rose continued that he had met John Sullivan, Buckinghamshire's first choice as ambassador, who informed him that Amherst was 'instructed to act precisely as Lord Macartney' (Colchester, 1861, vol. 2, p. 562). Rose added that this 'led me to say his Lordship had then better stay at home'. Amherst's only chance for a successful mission, in Rose's opinion, was to adopt a more conciliatory attitude towards the Jiaqing emperor than Macartney had shown to the Qianlong emperor where his:

> infinite ill-humour … excited by [his] temper and unbending disposition … certainly did not give fair play to the chance of effecting the objects of his mission; and I am quite clear that an opposite course should be adopted now. (Colchester, 1861, vol. 2, p. 563)

On 30 December 1815, Amherst was sworn in as a privy counsellor.[27] Lord Sidmouth congratulated him on his appointment and apologised for not attending the ceremony. He referred to the upcoming embassy and assured Amherst that he had no doubt of its success due to 'the judgment, temper and address of the Person, in whose hands this important entity is fortunately placed' (Lord Sidmouth to Amherst, 31 December 1815, in BL IOR MSS EUR F 140/35). Amherst thanked Sidmouth for his 'kind and flattering attention' and for:

---

25 Sir George Henry Rose (1771–1855), First Secretary, British Embassy, the Hague (1792–1793); Charge d'Affairs Berlin (1793); envoy extraordinary to the United States (1807–1808); British Minister in Munich (1813–1815) and Berlin (1815).

26 Charles Abbot, 1st Baron Colchester, was the speaker in the House of Commons (1802–1817) and a close personal friend of Amherst.

27 The Privy Council consisted of a board of high-ranking dignitaries who advised the British monarch on state affairs. Staunton was very bitter that he was never awarded the honour, especially after Ellis was appointed to the council in the 1830s. Staunton thought this was because he had no 'personal friend' in the Cabinet to further his cause. He added that such Royal favour would have been particularly pleasing had it been conferred on him after the Amherst Embassy while his mother was still alive and where he was still 'young enough to form and hope to realise fresh projects of ambition' (Staunton, 1856, pp. 176–183).

> the good wishes which you do me the honour and favour to express for the successful termination of my Embassy and for my safe return to my family … The best mode of repaying your Lordship's kindness will be to exert every faculty I possess in the honourable and faithful discharge of the duties entrusted to me; and my chief reward will be the approbation of those who, like your Lordship, deserve and acquire the applause and esteem of their Country. (Amherst to Sidmouth, n.d., in Devon Heritage Centre (South West Heritage Trust), 152M/C1816/OF1)

Rose, meanwhile, kept up his attack on the conduct of Macartney at the time of his embassy and told Lord Colchester:

> I feel quite confident, if the ambassador is to act as Lord Macartney did (whose steps Mr. Sullivan told me he [Amherst] is to follow exactly), he will not have even a chance of obtaining anything; and much is to be obtained if the Chinese Ministers will open their eyes to the true interests of their country. I was present at long and repeated conversations between Mr. Pitt and Lord Macartney, after the return of the latter, and Mr. Pitt was entirely convinced that the unbending conduct of his Lordship rendered his success hopeless. (Colchester, 1861, vol. 2, p. 566)

Final Instructions on the Performance of the Kowtow

Amherst received two 'enclosures' of instructions 'for your guidance in the discharge of Duties' at the Court of Peking from the Foreign Secretary, Lord Castlereagh, dated 1 January 1816. Amherst was reminded that there was a danger of commerce at Canton failing 'altogether' and that his mission was 'the only remedy that was likely to be effectual in order to place the [trade and] intercourse upon a satisfactory and stable footing' (Castlereagh to Amherst, Foreign Office, 1 January 1816, in BL IOR MSS EUR F 140/43 (a); also cited in Morse, 1926/1966, vol. 3, p. 279). His objects were to negotiate assurances of protection of the Company members at Canton from the violence and injustice of the local government; to more accurately define and detail their privileges; to guarantee freedom from intrusion of the Chinese provincial government at Canton into the British Factory; and to secure an open channel of communication, in the Chinese language, in all addresses and representations to the Chinese Government. A copy of the proceedings of the Macartney Embassy was also enclosed from which 'a careful perusal of the correspondence of his Lordships, you will receive the most valuable suggestions' (Castlereagh to Amherst, Foreign Office, 1 January 1816, in BL IOR MSS EUR F 140/43 (a)). Amherst was instructed:

> In the pursuit of these objects, you will regulate your conduct, by such information as you may receive from the Company Supercargoes, on the habits and customs of the Chinese government and people; and I am persuaded that in the knowledge and experience of the Supercargoes you will find the means, under the exercise of your own judgment and discretion, of adapting a course, the best calculated to affect the essential purposes of your Embassy. (Castlereagh to Amherst, Foreign Office, 1 January 1816, in BL IOR MSS EUR F 140/43 (a))

Castlereagh issued two important instructions. The first was identical to that given to Macartney revealing a lack of any further thought on the part of the Foreign Ministry. Thus, Amherst was informed to follow the 'punctilio' or procedures of ceremony at the emperor's court and conform 'to all the ceremonies of that Court, which may not commit the honour of your Sovereign or lessen your own dignity, so as to endanger the success of your mission' (Castlereagh to Amherst, Foreign Office, 1 January 1816, in BL IOR MSS EUR F 140/43 (a)). The historian Tuck (2000, p. xx) has pointed out the 'vagueness and ambiguity' of such instructions. Further 'ambiguity' followed with Castlereagh instructing Amherst to 'take the earliest opportunity to declare … [that] the Prince Regent had entirely approved of the ceremonials performed by the Earl Macartney to the August Father of the present Emperor' and had especially commanded him to 'adopt that precedent upon' his mission 'to His Illustrious Son' (Castlereagh to Amherst, 1 January 1816, in BL MSS EUR F 140/43(a)). Castlereagh's second instruction regarded Amherst's rank in the embassy where he was to 'consider yourself at liberty to act upon your own responsibility, in case of any difference of Opinion between you and the other Commissioners' (Castlereagh to Amherst, 1 January 1816, in BL MSS EUR F 140/43(a)). The Secret Commercial Committee of the Company similarly stressed that the first commissioner, namely, Amherst, 'was to possess an extraordinary power of acting on his own responsibility in opposition to the sentiments of his Colleagues' (Secret Commercial Committee to Amherst, 17 January 1816, in Morse, 1926/1966, vol. 3, p. 294). These instructions endowed Amherst with the flexibility to override Company interests if he deemed it expedient to do so. Ultimately, Amherst answered only to the Prince Regent who had appointed him.

Amherst's notes reveal his continued confusion over these instructions, especially regarding the performance of the kowtow. He wrote to Buckinghamshire for clarification on its performance, but Buckinghamshire's reply was not particularly helpful (Buckinghamshire to Amherst on the Ceremonies of Lord Macartney, 12 January 1816, in BL IOR MSS EUR F 140/35). After some deep thought on the issue, he had decided that:

> due to the absurd prejudices and customs of the Chinese ... I can't define which ceremonial would be considered as committing the honour of the sovereign or lessening the dignity of the emperor. (Buckinghamshire to Amherst on the Ceremonies of Lord Macartney, 12 January 1816, in BL IOR MSS EUR F 140/35)

Amherst was informed that because it was impossible to anticipate the 'circumstances you [will] find yourself in' it was necessary that he 'exercise your own discretion' (Buckinghamshire to Amherst on the Ceremonies of Lord Macartney, 12 January 1816, in BL IOR MSS EUR F 140/35). Buckinghamshire was convinced, however, that it was unwise to include any official reference to Macartney's ceremonials in the Prince Regent's letter to the Jiaqing emperor as this would serve 'to embarrass [rather] than facilitate' (Buckinghamshire to Amherst on the Ceremonies of Lord Macartney, 12 January 1816, in BL IOR MSS EUR F 140/35). He added, reassuringly, that Macartney acted 'with full confidence in the support of his government' (Buckinghamshire to Amherst on the Ceremonies of Lord Macartney, 12 January 1816, in BL IOR MSS EUR F 140/35). Amherst thanked Buckinghamshire for his advice and 'for clearing up some doubts relative to the latitude afforded me under my ... instruction relating to the ceremonial of my presentation to the emperor of China' (Amherst to Buckinghamshire, 19 January 1816, in BL IOR MSS EUR F 140/35).

Buckinghamshire had sent Amherst a private letter two weeks earlier from Bath, writing:

> My most anxious wishes for the success of your Mission, not only on account of the Public, but because I feel deeply interested on your account. I certainly am sanguine in my expecting, and not

> the less so, from a conviction that by placing the business in your hands we take the best security against failure. (Buckinghamshire to Amherst, 5 January 1816, in BL IOR MSS EUR F 140/43 (a))

On 4 February 1816, Buckinghamshire suffered a fatal stroke while riding in Hyde Park. He had informed Amherst five days earlier of a 'most serious attack, but hope I am doing well' (Buckinghamshire to Amherst, 30 January 1816, in BL IOR MSS EUR F 140/35). Expectations of a successful mission were muted with little overt optimism, but Amherst had done all he could by way of background research and preparation to ensure that he had a flexible strategy in place should the opportunity present itself.

Amherst's Notes: 'The Course Which I Shall Have to Pursue Will Be as Follows'

Amherst read his brief in the following terms. His 'great objective' was to 'open a direct communication with Pekin'. He wrote in his notes, 'I must not lose sight of this' (Amherst, 'Notes on policy to be pursued by the British Embassy to China' in BL IOR MSS EUR F 140/36). He noted further that although the Qianlong emperor had:

> absolutely refused to permit an English Resident at his Court, I see nothing in the transactions of the former Embassy which would render hopeless an application for permission to open a direct communication between the members of the Factory and one of the tribunals or public departments at Pekin. No such demand appears to have been made by Lord Macartney & consequently there are no traces of any objection on the part of the Chinese government to such a measure. (Amherst, 'Notes on objects of the Embassy' in BL IOR MSS EUR F 140/36)

Amherst listed the course he was to pursue:

1. announce to the emperor that he was appointed by the Prince Regent and explain his desire to renew the amicable relations that existed between the respective fathers and that the Prince Regent had chosen this time to send an ambassador due to the restoration of tranquillity in Europe

2. 'solicit the emperor's protection to the subjects and commerce of England'

3. 'bring forward propositions for the future regulation of trade, and therein the prevention of former evils'. Amherst added in a pencilled note, '(introducing the subject perhaps by the disavowing of the proceedings of the *Doris*)'.

He added that to accomplish his last objective he would propose:

1. a British resident at Peking
2. open communication in the Chinese language between the Factory and a Tribunal at Peking or a Chinese minister in England
3. a consul at Canton.

Success in one or the other, Amherst continued, would be the best means of obtaining:

1. protection from violence or injustice and a more accurate definition of Company privileges
2. security for trade against the sudden and capricious interruptions and the privilege of dealing with such merchants as the Factory may think fit
3. free communication with a resident at Peking or by written representations in the Chinese language, and the right to use that language in all addresses to the local government.

Amherst's greatest wish, only to be promoted in the event of the above being achieved, was the opening of a 'port to the north-wards of Canton and a Resident Minister at Pekin and a Chinese Minister to England in return', reflecting a British belief in the value of mutual self-interest in achieving British aims. A secret report prepared at Canton by Samuel Ball, Inspector of Teas, was prepared on this subject and handed to Amherst on arrival in China.[28] A further objective was the 'extension of British manufactures' into China. Above all else, Amherst reminded himself, was the need to 'avoid the language of complaint' in his negotiations with the Qing court (Amherst, 'Notes on policy to be pursued by the British Embassy to China' in BL IOR MSS EUR F 140/36). While the general objective of his embassy was stated in his instructions, Amherst's actions were to be left largely to his own discretion and judgement to be decided at the time.

---

28 This report is reproduced in Appendix D.

As the time of departure for China drew near, Amherst became more and more concerned at the delays caused by the refitting and loading of the ships. Instead of leaving England by 1 December 1815 as initially planned, the date was pushed back to early February 1816, which left little time for the embassy to arrive in northern China before the onset of the typhoon season. Amherst told the Company chairs five days before sailing:

> I do not recollect any former period of my life to have looked with so much anxiety to any event, as I now feel for our arrival at a proper season in the Bay of Pe-tchee-lee … [as] we need to arrive at the mouth of the White River before the change of the Monsoon. (Amherst to the Chairman and Deputy Chairman, 3 February 1816, in BL IOR G/12/196 (Reel 1) F 131)

Refitting of the *Alceste* was completed on 3 February 1816 and Amherst and his suite came on board the following day (Journal of Sir William Fanshawe Martin, 1817, pp. 1–2, in BL ADD MSS 41346-41475). The embassy sailed on 8 February 1816. On the day of departure, Captain Maxwell sent a letter to the Company chairs pledging his utmost 'zeal and energy' to the task of providing for the comfort of Amherst and his entourage. He further reassured them that he would 'endeavour to conform to that liberal motto of old English hospitality [of] "spare not, waste not" which you requested should be my guide' (Maxwell to the Chairs, 8 February 1816, in BL IOR G/12/196 (Reel 1) F 135). Amherst wrote to his wife on the same day from Portsmouth:

> My dearest love, Our bitterest parting is over. Let us support ourselves till we meet again by the consciousness of having done a duty now, which will sweeten the rest of our lives … The sun was setting gloriously one side of me and the Moon rising in almost equal splendour on the other. I thought they seemed to shed a favourable influence of the journey I am undertaking, and in that belief I will bid you goodnight. (Amherst to Sarah Amherst, in BL Box 130 946c Ref 5562)

6

The Voyage from Portsmouth to 'Hong Kong'

The three ships carrying the British embassy to China set out from Portsmouth on 8 February 1816 on the five-month voyage that sailed via Madeira, Rio de Janeiro, Cape Town and Batavia. Lord Amherst; his 14-year-old son Jeffrey; Henry Ellis, Secretary to the Ambassador; Clarke Abel, Surgeon and Naturalist; and Henry Hayne, Private Secretary to the Ambassador, travelled on the man-of-war HMS *Alceste*.[1] Also on board, it has been noted, was the wife of the boatswain, whose presence was described by one of the *Alceste*'s crew as 'the Dammablest thing a man can be troubled with but she stood it like a Brittan'.[2] Charles Abbot, the son of the speaker, as well as Captain Maxwell's son were among the midshipmen. The *Alceste* was joined at Spithead by the naval brig HMS *Lyra* under the command of Captain Basil Hall. One of her midshipmen, William Hutcheon Hall (no relation), later commanded HMS *Nemesis* at the time of the First Opium War.[3] The Company ship *General Hewitt*, commanded by Captain Walter Campbell, carried the presents sent by the Prince Regent to the Jiaqing emperor.

---

1 Henry Hayne (n.d., vol. 1, p. 3) listed the other members of the embassy on board the *Alceste*: Mr Griffith, Chaplain and Jeff's tutor; Doctor Lynn; and Havell, the embassy's draughtsman.
2 This was quoted in a 13-page manuscript written by the carpenter on board the *Alceste* to his father that was auctioned at Christies on 26–27 September 2007 (see *Christie's Sale 7470: Exploration and Travel 26-27 September 2007*, www.christies.com/lotfinder/Lot/china-lord-amhersts-embassy-to-china-4966662-details.aspx).
3 The HMS *Nemesis* was the world's first ironclad steam-powered warship. On 7 January 1841, the *Nemesis* engaged in action against Chinese forces in the Pearl River with other British warships and routed the Chinese war junks sent against them. The *Nemesis*'s shallow draught showed the utility of such vessels in shallow waters and 'demonstrated conclusively the enormous gap' between Chinese and British military might (Marshall, 2016, p. 89).

Life on board the *Alceste* on the outward voyage helped build an esprit de corps forging the members of the embassy into a close-knit group united in their mission. The spirit of camaraderie was enhanced further by the arrival of the men from the British Factory at Canton who joined the embassy when the ships arrived at the islands off Macao on 13 June 1816. Such high spirits were mostly due to Amherst's leadership derived from his civility, reasonableness and sense of humour. In modern management parlance, Amherst would be regarded as an inclusive leader and a team player who extensively consulted his commissioners and other members of his retinue to make decisions based on the fullest possible range of information and views.

Ellis and Clarke recognised the challenges of a long voyage to the other side of the world and the uncertainty of their reception once they reached China. Their views, no doubt, reflected those of the others in the mission. Ellis (1817) wrote:

> The voyage must in fact occupy so many months, that the most sanguine cannot yet dwell upon the scene awaiting them at its termination with any degree of interest; and those who have perused the accounts of the former Embassy, commenced too as it was under better prospects, can scarcely anticipate either public success or private gratification from any events likely to occur during our progress through China. (p. 1)

Clarke Abel, the surgeon and naturalist, later lamented:

> In passing the shores of the Isle of Wight, my imagination dwelt painfully on the white cliffs and verdant slopes, which but three days before I had visited with friends who gave the best value to my existence, and from whom I was separating, perhaps for ever. (1818, p. 1)

Amherst's initial thoughts concerned his personal wellbeing. His dislike of sea travel was revealed in a letter to his wife written at Dover in 1806:

> Many people go from hence over to the French Coast, but you know I am no admirer of a sea voyage and shall content myself with seeing them from Terra firma. (Amherst to Sarah Amherst, 1806, in Letters from the Yale Collection of American Literature)

Suffering dreadfully from sea sickness during the first days of his voyage to China, Amherst complained of the 'rolling' of the ship making writing impossible and forcing him to retire to his 'cot for 5 days and … sit out two dinners':

> both my head and stomach are … exceedingly confused … [the] noise of the bulk heads … [the] creaking of the wood is such as to intercept all conversation across the table … [one has to] exert your lungs to the utmost to be heard by your next neighbour. (Amherst to Sarah Amherst, 16 February 1816, in BL Box 130 946c Ref 5562)[4]

Abel also suffered chronic sea sickness, but William Havell, the artist for the embassy, soon recovered and, after the first day, 'was the life and soul of the party' (Hayne, n.d., vol. 1, p. 4).[5] Despite his indisposition, Amherst remained positive and wrote, 'Nothing can exceed the harmony and good humour that prevails amongst us' (Amherst to Sarah Amherst, 16 February 1816, in BL Box 130 946c Ref. 5562). Jeffrey's presence, as predicted by Lord Boringdon, was a great comfort to his father:

> Without him I should have been a very wretch … From nine o'clock till three I do not see a human being in the ship except Jeff who comes from his French lesson and Captain Maxwell who brings the Chart to show me where we were at 12 o'clock. (Amherst to Sarah Amherst, 22 February 1816, in BL Box 130 946c Ref. 5562)

Amherst and Jeffrey spent a lot of time walking up and down the quarter deck looking out for the *Lyra* and the *General Hewitt*. Amherst wrote on 16 February, 'the Indiaman sailed along side us … for 2 or 3 hours, near enough to nod to each other, but the weather was too rough to admit to conversation' (Amherst to Sarah Amherst, 17 February 1816, in BL Box 130 946c Ref 5562). Amherst's optimism about his mission improved steadily after gaining his sea legs. He told Sarah:

---

4   Hayne (n.d., vol. 1, p. 4) noted that Amherst appeared on deck for the first time on the afternoon of 14 February.
5   William Havell, born in 1782, worked in his family's London-based engraving firm and was an established artist. He left the embassy at Manila on its return voyage in February 1817 after an altercation with one of *Alceste*'s officers and travelled separately to India where he remained for eight years earning a living as a portrait artist. He returned to England in 1825, living in reduced circumstances and died in December 1857 (Owen, 1981).

> I am so convinced that what we have done is right, and so confident, humbly confident, that we shall be rewarded for it, that hope was never so buoyant with me before. (Amherst to Sarah Amherst, 17 February 1816, in BL Box 130 946c Ref 5562)

He also felt well enough to inform her of some choice gossip regarding the details of Lord Buckinghamshire's will. Informed by Ellis that Buckinghamshire had 'not left a single shilling to the present lord' and only a 'small legacy to Mr Ellis and his elder brother', he added that 'Lady Buckinghamshire has a handsome provision [but] I dare say you have heard all this from Lady Macartney' (Amherst to Sarah Amherst, 17 February 1816, in BL Box 130 946c Ref 5562).

Madeira

The ships reached Madeira on 18 February 1816 where they found two British men-of-war, recently arrived from Portsmouth, waiting in the Funchal Roads. On board the HMS *Niger* was Sir Charles Bagot, newly appointed British Ambassador to the United States on his way to Washington. Bagot knew Amherst and had commented earlier on his dire financial circumstances.[6] Sir Hudson Lowe, on board the HMS *Phaeton*, was on his way to St Helena to take up the post of governor in charge of Napoleon's exile.[7] Amherst, anxious to set sail and get underway, declined their invitations to visit Madeira as nothing 'shall interfere with the main object of our voyage' of a speedy passage to China (Amherst to Sarah Amherst, 18 February 1816, in BL Box 130 946c Ref. 5562). Jeffrey recorded in his journal that the town of Funchal appeared 'very clean and large' from a distance, but learned from others that the reverse was true: 'like most Portuguese towns, it is excessively filthy' (Journal of Jeffrey Amherst, son of Lord Amherst, on his father's mission to China, n.d., n.p. in BL IOR MSS EUR F 140/37, hereafter referred to as 'Jeffrey Amherst, n.d., n.p.'). Regardless of Amherst's immediate concerns and those of the Company Directors, time was found to load a store of Madeira wine on board the *Alceste* before sailing that evening for Rio de Janeiro.

---

6   Charles Bagot was later to enjoy a pension of £4,000, in contrast to Amherst who received a hereditary pension of £3,000 (Wade, 1835, pp. 510, 507).

7   Napoleon was taken to St Helena on board the HMS *Northumberland* under the command of Sir George Cockburn who was entrusted with his safe custody until the arrival of Sir Hudson Lowe. Lowe arrived at St Helena in April 1816 (Seaton, 1898, p. 37).

Sailing into fine weather, the squadron made good time. Dinner was heralded by the sound of a horn and the band playing the 'Roast Beef of Old England' (Hayne, n.d., vol. 1, p. 6). Embassy personnel were joined by two or three officers of the watch and evenings were spent playing backgammon (Hayne, n.d., vol. 1, p. 5). A festive mood was felt throughout the ship (Amherst to Sarah Amherst, 25 March 1816, in BL Box 130 946c Ref. 5562). Amherst wrote:

> For the last two evenings there has been dancing upon the deck from about 6 to 8, the gentlemen and officers on the quarter deck and the sailors on the gang-way and forecastle. I don't know which party enjoy it most, but the sailors are a little puzzled with the French country dance tune. One fellow last night amused himself with dancing upon his head. (Amherst to Sarah Amherst, 22 February 1816, in BL Box 130 946c Ref. 5562)

'Much mirth and humour' accompanied the crossing-the-line ceremony on 4 March (Amherst to Sarah Amherst, 22 February 1816, in BL Box 130 946c Ref. 5562). Sounds symbolic of British power swept the waves as the embassy band played 'God Save the King' and 'Rule Britannia' when King Neptune came on board (Hayne, n.d., vol. 1, p. 17). Novices dressed up in women's clothes lent by Mrs Low (Hayne, n.d., vol. 1, p. 17) and were ordered to be smeared with an oatmeal paste that was shaved off 'with a rusty iron hoop, full of notches' followed by a ducking match (Hayne, n.d., vol. 1, p. 19). Amherst's exemption from the ceremony was bought at a cost of 'a double allowance of grog to the sailors for two days', much to the delight of the crew (Jeffrey Amherst, n.d., n.p.). The *Lyra* and *General Hewitt* left the *Alceste* soon after on 10 March and followed a course directly to the Cape of Good Hope, while the *Alceste* headed west to Brazil in order for Amherst to pay a courtesy call on the Portuguese royal family who were living in exile at Rio de Janeiro under British protection. Such a detour, it was felt, would not jeopardise the mission as the *Alceste*'s speed and favourable southeast trade winds would ensure ample time for a rendezvous with the rest of the squadron at Cape Town (Ellis, 1817, p. 2).

The New World: Rio de Janeiro

British reactions to Rio de Janeiro, their first port of call in the New World, provides a useful touchstone against which to compare their later views on China. British responses to their alien environments need to be placed within the framework of Regency values and assumptions. Visual reactions to scenery were important for classifying interest or otherwise in a country. Other sensory sensations, especially unpleasant odours, immediately indicated an uncivilised and coarse society deprived of order and civility. Appearances were especially important for determining people as respectable or otherwise. Henry Hayne, Amherst's private secretary, wrote of Rio de Janeiro, 'nothing reminded me more of the uncivilised country where I was than their appearance' (Hayne, n.d., vol. 1, p. 57). He added that the American minister met at Rio looked more 'like an English barber than a minister ... [of] the Corps Diplomatic' (Hayne, n.d., vol. 1, p. 55).

British reactions to the new environments they encountered, revealed especially in their later responses to and perceptions of China, were shaped also by other more pressing concerns. Amherst, for example, did not respond to the sights of Brazil in the same way as others in his mission due to his anxiety about reaching northern China before the onset of the typhoon season and his preoccupation with immediate official duties connected with meeting the exiled Portuguese royal family in Rio de Janeiro.

Rio de Janeiro's physical appearance, in particular the Sugar Loaf, was described by Ellis as 'indescribably sublime and beautiful': 'The eye wandered in rapturous observation over an endless variety of picturesque combinations, presenting a totality of wondrous scenery ... [which defied] pictorial and verbal description' (Ellis, 1817, p. 3). Hayne (n.d., vol. 1) referred to Barrow's experience when visiting Rio and, like him, was 'lost in admiration of the magnificent scenery' (p. 35). Hayne and Ellis were enchanted when they came across the wife of the Russian Consul reading a book with a small child in a jungle clearing. Ellis described:

> On approaching the stream ... we observed an European lady, with her nurse and child, in a recess of the rock; her dress, appearance, and occupation (that of reading), presented, from their civilized combination, a most striking contrast to the uncultivated grandeur of the scene which surrounded us. (Ellis, 1817, p. 6)[8]

Ellis's response to the New World seen in this passage reveals early nineteenth-century British cultural predispositions for interpreting new sights that were later applied to China. Struck by the incongruous and contradictory sensory and Romantic image of an unexpected scene

---

8   The lady was Mrs Langsdorf, wife of the Russian Consul.

of a European mother and child reading in the wild Brazilian jungle, Ellis reverted to notions of civilisation, progress and sentimentality. For him, the European lady's presence imposed a sense of order on the uncultivated and wild landscape. The external appearance of fine dress and the refined occupation of reading further engaged Ellis's sensibilities, while the presence of the child suggested the finest values of familial love and affection.

While the *Lyra* did not visit Brazil (proceeding directly from Madeira to Cape Town), her captain, Basil Hall, clearly recognised the cultural insularity of the common British sailor when exposed to a foreign culture. He wrote as a general observation:

> It is Jack's custom, wherever he goes, to call every one he encounters abroad a mere outlandish-man, forgetting that it is himself alone who is so … Should the people he meets with happen to understand a word or two of English, he is satisfied, and they are set down for sensible people; otherwise he pities their ignorance, and laughs at the folly of their designating common things by names strange to their ears. I remember once overhearing the conversation of two of my sailors in the streets of Valparaiso, who had only been a few days in the country; one said to the other, 'What do you think of these people?'—'Why', replied his companion, with a look of thorough contempt, 'will you believe it—the infernal fools call a hat Sombrero!' (Hall, 1840/1865, p. 10)

Amherst had little time to contemplate Brazil's novelties. Cannon fire heard by those on board the *Alceste* as she approached the harbour was revealed as a salute announcing the death of the Queen of Portugal. The town of Rio de Janeiro was clouded in a 'character of noisy and luminous melancholy' as ships in the harbour fired their guns every five minutes as a mark of respect (Abel, 1818, p. 10). Amherst prepared himself for the Queen's funeral but was also taken by the British consul on a sightseeing tour of the area where he noted the splendour of the botanic gardens and made reference to a few 'Chinese gardeners' who were cultivating the 'Tea-plant' with great success (Abel, 1818, p. 18).

British reactions to Rio were affected specifically by the presence of numerous slave markets where vast numbers of slaves generated considerable moral outrage. The *Alceste*'s physician, John M'Leod, thought slavery was contrary to 'reason and natural light'. He complained further of Brazil's despotic government and the 'swarms' of Catholic priests who hung about the streets in clusters (M'Leod, 1818/1820, p. 8). The filth of Portuguese towns was also confirmed by Abel (1818):

> The strongest efforts of the imagination cannot picture any thing so heavenly as the country, or so disgusting as the town ... I almost lamented that I had an organ of smell. [I can] give no idea of the stench which exhales from the accumulated odure [sic] of its streets. (p. 23)

Cape Town

The *Alceste* reached Table Bay, South Africa, in record time, arriving on 30 April 1816 (Jeffrey Amherst, n.d., n.p.). Cape Town's character as a 'completely European' settlement evoked little interest for Ellis (1817, p. 18). Amherst was entertained by Lord Charles Somerset, Governor of the Cape, and two sailors jumped ship from the *General Hewitt*. After the squadron left the Cape bound for Java on 11 May 1816, Amherst's anxiety grew as the *Alceste* drew closer to China. He wrote to Sarah:

> I get exceedingly nervous as we approach the Straits of Sunda and advance towards Canton. I cannot feel confident that we shall be allowed to go up the Gulf of Pechelee. If we are required to land at Canton I know it was the opinion in England that it would be fatal to the success of the Embassy. (Amherst to Sarah Amherst, 11 May 1816, in BL Box 130 946c Ref. 5562)

Batavia

The Dutch East Indies were reached on 10 June 1816 and the ships anchored in the Anjere Roads. Amherst and some of his suite travelled overland to Batavia and were fascinated by scenes of rice fields, sugar and bamboo plantations and wild jungles. Arriving at Batavia, Amherst noted the port's Chinese 'middling classes', described by Ellis (1817, p. 25) as the descendants of 'Fo-kien province' who 'surpass[ed] the rest of the [Chinese] nation in enterprise' due to their willingness to travel and establish themselves in foreign countries. The children were of 'mixed race', as there were no Chinese women in Batavia, and were sent to China for their education (p. 26).

Despite Batavia's numerous novelties, the British were impressed primarily with the effect of good British governance on the Javanese population following their occupation of the East Indies between 1811 and 1816.[9] Dutch rule was condemned for its mismanagement and exploitation of the native population and natural resources and for its indifference to the rights and happiness of their subjects (Ellis, 1817, p. 34). Ellis thought that the imminent departure of Sir Stamford Raffles and the British administration from the islands was a 'matter of mutual regret' because Raffles was 'idolised' by the Javanese who thought of the British not as their masters, but as their benefactors (p. 36).

Amherst's attention now focused on the arrangements for the secret rendezvous with the embassy's Canton-based contingent off the coast of Macao. He addressed a letter dated 9 June to the president of the Select Committee informing him of the impending arrival of the embassy. This was handed to the captain of an American ship bound for China. The *Lyra* was sent on ahead to meet up with the Indiaman *Orlando* in Chinese waters to confirm arrangements for rendezvousing with the two Company ships, the *Discovery* and *Investigator*, scheduled to join the embassy. The *Alceste* and the *General Hewitt* departed Java 10 days later bound for China.

Reaction to the Embassy at Canton

Early rumours of another embassy reached Canton in January 1816. Barrow had alerted Staunton that an embassy was 'still in contemplation' and it appears he suggested that Staunton would be its leader (*Staunton Letters*, Macao, 18 January 1816). Staunton had just been promoted to president of the Select Committee after Elphinstone's departure for England in early 1816. His new position, Staunton informed his mother, was one 'I never either coveted or expected', while his new responsibilities made it very difficult 'to leave this spot … to form an Embassy' (*Staunton Letters*, Canton, 21 February 1816). British relations with the Cantonese authorities were currently very cordial in part due to the arrival of the son of Staunton's old friend Sungyun, the former governor-general at Canton, who in 1811 had bestowed extra favours on

---

9   Amherst had brought a duplicate set of dispatches ordering the evacuation of British troops from Java.

the British. Sungyun's son, whose rank was higher than the viceroy, was on a special assignment as the Imperial commissioner sent to try appeals against some provincial officials. He sent Staunton some small presents and invited him to visit his pleasure boat which Staunton refused on the grounds that this was 'unbecoming' to his status (*Staunton Letters*, Macao, 18 March 1816).

Official news that an embassy was on its way was received at Canton on 25 May 1816, only 45 days before Amherst arrived at the islands off Macao.[10] The Select Committee, fearful of unofficial news of the embassy's imminent arrival coming to the notice of the Chinese authorities through Indian newspaper accounts arriving at Macao, immediately sprang into action.[11] The governor of Guangdong, called the 'acting viceroy' or 'Foo-yuen' by the British, was notified officially of the approach of the embassy.[12] It was assumed another British embassy was acceptable to the Chinese Government following the Qianlong emperor's edict of 1796 signifying his approval of such a mission. The embassy's aim was to inform the Jiaqing emperor of 'the happy restoration of peace among the nations of the West'.[13] The Indiaman *Thomas Grenville* arrived from Bengal with Buckinghamshire's official letter to the viceroy two days later (Morse, 1926/1966, vol. 3, p. 258). Staunton, along with the other Factory members scheduled to join the embassy, travelled immediately to Macao to wait for Amherst's arrival.

Metcalfe's Meeting with the Fuyuan or Governor of Guangdong

Thomas Metcalfe, the second member of the Select Committee, arranged a meeting with the Fuyuan for the official handover of Buckinghamshire's letter. The Fuyuan was to be reminded of the superior status of the British

---

10   This news was brought by HIC *Orlando*. Amherst arrived at the Lemma Islands off Macao on 10 July 1816.
11   Newspapers from India with the news of the embassy arrived on 2 June 1816.
12   The Fuyuan is typically referred to as governor of Guangdong. It is unclear here whether the British made a mistake or whether this governor was acting as governor-general of the Liangguang at this time.
13   The Select Committee informed the 'Foo-yuen' of the Qianlong emperor's invitation, dated the 6th day of the 11th moon of the 58th year (December, 1793), where it was signified to Macartney that the court was agreeable to receiving another British ambassador (see Ellis, 1817, pp. 493–494, Note No. 1).

nation in contrast to the 'lesser respectability' of the traditional vassal states who regularly sent embassies to the imperial court (Metcalfe to the Select Committee, Canton, 4 June 1816, in BL IOR MSS EUR F 140/45). Metcalfe, accompanied by Morrison as interpreter, was met at the Canton city gates by the Hong merchants who, aware that this was the first time the Englishmen had entered the city, allowed extra time for sightseeing before proceeding to the governor's palace (Metcalfe to the Select Committee, Canton, 4 June 1816, in BL IOR MSS EUR F 140/45). The meeting with the Fuyuan was short, lasting only 20 minutes. The British were not offered chairs and remained standing while the five senior mandarins remained seated. After making a specific point of taking off their hats and bowing before replacing their hats, Metcalfe opened the box carrying Buckinghamshire's letter and delivered it to the Fuyuan who looked at it briefly before passing it to the Hoppo who passed it to another senior mandarin. Metcalfe recorded that the Fuyuan 'mentioned with seeming satisfaction the former Embassy' (Metcalfe to the Select Committee, Canton, 4 June 1816, in BL IOR MSS EUR F 140/45). After handing over a Chinese translation the British retired. Metcalfe was anxious to leave the palace as quickly as possible to dodge being questioned further about the embassy's purpose and to avoid giving the Chinese the impression that this was a Company initiative rather than one sent on behalf of the British Crown (Metcalfe to the Select Committee, Canton, 4 June 1816, in BL IOR MSS EUR F 140/45).[14]

The Hong merchants Howqua and Puankhequa visited Metcalfe the following day with a list of questions regarding the embassy including some about the nature of the presents for the emperor and whether the ships planned to follow Macartney's itinerary by stopping at Zhoushan. Questions were then asked about the 'real object' of the mission (Metcalfe Report of Meeting with Howqua and Puankhequa, in BL IOR MSS EUR F 140/45). Metcalfe stuck to the party line and reiterated that its objective was to announce the peace in Europe and the Prince Regent's desire to preserve the bonds of friendship between Great Britain and China (Metcalfe Report of Meeting with Howqua and Puankhequa, in BL IOR MSS EUR F 140/45). Other private conversations between Metcalfe and the Hong merchants held later in the week, however, focused on Staunton's inclusion in the embassy. Metcalfe was informed

---

14   Morrison (1820) wrote that Metcalfe asked for questions to be sent to the Factory to 'afford more time to give suitable answers' (p. 11).

that the emperor did not approve of Staunton visiting Peking after his role in the recent altercations at Canton, but Metcalfe replied that Staunton's inclusion in the embassy was ordered by the British sovereign and could not be disobeyed (Morse, 1926/1966, vol. 3, p. 259). Metcalfe informed Amherst in a private letter that Chinese displeasure regarding Staunton's participation in the embassy originated with the Hong merchants and not from the government due to the 'merchants who have always a wish to lower the Company's Servants in the Eyes of the Mandarins' (Metcalfe to Amherst, 10 July 1816, in BL IOR MSS EUR F 140/38 (a)).

Staunton was also visited by some senior Hong merchants at Macao who questioned the embassy's plan of travelling directly to Tianjin rather than calling first at Canton. They were informed that this was necessary due to the nature of the presents whose bulk and delicate nature required they travel by sea as they would be damaged if they proceeded overland. They were also informed that Buckinghamshire's letter ordered a direct route to Tianjin and could not be disobeyed.

Meanwhile, rumours at Macao began circulating while the Select Committee waited for official approval from Peking, which was expected around 15 July. Howqua became increasingly anxious over the inclusion of both Staunton and Morrison in the embassy and warned this could result in 'evil consequences' with 'something unpleasant' occurring as the emperor would not be pleased at learning that Staunton, in particular, was travelling to Peking (Metcalfe Report of Meeting with Howqua, 13 June 1816, in BL IOR G/12/196 (Reel 1) F 275). Staunton, however, read his concern as indicative of the desire of the merchants to protect themselves in the face of imperial displeasure.

Staunton's withdrawal from the embassy, the British thought, would only confirm Chinese suspicions and would be tantamount to labelling him as a traitor when in fact he was only doing his duty and following his sovereign's orders. The Hong merchants' attitude was interpreted as yet another example of Chinese interference in the internal affairs of the British Factory. Such 'low cunning and intrigues', the Select Committee felt, had to be defeated at all costs. It was imperative that 'Sir G. Staunton and suite should embark and proceed to some rendezvous to join the Embassador; apprising the Mandarins of the circumstance, but to move out of reach of any reply' (Morse, 1926/1966, vol. 3, p. 260).

Staunton sent the Fuyuan an official letter informing him that he was proceeding immediately to join the embassy ships that were sailing directly to Tianjin. Their exact location was kept secret from the Chinese Government, which had taken the precautionary measure of sending Chinese troops to military posts in the area following rumours spread by the Portuguese at Macao of suspicious British intentions (Ellis, 1817, p. 55).[15]

Staunton's immediate reaction on learning that he was not to lead the embassy is not known. He informed his mother in a brief note dated 6 June 1816, 'I am at this moment full of business preparing for the expected Embassy—and likewise being chief of the Factory … but [I am] in good health' (*Staunton Letters*, Macao, 6 June 1816). His next letter is dated 6 July. The gap in correspondence is uncharacteristic, especially given the importance of such a mission for the Staunton family. Nevertheless, he was delighted to receive a private letter from Amherst, delivered by the American ship sent from the Straits of Sunda, that reached him on 24 June, informing him that Amherst had visited his mother in London before departing on the mission: '[I am] well pleased at this mark of politeness and attention' (*Staunton Letters*, Macao, 6 July 1816). The embassy was due to arrive at any moment and it was important he 'should lose no time in this neighbourhood. I am going to embark tomorrow on board one of the Company's cruising ships stationed here, in order to proceed with his Lordship to his destination' (*Staunton Letters*, Macao, 6 July 1816). Staunton's earlier doubts about the prospects of the embassy had not changed, but his naiveté remained:

> I do not flatter myself that much is to be gained at present by an Embassy, but I have little doubt of the Chinese receiving us handsomely—and with the proper attention due from one great nation to another. (*Staunton Letters*, Macao, 6 July 1816)

---

15 Dutch and Portuguese 'jealousy' at Macao was also detected at the time of the Macartney Embassy. Macartney commented on the Portuguese that 'we had to expect from them every ill office and counteraction in their power' (Cranmer-Byng, 1962, p. 64).

Staunton's position in the embassy had still to be determined. His role had not been approved by the Company due to fears of Chinese displeasure after the part he played in the recent altercations at Canton and Macao. Accordingly, it was left to Amherst to decide Staunton's position.[16]

Amherst Overnights in Coastal Waters off Hong Kong

Amherst's arrival in the South China Sea was shrouded in secrecy. The *Alceste* met up with the *Lyra* and *General Hewitt* and the two Company ships, the *Discovery* and *Investigator*, with the members of the British Factory on board at a prearranged location on 10 July 1816.[17] The ships moved that evening to a small rocky island known as 'Hong Kong' for the purpose of watering. Staunton was due to visit Amherst on board the *Alceste* the following morning, but in the meantime Basil Hall wrote in a private capacity to his friend, Lord Sidmouth, on the prospects of the embassy based, no doubt, on information from the members of the Canton contingent who had joined the *Lyra* that day.[18] He informed Sidmouth:

> It would give me pleasure could I furnish your Lordship with any accurate information as to the probable success of our mission; but it is difficult to get this free from prejudiced views. Along with Sir George [Staunton], there have come several men of great acuteness, & local knowledge. I can readily observe that they have not any expectation of our succeeding. They seem to think it quite hopeless our even finding this government treating us on an equal footing with themselves; under a show of cordiality & good faith, they disguise the worst possible opinion of us, & all sorts of treachery; therefore, without some motive to induce them to

---

16   Only Toone and Davis had been officially instructed to attend the mission (Staunton, 1824, p. 8). Morse (1926/1966) stated that Buckinghamshire appointed Elphinstone second commissioner and Staunton third commissioner. On the departure of Elphinstone to England, the vacancy was to be filled by Ellis, originally secretary to the ambassador.

17   The Macartney Embassy arrived in Chinese waters on 20 June 1793 and anchored off Macao. In contrast to the secrecy surrounding the Amherst mission, the Qianlong court had ample warning of its arrival. Three members of the mission, including Sir G. L. Staunton, went ashore immediately and returned the following day with news that the Qianlong court planned to give it a most hospitable and honourable reception (Cranmer-Byng, 1962, p. 63).

18   Henry Addington, 1st Viscount Lord Sidmouth, had served as prime minister from 1801 to 1804, and was the home secretary at the time of the Amherst Embassy. He was a close friend of both Amherst and Basil Hall. Hall's letter was sent in a private capacity.

behave better, we perhaps lose ground by these acknowledgments of their right to treat us as inferior. The Portuguese of Macao appear to be guided by the wildest jealousy imaginable—their accounts of the object of this Embassy have produced strong apprehensions that it is merely the precursor of an invasion. (Hall to Sidmouth, HMS *Lyra* off Macao, 9 July 1816, in Devon Heritage Centre (South West Heritage Trust), 152M/C1816/OF2)

This letter is important as it represents the only document reflecting the up-to-date and private views of the Englishmen based at Canton that were no doubt also relayed to Amherst. Amherst's task ahead in dealing with an arrogant and suspicious imperial court was considered daunting in spite of the inclusion of Britain's foremost sinologists and contradicts Staunton's view of an expected cordial, if fruitless, reception. Chinese suspicions of British motives were reinforced by the Select Committee's tactics of secrecy and evasion that provided no specific information on either the movements of embassy personnel or the ships transporting them. Further, the role of Portuguese propaganda and the presence of unusual British shipping activity in the waters of the Lemma islands near Hong Kong had alerted local authorities. The *Alceste*, *Lyra* and *General Hewitt*, as well as the Company ships *Discovery* and *Investigator*, were joined for a brief time by the Company ship *Thomas Grenville*, which was on its way to Europe. Jeffrey recorded in his journal, 'Such an assemblage of English ships had I suppose never before met together at Hong Kong' (Jeffrey Amherst, n.d., n.p.).

Staunton learned of Ellis's position as the second commissioner in the embassy upon the arrival of the *Alceste* on 10 July 1816. His disappointment, as well as his delay in visiting the *Alceste* and meeting Amherst until the following morning, has been interpreted by Platt (2018, p. 161) as a sign of great petulance where 'he initially refused even to speak' to Amherst. However, there is no evidence to support this assertion. Staunton (1824, p. 7) gives a more plausible and practical reason for his delayed arrival on board the *Alceste*. First, Amherst had just received reports and intelligence from Canton on 10 July and needed time to study these, especially regarding the expediency of including Staunton in the embassy. Second, Captain Maxwell was anxious for all the ships of the squadron to proceed as quickly as possible to 'Hong Kong' to re-water. Once on board the *Alceste*, Staunton proceeded to spend 'a considerable time in consultation with Lord Amherst and Mr. Ellis, relative to the future arrangements and constitution of the Embassy' (Staunton, 1824, p. 7). At issue was his rank and position in the embassy. Staunton argued that the subordinate position of third commissioner would lower his status in the eyes of the Cantonese Government and he was especially concerned that Ellis was nominated with dormant credentials of minister plenipotentiary, meaning that he would be the ambassador in the event of Amherst's death. Fortunately, both Amherst and Ellis agreed readily with Staunton's wishes. He was delighted and told his mother in a letter, also quoted by Platt (2018, p. 161) who omitted the following three lines, thus changing the emphasis of Staunton's positive remarks about his first meeting with Amherst and Ellis:

> The conduct of both these Gentlemen is everything I could properly wish—nothing could be more obliging and kind than Lord Amherst's reception—or more conciliatory than Mr. Ellis … You will perceive that I am established the Second, and <u>First</u> of the Embassy—Lord Amherst also said verbally—'You are in a higher situation than your father was because you are actually … in the Commissioners of Embassy … whereas he was only Secretary of Legation'. (*Staunton Letters*, On board *Discovery*, 12 July 1816)

Staunton's emphasis on the importance of rank and his pride at surpassing the status of his father in the Macartney Embassy is made clear in this letter. He concluded by persisting in his belief that, while he was not sanguine about the embassy's prospects, he nevertheless remained confident that it would be 'received as well at least as the former Embassy' (*Staunton Letters*, On board *Discovery*, 12 July 1816). While Amherst's decision to appoint Staunton as his number two, in Tuck's (2000) view, may have 'doomed the Embassy from the start' (p. xxi), it needs to be noted that, contrary to the views of historians such as Platt (2018) and Gao (2016), the camaraderie that existed on the outward voyage continued to characterise the relations within the embassy suite, which would remain positive and professional throughout the remainder of their time in China.

However, Amherst had his doubts regarding the inclusion of Thomas Manning in the embassy. He was instructed to take only Toone and Davis on the mission and was concerned with Manning's 'peculiar costume and appearance' of a long beard and Chinese dress (Staunton, 1824, p. 9). Staunton reassured him that, although some Hong merchants had previously objected to Manning's appearance, the Chinese Government had taken no notice of him, either at Canton or during his time in Tibet. His knowledge of Mandarin, Staunton thought, would be a valuable asset in future dealings with the Chinese. Manning, however, acknowledged his 'insufficiencies' and referred to Morrison as the person possessing the 'most able of all' skills. He praised Morrison's fluency in Mandarin, as well as his 'peculiar attention' paid to the habits of the Chinese people and practical experience of current affairs at Canton (Manning to Staunton, Accepting the Offer, Macao, 25 May 1816, in BL IOR G/12/196 (Reel 1) F 229). Nevertheless, the embassy's importance required the inclusion of all available talent if it were to fulfil its mission and Manning was hired at a fee of $2,000 (Manning to Staunton, Accepting the Offer, Macao, 25 May 1816, in BL IOR G/12/196 (Reel 1) F 229).

Watering in a 'Sheltered' Bay: Hong Kong, 11–13 July 1816

Hong Kong was the first Chinese territory seen by those who had come directly from England. Inhabited by only a few scattered fishing villages, the harbour impressed the British naval officers who thought that it afforded an 'admirable shelter for ships of any burden'. Its geographical topography of being 'land-locked on every side by lofty islands' was acknowledged as an ideal haunt for pirates (Hall, 1840/1865, p. 6). Reference to 'Hong Kong' at this time, as noted earlier, was its first citation in published English literature.[19]

Abel, in keeping with his earlier impressions of Rio de Janeiro, was impressed with the 'high conical mountains, rising in the centre, and … a beautiful cascade [of water] which rolled over a fine blue rock into the sea' (1818, p. 60). The Chinese fishing boats that gathered around the British ships caught Jeffrey's attention; he described their curious shape and the large painted eye on their bows. Revealing British amusement at the use of pidgin English at Canton and the perceived superstitious mentality of the Chinese he wrote: 'When asking them the reason [for the eye] they answered in broken English, "How can see the rocks when no have got Eye?"' (Jeffrey Amherst, n.d., n.p.).

Several embassy members took the opportunity to go ashore while the crews were collecting fresh water from the waterfall. Abel gathered rock samples and plant specimens, including a variety of fern that gave a distant impression of a green and fertile island. Closer inspection,

---

19 Morse (1926/1966, vol. 3, p. 260) identified the spot where the ships of the Amherst Embassy moored as 'Malihoy Bay abreast the Waterfall at Hongkong in the Channel between Hongkong and the North end of Lemma Island'.

however, revealed a 'remarkabl[y] barren' place (Abel, 1818, p. 60). The heat and humidity were overwhelmingly oppressive and Abel recorded a temperature of 120 °F (48.8 °C) during a hike on the mountain. Hong Kong, on closer inspection, had none of the tropical wonders of Brazil or Java and, apart from the waterfall, had no other picturesque features.

Abel's first contact with native Chinese was also an anticlimax. The only inhabitants were 'some poor and weather-beaten fishermen, spreading their nets, and drying the produce of their toils on the rocks which supported their miserable mud-huts' (Abel, 1818, p. 62). Davis noted the good manners of the locals, which he thought were far more acceptable than those of the impertinent Cantonese. Their 'quiet and civil' behaviour, Davis (1841, p. 7) thought, was due to the island's isolation where a European visitor was a 'novel' occurrence.

Havell, meanwhile, had his sketchbook and tried to draw the local people who had gathered around him 'in all eagerness and insatiable curiosity' (Davis, 1841, p. 7). His task, according to Davis, proved difficult, as the subject being drawn immediately 'wheel[ed] round to the rear to look over the artist's shoulder and observe progress' (p. 7). Havell, described as 'not the most patient of his profession', became frustrated and the whole scene 'became rather ridiculous' (p. 7).

Wet and unsettled weather greeted the British the next morning. Imperial permission to proceed to the north of China had yet to arrive and the British were growing increasingly anxious that their location would be discovered by Cantonese authorities who would halt the embassy and divert it to Macao. Hall was concerned that the 'well-known practice of the Chinese, whose constant study it had been to render access to the court as difficult as possible' made their next move a total gamble. He added:

> It was finally resolved, after much discussion, to put the most favourable construction on the matter; to take it for granted … that the ambassador was to be favourably received, and to push on without delay for the Pei Ho river, the nearest to Pekin of any part of the sea-coast of China. It was contested, that once fairly on the threshold of the celestial empire, we should be less exposed to the operation of those multifarious intrigues, through which … everything must pass, if discussed at Canton. (Hall, 1840/1865, p. 6)

The British, concerned at the lateness of the season, decided to take their chances and set sail for the north of China despite having not received official permission to do so. The ships were about to depart when a fast sailing boat, sent by the British at Macao, approached them with news that the emperor's edict had been received granting permission for the embassy to proceed. Metcalfe's accompanying letter was optimistic. The Chinese at Canton, Amherst was informed, thought the emperor's response to the embassy was extremely favourable (Staunton, 1824, p. 10). Staunton read the emperor's edict before passing it to Morrison for translation and concluded it was expressed in the 'usual strain of arrogance and affected superiority' representative of all such correspondence. Dated 24 June 1816 the edict stated:

> As the English nation offers presents, and tenders its sincere good will with feelings, and in language respectful and complaisant, it is doubtless proper to allow the Embassy and presents to enter China, and the ship bearing them to proceed to Teen-sing, that the ambassador and suite may disembark. (Abel, 1818, p. 380, Appendix C)

The British, understandably, were ecstatic and greatly relieved. Amherst wrote to Sarah:

> In the midst of my anxiety what should burst upon me but a dispatch beginning Huzzu! Huzzu! [Hurrah! Hurrah!] with the intelligence that the Imperial answer … had arrived at Canton on the 9th and expressed the Emperor's high gratification at the honor intended him by the Embassy - that three Mandarins were dispatched to the province of Pe-che-tee and particularly one to Tien-sing [Tianjin] on the White River to wait our arrival and to conduct the Embassador with due honor to Pekin. (Amherst to Sarah Amherst, 'At Anchor off the Island of Hong-Kong', 12 July 1816, in BL Box 130 946c Ref. 5562)[20]

The squadron departed Hong Kong for the north of China on 13 July 1816 in rain and unsettled weather. Staunton and Morrison had since joined Amherst and Ellis on board the *Alceste* where discussion soon turned to the strategies to be employed on the mission, in particular, the crucial issue of the kowtow.

---

20 It would appear that this letter was placed with Captain Maxwell for dispatch with the first ship leaving China for England after the *Alceste* arrived back at Canton in early November 1816.

7

Up the Coast of China and Arrival at Tianjin

On 13 July 1816, five British ships left Hong Kong Island and set a course for the Gulf of Bei Zhili in northern China.[1] The initial British encounter with China after the embassy arrived in the north and before it was embroiled in the kowtow controversy was largely informal and cordial. Ensuing stressful confrontations with Chinese officialdom, however, simply reinforced British stereotypes of the Chinese. Perceptions of China soon came to duplicate Barrow's views portrayed in his book *Travels in China* (1804). This account functioned as a primer assisting British understanding of the novel environment in which they now found themselves, and was referred to constantly by members of the Amherst Embassy during their journey.

The intrusion of British ships into China's northern seas represented a physical demonstration of British technical and military superiority seen only once before at the time of Macartney in 1793.[2] While the ships were following Macartney's route, there were still considerable dangers for such large vessels in little-charted waters. Captain Basil Hall complained that the best charts were 'nearly useless … we frequently stumbled upon large groups of islands, headlands, and bays, of which no mention had ever

---

1   Bei Zhili literally means 'northern directly ruled' province. There was a Nan Zhili or 'southern directly ruled' province around Nanjing.
2   Earlier British naval expeditions to the north Asian region included Captain Cook who had sailed down the eastern coast of Japan on his way to Macao during his third voyage in 1776–1780, and Captain William Broughton who stopped at Macao in 1796–1797 during his exploration of the Japanese islands.

been made' (1840/1865, p. 7). Assisting navigation was 'Massey's patent sounding machine', the latest British scientific tool used for measuring sea depths (Hall, 1840/1865, p. 7). Hiring Chinese pilots had been canvassed briefly in London, but was soon dismissed on grounds of the need for keeping the mission a secret from Chinese authorities, as well as doubts over their competency to navigate large ships in waters north of Guangdong province.[3] Trust was placed instead in British seamanship and technology to steer the embassy safely to the Yellow Sea.

Fast progress was made through the Straits of Formosa, passing along the coasts of Guangdong and Fujian provinces until the ships entered the Donghai or Eastern Sea (M'Leod, 1818/1820, p. 21). Jeffrey wrote in his journal that the *Alceste* and *General Hewitt* often towed the *Discovery* and *Investigator* 'by which means we got on rather faster' (Jeffrey Amherst, n.d., n.p.). The British were in a buoyant mood due to fine weather and the prospect of encountering new and 'stirring scenes' of China (Davis, 1841, p. 10). Chinese fishing boats periodically approached the *Alceste*, but, according to Jeffrey, British attempts to bargain with them failed as 'they did not like to have any dealings with us' (Jeffrey Amherst, n.d., n.p.).

The ships cleared the Formosa Straits on 17 July and passed the Zhoushan Islands the following day. Swift progress continued. Several geographical landmarks named by Captain Erasmus Gower of the HMS *Lion* during the Macartney Embassy were noted. These included Staunton's Island, Cape Gower and Cape Macartney. Captain Maxwell followed Gower's example and named a cape situated at the point of the promontory of the Shandong peninsula 'Cape Amherst'. The naming of the China coast after British officials appears incongruous given the cultural antiquity of the sea route, but little shipping was seen apart from fishing boats, which gave an erroneous impression that the coast was deserted. A vigorous local coastal trade, pointed out by Samuel Ball in his secret report,[4] was taking place much closer to shore out of sight of the British ships.

---

3   The Macartney Embassy sought to procure Chinese pilots at Zhoushan to conduct the mission to Tianjin. They had little nautical skill, however, and the British had to rely on their own resources (Cranmer-Byng, 1962, pp. 65–66).
4   This report, as noted above, is reproduced in Appendix D.

7. UP THE COAST OF CHINA AND ARRIVAL AT TIANJIN

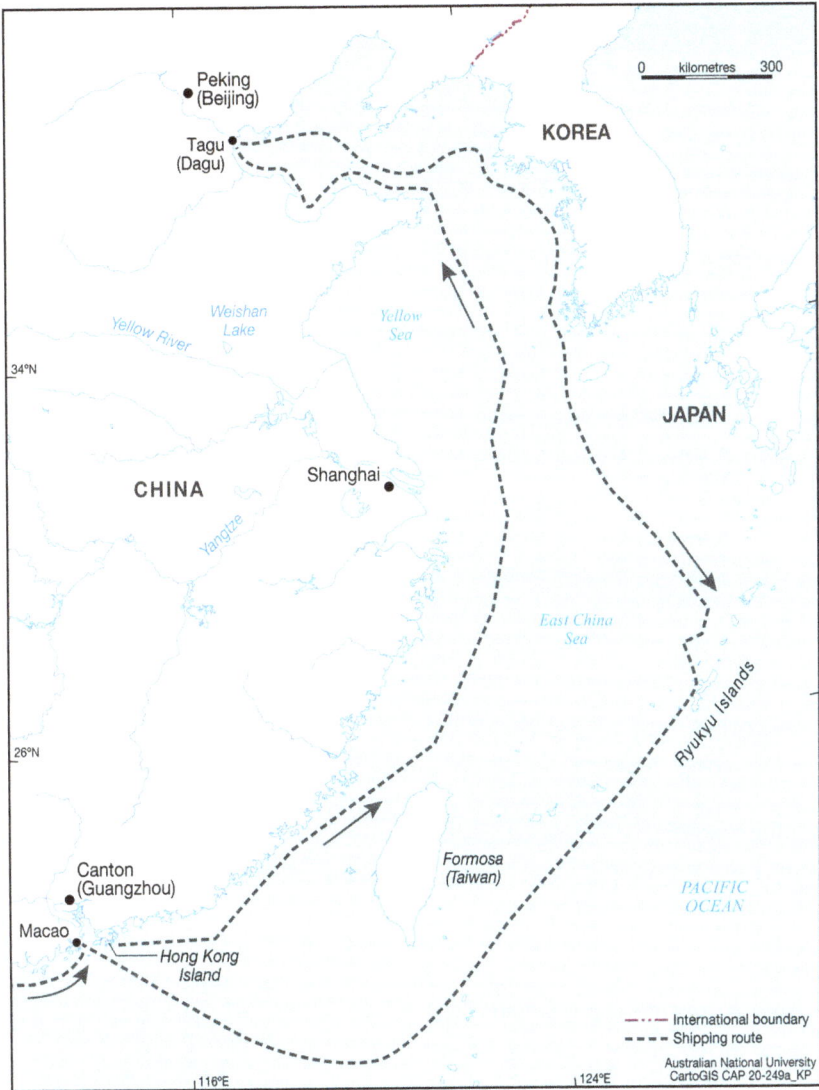

Figure 5: Route taken by the British ships to the Gulf of Bei Zhili in northern China.

Note: After depositing Amherst and his embassy at 'Tagu', the HMS *Alceste* and HMS *Lyra* proceeded to chart the coast of Korea and the Ryukyu Islands before travelling onto the Canton port of Whampoa to collect the embassy.

Source: CartoGIS, College of Asia and the Pacific, ANU. Based on map in M'Leod (1818/1820, p. 28).

The Yellow Sea

The British reached the Yellow Sea in only 12 days. Little of China had been seen apart from a thin ribbon of land that came in and out of view as the ships passed. Davis wrote later on the occasion of sailing past the Fujian coast:

> We cast a wistful eye from our ships at the China coast, a few miles off, and with the help of a glass could discover a few scattered villages, apparently fishermen's houses. The shore was generally low, with barren hills a little way inland. (1841, p. 12)

Of more immediate concern was the severe discomfort from extreme humidity endured by the English. Abel wrote:

> I can … give no better notion of the excessive moisture of the atmosphere in the China seas during the S.W. monsoon, than by stating the Leslie's hygrometer is not graduated to a sufficient extent to mark its degree, that our clothes were as wet as if they had been exposed to a smart shower of rain. (1818, p. 64)

The squadron finally came to a halt in the Gulf of Bei Zhili, called 'Pe-che-lee' by the British, on 26 July 1816. Amherst took the opportunity of following Macartney's precedent and called on all the 'gentlemen, servants, musicians, and guard of the Embassy to be assembled on the quarter deck' where he addressed them on 'the importance, and indeed the absolute necessity of conducting themselves with sobriety and decorum during their residence in the Chinese dominions' (Ellis, 1817, p. 63).[5] Further, trade with the Chinese was strictly prohibited as it was imperative to remove any suspicion that the prime aim of the embassy involved commercial interests.

---

5   Macartney ordered that a similar proclamation be communicated to the crew of the *Lion* and *Hindostan* on 16 July 1793 (Cranmer-Byng, 1962, p. 66).

First Contact with the Chinese: Fishermen and Mandarins

The *Lyra*, meanwhile, had been sent on ahead to announce the approach of the embassy and anchored in three fathoms of water, six miles from shore. The rest of the fleet anchored in five fathoms of water, 15 miles from the mouth of the Baihe River (Ellis, 1817, p. 63).[6]

Captain Hall and Francis Toone, the interpreter on board the *Lyra*, were instructed to make contact with the local mandarins to inform them of the embassy's arrival by way of an official letter written by Amherst and placed in Toone's care. The letter, following Chinese protocol, contained the names of the embassy's officials and included a list of the presents. Amherst referred to the Macartney Embassy and requested that a similar number of boats be made available for the transport of his embassy to Peking (Ellis, 1817, p. 63). Toone, however, was instructed not to visit the shore to avoid the prospect of some questions of an 'insidious and embarrassing character' on the motives of the embassy (Ellis, 1817, p. 63). The pair set off in a rowboat from the *Lyra* for the distant mouth of the Baihe River, hoping to find some way of notifying the local authorities of the embassy's arrival.

28 July 1816

Hall and Toone decided to approach a Chinese fishing junk lying at anchor near the *Lyra*. Chinese reactions at noticing some Europeans rowing towards them can only be imagined. British sensibilities, on the other hand, were shocked at the discovery that the fishermen were as 'naked as savages' wearing only a jacket over their shoulders but 'no clothing for the lower part of the body' (Morrison, 1820, p. 16). The moral assessments are Morrison's as Hall neglected to mention this point in his account, perhaps out of sensitivity to the possible response of his readers. The fishermen received the Englishmen most cordially and invited them on board where they were offered a seat on a bench placed on the quarterdeck. Communication at first was difficult as Toone did not understand their dialect, but matters resolved themselves when he reverted

---

6   The Baihe or White River is now known as the Haihe or Ocean River.

to the use of Chinese characters where 'every man in the boat understood him' (Hall, 1840/1865, p. 7). While Toone was busy communicating with the head fisherman, Hall described 'falling into the hands' of the crew whose curious attention focused on his dress. Particular interest was shown towards his shoes, which Hall removed for examination while his epaulettes were unbuttoned and drew the 'greatest wonder'. Hall's pocket compass was also discovered and its purpose comprehended immediately by the fishermen: 'three or four of them carried it off to compare with their <u>own</u> needle' (Hall, 1840/1865, p. 7, emphasis in original). The fishermen's delight on recognising the function of the compass was commented on by Hall who acknowledged the important role of common understanding and awareness serving to break down cultural barriers. The fishermen returned the compass to Hall 'with much complacency' (Hall, 1840/1865, p. 7).

A sudden downpour forced Hall and Toone to take shelter inside the junk's cabin, which represented one of the few occasions during the travels of the embassy in China where the English were privileged to see inside any local abode. The cabin was 'a neat little apartment, round which were spread a few fur skins, and very comfortable pillows in small pigeon-holes, or sleeping berths' (Hall, 1840/1865, p. 7). Threads of copper coins were noticed on a table and numerous Chinese books were scattered around the room. Hall was fascinated with the Chinese hairstyle described as the 'well-known long tuft or tail, reaching from the back of the head nearly to the ground; all the rest of the head being shaved' (Hall, 1840/1865, p. 8). Chinese reaction to the British, on the other hand, centred on the absence of 'tails'. Hall wrote perceptively:

> Such is the effect of custom, that nothing in our dress or manners excited so much surprise in these people, or appeared more preposterous in their eyes, than our contriving to exist without long tails. (1840/1865, p. 8)

The cordial meeting came to an end when the fishermen refused to accept Amherst's letter or take it to the local authorities. Hall and Toone offered some silver dollars as thanks for their hospitality but the coins were not recognised and the fishermen tried to hand the money back. 'The fishermen', Hall wrote, 'finding us determined not to take back the money, very unceremoniously pitched it into the boat as we rowed away' (1840/1865, p. 8). M'Leod, the physician accompanying the *Alceste*, noted that the universal currency of Spanish silver dollars held no meaning for the Chinese; rather, these coins were 'melted down, the moment [they fell] into the hands of a Chinese at Canton' (M'Leod, 1818/1820, p. 34). The British, meanwhile, decided to send a boat to the river entrance on the following day in an attempt to make contact with local officials.

29 July 1816: The Mandarins Come On Board

Two large junks approached the *Lyra* the following morning and Hall described 'two Chinese officers, middle-aged, portly, comfortable-looking … with very dark mahogany-coloured faces' who came on board. Their names were Chang-wei and Yin. Chang-wei was Chinese and a civil officer who wore a blue button, while Yin was a Manchu military officer who wore a red button.[7] Their appearance, Hall related, caused a sensation among the British crew because this was the first time they had seen 'Chinese dress … except on teacups and saucers' (1840/1865, p. 7). His perceptive comment reflects that British images of 'China' and its people for the majority of Englishmen were formed exclusively from their representations on the export wares from Canton that flooded the British market during the eighteenth century.[8] British astonishment expressed on board the embassy ships can also be read as signifying the difference noted in Chinese identity between the mandarins or 'gentlemen' who came on board the British ships at this time, with those Chinese seamen seen previously at Batavia or on the local fishing boats.

The first social encounter between the British and the mandarins was an enjoyable occasion due largely to the personality of Chang-wei, the younger official, who 'made himself at home in a moment. He laughed,

---

7   Tuck (2000) noted that Staunton and Ellis grew to like both mandarins whose junior rank spared them any repercussions from the emperor at the time of the eventual dismissal of the embassy. Tuck further noted that Chang-wei was promoted to a judicial commissionership in Shantung soon after the embassy's departure and left the embassy on 12 September 1816. Yin left the embassy on 17 September 1816. 'Their task seemed to be to see to the daily wants of the Embassy … and to keep the Embassy in touch with the two great officials conducting the mission to Peking' (p. xxvii).

8   William Alexander (1767–1816), the draughtsman with the Macartney Embassy, produced over 2,000 sketches of images and scenes depicting China and Chinese life that were first published in Sir G. L. Staunton's (1797a) *Authentic Account* and subsequently in 1805 and 1814. Access to these was, of course, restricted to the most privileged classes of British society. Alexander's artwork can be found in Legouix (1980).

joked, and skipped about, examining everything more like a child than a grave public functionary' (Hall, 1840/1865, p. 7). Chang-wei enjoyed himself especially in Hall's cabin. Here he:

> placed himself unceremoniously, but not rudely, at the head of the table, and reaching his arm out, drew a book from the library, opened it, and, with great affected formality, turned the leaves backwards and forwards till he lighted upon the title page. He then held it up before him, examined it with his eyes nearly closed,—turned it upside down, sideways and in every direction,—twisting his face into all sorts of ridiculous forms, expressive of his amusement and surprise at the strangeness of what he saw;—then jumping on his feet, displayed the book to his wondering attendants, who had taken possession of the skylight, and were thrusting their heads down to see what was going on. (Hall, 1840/1865, p. 7)

Harmonious and jovial relations between the mandarins and the British were improved further with the arrival of a couple of bottles of cherry brandy. The mandarins, Hall related, 'no sooner drank, than they filled their glasses again, and were not contented till all their attendants had followed so good an example' (1840/1865, p. 7). Eventually, Hall added, it was high time to come to business. Predictably, after all the cherry brandy, the mandarins declared their willingness to take charge of Amherst's letter and return with it to Dagu to place it in the hands of the senior legate. Communication with the mandarins was difficult and Toone once more reverted to the use of Chinese characters to get messages understood, much to the mandarin's surprise and amusement (Jeffrey Amherst, n.d., n.p.).[9] The practice was taken up by Chang-wei, who finding himself misunderstood and seeing no ink or paper, improvised by 'dip[ping] his finger, without apology, into his neighbour's glass [of cherry brandy]—for the contents of his own had long disappeared—and painted the symbols on the table' (Hall, 1840/1865, p. 8).

The Chinese guests were not easy to get rid of. Hall wrote that while the mandarins were:

---

9   Jeffrey wrote that the mandarins were 'much surprised and amused at seeing Mr. Toone talk and write in the Chinese language'.

pledging the emperor in cherry brandy, the boatmen were taken in charge by the sailors who, in like manner, were initiating them, with great success, into the mysteries of grog and salt-beef. (1840/1865, p. 8)

The mandarins, armed with Amherst's letter to the local governor, finally departed. The *Lyra* weighed anchor and set out to rejoin the rest of the squadron anchored 10 miles out at sea.

Captain Hall came on board the *Alceste* the following morning with news of the mandarins' visit to the *Lyra*. Amherst was informed that the governor-general of Bei Zhili had signified his readiness to receive the embassy at the mouth of the Baihe River. Bad weather, however, prohibited any further communication from shore and the British had a couple of anxious days waiting for news. Time was spent observing the great number of junks and boats that passed by them on their way to Tianjin. The Chinese were initially shy in approaching the British squadron, 'alarmed perhaps by the novel appearance of our ships', but gradually became bolder and approached near enough for close mutual inspection (Jeffrey Amherst, n.d., n.p.). Jeffrey, no doubt parroting the sentiments of his father, was pleased that the cooler weather allowed them to 'dress something like Englishmen—before we need[ed] to go without our coats and waistcoats' (Jeffrey Amherst, n.d., n.p.). He also joked about the happy disposition of Hall's mandarin visitors who were 'always laughing and cherry [sic]' (Jeffrey Amherst, n.d., n.p.).

31 July 1816: The Embassy Conductors Come On Board

On the morning of 31 July, a small junk with streamers and flags portraying 'a dark coloured dragon' approached the *Alceste*. On board were four mandarins, including Chang-wei and Yin (Ellis, 1817, p. 65). This visit represented Amherst's first direct contact with the Chinese authorities. The mandarins were kept waiting in Captain Maxwell's cabin where 'they were regaled with wines' and engaged in conversation with Morrison while Amherst prepared himself for their reception (Jeffrey Amherst, n.d., n.p.). Amherst wore his Parliamentary robes while the other civilian members of his suite wore their Windsor uniforms. The mandarins were subsequently conducted by Morrison, who acted as the interpreter at the meeting, 'through a passage formed by the other gentlemen of the

Ambassador's suite' to Amherst's cabin where Amherst, Staunton and Ellis were waiting to receive them (Abel, 1818, p. 69). Amherst, according to Jeffrey, was seated on the sofa with Staunton on his left, the place of honour in China. Ellis sat on Amherst's right while Jeffrey 'stood behind the sofa ready to carry [his] father's train' (Jeffrey Amherst, n.d., n.p.). The mandarins made a very low bow on entering the cabin and seated themselves where they were served cherry brandy as the British had no means of serving tea in the Chinese fashion. The choice of beverage was 'by no means to the[ir] dissatisfaction' (Ellis, 1817, p. 67). Jeffrey, meanwhile, was a focus of attention. He wrote that Morrison had taught him 'the Chinese for 14 which was my age … and … it turned out, [that] one of the mandarins asked me my age as soon as I was presented to him and was not a little amused at my answering him in his own language' (Jeffrey Amherst, n.d., n.p.).

The British believed the purpose of the meeting was largely complimentary as its chief objective was to enquire about the number of people in the embassy and the nature of the presents (Ellis, 1817, p. 66). Such an enquiry in Chinese terms formed part of a body of fundamental protocols governing the reception of any prospective embassy at the Qing court. The British were informed that the superintendent of salt duties at Tianjin, a mandarin appointed by special commission to the embassy, was waiting to receive Amherst on shore. His name was Guanghui, referred to as 'Kuang' or the 'legate' by the British, who was destined to escort the embassy to Peking and back to Canton.[10] Immediate arrangements were made for Morrison and Cooke to return to shore with the mandarins to meet with Guanghui to make arrangements for the disembarkation of the embassy. Two other pieces of information were relayed at the meeting. The first was the disturbing intelligence that the current governor-general of Bei Zhili had been removed and was due to be replaced by a man named Sulenge, called 'Soo' by the British, who had been the recent viceroy at Canton and whose disposition towards the British was particularly hostile. Ellis thought this change would be most unfortunate as the viceroy 'will probably be disposed to connect the present embassy with the late discussions at Canton in which he was so

---

10 Tuck (2000, p. xxviii) pointed out that Guanghui was referred to as 'Kwang' by Ellis, as 'Quang Ta-zin' by Staunton and as 'Quong' by Amherst. He was a Manchu and a bond servant of the imperial household.

actively engaged' (Ellis, 1817, p. 66).[11] The second piece of intelligence was that the Jiaqing emperor was due to depart for his summer retreat at Jehol on 9 September, leaving little time for embassy business at Peking.

Evidence that the Chinese had studied 'the minute circumstances relating to the former Embassy' was shown when one of the mandarins asked if there was a portrait of the emperor on board. A print of the Qianlong emperor from the time of the Macartney Embassy was produced at which time the mandarins became very anxious and 'displayed the greatest embarrassment' (Davis, 1841, p. 32). Davis recalled that they rose from their seats and begged that it be put away or otherwise it would be necessary for them to 'perform the prostration' before it (1841, p. 32). The mandarins also spent time looking around the cabin where their gaze fell on some fine pieces of English bone china. They were astonished to learn that these were made in England and not at Canton; even greater disbelief was expressed by the mandarins when being told that finer specimens of china were available in England.

Ellis was disappointed with his first encounter with Chinese officials:

> Their dresses were common; and certainly, their general appearance was neither respectable nor elegant: comparing them with persons of correspondent rank in Persia, Arabia, or Turkey, I should say they were inferior in outward respectability. The most remarkable part of their dress is the straw conical bonnet, with hair dyed red, hanging over it. Their complexions were dark and their features coarse. (1817, p. 66)

The mandarins, according to Jeffrey, were 'pretty fresh' by the time they departed the *Alceste* but were still capable of 'measuring the length and breadth of the *Alceste* and in counting the number of guns she carried' (Jeffrey Amherst, n.d., n.p.).

---

11 The British later discovered that 'Soo', or Sulenge, had not been a governor at Canton but rather the Hoppo who had received Macartney at Canton at the completion of his embassy. He was currently a most senior mandarin holding the position of president of the Board of Public Works.

31 July 1816: Morrison and Cooke Visit the Mainland

Morrison and Cooke travelled to Dagu in a boat from the *Discovery* manned by Lascars under the command of Captain Crawford. Arriving at the port, described by Morrison (1820, p. 16) 'as a poor village', the accompanying mandarin displayed 'the most civil behaviour' in attempting to shelter the Englishmen from the heavy rain. After an uncomfortable journey in Chinese carts along wet and muddy roads, Morrison and Cooke reached the temple where Guanghui and the other mandarins delegated to escort the embassy, including Chang-wei and Yin who had earlier visited the *Lyra*, were waiting.

Guanghui, or the legate, described by Morrison (1820, p. 18) as a Tartar and 'a little man, about 58 years of age; pleasant and conversable … but artful and fraudulent' opened proceedings.[12] Morrison was asked 'in a cheerful tone' a number of questions customarily addressed in Qing diplomacy: How far had the embassy come? Had the embassy stopped at Macao? Had the embassy met the ships that he had sent and how many British ships and how many people were in the embassy's entourage (Morrison, 1820, p. 18)?[13] On learning that the embassy had 75 members, Guanghui requested that the number be reduced to 50 by dispensing with the guard and the band, to which Morrison replied that an extra 25 people could be of little consequence to so great an empire, leaving the legate with little choice but to agree (Morrison, 1820, p. 18). The meeting closed with an announcement that Chang-wei and Yin would pay a call on Amherst the next day. Morrison thought the meeting was an 'intended haughty reception'. He and Cooke retired and had dinner in the 'Chinese manner' (Morrison, 1820, p. 18).

The Englishmen climbed the stairs to the upper storey of the temple after dinner to admire the view where Morrison met a minor Chinese mandarin who was an excellent source of unofficial intelligence. He learned on this occasion that the embassy would not be staying long at Peking and,

---

12   Platt (2018, p. 168) referred to Guanghui as 'Zhang' and the 'handler' of the embassy. 'Zhang' is the only mandarin referred to by Platt, apart from the high ranking Heshitai, known as 'the Duke' who encountered the British for the first time at Tongzhou on 20 August 1816.
13   Morrison noted that no Chinese ships had been sent.

unlike the Macartney Embassy, would not be travelling to Jehol. Rather, it was the Qing court's intention to receive and dismiss the embassy as quickly as possible.

Following a very uncomfortable night spent at the temple with only a bench to sleep on and no blankets or pillows, Morrison and Cooke travelled back to the river in 'the wretched carts of the country' before enduring a very rough sea passage back to the British ships (Morrison, 1820, p. 19). Morrison was so fatigued from his trip ashore that he had to rest for the next couple of days. He later received an apology from the Chinese for their impolite hospitality towards him and Cooke.

4 August 1816: The Mandarins Visit Amherst

Final arrangements for the embassy's disembarkation were delayed by the 'blowy weather' preventing the mandarins from travelling out to the *Alceste* (Jeffrey Amherst, n.d., n.p.). Calm weather returned on 4 August and several large junks, bearing red flags announcing the presence of Chang-wei and Yin, finally approached the *Alceste*. Yin had brought his 11-year-old son.[14] British protocol was broken on this occasion with the seven-gun salute being fired as the mandarins approached the ship, rather than when they came on board, in order to not 'needlessly shaken [their] tender nerves' (Hall, 1840/1865, p. 9). The *Alceste*'s quarter deck was lined with two columns of British marines. The band played while the mandarins scrambled up its sides with great difficulty 'owing to the load of state-robes with which they had encumbered themselves for the occasion' (Hall, 1840/1865, p. 9). Captain Maxwell, resplendent in his full uniform, greeted the mandarins who showed much 'involuntary surprise' when inspecting the marines and witnessing the presentation of arms. The full military reception impressed Abel who drew a comparison between British splendour and the mandarins' appearance:

> They gave me no very exalted notions of Chinese magnificence … plainly dressed, and attended by a train of very shabby looking fellows … the appearance of the whole party was strikingly

---

14   Yin was later described by Abel (1818, p. 144) as 'an old soldier, with ruddy complexion and laughing eyes, [who] cared very little about the arts or sciences of his own or any other country. The only produce of Europe that seemed to interest his attention was port-wine or cherry-brandy'.

> contrasted with the very tasteful and imposing splendour which surrounded them on board the Alceste. Her clear and ample decks, her well arranged rigging, her formidable artillery, her men prompt and orderly, and her officers in full uniform, formed a picture of propriety and order, of magnificence and power. (1818, p. 70)

Staunton and Ellis conducted the mandarins to Amherst's cabin and Amherst greeted them wearing his ceremonial robes. Guanghui had sent his apologies, explaining that his exalted rank freed him from the obligation of travelling 'eight or ten miles on the open sea to pay a visit of ceremony' (Hall, 1840/1865, p. 9).

The mandarins were seated in the place of honour on Amherst's left following Chinese protocols, while Staunton and Ellis sat in a row of chairs situated on the right-hand side. Morrison overheard Chang-wei tell his servant that he would have far rather preferred to have been placed in line with the ambassador, indicating the problems implicit in protocols of seating arrangements that continued to be a major concern in future official meetings between the British and Chinese (Morrison, 1820, p. 20). The diplomatic encounter soon turned into a farce due to interruptions by Chang-wei and Yin's numerous attendants, who, curious to catch a glimpse of the ambassador, kept trying to enter the cabin where they were resisted by the British. British sensibilities at this time were also offended by the 'disagreeable odours' emitted by the Chinese, both of 'garlic and asafoetida', as well as the 'repulsive atmosphere' that surrounded them resulting from 'a want of cleanliness' (Abel, 1818, p. 70).

Curiosity over dress was not confined to Chinese fishermen. The mandarins' appearance of long beards and 'two enormous claws on the left hand', described by Morrison as rendering 'the limb useless to them', was particularly disconcerting to the British (M'Leod, 1818/1820, p. 24). M'Leod (1818/1820) thought they 'resembled bulky old women with their clumsy boots' (p. 24). The mandarins, in Morrison's (1820) opinion, were embarrassed by the 'novelty of their situation' because they had never seen Englishmen before (p. 20). He picked up also on the nuances of meaning in the discussions held among the Chinese as they worked out their answers. He wrote that 'An old servant, in a loud tone, stood prompting and explaining for Yin'. Morrison checked him by saying 'he understood the master better than the servant' (p. 20).

Chang-wei asserted that his government's lack of preparations was due to the premature arrival of the embassy in northern China. Nevertheless, Amherst was informed that a highly ranked minister of state was waiting at Tianjin to receive him, and confirmed Morrison's earlier intelligence that the embassy's imperial audience was scheduled for Peking rather than Jehol. After receiving a list of embassy personnel and presents, Chang-wei asked the British about the objective of the embassy. Its purpose, the British affirmed, was to confirm and strengthen the friendship and alliance of the two courts. A formal letter with a detailed explanation of British goals was being prepared and would be presented to the minister at Tianjin along with a translation of the Prince Regent's letter to the emperor. The next question concerned the proposed manner for the embassy's return. Amherst replied that it was intended to follow Macartney's precedent and travel overland to Canton. The mandarins, on learning this information, 'made no reply' (Amherst to Canning, 8 August 1816, in BL IOR G/12/196 (Reel 1) F 193).

Chang-wei and Yin next raised the unwelcome issue of the ceremony. Amherst wrote later in his official report:

> Next came a question which altho' prepared for its early discussion I hardly expected would have been put to me so soon. I was asked as to my knowledge of the Ceremony to be performed at the time of my presentation to the Emperor, and was expected to be ready for its performance. I said that I should be prepared to approach the Emperor in the most respectful manner possible, and being anxious to avoid entering at that time into further particulars an endeavour was made to turn the conversation to other subjects. (Amherst to Canning, 8 August 1816, in BL IOR G/12/196 (Reel 1) F 193)

The mandarins were diplomatic. They told Amherst:

> That England was an important Country, and that the attention which the emperor was about to shew us were not bestowed on embassadors from every nation. Lest however this compliment should be treated too high something was said as if the long and fatiguing voyage we had made was to be considered as our special title to His Imperial Majesty's favour and attention. (Amherst to Canning, 8 August 1816, in BL IOR G/12/196 (Reel 1) F 194)

Staunton, ironically given his fame as the 12-year-old at the Qianlong court, failed to mention Yin's son in his account of the embassy. The boy knelt before Amherst on one knee 'with much grace and modesty' suggesting that he had been instructed in the British custom of respect and had been told by his father to honour it (Ellis, 1817, p. 74). Jeffrey, in return, was presented to the two mandarins who 'seemed highly pleased with him' (Davis, 1841, p. 37). The two boys 'made acquaintance with each other' and Hall commented on the effect of children breaking down the 'ice of ceremony' among cautious and distrustful people (1840/1865, p. 9). Jeffrey's presence served to delay the mandarins' departure while they engaged in cheerful conversation with the British relieving them of 'much needless formality' (Hall, 1840/1865, p. 9). The mandarins promised a delivery of provisions and left the *Alceste*. Ellis complained once more of the oppressive stench emitting from the departing Chinese that reminded him of 'the repose of petrifying garlic on a much used blanket'. He agreed with Barrow's assessment that the Chinese were 'a frowzy people' (Ellis, 1817, p. 74).

Hall, who had the 'leisure to watch what was going on', observed the return of the mandarins to their boats (1840/1865, p. 9). Yin, Hall wrote, had no sooner returned to his junk than he:

> flung off his robes, his crape petticoat, his great unwieldy velvet boots with soles an inch thick, and his fantastical cap, and issuing forth with his pipe hanging out of one side of his mouth, and a pair of slippers on his feet, appeared on the deck of his vessel without one trace of grandee left. So anxious indeed was he to remove from our minds the idea of his being naturally the grave and austere personage we had seen before, that he immediately set about monkey tricks, as they are called at sea, and diverted himself with throwing peaches to the young midshipmen, who, in a correspondent taste, had climbed into the rigging, and were not slow to better this instruction. (p. 9)

A procession of eight large junks with red swallow-tailed flags and one bearing the ensign of the imperial dragon approached the British ships soon afterwards bearing a present from the emperor that included 10 bullocks, 20 sheep, 20 hogs, 100 ducks and fowls, a great store of vegetables and many boxes of tea (p. 9). The Chinese carriers who came on board with the produce were warmly received by the British sailors who:

paid them the most obsequious attention, escorting them around the decks like ladies, smoothing down their long tails, joking and talking with them ... not caring whether John Chinaman ... understood them or not. (p. 9)

The Chinese visitors were invited to sit down in the midshipmen quarters but when they attempted to rise from their seats they 'found themselves like Gulliver, for their wicked entertainers had tied each by his long tail to the back of his chair' (p. 9). Initially angry at such abuse, the Chinese soon saw the humour of the occasion and all parties 'joined in the laugh' (p. 9). The British trick, according to Hall, hereafter became well known among the Chinese who, on subsequent visits to British ships, took the precaution of 'coiling their tufts around their heads, out of the reach of practical jokes' (p. 10).

Some of the bullocks sent by the emperor had drowned on the outward passage. The British waited until the Chinese had departed before throwing the carcasses overboard and were astonished when people on passing junks scooped them up and proceeded to prepare them for cooking. M'Leod thought the practice disgusting and although he had yet to set foot in China had already judged that the Chinese 'eat in a putrid state, dogs, cats, rats, and in fact, all manner of carrion and vermin' (1818/1820, p. 27). He added that the British much preferred to live 'on our own salt beef' (p. 27).

The junks that brought the mandarins, as well as those that had brought the supplies, remained moored beside the British ships. The larger junks, the British learned, were scheduled to offload their luggage and the emperor's presents the following day. The Chinese carriers were astonished at the amount of luggage and furniture required by the British on their mission, leading Davis (1841) to comment on their 'self-denying and frugal habits' compared with their British counterparts:

> A mat to spread out as a bed, and a hard, hollow pillow of woven rattans, together with the smallest possible box for garments, is all that they generally want for themselves. (p. 39)

Amherst invited the mandarins to dine on board the *Alceste* but this was declined due to Chang-wei's dread of 'passing from one vessel to another' in the choppy seas (Morrison, 1820, p. 21). Chang-wei's language, according to Morrison, was more civil than Yin's coarse and boisterous military manner (Ellis, 1817, p. 75). The mandarins sailed for shore that evening.

Hall was invited to breakfast on board a junk anchored close to the *Lyra* the following morning. Initially deterred by stories of Chinese eating 'bow-wow pies' and 'ragouts of cats', he bravely 'put on a good face' and accepted the invitation. He was very pleasantly surprised to find the deck spread with a grass mat on which was placed five or six bowls of finely boiled rice 'as white as snow' accompanied by a 'variety of savoury hashes and stews' (Hall, 1840/1865, p. 10). In the middle of the dishes was a large smoking platter containing 'what looked very like an omelette'. Shamsu wine was served in diminutive teacups and Hall thoroughly enjoyed himself, recording,

> I had intended merely to go through the ceremony of tasting a morsel of rice to please these kind people, but ended by making a hearty meal, to the unspeakable delight of the Chinese boatmen. (1840/1865, p. 10)

Davis and Lieutenant Cooke went ashore a couple of days later to supervise the boats transporting the embassy and the presents to Tianjin. They were met by a civil mandarin wearing a light blue button and greeted with a three-gun salute fired by a company of Chinese soldiers. Vast crowds hoping to catch a glimpse of the English had gathered on the riverbank. Refreshments of tea and sweetmeats were served. Twenty-two boats were ready for the transportation of the embassy to Peking, including the baggage and presents for the emperor. A 'dinner-boat', suitable for the embassy suite to dine together, was promised at Tianjin (Davis, 1841, pp. 41–42).

Davis was not surprised to notice that the flags on the boats bore the Chinese characters for 'Koong-she' (*gong shi*) or 'Tribute Emissaries' but, being unauthorised to speak on the subject, made no comment (Ellis, 1817, p. 75). The emperor, he was informed, wished to meet Amherst without delay and Minister Sulenge was waiting at Tianjin to receive the embassy (Ellis, 1817, p. 75). Davis and Cooke were presented with gifts of apples, pears and peaches and returned to their ships in a journey that took five hours (Davis, 1841, p. 43).

The unloading of the presents and the embassy's baggage onto the junks took a couple of days. The cheerful attitude of the Chinese workers and the orderly manner in which they carried out their task impressed the British and Ellis wrote that 'the lower orders, though curious, are by no means intrusive or impertinent' (1817, p. 77). Chinese insolence shown towards Europeans was obviously confined to the Cantonese: 'here, the men in the boats, and others of the same class, appear aware of the conduct required to persons of superior station' (Ellis, 1817, p. 77). Pressure was placed on the embassy to speed up its arrangements for leaving the ships due to the emperor's wish to meet them as soon as possible before leaving for Jehol. Amherst was informed that the emperor was especially looking forward to meeting Jeffrey and was planning a play and other amusements for him at Peking. He also enquired if Jeffrey 'had read any Chinese books', indicating that Staunton's impact at the Qianlong court had not been forgotten (Amherst to the Chairman and Deputy Chairman, sent from the 'Gulf of Pe-Che-le', 8 August 1816, in BL IOR G/12/196 (Reel 1) F 196).

Discussion on the 'Kowtow Question'

Their imminent departure from the British ships provided the last opportunity for Amherst and his commissioners to discuss strategies in a free and unrestrained environment. Hints dropped by Chang-wei and Yin convinced Staunton that the Chinese expectation of the English performing the kowtow had changed from a probability into a certainty:

> A great deal of anxious conversation [took] place between Lord Amherst, Mr. Ellis, and myself on the subject to the mission ... in all its bearings, and to contemplate all the possible contingencies by which its success may be either retarded or promoted ... so as to provide against being taken by surprise or off our guard; at least with respect to all the *probable* points of discussion—Among these, from the first, there was none which appeared more important, or more likely to be brought into early and serious discussion, than the question of compliance with the Chinese ceremony of prostration. (Staunton, 1824, p. 29)

Amherst's ambiguous instructions regarding the kowtow were noted where Barrow and Castlereagh instructed him to follow Macartney's precedent of bowing on one knee as ordered by the Prince Regent, while Buckinghamshire said he was free to perform the kowtow if expedient to do so for the attainment of his mission's objectives (Staunton, 1824, p. 30). As acknowledged earlier, Castlereagh's orders muddied the waters even further by stating that Amherst conform to the ceremonies of the Qing court 'which may not commit the honour of your Sovereign or lessen your own dignity' (Castlereagh to Amherst including two enclosures: Instructions, No. 1, 1 January 1816, in BL IOR MSS EUR F 140/43 (a)).

Staunton's presence in the embassy brought a new perspective to the issue as his local experience and deep reflection on the subject claimed authority over the views of the other embassy members. Following Amherst's request for his opinion, Staunton delivered a letter on 8 August with his view on complying with the Chinese ceremony of prostration. His prime concern was:

> The effect it may have on the British character and interests at Canton, I beg to state that I feel strongly impressed with the idea that a compliance … will be unadvisable, even though the refusal should be attended with the hazard of the total rejection of the embassy. I am fully sensible of the importance of the objects of the present mission; but I cannot bring myself to believe that their attainment would in the smallest degree be promoted by the compliance in question: and the mere reception (it could hardly be termed honourable reception) of the Embassy, would I think be too dearly purchased by such a sacrifice.

Staunton (1824) added:

> There are some expedients by which the chief objections against the ceremony would be removed, but I am persuaded that the Chinese government is more likely to waive the ceremony, than to accede to any arrangement of that nature, that could be accepted as satisfactory. (p. 24)

Staunton's continuing belief that British exceptionalism would result in a possible dispensation from the strict protocols of Qing tributary ceremonial is evident in his statement. He argued strongly, however, that:

> To recede at present from the precedent of Lord Macartney's Embassy, by a compliance unaccompanied by any condition similar to that for which Lord Macartney had stipulated, would be a sacrifice of national credit and character; and as such would operate injuriously to the trade and interests of the East-India Company at Canton; that such compliance (judging from my general knowledge and experience of the Chinese character, and

more especially from the result of the Dutch Embassy in 1795) would not be likely to promote the attainment of any one of the objects we have in view, or in any way to benefit our national and commercial interests. (1824, p. 32)

Ellis, who thought it expedient for Amherst to perform the kowtow if this gained access to the emperor, followed up with his views on the issue in a letter dated 11 August. He thought the performance of the ceremony rested on 'matters of expediency' and that it was important to arrive at a consensus in order 'to clear the question of all personal feelings, which might lead us into a course of proceeding not quite in unison with the sentiments of the authorities at home' (1817, pp. 84–85). He concluded:

> I have, however, such perfect reliance on Sir George Staunton's judgment and local experience, that I shall not hesitate in giving way on every point connected with Chinese usages and feelings, where my individual opinion might lead to a different conclusion. (pp. 84–85)

Staunton's and the Company's view, on the other hand, recognised that notions of British sovereignty were at stake. Metcalfe, the acting president of the Select Committee at Canton in Staunton's absence, succinctly summed up the Company's position: kowtowing before the Chinese emperor functioned as an acknowledgement of his rank as the 'Sovereign of the Universe', implicitly degrading the British sovereign and British envoys to the rank of tributary vassals (Metcalfe as quoted in Morse, 1926/1966, vol. 3, p. 263). Performing the kowtow would result in demoting British status, thereby allowing the Hong merchants at Canton the upper hand in acting roughshod over Company merchants. Discussion on the kowtow continued with Amherst deciding eventually:

> That we should take the subject of compliance with ceremony into our consideration, unshackled by any reference to the instructions in question; and view it as a mere question of expediency, with regard to its influence more especially on the commercial interests of the East-India Company at Canton. (Staunton, 1824, p. 31)

The kowtow question remained open. Amherst, it was agreed, was free to perform the kowtow if the success of the mission was thought to depend on it (Staunton, 1824, p. 30). Relationships among Amherst and the commissioners were exceedingly close. Staunton wrote to his mother from the *Alceste* on 7 August 1816 that all the 'preliminary arrangements' of the embassy had been settled in 'a manner quite agreeable to my wishes'. Showing no signs of jealousy or resentment that Amherst had been appointed ambassador over him, Staunton continued:

> I have found Lord Amherst everything I could possibly wish— He has not only been exceedingly kind and attentive to me personally, but appears disposed to pay every consideration to the suggestions and representations that I have occasion to make him. His Lordship's conduct and manner throughout is extremely conciliating … yet without any sacrifice of dignity—and I therefore really think that our Government has been very fortunate in its selection. (*Staunton Letters*, HMS *Alceste*, on anchor in the Gulf of Pechelee, 7 August 1816)

Staunton also praised Ellis:

> Mr Ellis is also [a] very pleasant, and intelligent young man, and I have little doubt of our continuing to act together with the greatest cordiality. The rest of the Gentlemen are likewise pleasant and respectable men, and form, with those who have accompanied me from Canton, a society of 20 persons—the whole party— Servants, Soldiers and Musicians being 75. (*Staunton Letters*, HMS *Alceste*, on anchor in the Gulf of Pechelee, 7 August 1816)

Amherst, meanwhile, was uneasy about his forthcoming reception at Tianjin. Sulenge's exceptionally high rank raised concerns about the future of the embassy. Amherst wrote:

> I am a little apprehensive that [Sulenge's appointment] … is not to be considered altogether as a compliment, but rather as a design to introduce matters of ceremony or others such as was done in the case of the Russian Embassy in 1805 before our arrival at the Capital and possible to prevent our ever reaching the Capital at all. (Amherst: First Dispatch, to the Chairman and Deputy Chairman, sent from the 'Gulf of Pe-Che-le', 8 August 1816, in BL IOR G/12/196 (Reel 1) F 197)

Ellis also sensed that the presence of a high-ranking minister at Tianjin suggested 'that some propositions of importance, more especially touching the ceremony, were to be made there'. Fearful that the agenda at Tianjin left little time for negotiations, he predicted, 'The tempest is gathering, and it is difficult to say whether we should carry through it, or strike our masts and make everything snug' (1817, p. 73).

Regardless of the diplomatic outcome of the embassy, the British were determined to travel back to Canton on the overland route followed by Macartney. Accordingly, plans had been made at the Admiralty in London to circumvent any Chinese attempt to force the embassy to return by sea by arranging for the early departure of the British ships. The *Alceste* and *Discovery* were to head north to explore the Manchurian and Korean coasts, while the *Lyra* and *Investigator* were to head south towards the Yellow Sea. It was then proposed that the ships would rendezvous at a point along the coastline of Shandong Province where they would separate. The ships of the Royal Navy, namely, the *Alceste* and *Lyra*, would head east towards the Ryukyu Islands, while the Indiamen sailed south to Macao, in the wake of the *General Hewitt*, which was tasked with sailing directly to Whampoa to collect tea (Tuck, 2000, p. xli, fn. 70).[15]

The members of the embassy enjoyed a fine dinner on board the *Alceste* and disembarked onto the boats carrying them to the port of Dagu on the morning of 9 August 1816 where they were 'to commit themselves, for a period of about six months, to Chinese hospitality' (Davis, 1841, p. 43). Amherst had made it his duty to 'make the situation of everybody in the Embassy as comfortable as possible' and reminded all who were travelling with him that the good conduct of the last embassy had 'excited the admiration' of the Chinese (Journal of Sir William Fanshawe Martin, 1817, p. 23, in BL ADD MSS 41346-41475).

The embassy ships had been fully stocked with supplies arranged between the quartermaster of the *Alceste*, Mr Hickman, and the Chinese authorities. Maxwell told Amherst that Hickman had negotiated with a 'very civil mandarin'. He added:

> How they came to understand what they said, I do not exactly know, but Hickman seems positive beef, mutton, greens and fruit were amongst the … good things intended to be sent us by His Imperial Majesty. (Maxwell to Amherst, the Yellow Sea, Saturday, noon, 10 August 1816, in BL MSS EUR F 140/38 (a))

Maxwell requested, with a wink and a nudge, that Morrison give a mandarin 'a hint' that the sooner 'the supplies came the better':

---

15 Captain Murray Maxwell's obituary in 1831 noted the contribution made to British hydrography by these voyages. For example, the 'mainland of Corea was found more than a hundred miles to the eastward of the spot on [former] charts' (*Gentleman's Magazine*, September 1831, vol. 101, pt. 2, p. 273).

> As we are very anxious to move away from this very dangerous anchorage, (where betwixt your Lordship and myself, I would venture to ride, at any time a whole summer without the smallest apprehension) all the ships are getting very short of water. We shall therefore be on our way out of the Yellow Sea endeavouring to procure some … The Pekin government may despair of catching us at Chusan [Zhoushan] above a very few days, but should your Lordship have any commands for me, a letter directed there might reach me. (Maxwell to Amherst, the Yellow Sea, Saturday, noon, 10 August 1816, in BL MSS EUR F 140/38 (a))

The embassy ships, soon after disembarking Amherst and his suite, 'slipped anchor, evaded the maritime authorities and made for the open sea' (Tuck, 2000, p. xxviii).[16]

9 August 1816: The Embassy Lands in China and Early Negotiations on the Kowtow

Seventy-five Englishmen left the British ships on the morning of 9 August 1816, bound for Dagu.[17] Twenty gentlemen made up the ambassadorial suite while the remainder of the party comprised 17 servants, 12 musicians, 23 marines and three mechanics (Staunton, 1824, pp. 36–37). The group was joined on its first night ashore in China by some men from the ships, including captains Maxwell, Hall and Campbell, who accompanied it to Dagu before returning to their ships the next day to prepare for weighing anchor and setting off on their respective missions on 11 August 1816.

Amherst's departure for the Chinese mainland was marked with an elaborate display of British pomp and ceremony. The British ships fired a 19-gun salute while cheering crews lined the decks. Amherst and the two commissioners were seated in the *Alceste*'s barge bearing the English standard at the fore and the Company's ensign at the mizzen. They led a procession of two lines of boats carrying the rest of the embassy personnel, the marine guard and the band playing martial songs. Davis noted later, 'The Embassy never again made so respectable an appearance until the

---

16   The ships left on 11 August 1816 and rendezvoused on 29 August 1816 in the waters off the southern coast of Shandong Province.
17   This number was 20 less than Macartney's entourage which included five German musicians and 53 military personnel.

same boats met it on its return, in the river near Canton, and conducted it to the British Factory' (1841, p. 44). Nearing Dagu, the embassy suite transferred to Chinese junks for the final stage of their journey to the Chinese mainland.

Four to five hundred Chinese troops with their colours flying and music playing were lined up at the entrance of the river to Dagu where a three-gun salute from a Chinese shore battery greeted the arrival of the British (Staunton, 1824, p. 33). The Chinese soldiers, in Ellis's view, appeared 'respectable' from a distance but Jeffrey noticed they were armed only with bows and arrows. Closer inspection, he reported, revealed they were not of:

> A warlike appearance; first of all from their dress, and secondly from the slovenly way in which they stand; some with their toes turned in, others from their hands in their pockets and so on. (Jeffrey Amherst, n.d., n.p.)

Abel was dismissive also of their 'gaudy appearance' and observed that the troops were constantly moved up to the next point of the river once the embassy had passed (1818, p. 74).

Amherst was met at Dagu by a great number of mandarins who directed the British onto the Chinese barges carrying them to Tianjin. Flags bearing characters denoting 'Tribute Bearers' flew from the mastheads but the British decided not to comment (Abel, 1818, p. 73). Guanghui, the legate in charge of the embassy, visited Amherst and announced his regret that 'an ignorance of each other's language, prevented a more intimate and familiar conversation' and was disappointed on discovering that Jeffrey could not speak Chinese (Staunton, 1824, p. 34). 'The emperor', Jeffrey wrote, 'fully expected I could, because Sir George Staunton when he accompanied the last Embassy was about my age and could speak the language' (Jeffrey Amherst, n.d., n.p.). Guanghui was affable and well-mannered and stressed that his early visit was purely complimentary, but hinted that an imperial banquet was scheduled at Tianjin.

Amherst repaid the visit that evening where he met the high-ranking mandarin, Sulenge, for the first time. No formal discussion took place and Sulenge departed for Tianjin soon after. Jeffrey wrote:

> Su entered his palanquin carried by four bearers and accompanied by an escort of horse archers, and set off on the eighty mile journey to Tien sing in order to receive the Embassy there. (Jeffrey Amherst, n.d., n.p.)

The boats assigned for the embassy were a mixture of large, roomy vessels for Amherst and the commissioners, while the others were small and indifferent (Staunton, 1824, p. 35). Morrison (1820) described them:

> They were divided into rooms: first was a kind of anti-chamber for servants; next a room in which to receive visitors; and farther back a bed-room. Some had four apartments, beside a place at the stern occupied by the boatmen, and used as a cooking-room. The Embassador's and Commissioner's boats were large and handsome, with streamers in the Chinese manner. Most of the others were too small for two persons, which was the general arrangement. (p. 25)

The first evening in China presented an immediate challenge to British culinary sensibilities on the presentation of a gift of cooked dishes for the evening meal chosen by Guanghui. Notable for the absence of cats and dogs, these nevertheless included trays of stewed shark fins, stag sinews, bird's nests and sea slugs (Abel, 1818, p. 74). Abel (1818) wrote, 'as it was the first time of partaking of Chinese fare, curiosity induced us to taste the made dishes, but their flavour did not tempt us to do more' (p. 74). Other unappetising offerings consisted of 'varnished' sheep, pigs and fowls (p. 74).

Regardless of the novelty of the food, the dining experience was unsatisfactory and chaotic for other reasons. The crates with Amherst's cutlery, crockery and table linen had been sent on to Tianjin. Jeffrey wrote, 'Many of our party were obliged to eat with the Chinese chopsticks [and] made pretty work of it' (Jeffrey Amherst, n.d., n.p.). There were no chairs or dining tables and Chinese tables had to be pushed together and stools were used as chairs. Beds and bedding had also been sent to Tianjin along with many boxes holding personal belongings. Servants rummaged through boxes and bags searching for their master's possessions, which left things in a considerable mess. The British spent their first night in China sleeping on bare boards in cold conditions with no blankets or pillows and plagued by hordes of mosquitoes. An added blow to British comfort was being prohibited by Chinese soldiers from taking a walk after dinner. Abel commented, 'We had little cause to look forward with much pleasurable anticipation to the liberty which we were likely to enjoy during our passage through China' (1818, p. 75).

First impressions of the Chinese countryside were disappointing, especially when compared with the picturesque scenery of Rio de Janeiro. Abel thought Dagu was 'destitute of interest' with flat, barren shores and mud houses. Crowds of silent people lined the riverbank and thousands of junks covered the waterway, impeding the progress of the embassy (Hall, 1840/1865, p. 10). Ellis, on the other hand, noted improvements as the embassy barges approached Tianjin. Not only did the countryside appear well cultivated, but also some 'small inclosures in places remind[ed] us of England' (1817, p. 82). Ellis's tone even implied some warmth towards Chinese children noted in his observation that 'Chinese children must have a peculiar satisfaction in being dirty, as we observe them every where either sliding down the bank, or rolling themselves in mud' (p. 83). On the whole, Ellis's assessment of the Chinese at this early stage was positive and he wrote that 'My good opinion of the ordinary habits of the Chinese increases: they are orderly and good humoured to each other, and to strangers; not a single dispute has yet occurred' (p. 83). His perceptions had been softened by an earlier acquaintance with India and he was not as shocked as his compatriots with the appearance of the boat trackers described by Abel (1818) as 'miserable objects of wretched and naked men, tracking our boats and toiling often through a deep mire under a burning sun' (p. 76). Morrison (1820) painted an even bleaker picture of the boats propelled by human effort where groups of 20 or 30 'poor miserable-looking men' passed cords across their shoulders and walking forward in a leaning posture pulled the cords tied to the masthead of the vessel (p. 25). Jeffrey referred to seeing a body floating in the river that drew no reaction from the Chinese and thought it was the custom for poor Chinese to dispose of their dead in this fashion, accounting for 'the many dead bodies which we passed in our progress through China' (Jeffrey Amherst, n.d., n.p.).

12 August 1816: Arrival at Tianjin

The barges came to a halt at Tianjin at half past four in the afternoon of 12 August 1816, three days after leaving Dagu. Midshipman Martin wrote of British annoyance at the 'number of pleasure boats which flocked round our junks with parties in them who amused themselves by passing their remarks on us and criticizing our dress' (as quoted in Morrison, 1820, p. 29). A party of mandarins dressed in their ceremonial robes was waiting to greet the embassy, catching Amherst unprepared and in his dressing gown. Embarrassed, Amherst hastily retired to dress, leaving Morrison to explain British etiquette where the reception of visitors occurred sometime after a first arrival at a destination. Toone, Davis and Morrison were sent to meet Guanghui and Sulenge. Sulenge was described as a stooped old man of 70 who wore a red button. His complexion was marked with 'the small pox' and he was in the habit of deferring to Guanghui (Morrison, 1820, p. 27).

The British were received with a pleasing formality and were honoured with chairs situated to the left of Sulenge. The emperor, Guanghui informed them, regarded the British highly and favoured those who had travelled from such a great distance to pay their respects to him but, he supposed, they must be in a great hurry to return to England (Morrison, 1820, p. 27). Morrison replied that an extra month or so was of no matter considering the distance the embassy had come and that Amherst would be insulted if he was forced to leave Peking before the customary 40 days allotted traditionally to foreign embassies. Guanghui next raised the subject of the king's letter to the emperor and pointed out that Macartney had already delivered his letter by this time during his embassy. Morrison corrected him. Macartney's journal stated clearly that the king's letter was delivered into the hands of the ministers at Jehol some weeks after the embassy had first arrived in northern China. Declining to comment, Guanghui's final questions concerned the rank of Jeffrey Amherst, as well as that of other members of the ambassadorial suite. These questions were later interpreted by the British as an attempt to confirm Staunton's presence and status within the embassy.

Morrison, Toone and Davis returned to the boats to inform Amherst that Sulenge and Guanghui were about to make a call. The legates were received by the British with 'great ceremony'. Amherst was informed of the emperor's intention to receive him and his embassy with even greater honours than those offered to Macartney at the Qianlong court. Focus at the meeting fell again on the presentation of the Prince Regent's letter to the emperor. The legates, Amherst was informed, were authorised to receive the letter at Tianjin rather than waiting to hand it to the ministers, as Macartney had done, at Jehol. Amherst, who had always planned to use the occasion of handing the letter personally to the first minister at Peking as the opportunity to raise the subject of the embassy's objectives, specifically those concerning trade, said he intended to wait until he met the minister. This, Sulenge informed him, was impossible. All business was to be conducted through him and Guanghui and there would be no dealings between the embassy and government ministers (Morrison, 1820, p. 27). Amherst, on being informed of this, agreed to deliver a copy of the Prince Regent's letter to them on the following day. Sulenge then enquired after the identity of a young boy called Thomas Staunton that he remembered at the time of the Macartney mission and enquired if Staunton was he. Morrison, who was interpreting, hesitated to answer at which point Staunton came forward 'to introduce himself' (Staunton, 1824, p. 43). Staunton explained that he had been reluctant to speak until this time as his facility in the Chinese language had suffered due to long stays in England. Guanghui proceeded to compliment Staunton and told him that he had heard a great deal about him from his good friend, Sungyun, the late viceroy of Canton (Staunton, 1824, p. 43). Sulenge, Davis (1841) wrote, 'feigned surprise' at discovering Staunton's identity 'though there was every reason to suppose that the accounts from Canton must have long since put him in possession of this piece of information' (p. 64). Revealing his identity, however, was a great relief for Staunton, as every interview with the Chinese had been 'awkward and equivocal' (Staunton, 1824, p. 44). 'Whether or not', Staunton wrote, this was a preconceived plan of the legates to 'ascertain whether I meant to avow or conceal my identity with the youth in question, it is difficult to say' (1824, p. 44).

Staunton, meanwhile, had picked up some of the nuances in the legates' conversation regarding their invitation to the whole embassy to attend a banquet feast arranged for the next morning. He informed Amherst that the words '*tse-yen*' (*ciyan*) or a 'repast conferred' meant that the banquet was more than an ordinary event. Indeed, Staunton added ominously, it forced British attention on 'the description of the imperial breakfast' that had proved so fatal to the Russian embassy in early 1806, after which Golovkin and his embassy were expelled immediately from China for refusing to kowtow (Staunton, 1824, p. 44). On the legates' departure, Amherst and the commissioners once more discussed the strategy to be pursued at the imperial banquet the next day. While the kowtow before the emperor remained an open question, unanimous agreement was reached that performing the ceremony before an imaginary presence of the emperor represented by a yellow curtain was totally inadmissible (Staunton, 1824, p. 44).

8

The Imperial Banquet of 13 August 1816 and Progress to Tongzhou

Amherst's arrival at Tianjin marked the start of official negotiations with the Chinese Government on the occasion of an imperial banquet that Macartney had managed to avoid at the time of his embassy.[1] Historians have ignored the critical role and significance of the banquet that served as a site of generic diplomatic conflict and a carefully planned diplomatic ambush for the British from which the embassy never fully regained its forward momentum.[2] Chinese tactics at the time confirmed British views that they were dealing with a devious and inflexible 'Tartar court' that was determined to ensure that access to the emperor conformed to the protocols of the tribute system. These assessments were reinforced for the British as the embassy proceeded to Tongzhou, situated 12 miles from the emperor's Summer Palace of Yuanmingyuan.

---

1 Macartney was invited to a banquet at Dagu on 5 August but pleaded illness. He wrote, 'The Mandarins, Wang and Chou … now came to visit us, and pressed us much to accept their invitation to a banquet … which had been prepared for us, but being a good deal fatigued I declined it' (Cranmer-Byng, 1962, p. 73). Serious discussion of the ceremony to be performed before the Qianlong emperor did not take place until 8 September at Jehol (pp. 118–119). In contrast, Amherst was confronted about the kowtow within three days of arriving in China. Barrow commented later in the *Quarterly Review* that 'Lord Macartney … was more fortunate than Lord Amherst in escaping the yellow screen and the five clawed dragon of Tien-sing, where all the misfortunes of the latter originated' (1817, p. 479).
2 For example, Eastberg (2009) made no specific reference to the banquet while Gao, in his article 'Inner kowtow controversy' (2016), devoted only a paragraph to it but correctly concluded that Amherst 'paid some reverential bows without indicating he would perform kowtow before the emperor himself' (p. 601).

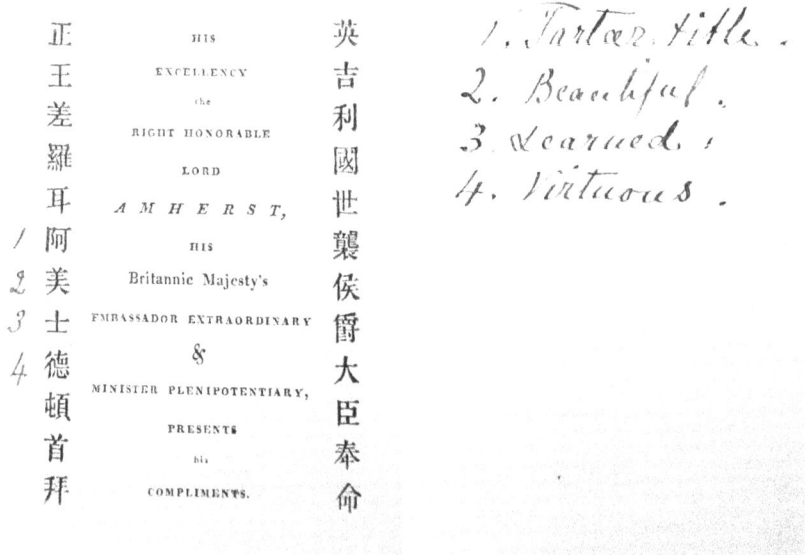

Figure 6: Amherst's official visiting card (front and back views) with an explanation of the Chinese rendering of his name.
Source: British Library.

13 August 1816: The Imperial Banquet

The imperial banquet hosted by the legates Guanghui and Sulenge at Tianjin on 13 August 1816, held only three days after the embassy disembarked at Dagu, represented the first of only two formal receptions granted to the Amherst Embassy in China and was the only one held in northern China.[3] Amherst and Staunton recognised that it was no ordinary civil reception; rather, it was a test on their readiness to comply with the kowtow ceremony (Staunton, 1824, p. 44; Amherst to Canning, 12 February 1817, in BL IOR G/12/197 (Reel 2) F 218). The day was also very hot, with Hayne (n.d., vol. 2, p. 20) recording an afternoon temperature of 93°F (33.8°C). For the British, the occasion presented an opportunity to make a suitable display befitting the embassy's first public appearance in China. Leading the parade on horseback were lieutenants Cooke and Somerset, in full uniform and bearing the Colours of England. The marine guard marching two by two followed, accompanied by the band. Amherst, the commissioners

---

3   The second reception was at Canton on 7 January 1817 after Amherst's return from Peking.

8. THE IMPERIAL BANQUET OF 13 AUGUST 1816 AND PROGRESS TO TONGZHOU

and Jeffrey were borne by Chinese palanquins. Amherst wore his 'peeral' robes over his Windsor uniform; Staunton was in the gown and cap of the Fellow Commoner of Cambridge; and Ellis wore his Windsor uniform without a sword. The rest of the suite were resplendent in the blue and scarlet embroidered uniform of the embassy, with gold lace coats, round hats, pantaloons and boots (Hayne, n.d., vol. 2, p. 20). Chinese soldiers cleared a path through the immense though silent crowd that had gathered as the procession made its way through the narrow streets of Tianjin.

The reception took place in a makeshift building of bamboo and plaited matting purposely built for the banquet. This venue represented a stark contrast to the grand stone buildings of Europe normally associated with diplomatic receptions. A hushed crowd at the entrance watched as the British alighted and entered an outer court lined with Chinese bowmen. Several mandarins dressed in their ceremonial robes stepped forward to meet the British and conducted them to a large hall.[4] Staunton's earlier suspicions were confirmed. Amherst wrote:

> The first thing that caught my eye on entering the room was a table covered with yellow silk evidently intended as a symbol of the Imperial Presence. Having read in a journal of the Russian Embassy in 1805 that the Russian ambassador soon after passing the frontier had been invited to a banquet, and then had been required to perform the Ko-tow … I concluded it was intended to put me to the same test, and having made up my mind, whatever ceremony I might afterwards submit to in the presence of the Emperor himself, to refuse prostration to any mere representation of the Imperial Person, I anticipated a similar fate to that of the Russian Embassy and was prepared to find, at Tien-sing, a final termination to our progress. (Amherst to Canning, 12 February 1817, in BL IOR G/12/197 (Reel 2) F 219)

Amherst, Staunton, Ellis, Morrison and Jeffrey were conducted into an inner apartment where the two legates Sulenge and Guanghui and four other mandarins were waiting. The Chinese sat on the left side of the room and gave the British seats on the less honourable right-hand side. The British, Guanghui emphasised, were being honoured by an imperial banquet expressly commanded and given by the emperor and it was to be assumed that the emperor himself was present. Accordingly, the kowtow was to be performed in return for the emperor's benevolence.

---

4   State banquets and the food served were managed by the Court of Banqueting, an agency of the Board of Rites (see Rawski, 1998, p. 43).

Amherst replied that his orders came directly from the King of England and he was unable to comply with the Chinese request to kowtow. Rather, he intended to show the same respect to the emperor as he would to his own sovereign and would follow Macartney's precedent as commanded by the king. In the presence of the emperor he would kneel on one knee, bow his head and kiss the emperor's hand as a mark of affection.[5] But on the present occasion, where the physical presence of the emperor was absent, he would perform the same ceremony paid by the Lords before the vacant throne of the British sovereign in the House of Lords, a low bow. As a conciliatory gesture to the mandarins, Amherst agreed to bow nine times in unison with the number of 'kneelings' performed by them (Morrison, 1820, p. 29).

Kissing the emperor's hand, the mandarins replied, was unacceptable and asserted, with what Jeffrey described as the 'the most obstinate perverseness', that Macartney had kowtowed, not only in the presence of the emperor but at other times as well, whenever the occasion demanded (Staunton, 1824, p. 46; Ellis, 1817, p. 92). Sulenge recalled that he remembered Macartney performing the kowtow at Canton and appealed to Staunton, who had been present on that occasion, to vouch that this was the case (Staunton, 1824, p. 47). Staunton was evasive. The embassy was so long ago, and he had been so young, that he could not remember which ceremony had been performed, but he was certain that it was not the kowtow (Staunton, 1824, p. 47).[6] He reaffirmed Amherst's position

---

5   The tradition of a ceremonial kissing of the hand in European diplomacy was an act of submission performed by the great lords of the realm (see Ruiz, 1985, p. 125).

6   Historical controversy surrounds the question of whether Macartney kowtowed before the Qianlong emperor in 1793. An entry in Staunton's boyhood diary, dated 14 September 1793, describes the British standing by the side of the road as the emperor passed where, he wrote, 'we went on one knee and bowed our heads down to the ground'; 'down to the ground' is crossed out. Later that day, at a reception before the emperor, Staunton referred to 'making the proper ceremony', assumed by some to suggest the Chinese ceremony of the kowtow. But, on 30 September, Staunton referred to performing 'the usual ceremony of Bending one knee'. Back in Canton, the mandarins made nine bows and three genuflections before a throne representing the emperor where the British, according to Staunton, 'followed their example' (Sir George Thomas Staunton, *Diary 1792–1793: Journey to China, 1792–1793*, London, England: Adam Matthew Microform Publications (China Trade, Politics & Culture, 1793–1980 database). Retrieved from www.china.amdigital.co.uk). These descriptions have led some historians, including Rockhill (1897, 1905) and Pritchard (1943), to conclude that Macartney kowtowed. Rockhill (1905, p. 31) based his claims on a report by a Russian interpreter, Vladykin (based in Peking at the time), that claimed Macartney had performed 'the detested prostrations'. Pritchard (1943, p. 166) referred to a French savant, M. Pierre Abel-Ramusat, who, following Russian sources, also reported that Macartney had kowtowed. A more realistic assessment is made by Peyrefitte (1992, pp. 224–225) who correctly points out the physical impossibility of Macartney—53 years of age, overweight, gout ridden and wearing tight silk trousers—kowtowing. Further, it is almost impossible for the average person to touch the ground with their head while kneeling on one knee!

that the British would follow Macartney's precedent, recorded in his official report, which was the most authentic authority on the subject. 'However mortifying to his feelings', Amherst said, he had no choice but to decline the honour of the emperor's invitation and would forego the banquet altogether (Ellis, 1817, p. 93). This, Staunton wrote later, would 'get rid of the difficulty for the present', but, by doing so, the mandarins had argued, he would be treating the emperor's kindness with contempt (1824, p. 47).

Discussions on the subject dragged on for two hours, made especially tedious, it would seem, by the logistics of interpreting and the very hot weather. The mandarins appealed to Amherst's paternal feelings, suggesting it would be a great shame if Jeffrey was deprived of the opportunity of seeing the emperor (Ellis, 1817, p. 94). Macartney had kowtowed, the mandarins argued, and it was necessary for Amherst to practise the ceremony. Amherst 'strenuously denied' such claims and diplomatically pointed out that the obeisance Macartney paid to the Qianlong emperor should be acceptable to his son. The mandarins refused to accept Amherst's argument and pointed out, significantly, that the Jiaqing emperor had been present on the occasion of Macartney's audience with his father and would vouch that Macartney had kowtowed.

Amherst next proposed that he would prepare a letter stating his reasons for not kowtowing and would present it to the emperor at Peking, but this was not acceptable. The Qianlong emperor, Amherst was informed, was most unhappy with Macartney's European homage and had been adamant that it should not become a precedent for future occasions. 'The Emperor', Guanghui added, 'would be angry with the King of England', which so offended Morrison that he dared not translate it (Morrison, 1820, p. 30). Amherst, however, read the admission of the Qianlong emperor's disapproval as proof that the mandarins had lied in their assertions that Macartney had kowtowed. A compromise was suggested. He would bow before the altar table the same number of times as the mandarins kowtowed, thereby showing his respect to the emperor, but he would not transgress his sovereign's orders. The emperor, he was confident, would understand his position. His embassy, he pointed out, had been in China for only three days after a six-month voyage—surely the emperor would not be so unreasonable to expel the embassy. This proposal was eventually accepted 'with good grace'. It was agreed that Amherst would make nine bows before the imaginary presence of the emperor (Amherst to Canning, 12 February 1817, in BL IOR G/12/197 (Reel 2) F 227).

The party adjourned for lunch and returned to the banquet hall. Guanghui told Amherst that he was very unhappy with his decision not to kowtow and cautioned that it would be wise for him to 'reconsider the consequences that might result' from a refusal to perform the correct ceremony (as quoted in Ellis, 1817, p. 96). Morrison (1820) quoted the legate as saying:

> Return thanks in your own way, and whatever it be, we shall report it to the court … you will give offence if you do not conform; we warn you of the consequences; do not reflect on us hereafter. (p. 30)

Morrison described Sulenge as 'screwing up his arch mouth', and saying in a serious tone, 'Do conform! Imitate us! If you do not, it will not be well!' (p. 31). Negotiation on the subject had reached a crisis point. It was clear, Staunton thought, that there was no chance for any 'reconsideration or consultation, as we had no option' (Staunton, 1824, p. 96). Jeffrey thought his father's refusal to perform the kowtow was likely to result in the embassy being 'sent back without seeing his Imperial Majesty' (Jeffrey Amherst, n.d., n.p.).

With the prospect of the ceremony taking place beside the altar, Amherst informed the others of his suite that they were to follow his example, 'by bowing in the same respectful manner we should do to our own Sovereign' (Hayne, n.d., vol. 2, p. 25).

The British were confronted with an altar table covered in a yellow silk cloth embroidered with gold dragons. A lighted censer that spewed smoke sat on top of the table. Placed behind the table was a carved screen 'of curious workmanship, representing a vine in full fruit' and made up of glass gems of different colours (Abel, 1818, p. 81). Abel (1818) noted that this represented the 'symbolic presence of His Chinese Majesty' (p. 81). Situated on the floor in front of the table were several small, red-coloured rugs, placed to accommodate the 'faithful votaries' (p. 81). Two Chinese, standing beside the table, commenced the ceremony with a 'slow chant' (Jeffrey Amherst, n.d., n.p.). The six mandarins situated themselves on the right-hand side of the table. Amherst stood on the left-hand side while Staunton, Ellis and Morrison stood behind him. Abel wrote:

> At a signal given by an officer, who uttered a few words in an exalted and singing tone, the Mandarins fell on their knees, and inclining their heads, knocked them three times against the ground, and then arose. A second and a third time the signal was repeated,

and a second and a third time they knelt and knocked their heads thrice against the earth. The Commissioners and the gentlemen of the suite bowed respectfully nine times. (1818, p. 83)

At the conclusion of the ceremony, the parties adjourned for the meal, which was described by Ellis (1817, p. 96) as 'handsome' and served in the Chinese style. Amherst, Jeffrey and the commissioners were invited to the upper part of the hall where they sat on cushions, six or eight inches from the ground before very low tables barely 12 inches high, facing the mandarins seated opposite them on the left-hand side (Morrison, 1820, p. 32; Hayne, n.d., vol. 2, p. 27). They had their own separate table where they dined alone with no opportunity to converse with their fellow diners, representing an inversion of Western dining protocol. The rest of the embassy suite sat on the ground on which a red felt cloth was placed. Sitting on the floor for the British dressed in their heavy robes was exceedingly difficult and even painful. Morrison wrote:

> We were compelled by this arrangement to sit cross-legged. Some of our party, incapable of this, stretched their legs under the tables … from the awkward posture in which we sat, it was a most uncomfortable meal. (1820, p. 32)

Figure 7: The frontispiece of an anonymous critique of the Amherst embassy, *Sketches of China* (1820), depicting Amherst kneeling before the altar table while the mandarins kowtow.
Source: British Library.

Martin added that they were 'forced to sit ... Tartar fashion cross-legged like our English taylors' (Journal of Sir William Fanshawe Martin, 1817, p. 32, in BL ADD MSS 41346-41475). Sennett's (1994, p. 340) observation that comfort for Europeans in the late eighteenth century meant freedom of movement, even when sitting, illustrates the practical difficulties confronting the British on this occasion. The meal lasted about an hour. 'Strings of trays were brought and fitted in the square tables before us, each one for 2 persons with a dozen basons or small dishes each' (Hayne, 1820, vol. 2, p. 27). The food, according to Staunton (1824), was 'exceedingly well dressed'. He added:

> Those of our party, who had no prejudice against Chinese cookery ... and were enabled to use the chop-sticks in the absence of the knife and fork, partook of the feast very heartily. (p. 50)

Ellis did not enjoy the food, although he found the first course of preserved fruits and custard 'very palatable'. The shark fin was not to his taste and he thought the 'bird-nest soup ... too gelatinous and insipid'; it even remained bland even after the addition of 'shrimps, eggs, &c' (Ellis, 1817, p. 102). Hayne, on the other hand, found the food 'remarkably good ... especially the birds nest and shark's fin' (Hayne, n.d., vol. 2, p. 27). Other dishes served included a soup made of mare's milk and blood, heart sinews 'and other viands used by the Chinese for their supposed aphrodisial virtues' (Abel, 1818, p. 84). Ellis and Staunton enjoyed the warm Chinese wine and the mandarins 'were very attentive in pledging the Ambassador and commissioners every time the cups were presented' (Staunton, 1824, p. 50). Martin described their Chinese hosts 'encouraging us to drink by showing us the bottom of their cups' (Journal of Sir William Fanshawe Martin, 1817, p. 32, in BL ADD MSS 41346-41475).

The guests were entertained by a Chinese orchestra and a play whose plot was indecipherable to the British, although the well-presented stage sets and colourful costumes were admired. These, Abel thought, resembled the clothes of the Chinese before the Tartar conquest (1818, p. 84). The music, consisting of a 'hubbub of noises proceeding from gongs, drums, cymbals, and everything else calculated to deafen the ears' offended British sensibilities (Davis, 1841, p. 70). Ellis was reminded of bagpipes and thought it 'might have been tolerated by Scotsmen, [but] to others [the music] was detestable. Of the same description was the singing' (1817, p. 102). The Chinese tumblers, on the other hand, were greatly admired for their strength and agility (p. 102).

At the meal's conclusion, Amherst, Jeffrey and the commissioners were invited once again into the inner apartment to resume discussion on the kowtow ceremony. 'The test of the yellow curtain', Staunton wrote, 'had failed to produce the desired effect' (1824, p. 50). The legates 'now pressed for a verbal pledge' of the ceremony the English proposed to perform in the actual presence of the emperor (p. 50). Repeating that he planned to follow Macartney's precedent and bend one knee as he would before his sovereign, Amherst was requested to give a demonstration of the British ceremony before the mandarins to enable them to make an accurate report to the emperor. Amherst replied that this was not possible. An impasse was averted when:

> Sir George Staunton ... happily suggested, that Lord Amherst's son should perform the proposed ceremony before his father. Chinese usage was so completely in accordance with this manifestation of respect from a son to his father, that every difficulty or objection to any previous practice by Lord Amherst was removed, and the proposition was instantly admitted. (Ellis, 1817, p. 97)

A carpet was produced and Jeffrey performed the ceremony. The mandarins, in Jeffrey's opinion, were 'still very dissatisfied, and complained that we did not shew the Emperor proper respect' (Jeffrey Amherst, n.d., n.p.). Amherst was asked to clarify if he proposed to repeat the ceremony nine times. Amherst agreed to do so but pointed out that this was more than he would perform before any European monarch. The mandarins asked if Jeffrey could repeat his earlier bow but perform it nine times. Amherst refused, telling the mandarins that he had no wish to 'trifle with a ceremony' that he considered a serious one (Amherst to Canning, 12 February 1817, in BL IOR G/12/197 (Reel 2) F 231). The mandarins insinuated that a refusal to kowtow could have serious consequences for the wellbeing of British trade at Canton. Amherst ignored such threats. Staunton had assured him earlier that a performance of the kowtow would be much more damaging to Company interests than non-compliance. Amherst's refusal to change his mind brought discussion on the ceremony to a close. The legates were handed a copy of the Prince Regent's letter to the emperor and the conference concluded.

An Analysis of the Banquet

Scholarly reference to the Amherst Embassy has been confined to the context of the 'kowtow question', but little attention has been given to its initial reception at the banquet just described. The occasion of the banquet represented an important site where knowledge about each other was produced for both the British and Chinese and where each other's intent was weighed and gauged (Hampton, 2009, p. 4). Each side scrutinised the other through performance and both were highly sensitive to this intense scrutiny. The British arrived with a splendid display of pomp and pageantry but, on entering a Chinese space, found themselves forced to respond to Qing pressure over the kowtow. Jonathan Spence (1998, p. 43) refers to the official banquet as one of the most central and solemn moments of ritual in Chinese diplomatic intercourse. The banquet's importance for the Amherst Embassy was a critical test and served to dispel British notions that it was possible to negotiate as equals with the Qing court.

The British, it was seen, travelled to the banquet hall within the reassuring space of a formal European cortege insulated from the Chinese crowds. Abel (1818) described his efforts to scan the crowd for glimpses of women and was surprised that many of the 'well-dressed and interesting children [had] so little of the Chinese character in their faces, that they would scarcely have attracted attention in an English crowd' (p. 80). 'The men', Abel thought, were 'generally well made and frequently tall [and I] did not observe in them that uniformity of countenance which I had been led to look for in the Chinese' (p. 80). Hayne was of the same opinion:

> I had here a better opportunity of contemplating innumerable faces, & I must do them the justice to say that they were by no means an ill-looking race one with the other, nor so dark as those in the country we had passed. I think any unprejudiced person would come to the same conclusion after making allowances for the shaved head, [and] ugly dresses both of which we have been unaccustomed to see. (n.d., vol. 2, p. 22)

Hayne and Abel were reassured with the sight of physically attractive people. The sociologist Erving Goffman's insight referring to peoples' reaction to being among crowds is relevant to the British frame of mind at this time:

> By scanning one's surroundings through an image repertoire, subjecting the environment to simple categories of representation, comparing likeness to difference, a person diminishes the complexity of [alien] experience. (as quoted in Sennett, 1994, p. 366)

On arrival at their banquet destination, the British left behind the secure confines of a British space, represented by the military order of the marine guard and procession, and entered into the Chinese-controlled space of the banquet hall. The visual and olfactory markers, such as cooking smells and incense smoke, were especially confronting to the British and exacerbated preconceived cultural images and meanings of China. The visual impact of the hall's interior was commented on by Abel:

> It is difficult to describe the glittering and tawdry magnificence which now suddenly opened upon us. An immense number of painted lamps, pictures, and other ornaments, in all colours of the rainbow, hung about us on every side; whilst a crowd of Mandarins, in their dresses of ceremony, rendered the animated part of the scene no less striking. (1818, p. 80)

Hayne and Abel, as well as others in the British party, were free to wander around the hall and courtyard while Amherst and the commissioners were engaged in negotiations in the conference room. British attempts were made to come to terms with Chinese culture where little of worth was seen apart from some beautiful painted lanterns and a picturesque display of presents for the embassy consisting of rolls of coloured silks 'prettily arranged in trays' on a table (Hayne, n.d., vol. 2, p. 23). The low square dining tables neatly arranged for the forthcoming meal caught Hayne's attention, while Abel (1818) described the 'pots of flowers and dwarf trees … distributed over the room, [which] were often mingled with pieces of limestone' (p. 81). Appearances for the British were important, especially for classifying Chinese dignitaries. The historian James Epstein (1989, p. 77) has written of the importance for the British of 'flags and banners, hats and caps, ribbons and medals' during the early nineteenth century for defining state and civil power brokers. Accordingly, members of the embassy sought clues to the rank of the various mandarins by a close scrutiny of their dress. Hayne (n.d., vol. 2, p. 24) referred to badges of rank consisting of 'a tiger or Dragon for the orders of the Military and a bird for that of the civil'. Abel (1818, p. 82) also described the mandarins' finely embroidered silk petticoats 'beautifully interwoven with gold and silk, in the forms of dragons and flowers. Their boots were of satin, and served them for pockets'. The mandarins' hats, described as 'small and conical, covered with long red hair, and surmounted with a globe, whose colour indicated their rank' (p. 82), were of specific interest.

The different coloured hat buttons worn by the mandarins were similarly important signifiers for British recognition of rank and status of the officials they encountered, and reference was made often to the 'Red Book' that explained the colours.[7] While Hayne was correct in his assertion that dragons and tigers indicated military men, he was not sufficiently educated on Chinese culture to recognise their symbolic meaning or gradations of rank (Forge, 1973, p. xiv).[8] Patricia Bjaaland Welch's (2008) work on symbolic meanings in Chinese art explains that high-ranking officials of 'one to three were allowed the use of the five-clawed *lóng* dragon, while the lower ranks (four down) were only allowed the use of the four-clawed *mǎng* dragon. These dragons are virtually identical in terms of majesty and composition, the main difference being the number of claws' (p. 125). Similarly, the tiger represented 'strength, power, and courage, and, in particular, military prowess. The tiger is therefore regarded as a protector and guardian' (p. 145). While the British made a connection with the presence of dragons at the banquet with the emperor, the symbolism found on the mandarins' robes was read only in British terms as attractive and effeminate pieces of embroidery. Also noted were the girdles worn around the waists of the military mandarins from which hung 'fans, pipes, and chop-sticks' (Abel, 1818, p. 82). The contrast with the bearing of the British officers, which the British regarded as manly and military, marked a clear distinction with their Chinese counterparts on show at the banquet.

The banquet's political function, namely, to secure British compliance with the ritual performance of the kowtow, was recognised immediately by Amherst and Staunton. As explained previously, Amherst's public performance of the kowtow would have affirmed the demotion of the British sovereign to the status of a tributary vassal of the Chinese emperor. Sulenge admitted this fact in his memorial to the Imperial Government

---

7   The 'Pekin Red Book' was referred to by the British for information on Chinese ranks and family background. Ellis noted their research on Guanghui: 'On reference to the Pekin Red Book, it was found that the Chin-chae [Guanghui] is connected with the imperial family; his rank as a Mandarin is low' (1817, p. 69).

8   Forge, an anthropologist, writes in the context of art appreciation: 'Most anthropologists would suggest that it is impossible for a member of culture A to know with any meaning of a work produced in culture B unless he has had considerable experience of that culture' (1973, p. xiv).

following the banquet. He stated he had informed Morrison, 'if the envoy knew the true meaning of reverence, he should follow us in performing the same ritual; it was only then, we said, that he could properly be regarded as having assumed an inferior status' ('Su Leng-eh and Kuang-Hui: The Kowtow Controversy', a memorial submitted to the Imperial Government on 13 August 1816 in Li, 1969, pp. 46–47).

Amherst was ill at ease on entering the banquet hall. He had moved from a secure British space into one where his personal status as a British ambassador was in danger of being undermined as he was pressured to undergo a rite of incorporation into the Chinese politico-cultural realm (Gluckman, 1966, p. 3). The sight of the altar table draped in yellow silk alerted Amherst immediately to Golovkin's expulsion in 1806 and he braced himself for difficult negotiations with the mandarins. The censer spewing smoke on the altar table served further to remind the Protestant British of the abomination of Catholic and pagan practice. 'Kneeling' also evoked in them images of Islam or cowardice (Rawski, 1998, p. 22).[9] Kneeling thus symbolised subjugation and touching the ground with one's head held connotations of uncleanliness and insult equating human behaviour with that of savage barbarians (Hevia, 1995, p. 234).[10] Sennett (1994, p. 82) has pointed out that some forms of ritual function to give bodily performance precedence over the spoken word. Diplomacy for the British was not established by the oppression of the prostrate body, but on a belief in equality based on the strength of negotiation and rational argument where participants were held responsible for their spoken words, which were recorded and documented.

Regardless of bodily positions and connotations of pagan ritual, the fundamental question concerning the performance of the kowtow, from the British point of view, was the fact that it was not reciprocal and signified subjugation of the British monarch to the Chinese emperor. This had been shown during the Macartney Embassy when the suggestion that a Chinese minister of equal rank to Macartney kowtow before a portrait of George III was refused. The kowtow, the British asserted:

---

9   Rawski (1998) referred to 'the ritual of submission before the emperor [being] inspired by Muslim pilgrimage traditions and thus bore religious connotations' (p. 22). It will be seen that Captain Maxwell, at the time of firing at the Bocca Tigris forts, commented on the cowardly Chinese falling on their knees in a stage of fright 'like Persians at sunrise' (Hall, 1840/1865, p. 71).
10   Hevia (2009) also quoted Stallybrass and White who argued that the kowtow represented the 'the feminization of servitude in the figure of the kneeling chambermaid' (p. 222).

> If ... not reciprocally performed ... express[ed] in the strongest manner, the submission and homage of one person or state to another and [it is] in this light the Tartar Family now on the throne of China considers the ceremony call'd San-Kwei-Kew-Kow - thrice kneeling and nine times beating the head against the ground. (Anonymous, Handwritten background notes on the Amherst Embassy, n.p., in PRO FO 97/95)

The Amherst Embassy's fate was sealed at this early time. The legates next made a fundamental mistake in permitting the embassy to proceed towards Tongzhou before receiving official approval from the Jiaqing emperor, and before receiving confirmation of Amherst's intentions on the performance of the kowtow in the physical presence of the emperor. Amherst had kept his options open, which ensured that future diplomatic discussion would focus only on this question until a mutual agreement was reached. British objectives for the embassy were now destined to be neglected and overlooked, although they still believed that an audience before the emperor would open the door for negotiation. The banquet of 13 August had resulted in setting the diplomatic agenda where the Amherst Embassy from now on found itself on the back foot in its dealings with Qing officialdom.

Aftermath of the Banquet

Amherst, nonetheless, was very pleased with the outcome of the conference at the banquet. He had escaped Golovkin's fate and had not been expelled from China for refusing to kowtow. Importantly, he was to proceed to Peking, 'conceiving that every day of progress toward the Capital added some probability of our ultimate reception' (Amherst to Canning, 12 February 1817, in BL IOR G/12/197 (Reel 2) F 219). His reception had been civil and 'there was no mixture of rudeness or acrimony or any indication of ill-will, such as Lord Macartney had reason to complain' (Amherst to Canning, 12 February 1817, in BL IOR G/12/197 (Reel 2) F 232). Ellis (1817) recalled the fate of the Dutch embassy of 1795 where compliance with the kowtow ceremony had resulted only in the most degrading of circumstances, whereas Amherst had 'sufficiently establish[ed] the expediency of resistance' (p. 99). Hayne was impressed with Amherst's efforts to brief the rest of the embassy:

[Of] everything that might interest them, & even to gratify any reasonable curiosity or something to this effect which of course gave universal satisfaction & raised him still higher in the estimation of everyone. The contest was severe indeed on the disputed point, which made us glory more in our victory. (n.d., vol. 2, p. 31)

Hayne's assessment of Chinese actions reflected wider British opinion where lying and low cunning was:

> characteristic of the Nation, who from beginning to end think no more of a lie than we do of eating our breakfast, which of course has done away with every thing like mutual confidence. (p. 32)

Ellis read Sulenge's assertion that Macartney had kowtowed as a deliberate attempt by the mandarins to trap Staunton into contradicting himself. To have done so, Ellis added, would have had the effect of attributing British resistance to the ceremony to his suggestions, thus undermining Amherst (Hayne, n.d., vol. 2, p. 32). The legates' acceptance of a copy of the Prince Regent's letter to the emperor signified that the embassy was still on track to proceed to Peking. But there was no guarantee that the emperor would accept the proposed British ceremony of respect.

The embassy travelled 19 miles up-river towards Tongzhou the following day and the British were astonished by the large number of junks loaded with grain destined for the Peking granaries (Ellis, 1817, p. 105). Sulenge and Guanghui informed Amherst during an evening visit that the emperor was unlikely to agree to his terms over the performance of the kowtow. Sulenge's appointment to the embassy, it was pointed out, was an unprecedented honour and indicated the emperor's high regard for Amherst because his rank was superior to any official appointed to the Macartney Embassy. Amherst, in reply, stressed that the nine bows he proposed to perform before the Jiaqing emperor represented a greater honour than the single bow traditionally paid by a British ambassador to the Russian sovereign. This gave the mandarins the opportunity to inform Amherst that the Russian embassy was expelled from China without an audience over the very question of the kowtow. Morrison wrote:

> Old Soo threw out, in a rather gruff tone, that the Russians had been rejected for their non-compliance, and their commerce interrupted; and hinted that it would be the same with us. (1820, p. 35)

Guanghui added that as there was only one Sun in the universe so there was only one Sovereign in the world; this Sovereign was the Emperor of China to which all other sovereigns owed homage and submission (p. 35).

While this statement resulted in an 'excited murmur' among the Chinese present, the British thought this proposition was 'too ridiculous to be seriously opposed' (p. 35). Guanghui and Sulenge remained steadfast and informed the British that 'they did not think there was more of a chance in ten thousand' that the emperor would receive the embassy on the terms currently proposed (Amherst to Canning, 12 February 1817, in BL IOR G/12/197 (Reel 2) F 235). The copy of the Prince Regent's letter was returned as his address to the emperor headed 'Sir, My Brother' was inappropriate and had to be changed (Staunton, 1824, p. 53). The British agreed to delete the term.

The legates next requested to see the box containing the Prince Regent's letter. The gold box, valued at £1,500 (equivalent to approximately £150,000 in today's values) and described as 'a magnificent thing of its kind' failed to attract attention whereas the appearance of the little gold silk purse given to Staunton by the Qianlong emperor evoked 'extreme veneration' and interest (Davis, 1841, p. 86).

Ellis (1817) wrote on the conclusion of the meeting that he was becoming increasingly concerned that the true objectives of the embassy were being ignored. The emphasis on ceremony and the kowtow indicated that the chances of negotiations on these were highly unlikely.

15 August 1816

The boats proceeded up-river towards Tongzhou for the second day. The question of the kowtow was raised again when Chang-wei and Yin visited Amherst on his barge during a stopover. Macartney, they admitted, had bowed before the Qianlong emperor on his first audience, but thereafter had kowtowed during the second audience at the time of the celebrations of the emperor's birthday. Amherst dismissed 'this admission', which he thought would have 'been of considerable importance had it come from higher authority' (Amherst to Canning, 12 February 1817, in BL IOR G/12/197 (Reel 2) F 237).

Discussions were interrupted with the arrival of the legates, Sulenge and Guanghui, who requested a private meeting. A vermillion edict written in the Jiaqing emperor's hand had just been received. The emperor thought there were too many people in the embassy and accordingly ordered that the band return to the ships. This demand, in Morrison's view, indicated the emperor's 'weak [and] capricious mind' (1820, p. 36).

Staunton thought his objection was a 'very ungracious act' as the band was a 'harmless addition' to the embassy's amusement and was necessary for its 'public state' (1824, p. 56). Amherst stood firm. He told the mandarins that he was responsible for the band's behaviour and wellbeing and it was impossible to separate it from the rest of the embassy. The emperor's letter, Amherst noted privately, was written at a date prior to any formal discussions over the kowtow and before the emperor had any reason to suppose that Amherst was not going to perform the ceremony (Amherst to Canning, 12 February 1817, in BL IOR G/12/197 (Reel 2) F 238). Ellis (1817) noted ominously, 'it was impossible to avoid supposing that it was only the first in a series of trivial exceptions that were about to be taken to the Embassy' (p. 111). British attitudes towards the emperor's disposition changed at this time. The emperor, in Hayne's opinion, was 'an illiterate, debauched sot, timid and tyrannical' who, due to three attempts on his life, was 'frightened at his own shadow, so that we have nothing to hope from such a man' (n.d., vol. 2, p. 43).

Serious concerns arose that evening with the arrival of Sulenge and Guanghui in a highly agitated state, described by Jeffrey as being in 'a considerable fuss' (Jeffrey Amherst, n.d., n.p.). Amherst was asked, in a most abrupt manner, 'what is become of your ships?' (Staunton, 1824, p. 56). Provisions had been sent to Dagu, but it was discovered that the ships had already left. Their departure, undertaken without imperial permission, was blamed on Amherst and was viewed as a 'great omission' on the part of the British (Staunton, 1824, p. 57). Concerned that they would be blamed by the emperor, the legates enquired how the embassy planned to return to England. Amherst's reply was cagey. He said that, as there had been no previous discussion on the question, he had assumed that the embassy was to follow Macartney's precedent and travel overland to Canton. The mandarins were informed that he had no authority over the movements of the ships, which were respectively under the command of the Royal Navy and the Company.[11] An early departure, Amherst added, was thought expedient due to the danger of inclement weather but that decision was beyond his control.

---

11   Staunton, as president of the Select Committee, ordered Captain Ross, Commander of the Company ship *Discovery*, to follow the orders of Captain Maxwell until the 'latitude of the N.E. point of Shan-tung, when you will be permitted to separate from His Majesty's ships, and are to proceed towards Macao with the Investigator under your orders, and to execute such parts of the survey … as you may find practicable, without giving any ground of suspicion or offence to the Chinese Government'. Orders were not to take a 'regular Survey' of the 'Gulf of Pe-chee-lee' but any 'observations' made will be 'exceedingly acceptable to the Honourable the Court of Directors' (Orders signed Geo. Thom. Staunton, HMS *Alceste*, 9 August 1816, in BL IOR G/12/196 (Reel 1) F 366).

Guanghui became increasingly irritated. Informing Amherst that his behaviour in concealing the movement of the ships was highly improper, he blamed Morrison for wrongfully translating British intentions. Guanghui pointed his finger at Morrison, exclaiming, 'It is your fault!' (as quoted in Morrison, 1820, p. 37). Morrison, according to Staunton, 'very properly said, that if such was his opinion he must decline any further interpretation' (Ellis, 1817, p. 114). Amherst now intervened using all his diplomatic skills. Staunton was requested 'to express to both Mandarins his sense of the injustice done to Mr. Morrison, and to inform them that he considered such observations personally offensive to himself' (p. 115). Morrison was offered an apology, which was accepted. The fact that Guanghui would be held accountable by the emperor for not preventing the ships' departure was obvious to the British (Amherst to Canning, 12 February 1817, in BL IOR G/12/197 (Reel 2) F 242). Amherst said he would write a letter to the emperor explaining that the ships had to leave due to the dangers of remaining at anchor in the shallow waters of the Gulf. Ellis added, 'We could not be surprised at the dissatisfaction shewn by the Mandarins at the departure of the ships, and still less at our silence upon the subject' (1817, p. 115). The mandarin in charge of the ships at Dagu, the British were informed, had since been demoted (Morrison, 1820, p. 38).

The departure of the British ships without imperial approval was a major reason for the subsequent treatment of the embassy. News reached the Select Committee at Canton in late September 1816 that the emperor had made up his mind to refuse any presents and had given directions for the embassy to be dismissed at this time (Extract from Public Consultations 1816/17, 21 September 1816, in BL MSS EUR F 140/48).[12]

16 August: Further Discussions on the Kowtow

Chang-wei and Yin visited Amherst the following morning. An imperial edict had arrived with instructions to dismiss the embassy if the kowtow was not agreed to (Staunton, 1824, p. 59). Sulenge and Guanghui were too distressed to come themselves and had deputised Chang-wei and Yin

---

12 News of this had serious repercussions at Canton where permission to load the *General Hewitt* with teas was refused by the Canton authorities. A standoff with the Select Committee lasted some months.

8. THE IMPERIAL BANQUET OF 13 AUGUST 1816 AND PROGRESS TO TONGZHOU

to deliver the emperor's message. Amherst said he would answer only to the legates but informed them that he was prepared to follow Macartney's precedent and enquired if a mandarin of equal rank would kowtow before a portrait of the Prince Regent. This, Chang-wei and Yin replied, was impossible, as Amherst would be in the presence of the emperor whereas the Chinese official would be paying homage to a mere picture (Amherst to Canning, 12 February 1817, in BL IOR G/12/197 (Reel 2) F 244). The proposal that a future Chinese ambassador at the Court of St James's kowtow in front of the British sovereign was also dismissed with the mandarins adding that they dare not suggest such a proposal to the emperor. Amherst called a halt to the meeting and said he would defer any further discussion on the kowtow until he met with the legates.

Sulenge and Guanghui arrived shortly afterwards. Staunton wrote that they appeared most dejected. Efforts were made to convince Amherst to kowtow by pointing out that the ambassadors of Japan, Siam and other independent countries all kowtowed before the Chinese emperor. Amherst recorded indignantly in his report that analogies made with the courts of Portugal or Russia would have been more appropriate.[13] Amherst, accordingly, refused 'any comparison to be drawn between the King of Great Britain and the feeble states which surrounded the Chinese Empire' (Amherst to Canning, 12 February 1817, in BL IOR G/12/197 (Reel 2) F 245). 'These nations', Ellis reminded the legates, 'could neither be classed in point of civilization nor power with the English' (1817, p. 118). This point was accepted by the legates who stressed again that the British were being received by the court with far greater honours than any other country. Amherst refused to compromise. He told the legates that he would record and forward his proposals in a letter to the emperor, but was told it was not possible to communicate with the emperor in this way. Moreover, the legates said, they had already been chastised by the emperor and dared not anger him further (Morrison, 1820, p. 39).[14] In that case, Amherst replied, he was left with no alternative but to return to England. Guanghui and Sulenge became most distressed at this turn of events and expressed their regret by saying repeatedly that such was 'the will of Heaven' (Amherst to Canning, 12 February 1817, in BL IOR G/12/197 (Reel 2) F 246).

---

13 Both of whom had refused to kowtow.
14 Morrison (1820) added that Amherst referred to the Kangxi emperor and the exception made at the time of the Ismailof Embassy where a mandarin kowtowed before an image of the Russian God, but Guanghui replied that, although he had heard of it, this was not in any authentic record.

Guanghui and Sulenge's refusal to forward any of Amherst's letters to the emperor, in Staunton's (1824) opinion, shifted the responsibility for the outcome of embassy onto the Chinese, 'at least according to all European notions of diplomacy'. The Chinese would now be 'completely responsible for the rupture, if a rupture ensued' (p. 63). In the meantime, Guanghui and Sulenge told the British that some mandarins of an even higher rank were being sent to conduct the embassy. The embassy was halted and ordered to turn back to Tianjin.

17–21 August 1816: The Continuation of the Diplomatic Impasse

Chang-wei and Yin remained the chief interlocutors with the embassy. Morrison described Chang-wei as 'grinding and gnashing his teeth' due to the situation having become 'extremely stern and severe' (1820, p. 41). Amherst was informed that the embassy's dismissal was considered most undesirable and appeals were made to him to reconsider his decision on the kowtow. Perhaps he could humbly request the emperor's permission to follow the Macartney precedent and kneel on one leg as ordered by the British sovereign. Further, Staunton was asked to confirm that, while he was too young to remember whether Macartney had kowtowed, he had heard that Macartney had not. The emperor may be 'induced to dispense with the strictness of the ceremonial, in consideration of such a solicitation' (Ellis, 1817, p. 125).

Staunton was then subjected to a long harangue from one of the mandarins. The Jiaqing emperor was disappointed, Staunton was told, that he had not used his influence to pressure Amherst into performing the kowtow. This action was the least Staunton could do considering the gracious notice he had received from the Qianlong emperor. Amherst interrupted. Staunton's opinion, he said, had nothing to do with his orders, which he received directly from his sovereign (Ellis, 1817, p. 124). Agreement was reached finally with Amherst undertaking to kneel three times accompanied by three bows. Amherst concluded the meeting and retired with his suite for breakfast.

News of the Appointment of Heshitai and Muketenge to Take Charge of the Embassy

Chang-wei and Yin paid another call immediately after breakfast with the news that the embassy was to proceed to Tongzhou where they would be met by two Tartar mandarins of the most senior rank who were taking charge of the embassy. The first was Heshitai (referred to as 'Ho' by the British) who held the title of *gongye*, translated by Staunton and Morrison as 'Duke' (Tuck, 2000, p. xxix).[15] Heshitai was also the emperor's brother-in-law and a Manchu of the Bordered Yellow Banner (Tuck, 2000, p. xxix). The second mandarin was Muketenge, referred to by the British as 'Moo', who was the president of the Board of Rites and one of the most senior administrators of the empire (Tuck, 2000, p. xxix).[16] Their specific orders were to instruct Amherst in the performance of the kowtow before permitting him to proceed to Peking.

Heshitai and Muketenge's appointment indicated to the British that Guanghui and Sulenge had failed in their handling of the embassy (Davis, 1841, p. 97). Amherst was informed that he was due to meet the senior mandarins where he was expected to perform the kowtow before a yellow screen and a dragon tablet (Staunton, 1824, p. 66). Such a rehearsal, Amherst thought, was a Chinese trick to induce him to perform the ceremony in a public space (Amherst to Canning, 28 February 1817, in BL IOR G/12/197 (Reel 2) F 254). Chang-wei and Yin next requested Amherst to practise the same ceremony he intended to perform before Heshitai and Muketenge at Tongzhou in front of them. Amherst 'flatly refused' and told them that the ceremony he would perform was a serious matter and was reserved for the emperor's presence. He added that he proposed to inform the emperor of his intentions in a personal letter. The offer 'of a written engagement for its performance', Amherst noted, 'seemed to give them great satisfaction' (Amherst to Canning, 28 February 1817, in BL IOR G/12/197 (Reel 2) F 255). He proposed to kneel on one

---

15   He was awarded the title due to his services in the defence of the Imperial Palace during a rebel attack in 1813.
16   Muketenge was also a Manchu of the Bordered Yellow Banner. Representing the highest rank of the Eight Banners, members of the Bordered Yellow Banner comprised the elite of the emperor's bodyguard (see Elliott, 2001, pp. 81, 366).

knee three times, and to thrice bow each time (Staunton, 1824, p. 67). The letter was composed by Morrison and signed by Amherst. Its delivery to the mandarins resulted in permission for the embassy to proceed to Tongzhou, arriving there on 20 August.

Davis is Visited by a Cantonese Mandarin

While Amherst was engaged in discussions with Chang-wei and Yin, Davis received an unexpected visit from a Cantonese mandarin that was regarded by the British as an intelligence gathering exercise. The mandarin wished 'to speak on the subject of the existing discussions', referring to the kowtow (Davis, 1841, p. 95). Davis informed him that he had no authority to speak on behalf of the ambassador but could inform the mandarin of the 'understood declaration' that the British could never perform the ceremony. This statement was met with a list of possible ramifications if Amherst did not agree to the kowtow. First, it would be a great pity if the British left China without seeing the emperor and the king would be 'incensed' when he found out how the British were conducting themselves in their negotiations with the Chinese. Davis was next asked about the ceremony he would perform in the presence of the British sovereign. Davis replied that it would not be the kowtow and that he wished to have no further discussion on the matter. The mandarin then raised the importance of the Canton trade to Britain, which was permitted only with the benevolence of the Chinese emperor. The trade, Davis replied, was mutually beneficial to China and Britain. The mandarin then departed, having failed, Davis believed, to learn any new intelligence about British plans (Davis, 1841, p. 97).

20 August: Arrival at Tongzhou, 12 Miles from Peking and Nine Days Before the Reception at Yuanmingyuan

The British boats anchored at Tongzhou at five o'clock in the afternoon. Guanghui and Sulenge called on Amherst to enquire further about the ceremony Amherst proposed to perform before the emperor. They said the emperor was in a very good mood and it would be a shame if some mutual arrangement could not be negotiated—everything would go smoothly once Amherst agreed to kowtow (Amherst to Canning, 28 February 1817, in BL IOR G/12/197 (Reel 2) F 254). The emperor's decision to send two mandarins of exalted rank to henceforth conduct the embassy was proof of his regard and an acknowledgement of the superior status of the British sovereign compared to the tributary princes. Amherst referred once more to the Macartney precedent, whereby he would kowtow if a Chinese minister of rank performed the same ceremony before a portrait of the Prince Regent, or if an imperial guarantee was received that any future Chinese ambassador at St James's would perform the kowtow in front of the British sovereign. He emphasised further that a British ambassador would never perform an act that could be construed by the Chinese as an act of homage from a dependent prince (Ellis, 1817, p. 140).

Guanghui and Sulenge were disappointed. Amherst reassured them that the exalted rank of the new mandarins was of little concern and that his decision was final. He would never be persuaded by any mandarin, no matter how exalted his rank, to change his mind (Ellis, 1817, p. 141).

The legates next made a fateful suggestion. Amherst was free to 'make any report he pleased on his return to England' regardless of whether he performed or did not perform the kowtow. The implication that Amherst would be prepared to lie before his sovereign met with predictable British outrage (Amherst to Canning, 28 February 1817, BL IOR G/12/197 (Reel 2) F 256). Amherst, Ellis (1817) pointed out, had 'seventy-four witnesses with him who would state the truth' (p. 141).[17]

---

17 The Chinese claimed that Macartney kowtowed before the Qianlong emperor at the second reception when only he and the Stauntons, as well as the Chinese interpreter Mr Plumb, were present. The fact that this was a tightly inclusive group, where a performance of the kowtow would most likely be kept secret, hardly needs to be pointed out. If Macartney had kowtowed, the three witnesses could be relied on to keep to the 'official' British story. The presence of other visiting envoys, however, as well as the close proximity of 10 Russians at the College in Peking, guaranteed that news of Macartney kowtowing would have eventually found its way to Europe, which, as noted earlier (see fn. 6 of this chapter), is what Rockhill (1905, p. 31) claimed.

21 August: New Mandarins Arrive to Take Charge of the Embassy, Seven Days Before the Embassy's Arrival at Yuanmingyuan

The two senior mandarins sent to witness Amherst rehearsing the kowtow arrived on 21 August. Heshitai was described as 'a young man of few words and of very firm character' (Morrison, 1820, p. 44).[18] Muketenge was 'a thin old man' who never spoke and was nicknamed the 'Silent Moo' by the British (p. 44). Their high rank impressed Morrison who noted that the embassy had three 'Shang-soo or Presidents' assigned to negotiate with the ambassador out of a total of seven in the Chinese Government (p. 44).[19] Amherst arranged to meet them the next day.

The British dined together that evening under a veranda in the court. Hayne wrote:

> Having got our plate, glass, and wine … we made a good display to the astonishment of the staring crowd who were mounted up in the surrounding trees overlooking our Court walls … watching every movement we made. (n.d., vol. 2, p. 57)

The meal was interrupted when Chang-wei appeared with news that a deputation of mandarins was waiting to call on the ambassador. Amherst, Staunton, Ellis and Morrison left the table and went to Amherst's apartment to greet them. Their visit, Davis wrote, 'sounded extremely formidable'. He added, 'it was right we should be duly prepared for such celestial colloquy sublime' (as quoted in Hayne, n.d., vol. 2, p. 57).

The 'Lads of Mougden'[20]

Six mandarins, dressed in their ceremonial robes, arrived. Some wore blue buttons and peacock feathers. Staunton and Ellis went forward to meet them but, much to their astonishment, were ignored as the mandarins

---

18 Morrison further described Heshitai as 'about 35 years of age, of the middle size; stout, and possessing apparently great bodily strength and warmth of temper' (1820, p. 44).
19 Morrison added that 'all three were destined to be dismissed from their employment' on account of the embassy (1820, p. 44). 'Shang-soo' is likely to be *shangshu*.
20 Mukden, present-day Shenyang.

'brushed rudely' past them and made straight for the sitting room where they 'seized on the chief seats without waiting for an invitation' (Staunton, 1824, p. 74). Davis wrote:

> We all stood aghast … when this half-dozen of savages rushed past without so much as a look, and proceeding to seize the six highest places, seated themselves down at once. (1841, p. 107)

Amherst, however, spectacularly 'out-manoeuvred them by taking the principal seat' at the other end of the room.

The mandarins, whom Jeffrey described as 'understrappers', were particularly haughty and acted in an 'exceedingly rude and overbearing manner' (Jeffrey Amherst, n.d., n.p.).[21] They enquired which of the Englishmen gathered before them was the ambassador for they had come to inform him that he was expected to perform the kowtow in front of Heshitai the following day. Amherst replied in an equally authoritative voice that he would only discuss such matters with Heshitai and Muketenge. The mandarins pretended not to understand and continued with a harangue about the importance of the ceremony to the Celestial Empire. Amherst repeated his answer in an even louder tone after which 'they [the mandarins] bounced up and strutted out of the room' (Davis, 1841, p. 108).

The meeting lasted only 10 minutes. The British made a point of showing their displeasure by 'treat[ing] them on their departure with all the disrespect we could' (Jeffrey Amherst, n.d., n.p.). The band was prohibited from playing and the marines were ordered to withhold their salute. The 'grotesque piece of diplomacy' they had witnessed astonished the British who remained in their seats for some time in what can only be interpreted as a state of shock. The group of six mandarins hereafter acquired a new nickname and were referred to by the British as the six 'lads of Mougden' (Davis, 1841, p. 108). Their attempts to bully the British into complying with the ceremony reinforced a fundamental difference between Western and Chinese diplomacy where negotiation over disputes was not an option. Any preconceived notion the British may have had of a fruitful diplomatic encounter was finally dispelled. Davis wrote:

---

21   *The Shorter Oxford English Dictionary* defines an 'understrapper' as 'a subordinate; an underling'.

> Nothing but the greatest ignorance of the character of Europeans could have led the Chinese to hazard such an attempt … Herein consists much of their weakness in negotiations; they are too proud to learn any thing about us, while we foreigners … never lose an opportunity of studying them in every relation of life … That 'power' which consists in 'knowledge', therefore, preponderates on our side. We know, above all, that the most complete want of faith, the most unblushing perfidy, is one part of the Chinese system in their negotiations with strangers; and unless this be carefully kept in view during the existing crisis, they may play us some sad tricks. (1841, p. 109)

British apprehension was reflected with Ellis having second thoughts over the wisdom of refusing to perform the kowtow ceremony. The fact that the kowtow had become the only question under negotiation was extremely worrying, but the dice was thrown and the British had to stand by their decision (Ellis, 1817, p. 145). Abel thought the 'despicable presumption of these men gave a foretaste of the treatment that His British Majesty's Representative afterwards experienced from their superiors' (1818, p. 93).

Amherst, who wished to sleep on board his boat, was requested with some urgency by Chang-wei and Yin to sleep ashore in the temple apartments arranged for him. Much to their relief, Amherst promised to do so once his furniture had been delivered. 'The Emperor', they said, 'has very long ears' and would suspect them of 'making false reports and punish them for it' (as quoted in Hayne, n.d., vol. 2, p. 61). Davis added in a superior tone, 'We were of course too polite, and had too sincere a respect for his Majesty, to dispute the application of this asinine attack' (as quoted in Hayne, n.d., vol. 2, p. 61). Amherst complained about the mandarins' rudeness earlier in the day and pointed specifically to the insult paid to Staunton when they pushed past him. Chang-wei explained that this behaviour was typical of those mandarins who remained at court and who had never served in the provinces; he and Yin had also been ignored, as had his offer to escort them to meet the embassy (Staunton, 1824, p. 146).

22 August: First Meeting with Heshitai and Muketenge

The meeting with the imperial commissioners, Heshitai and Muketenge, was arranged for midday. Amherst prepared himself for a termination of the embassy but still held a vague hope and a belief that a direct appeal to the emperor 'was the only way to obviate such a proceeding' (Amherst to Canning, 28 February 1817, in BL IOR G/12/197 (Reel 2) F 258). Ellis proceeded to draw up a letter that was carefully translated into Chinese by Morrison. With such in his possession, Amherst wrote, he accepted the invitation to a conference but stipulated 'that I should not be called upon, for either practice or performance of any Court ceremony' (Amherst to Canning, 28 February 1817, in BL IOR G/12/197 (Reel 2) F 258). His letter informed the emperor:

> The great affairs of empire being best conducted by precedent, his Royal Highness has instructed me to approach Your Imperial presence with the same outward expression of respect that were received by your dignified father Kien-Lung [the Qianlong emperor], from the former English Embassador, Lord Macartney, that is to say, to kneel upon one knee and to bow the head, repeating this obeisance the number of times deemed respectful. (Lord Amherst to the Emperor of China, August 1816, in Ellis, 1817, p. 497, Appendix 4(a))

Such a 'particular demonstration of veneration from English Embassadors' was shown only to Chinese emperors (Lord Amherst to the Emperor of China, August 1816, in Ellis, 1817, p. 497, Appendix 4(a)). 'I shall consider it the most fortunate circumstance of my life to be enabled thus to show my profound devotion to the most potent Emperor in the universe' (Lord Amherst to the Emperor of China, August 1816, in Ellis, 1817, p. 497, Appendix 4(a)). The letter concluded with a request that Amherst be received in an imperial audience to personally deliver the Prince Regent's letter. He hoped the emperor would 'graciously consider the necessity of my obeying the commands of my Sovereign' (Lord Amherst to the Emperor of China, August 1816, in Ellis, 1817, p. 497, Appendix 4(a)).

The meeting with Heshitai and Muketenge was due to be held at the Literary Hall situated in a small building in the middle of the city, some two miles from where the boats were moored (Morrison, 1820, p. 47).

Torrential rain was falling and the road was terrible. Amherst and the commissioners travelled in palanquins after refusing some 'primitive carts' drawn by mules. Chang-wei and Yin were fearful that this honour would come to the attention of the emperor given the close proximity of Tongzhou to Peking.

The Hall of Audience, the British noted, was 'a mean, dirty looking house, with the roof overgrown by grass' (Davis, 1841, p. 114). 'Crowds of mandarins' met the British in the courtyard where Amherst, Staunton, Ellis, Morrison and Jeffrey were conducted into a small hall to meet the imperial commissioners (Jeffrey Amherst, n.d., n.p.). The rest of the embassy had to wait either in the pouring rain or face the risk of 'suffocation in a crowded room of ill-savoured and importunate Chinese' (Abel, 1818, p. 96).

Heshitai, Muketenge, Sulenge, Guanghui and the six 'Lads of Mougden' were waiting to receive the British. Amherst was informed by Heshitai that he and Muketenge were sent to instruct Amherst on performing the ceremony and that he now wished to see Amherst perform it correctly. Amherst reiterated that he had never intimated that he would perform the ceremony and had been ordered by his sovereign to follow the same ceremony as Macartney that had been acceptable to the Qianlong emperor. Heshitai replied:

> What happened in the fifty-eighth year [1793] belonged to that year; the present is the affair of this Embassy, and the regulations of the celestial empire must be complied with; there is no alternative. (as quoted in Ellis, 1817, p. 148)

Amherst added he was confident that the Jiaqing emperor would accept the ceremony performed by Macartney before his father. Heshitai responded vehemently and informed Amherst:

> As in heaven there are not two Suns, so on earth there are not two Sovereigns. The Great Emperor is *Teen-tsze*, 'the Son of Heaven'; before him all Kings should bow down. (as quoted in Morrison, 1820, p. 48)

The commissioner then turned towards Morrison, who had earlier been seen reading a work by Confucius, and continued:

> You know it … [the ceremony] has existed from the highest antiquity, and cannot be altered. Without the performance of this ceremony, the Embassador and his tribute will be … rejected and cast out. (as quoted in Morrison, 1820, p. 48)

Heshitai, Morrison (1820, p. 48) noted, gestured with his hands in an outward motion as he pronounced the last word.

This belief, in the British view, was an 'absurd pretension'. Regardless of such absurdities, Amherst wrote, 'I did not think this a reasonable moment to assert the perfect equality of my own Sovereign' (Amherst to Canning, 28 February 1817, in BL IOR G/12/197 (Reel 2) F 258). Rather, he praised the emperor as 'one of the greatest Sovereigns in the world' and it was for this reason that the Prince Regent had sent him to compliment His Majesty (Morrison, 1820, p. 48). Heshitai, Morrison (1820, p. 48) reported, smiled at this moment, and gave Amherst a small purse from his belt. The Chinese Government, Heshitai responded, considered the British with greater esteem than other nations because they spoke Chinese and read Chinese books. This was demonstrated by the honour bestowed on the British of delegating mandarins of such high rank to escort the embassy (Staunton, 1824, p. 81). Nevertheless, the British must kowtow. Amherst remained calm and dignified. The British position on the ceremony was explained yet again. He told Heshitai that he had already written a letter informing the emperor of his position, but Guanghui now confessed that he had not dared pass it on to the authorities.

After 20 minutes, the British sensed the meeting was drawing to a close. Enquiring if another meeting was planned, Heshitai told Amherst that he never paid visits and that the present meeting was equivalent to one held before the emperor. He added, 'lips quivering with rage', that the embassy would be dismissed if Amherst did not comply with the proper ceremony (Ellis, 1817, p. 149). At this, Amherst placed his sealed letter to the emperor into Heshitai's hands and turned to leave the room. His actions, the British were pleased to note, had the desired effect. Heshitai was taken by surprise and the 'lofty tone assumed by the tartars was checked as their attention was arrested by the sight of the Emperor's name' (Amherst to Canning, 28 February 1817, in BL IOR G/12/197 (Reel 2) F 262). The British were shown a little more civility with the Chinese escorting them to the door. Amherst was confident that 'negotiation might be considered as still remaining open' despite all that had taken place at the meeting (Amherst to Canning, 28 February 1817, in BL IOR G/12/197 (Reel 2) F 262).

Heshitai's acceptance of Amherst's letter was encouraging, although doubt remained of it ever reaching the emperor. In the event that it did, the British hoped it might persuade the emperor to accept their position on the ceremony. If, on the other hand, permission to proceed to Peking was denied, the conciliatory tone of the letter was thought to at least ensure a civil return to Canton 'and allow us to part pretty good friends' (Davis, 1841, p. 116).

23 August: Amherst's Letter Dismissed

Chang-wei called on Morrison in the morning with news that Amherst's letter was being returned. The mandarins, Morrison was informed unofficially, had opened the letter on a pretext of legal protocol over the manner in which the emperor's address was written on the cover; while Amherst's title 'Ambassador' had been included, his name had not. Such an omission, the British were told, was defined under Chinese law as an anonymous address to the emperor and could never be delivered (Ellis, 1817, p. 150). The letter, Chang-wei admitted, was a 'very good one', but it could not be forwarded to the emperor (Staunton, 1824, p. 82). He enquired once again about Amherst's 'final sentiments respecting the ceremony', but Morrison told him that this would only be discussed after the ambassador had received a communication from the emperor (Staunton, 1824, p. 82).

Further strategic discussion took place among the British. As noted previously, Ellis, by this stage, was having serious doubts about the wisdom of refusing to kowtow. He wrote, 'The bearing of my mind, uninfluenced, and unaided by local knowledge, [began] to regret that the reception or dismissal of the Embassy should entirely turn upon the question of ceremony' (1817, p. 151). Regardless of Ellis's reservations, Staunton decided it was expedient to complain formally about the mandarins' refusal to send the letter to the emperor, pointing out that it was an official document and it would be the mandarins' responsibility should the embassy be expelled (Staunton, 1824, p. 82). A short statement on the exchange of presents 'and other arrangements' was planned in the hope of preserving good relations between Britain and China.

8. THE IMPERIAL BANQUET OF 13 AUGUST 1816 AND PROGRESS TO TONGZHOU

Negotiations at this time took place mainly between Chang-wei and Morrison, a fact that later drew criticism from one British commentator who pointed out, correctly, that Morrison was an interpreter and not vested with authority to conduct a diplomatic dialogue (Anonymous, 1818).[22] Chang-wei, meanwhile, made a second call later in the morning and handed Amherst's letter to Morrison, requesting that he add Amherst's name to the front cover. Heshitai had agreed to forward the letter to the emperor if this was done. Chang-wei again urged that Amherst comply with the ceremony but admitted privately to Morrison that he thought too much was being made of the issue. Morrison wrote:

> He did not seem at heart favourable to submission; he always called it 'their Tartar ceremony', and disclaimed the idea of it being Chinese. 'They were', he said, 'most tenacious of it; so much so, that old infirm people, who could no longer kneel or stand, were caused to raise themselves from the seat on which they sat, and fall down again with a bump, the number of times that others knocked their head'. (1820, p. 50)

Chang-wei explained that because the British had come to China in a voluntary capacity, it was the ceremony that was valued and not the presents. He added, significantly, that the Chinese could not make an exception for the Amherst Embassy as this would set a precedent for future diplomatic missions. Morrison replied that such ancient rules were no longer applicable to powerful nations—a good host would permit the British to observe their own ceremonies that, in turn, would serve to only increase the esteem of the emperor among foreign nations (Morrison, 1820, p. 51).

Chang-wei returned to the business at hand and suggested that Morrison change the wording in the letter from 'the King of England had cultivated amity with Keen-lung' to 'Keen-lung had treated the King of England amicably' (Morrison, 1820, p. 51). The British agreed to this change in the wording and also to the inclusion of Amherst's full name on the cover. Chang-wei next requested that the phrase referring to Amherst performing

---

22   *A delicate enquiry into the embassies to China and a legitimate conclusion* (1818) is an anonymously authored 30-page pamphlet published in response to the failure of both the Macartney and the Amherst embassies. Morrison was specifically criticised for not accurately relaying some of the mandarins' comments, thereby placing Amherst at 'his mercy'. The author argued that, had Amherst been properly informed, he would have immediately broken off negotiations and returned to England. Morrison's role was questioned: 'what right or authority [does] Mr. Morrison, [have] acting as interpreter?' (p. 2).

his ceremony on one knee be changed to 'two knees'. Morrison dismissed this proposal as childish because such a change would render Amherst's letter as useless (Morrison, 1820, p. 51).

Chang-wei now handed Amherst an extract from the imperial records that not only recorded that Macartney had performed the kowtow, but also that the Jiaqing emperor remembered his doing so. Ellis (1817) admitted, 'With this imperial assertion before us, however false or erroneous, it will be difficult, in the event of a renewed discussion, to press the precedent of Macartney' (p. 154).

Staunton, in a rare reference to Manning, described a private conversation Manning had held with an inferior mandarin who had visited him ostensibly on the pretence of grounds of civility. Manning soon realised his real purpose was to acquire some further intelligence on the intentions of the British regarding the ceremony. Manning listened to what the mandarin had to say before informing him of the reasonableness and the 'immutability' of the British decision (Staunton, 1824, p. 83).

24 August: An Attack on Staunton

Chang-wei visited Morrison early the next morning. Heshitai had refused to send Amherst's letter to the emperor and would only do so if the ambassador declared that he was prepared to perform the kowtow. The emperor, the British discovered, had seen the letter but had decided not to make a formal response, confirming instead that he had witnessed Macartney performing the kowtow before the Qianlong emperor. Amherst diplomatically suggested that because Macartney's ceremony was so similar to the kowtow that the Jiaqing emperor had probably mistaken one for the other. Further, he probably viewed the ceremony at some distance where his view was obstructed by the crowd and where Macartney's long robes would 'have the effect, in the eyes of His Imperial Majesty, of a salutation such as his Imperial Majesty required' (Amherst to Canning, 28 February 1817, in BL IOR G/12/197 (Reel 2) F 264).

Chang-wei paid yet another visit to Morrison in the afternoon. Amherst wrote, 'New matters [now] arose, such as to make every step taken by myself in conjunction with my colleagues the subject of serious reflection and deliberation' (Amherst to Canning, 28 February 1817, in BL IOR G/12/197 (Reel 2) F 264). The emperor, Morrison was informed, had received a report from Canton informing him of the presence of 'mere traders' in the embassy suite—the embassy, therefore, was not legitimate. Staunton specifically:

> Had been appointed … in consequence of his knowledge of the usages of the Celestial Empire; but [knowing these he] failed in his duty … as he did not inform the Embassador of them, and persuade him to comply with the ceremony. (Morrison, 1820, p. 52)

Amherst understood that the situation was now serious as British trade was being directly threatened by the Qing court. Chang-wei suggested that Staunton's time at Canton was limited unless he gave Amherst proper advice. Stories of Staunton's wealth had reached the court with reports of splendid apartments, fine aviaries, horses at Macao and that Staunton had bought his position in the embassy (Staunton, 1824, p. 85). Such information was symptomatic of the inaccuracies and shortcomings of Chinese intelligence as its facts were not true of Staunton but referred rather to another Englishman, Thomas Beale, a wealthy private trader and long-term resident of Canton who was also the Honorary Prussian Consul (Staunton, 1824, p. 89).[23] The British tried to stop this very 'improper harangue'. Amherst asserted that he resented such accusations, adding that the British Government and the Prince Regent could appoint whom it liked to its embassies. Amherst took the initiative and asked Chang-wei to provide a set date of departure if the embassy was not to be received. Chang-wei ignored the request and turned the conversation back to the topic of the ceremony, which was argued over again at some length with no resolution.

Chang-wei paid another call in the early evening. The Chinese wanted letters written to the captains of the British ships ordering them to stop at the next port they visited. Amherst agreed. The British suspected that the report regarding Staunton was written by the acting viceroy of Canton on the advice of a Portuguese judge whose 'badness of character' as well as 'his determined hostility to the English' were sufficiently known to justify the suspicion (Ellis, 1817, p. 161). Amherst and the commissioners refused to enter into any discussion on the matter, although Morrison privately informed Chang-wei that the report was of an absurd and scandalous nature (Staunton, 1824, p. 87).

---

23 Eastberg (2009) noted that Beale had made his fortune through the private opium trade. The association made by the Qing court of Staunton with Beale, Eastberg suggested, was a scheme engineered to associate the embassy with opium smuggling (p. 187).

The British read the personal attack on Staunton as a devious Chinese attempt to intimidate them and as a tactic designed to influence favourable outcomes. Staunton believed that such intelligence about him would never have been brought to the attention of the British had it not been for the impasse of the ceremony. He wrote:

> The Chinese know perfectly well that the rank and station of the East-India Company's senior servants at Canton is perfectly distinct from that of private merchants, and that the offices they hold are of a nature fully equivalent to those of their own magistrates, and this they have even specially acknowledged in a public edict … it is their object to seize upon any pretext to depreciate an Embassy they are threatening to dismiss; and thus their pretended objections to its constitution may be accounted for. (1824, p. 88)

25 August

Chang-wei informed the British that an imperial letter to the Prince Regent was in the process of being composed and it was planned to hand this to them in the event of the embassy's dismissal. Arrangements for the reception of the Prince Regent's presents also had to be organised. Chang-wei gave Morrison some hope that the presents might still be accepted and told him there were still some 'enlightened men in the emperor's councils' (Staunton, 1824, p. 90). Heshitai, however, was conspicuous by his absence and silence. The British had to sit tight and await events.

Chang-wei paid Morrison two more visits that day. News from his friends at the court reported that the emperor was 'extremely enraged' over the disappearance of the British ships. Further, the local viceroy had ordered the doubling of the guard around the British embassy to prevent Staunton from engaging in any communication with 'evilly disposed Chinese'. Staunton found this news 'rather mysterious and alarming', but as the British were due to receive a copy of the edict the next day, he reserved his opinion until he had read it (Staunton, 1824, p. 91). The presence of the Chinese troops, in Abel's opinion, kept the British in 'a state of uneasy feeling' but failed to alter Amherst's decision on the ceremony (Staunton, 1824, p. 97).

Meanwhile, reports of 'Two Russians, and a Frenchman in the service of Russia' hovering near the British quarters reached the British. They wore Chinese dress, spoke in French and were from the Russian College at Peking, but were prevented by the Chinese guards from getting close to the British (Staunton, 1824, p. 83). On the first day, the Frenchman managed to strike up a conversation with 'Vincent, the Negro drummer of the band' (Staunton, 1824, p. 83). He told Vincent that he had been in China for nine years and wished to talk with Amherst, but the British thought it best not to encourage any communication with him or the other missionaries (Ellis, 1817, p. 162). The motive for the visit was not known. The fact that Chinese troops prevented them from contact with the British suggested that they had not been sent by the court. On the other hand, it may have been a genuine attempt to engage the British for the latest news on international events.

26 August: Amherst is Confronted with a 'Severe Test'

Reports from the acting viceroy of Canton and the viceroy of Peking reached the British in the morning. The Canton report was a public version and contained none of the 'disparaging insinuations' mentioned by Chang-wei. On the contrary, Staunton wrote that it was favourable both to himself and to the embassy (1824, p. 92). But the report from the viceroy of Peking referred specifically to Staunton as 'an object of suspicion' as well as 'a person who certainly has the power, and *may* have the will, of combining with the natives against the government' (as quoted in Staunton, 1824, p. 92). Staunton attributed the suspicion and hostility shown towards him to the unsettled political state of northern China:

> The province in which we are in, has been lately in a state of open rebellion … and estimating the invariable jealousy and suspicion, which, in the most favourable and quiet times, the Chinese look upon foreigners, especially the English, and most of all, those who are acquainted with their language, and are therefore, supposed to have the means of detecting the real circumstances of the country;—it may perhaps be pronounced that there is nothing very extraordinary in the Pekin viceroy's edict. (1824, p. 92)

The fact that the British were permitted to read the document suggested an alternative interpretation—a deliberate Chinese attempt at intimidation. Staunton thought that 'the rejection of the Embassy [was] no longer the worst of the contingencies which may be apprehended' (1824, p. 93). Rather, there was a serious possibility that Staunton could be arrested. Staunton warned Amherst that the embassy now faced a 'severe test' (p. 93). Amherst, acknowledging Staunton's advice, wrote Heshitai a letter requesting specific notification as to whether or not the emperor intended to admit the embassy or expel it (p. 93).

Davis and Hayne delivered Amherst's letter to Heshitai's quarters where they handed it to Chang-wei. Amherst accepted an invitation to visit Heshitai the following day where a marked change in the commissioner's attitude towards the embassy was noted. Bullying had obviously not worked and Staunton thought the time had come for the British to 'decide finally upon the question of submission or resistance' (p. 94).

Amherst's Initial Thoughts on Performing the Kowtow

Some of the British read Heshitai's conciliatory gesture as an encouraging sign. The idea of performing the Chinese ceremony was even considered if the court gave a guarantee on the opening of negotiations on the embassy's goals. Amherst and Ellis were 'strongly against … closing the door to negotiation while anything like a hope remained of any of the objects of the Embassy being attained by concession' (Staunton, 1824, p. 94). Compliance, in their view, was 'preferable to damaging British interests at Canton by allowing the mission to fail' (Staunton as quoted in Tuck, 2000, p. xxxi). Further, Amherst, it appears, was following Lamiot's advice to delay as long as possible in giving into Chinese demands.[24] Staunton, however, stood firm on the decision not to kowtow, arguing that its performance would represent Britain's submission to the Jiaqing emperor, which would irrevocably threaten British honour and independence at Canton. He realised that being granted a mere audience with the emperor would serve no purpose and would result in only a few ceremonial pleasantries, at best, with no scope for serious negotiation

---

24 Lamiot's advice, as noted in Chapter 6 of this study, was referenced in Amherst's 'Notes on policy to be pursued by the British Embassy to China' (BL MSS EUR F 140/36).

on British goals. Staunton's stand on the kowtow question, however, provides the evidence for Tuck (2000) and other historians to blame him specifically for the failure of the Amherst Embassy.

27 August: Meeting with Heshitai

The conference between the imperial commissioner and Amherst held on 27 August 1816 had important repercussions for the future conduct of the embassy. Heshitai had concluded that Amherst, 'might be induced by certain concessions' to kowtow (Ellis, 1817, p. 195). The British were received with much civility (p. 169). Heshitai, Muketenge, Sulenge and Guanghui rose to greet the British when they entered the inner court. The British were conducted to their chairs, which were placed on the left side of the courtyard. Heshitai took the upper seat, while Amherst sat in the chair on the right. Such an arrangement, Staunton noted, placed Amherst opposite Sulenge, while Morrison was seated so far down the line that communicating with him was impossible. Accordingly, Heshitai called for another chair for Morrison to be placed alongside Amherst. All the other mandarins, including Guanghui, stood.

Heshitai began the conference with the customary polite questions enquiring how far the embassy had travelled and the distance between Britain and China. He then turned to the topic of the ceremony and wanted to make sure that Chang-wei had adequately explained all its details. The emperor was insistent, Heshitai explained, that Macartney had kowtowed to his father and would accept no other form of ceremony (Amherst to Canning, 28 February 1817, in BL IOR G/12/197 (Reel 2) F 265). Although Heshitai spoke in a more conciliatory tone, Staunton thought his displeasure was never far from the surface. The exalted rank of the emperor, Heshitai maintained, outranked the status of a king. Amherst replied that his allegiance was to his own sovereign. Heshitai told Morrison, 'take care how you persist, lest you expose your king himself to the emperor's displeasure' (as quoted in Staunton, 1824, p. 96). Staunton (1824) commented that Morrison 'very properly checked the duke immediately, by saying that he did not *dare* to interpret to the Ambassador such a remark' (p. 96). Morrison's decision not to inform Amherst of this fact once again incited later British criticism in a review of the embassy (Anonymous, 1818, p. 4).

Heshitai, attempting to 'deflect tensions', turned his attention to Jeffrey and called the boy to his chair. Jeffrey wrote that he 'condescendingly … [gave] me with his own hands four purses and his fan upon which he wrote some Chinese characters' (Jeffrey Amherst, n.d., n.p.). Davis was sceptical of the mandarin's kindness and thought it was proof of 'the low estimate which the Chinese generally entertain of European intellects and feelings, to suppose for a moment that they could be influenced in such a way' (Davis, 1841, p. 137).

The British took the opportunity to raise some of their objectives with Heshitai, specifically, the feasibility of opening consular representation in Peking, thereby enabling direct communication between the British merchants at Canton with one of the tribunals of the emperor's court. The emperor, Staunton pointed out, had always 'professed to extend his regard and protections to foreigners' (1824, p. 97). The British desired only those rights accorded to the 'meanest of the emperor's own subjects' who had the right to appeal through tribunals up to the highest authority to the emperor himself (p. 97). Heshitai thought this was a reasonable request and assured the British that he would be their 'friend and advocate' on this or on any other issue as long as they complied with the ceremony: 'Comply with the Tartar ceremony, and I am your friend at Pekin' (as quoted in Ellis, 1817, p. 170). But, he added, he could not anticipate the emperor's response to British demands:

> It might as well be asked of him, whether he thought it would rain or thunder to-morrow. The ways of the Son of Heaven were, like those of Heaven itself, inscrutable. (as quoted in Morrison, 1820, p. 54)

Testament to what was at stake, Amherst told Heshitai that he would reconsider his decision on the ceremony and would give a final answer in the afternoon.

The Final British Decision on the Kowtow

The British discussed the expediency of complying with the ceremony on return to their compound. Amherst and Ellis thought a performance of the ceremony in the emperor's presence was expedient if there was a possibility of the goals of the embassy being discussed. Staunton's (1824) memoirs explained their attitude in the context of the 'considerable sacrifice of private and personal feeling, to what they conceived to be the line of their public duty' (p. 99). Their approach, according to Staunton, was the result both of Heshitai's offer of support on one hand, and recent attempts to intimidate him personally and harm British commercial interests at Canton on the other (p. 100).

Amherst thought that his position was more complicated than it had appeared at the start of his embassy. Staunton's initial briefing on the kowtow, given on board the ships before the embassy landed in northern China, did not reflect on the possibility of either harm to the Company and trade at Canton, or on the contingency of a personal attack on Staunton as the Company's most senior executive. Amherst concluded:

> Such a result would indeed have produced the very mischief against which I have been specially cautioned. Not only former grievances would not have been removed, but new misunderstandings would have arisen, and new evils would have been incurred. (Amherst to Canning, 28 February 1817, in BL IOR G/12/197 (Reel 2) F 268)

Amherst now asked Staunton if he had changed his mind on the potential risks to the Canton trade if he went ahead and kowtowed before the emperor. Staunton realised that the responsibility for the future of the embassy now fell to him and decided to consult with the other Company members of the embassy from Canton. He wrote:

> Four of the five gentlemen who accompanied me had resided nine or ten years in China, and possessed such acknowledged talents, judgment, and local experience, as must necessarily entitle their opinions to considerable weight; and the fifth, Mr. Davis, though a young servant of the company, had displayed talents, and evinced a zeal in his application to the study of the language, which entitled his opinions to an attention beyond his years. (1824, p. 102)

Toone, Davis and Pearson were strongly against complying with the ceremony. Morrison and Manning had their reservations.[25] Morrison was strongly against the kowtow in principle, but thought on this occasion that Company interests might justify compliance (Ellis, 1817, p. 172,

---

25   Manning, as noted in Chapter 4 (fn. 6), had performed the ceremony of kowtow before the 'Grand Lama' (who was seven years of age) at Lhasa during his visit to Tibet in 1811 (Markham, 1876, p. 265). A distinction needs to be made here between Manning, as a private individual travelling in a non-official capacity, and Amherst, who was an ambassador appointed by the British sovereign.

note). On the conclusion of the consultations, Amherst decided to accept Staunton's advice and that of his colleagues and refuse to perform the prostration ceremony. He was swayed by Staunton's argument that to kowtow would not only represent a humiliating back down from the British position but would also 'encourage the local government at Canton to assume a tone of official superiority fatal to the independence of the trade' (Amherst to Canning, 28 February 1817, in BL IOR G/12/197 (Reel 2) F 270). Amherst wrote a note immediately to the mandarins informing them of his final decision not to kowtow. The historian Tuck (2000) has noted that, by this time, Heshitai had committed himself to 'ensuring the success of the Embassy' and had sent a misleading report to the emperor on 28 August that the embassy, 'despite not having rehearsed the Kotow, would certainly perform the full ceremonial at the imperial audience' (p. xxxi).[26]

Amherst, obviously unaware of Heshitai's report, wrote in his official report, 'From this time, I am at a loss to account for the proceedings of the Chinese Authorities' (Amherst to Canning, 28 February 1817, in BL IOR G/12/197 (Reel 2) F 270). Heshitai visited Amherst immediately on receipt of his note. Rather than bringing news that the embassy was to be expelled, he told Amherst that the emperor had ordered the embassy to pack up immediately in preparation for leaving for Yuanmingyuan the next day. Amherst checked to make sure that it was understood he would not be performing the kowtow. Guanghui, according to Morrison (1820), seemed to say 'yes' and bowed his head, which the British understood as affirming, 'You are to be received according to the forms you propose' (p. 54). Guanghui, according to Ellis (1817), replied:

> Both parties in the discussion had done their duty, but that now the affair was settled, and [the British] might be perfectly easy; the ceremony would not be again mentioned, and that [they] might rely upon the Emperor's kindness, whose heart was truly liberal and expanded. (p. 173)

---

26 Tuck's (2000) conclusion is puzzling as Heshitai had qualified his expression of support and had made it clear that he could not guarantee the attainment of any of the embassy's objectives. Staunton later wrote that Heshitai's assurances of support were quickly dismissed as unreliable and, after closer scrutiny, were not a sufficient basis on which to comply with the kowtow ceremony (see Minute of Sir George Thomas Staunton, 18 January 1817, in Morse, 1926/1966, vol. 3, pp. 303–304).

This was a pivotal discussion for the outcome of the embassy for it firmly established in Amherst's mind what was expected of him at any forthcoming imperial reception. He told Canning, 'My invitation to the Tartar Court had been given upon an express understanding that I should not be called upon for the performance of prostration' (Amherst to Canning, 3 March 1817, in BL IOR G/12/197 (Reel 2) F 280).

The British had another surprise. Chang-wei and Yin brought disturbing news that Guanghui and Sulenge were currently being investigated over the conduct of the embassy. The emperor had found them responsible for the expenses incurred by permitting the embassy to leave Tianjin and Guanghui had been stripped of his position in the Salt Department (Ellis, 1817, p. 174). Chang-wei added that further fatal consequences might befall Guanghui if the embassy did not arrive at Peking the following day.

Amherst refused to be hurried. His priority was to make a very dignified entrance at the Chinese capital and he was not prepared to leave Tongzhou until 'every thing connected with the public appearance of the Embassy had been dispatched to Pekin' (Ellis, 1817, p. 174).

So ended a couple of weeks of intense and stressful negotiations for both parties. Not only had Amherst been placed under increasing pressure to comply with Qing tributary diplomatic protocol, but the mandarins faced considerable pressure to ensure that the emperor's instructions were carried out. The negotiations had gone into overdrive at the beginning of the official banquet on 13 August 1816 when Amherst was confronted with a concealed diplomatic 'trip-wire' to establish if he was prepared to perform the kowtow. Amherst, to his credit, had recognised the trap immediately on entering the banquet hall as a result of his pre-departure research on the Golovkin Embassy of 1806, involving a table handsomely dressed in yellow silk with embroidered dragons said to represent the presence of the emperor.

In retrospect, Amherst had been variously pressured and threatened in relation to Staunton, as well as cajoled and induced to kowtow if he wished to secure an audience with the Jiaqing emperor and avoid the immediate expulsion of his embassy. The British had landed some counter-punches of their own by demanding their performance of the kowtow be reciprocated by a mandarin of equivalent rank to Amherst before a portrait of the Prince Regent, which was rejected by the Chinese. The departure of the

British ships on a reconnaissance mission to Korea and the Ryukyu Islands immediately after landing the party at Dagu had infuriated the emperor and meant that the Chinese Government was responsible for the cost and safety of the embassy's passage overland to Canton.

Admittedly, concessions and allowances had been made by both sides in an effort to keep the embassy on schedule for an audience with the emperor before his departure for Jehol. The dispatch of increasingly more senior mandarins by the Qing court as the embassy advanced closer to Peking indicated the court's determination to achieve a favourable outcome to the impasse over the kowtow. The British became puzzled when, on a number of occasions, it appeared as though they were to be expelled, only to have the order rescinded at the last minute. Thus, the final instruction in late August to proceed from Tongzhou to Peking caught the British by surprise and it was with not a little foreboding that they set off for Yuanmingyuan.

9

To Yuanmingyuan, Reception and Dismissal

The final leg of the Amherst Embassy's slow, uncomfortable and often hazardous journey to the Summer Palace of Yuanmingyuan ended badly. The embassy's reception, its expulsion and the immediate aftermath of its dismissal on its return journey to Tongzhou had a profound effect on British perceptions of the Qing court, confirming the futility of any future diplomatic overtures to achieve British objectives in China. The diplomatic encounter underlined the political and cultural differences between an increasingly powerful British national state whose diplomatic practice was based on notions of equality, free advocacy, negotiation and international law, and those of an ancient civilisation based on empire, Confucian values, obedience and despotic rule. Qing values and codes of behaviour were reflected in the actions and attitudes of high-ranking mandarins who, in British terms, represented the elite of courtly and civil society. Amherst himself was a courtier at St James's whose familiarity with British and European courts would have raised expectations of at least a gracious reception at Yuanmingyuan. His experience, however, exposed the critical difference between the status of an ambassador within the Westphalian system of diplomacy and that in the Qing court where an ambassador was received as a mere messenger sent to deliver their sovereign's letter and bear their presents or tribute to the emperor.

Figure 8: Portrait of the Jiaqing emperor (r. 1796–1820).
Source: Wikipedia Commons.

28 August: Preparations for Leaving Tongzhou and the Journey to Peking

The sudden and unexpected summons for the embassy to pack up and proceed to Peking engaged the British and the Chinese in immediate preparations for the 12-mile journey to the Summer Palace. Chinese packers worked throughout the night unloading the British presents for the emperor. Chang-wei's arrival the following morning with instructions for the embassy to hurry its preparations in order to leave as soon as possible because the emperor was waiting only added to the 'bustle and confusion'. Amherst's splendid carriage was unpacked and the coachman took great care to prepare it for the trip to the imperial capital, but Morrison (1820) thought that Bengal palanquins would have been better suited to the terrible roads and advised they be used in any future embassy to Peking (p. 55). Chinese wagons, pulled by teams of five horses, carried the embassy's luggage, while individual members of the embassy travelled in small carts drawn by mules. These, the British said, were 'bone breaking', while Abel (1818) complained that his horse was a 'miserable looking animal … having all his bony points extremely prominent' (p. 98). Davis and two British officers of the guard had planned to ride to Peking, but they too were disappointed with the very inferior horses provided. Further, Chinese saddles were most uncomfortable and the stirrups were far too short (p. 98). Similarly, Amherst's London coachman was mortified at the appearance of the four mules assigned to pull the ambassador's magnificent barouche. The coachman, according to Davis (1841):

> Having prepared the carriage … with as much care and pains as for a birthday at St. James's … gave an 'exclamation of despair' on first seeing the four mules provided to draw the carriage: 'Lord, sir, these *cats* will never do!' 'But they *must* do!' was the reply, for nothing better existed in the whole empire. The collars of the English harness hung down like mandarin necklaces, and the whole of the caparison sat like a loose gown. (p. 143, emphasis in original)

Jeffrey described the four mules as 'poor wretches [who] made a sorry figure, when caparisoned with the magnificent English harness … which was made for horses sixteen hands high' (Jeffrey Amherst, n.d., n.p.).

Other circumstances held up the embassy's departure including the arrangements for the transportation of two sick embassy personnel. The Chinese had provided two small wicker baskets carried by porters for their use, but these were considered as most unsuitable and Amherst accordingly allocated two of the palanquins (Staunton, 1824, p. 110). The sick men were also given large doses of opium to ease their pain.

The Embassy Sets Off for Peking

The embassy eventually left Tongzhou at four o'clock in the afternoon. Amherst, Ellis, Staunton and Jeffrey led the procession travelling in the barouche 'drawn by four stout mules, the coachman driving on the box, and the postilion riding on one of the leaders' (Staunton, 1824, p. 110). Four palanquins followed, including the two with the sick men. Next in line were Abel, Somerset and Lieutenant Cooke on horseback followed by 'one-man' carts carrying the rest of the embassy personnel. Bringing up the rear were the wagons carrying the band, servants, marines and baggage. Surrounding the procession were the 'mandarins and soldiers in chairs and carts, on horseback and on foot' (Abel, 1818, p. 99).

Progress was at a snail's pace. After skirting the city of Tongzhou, the procession eventually reached the paved granite road that led to Peking. While the road looked impressive, deep ruts between the large blocks of stone marred its surface and presented a danger to the barouche's wheels. Despite a few jolts, Jeffrey pointed out, the passengers travelling in the barouche were more comfortable than the occupants of the covered Chinese carts who were 'jumbled' into 'Mummies' and whose journey was 'quite intolerable' (Jeffrey Amherst, n.d., n.p.; see also Staunton, 1824, p. 111).

The embassy had travelled only five miles before it grew dark. 'It was evident', Amherst wrote, 'that altho' no reason was alleged for its' [sic] necessity, that we were to be exposed to the inconvenience of a night journey' (Amherst to Canning, 8 March 1817, in BL IOR G/12/197 (Reel 2) F 285). Abel's horse was so uncomfortable that he decided to walk but soon changed his mind when he was surrounded immediately by 'a crowd of Chinese soldiers and porters … and peasants who had assembled from the neighbourhood' (Abel, 1818, p. 100). He was rescued from the crowd's attention with the appearance of Vincent, the black drummer, who diverted their curiosity:

> This man, of a fine figure, six feet in height, of a jet black complexion, was an object of irresistible curiosity with the Chinese. Wherever he went, crowds followed, and left every other person of the Embassy to gaze upon him. To feel his hands, and to compare their colour with that of their own; to endeavour by signs to ascertain from what part of the world he came, was their frequent and eager employment. We always thought ourselves fortunate in our excursions when he had preceded us, and carried off the mob. (p. 100)

Walking in the dark, however, was difficult and after a couple of severe falls caused by holes in the road, Abel took refuge in the cart of a friend.

The procession came to a halt at an inn, described as a dilapidated building, at nine o'clock at night where the British were greeted by Guanghui and Sulenge and invited to dine. Amherst described the meal as 'a disgusting repast where a scramble was … made for such food as extreme hunger only would have rendered palatable' (Amherst to Canning, 8 March 1817, in BL IOR G/12/197 (Reel 2) F 286). Abel (1818) wrote of 'fowls served up whole, but without any instruments to carve them. We were consequently obliged, much to the amusement of the bye-standers, to separate the limbs with our fingers' (p. 100). Morrison (1820) added that the food was 'an attempt at English cookery, [but] it was neither English nor Chinese' (p. 56). Hayne (n.d., vol. 2) was less diplomatic and complained of an absence of knives and forks and chopsticks. No wines were provided and the only thing to drink was some water in a bucket. The table was covered with some 'nasty trash that none of us could touch [where] some hard boiled eggs and some of their bread were the only eatables' (p. 82(a)). He added:

> Nothing but L.A.'s [Lord Amherst's] extraordinary good nature & his natural incapability of doing a rude, offensive thing to another, would have induced him to attribute this reception to indifference on the part of Su & Quang [Sulenge and Guanghui] who had doubtless taken excellent care of themselves in a room behind, whilst we were in a place little better than a stable yard. (p. 83)

Rumours that the emperor was planning to receive Amherst the following day were circulating at the time of the dinner but were dismissed by the British as 'so strange and improbable … [we considered it] merely as a story invented at the moment, for the purpose of urging us upon our journey' (Staunton, 1824, p. 112). Chang-wei informed Amherst that their late arrival at Peking meant the city gates would be closed but the governor was waiting to conduct the embassy through the city to the Summer Palace of Yuanmingyuan and orders had been given to 'illuminate the city as [the Embassy] passed through' (Jeffrey Amherst, n.d., n.p.).

After an hour's rest, the embassy entourage took to the road once more. Several carts had been moved in the interim and the Englishmen had trouble relocating them. Many 'wandered [in vain] about for some time in the dark, without receiving any assistance … from the numerous Chinese … who only grinned on witnessing [our] dilemma' (Abel, 1818, p. 101). Staunton faced the rest of the journey with some trepidation. He wrote:

> Although to travel on during the whole of a dark night, on a strange and bad road, drawn by mules, never before harnessed to an English carriage, was not in itself a very agreeable or promising arrangement, it certainly seemed preferable to any longer stay at the dismal abode at which we had halted … we were almost as anxious as our Chinese conductors … to reach the termination of our journey. (1824, p. 113)

The Embassy Enters the Outskirts of Peking

British preconceived expectations of entering the Chinese capital in a grand style befitting the power and grandeur of the British sovereign were soon dashed. The embassy arrived at Peking's outer suburbs at 11 o'clock at night in darkness and in disarray, reaching the eastern gate an hour later. The governor was not there to greet them, but an immense though orderly crowd had gathered and Abel was worried about driving over people (Hayne, n.d., vol. 2, p. 85; Abel, 1818, p. 102). Some people held little red paper lanterns suspended on sticks in front of them, hoping to catch a glimpse of the Englishmen and were most impolite. Hayne (n.d., vol. 2) complained, 'If any of us spoke they endeavoured to repeat what we said which produced a loud laugh' (p. 85). Instead of entering the gate, the embassy was turned sharply to the right and proceeded northward to skirt the city wall on an outside track described by Amherst as 'a scarcely passable road between the wall and the ditch' (Amherst to Canning, 8 March 1817, in BL IOR G/12/197 (Reel 2) F 286). Jeffrey expressed British perplexity at the detour: 'What could be the motive of old Chong [Chang-wei], in inventing such a bouncing falsehood, I don't know'. He complained that the road:

> became worse and worse and we were in danger every moment of being upset. We were frequently obliged to get out of the carriage in order to lighten and enable the Chinese to lift [the carriage] out of the holes. (Jeffrey Amherst, n.d., n.p.)

An accident was waiting to happen. Lieutenant Cooke rode alongside Amherst's barouche to warn of impending dangers and Amherst and the commissioners had to vacate their carriage every five or 10 minutes. Staunton (1824) wrote:

> Our chief danger arose from the ignorance or inattention of our Chinese guides, who, not adverting to the precautions necessary with a carriage so differently constructed from theirs, often suffered us to quit the road, and then called upon us to attempt to regain it across steep banks, which were dangerous or impracticable. (p. 115)

The men travelling in the carts also suffered from the 'convulsive throes [of such a] primitive machine, without springs, on the rutted granite road' (Davis, 1841, p. 148).

The western road to Yuanmingyuan was 'broad, soft, and unpaved', but recent heavy rain had resulted in flooding that slowed the procession and caused vehicles to become bogged (Staunton, 1824, p. 115). Amherst and his commissioners had to leave their carriage on several occasions and wait on the side of the road while their carriage was pushed through the mud. He and his companions were tired and filthy while the mules pulling the carriage were exhausted.

29 August: Arrival at Yuanmingyuan

Yuanmingyuan came into view as dawn broke on the morning of 29 August 1816. The road improved and the weather had cleared. A scene of ornamental parks and gardens indicated the procession had arrived at the grounds of the Summer Palace. Abel (1818) wrote that, 'All the descriptions which I had ever read of the paradisiacal delight of Chinese Gardens occurred to my imagination' (p. 103).

The embassy came to a halt at the village of Haidian where accommodation had been arranged at a fine property owned by Sungyun, the viceroy previously at Canton and Macartney's 'amiable friend' who was currently 'absent in Western Tartary' (Morrison, 1820, p. 59). Much to their dismay, however, Amherst and the commissioners were not permitted to alight but were informed they were proceeding directly to the palace at Yuanmingyuan where the emperor was waiting to receive them. The rest of the embassy, waiting at Haidian, became concerned over Amherst's absence. Hayne (n.d., vol. 2) wrote:

> I waited some little time with Yin, & he then sent a man back again with me to our quarters. I rushed in to hunt for L. A. [Amherst] and all the party … Toone … and one or two of the servants arrived, but they knew nothing of L. A. … we began to fear some accident had happened, knowing, as I did, that he was only a quarter of a mile before I quitted him. (pp. 86–87)

Amherst's carriage came to a halt at five o'clock in the morning before a 'very large building in the best Chinese taste, seated in the middle of a park' (Staunton, 1824, p. 116). A large crowd of mandarins in full ceremonial dress surrounded the carriage where Sulenge 'begged' Amherst and the commissioners to alight (Staunton, 1824, p. 116). The British were astonished that they had not been taken straight to their quarters. Staunton (1824) wrote:

> Until now, it certainly never occurred to us, that the Chinese could think of taking us, after such an anxious, fatiguing, and sleepless night, spent in the carriage and on the road, to any other place than our intended lodgings; or that they would be guilty of such a breach of hospitality, and even common decency, as to attempt to call our attention to any kind of business until we had had some repose. (p. 117)

Sulenge was informed that Amherst wished to go straight to his apartment as he was tired and needed to rest, but this was not possible. Heshitai was waiting inside and wished to confer with Amherst briefly, after which, he would be free to retire to his accommodation. But for now, Amherst had to leave his carriage. He had no other option. Chinese insistence that Amherst follow the mandarins into the audience hall aroused British suspicion that 'the Chinese intended some treachery towards us' and that the date of reception planned for the following day was due to take place immediately (Jeffrey Amherst, n.d., n.p.). The British were conducted into a small room, 12 feet long and 7 feet wide, described by Amherst as 'a mean and dirty dwelling belonging to the Palace' (Amherst to Canning, 8 March 1817, in BL IOR G/12/197 (Reel 2) F 287).[1]

Amherst, accompanied by Staunton, Ellis, Morrison, Jeffrey and Lieutenant Cook who had escorted the carriage, took their seats on a hard bench covered in white felt. Crowds of princes and mandarins pushed towards them. Amherst complained of their 'rude and overwhelming curiosity' and of the 'wretched out-house' in which they were sitting (Amherst to Canning, 8 March 1817, in BL IOR G/12/197 (Reel 2) F 289). Ellis (1817, p. 178) referred to their 'brutal curiosity' treating the British more as 'wild beasts' rather than as 'mere strangers of the same species as themselves'. Jeffrey confirmed Ellis's view and described the mandarins:

> who from their badges must have been of high rank, and who came to gratify their curiosity by having a good stare at the monsters such they took us to be. (Jeffrey Amherst, n.d., n.p.)

---

1 Platt (2018) gave a different impression of the reception. He wrote of Amherst being received 'into a small, elegant waiting chamber with windows on four sides, about seven by twelve feet' (p. 175). This misquotes Abel (1818) who wrote that the party was 'pushed into a room, which, if a fair specimen of other parts, might induce the supposition that His Chinese Majesty was king of the beggars' (p. 104).

It became apparent that the British arrival at the palace was a deliberate Chinese strategy aimed to coincide with the assigned time set for an imperial audience. Staunton found the exposure of the British embassy in all its dishevelled appearance before the Chinese court 'mortifying', while Amherst wrote of the difference between expectation and the reality of his arrival at Yuanmingyuan:

> Instead therefore of the brilliant appearance which from its numbers and equipment the Embassy was calculated to make, it was intended to bring into the emperor's presence four persons only, fatigued and exhausted from the journey, in their travelling dress, and … without attendants of any description. I was, besides, without my credential letters, and was consequently unable to present myself in my public character. I therefore determined if possible to avoid the intended interview. (Amherst to Canning, 8 March 1817, in BL IOR G/12/197 (Reel 2) F 288)

Matters grew worse when Chang-wei arrived and informed Amherst that the emperor had changed the day of their audience to that morning. Amherst was told to prepare himself to meet Heshitai who was waiting to usher him along with Staunton, Ellis and Morrison into the emperor's presence. Amherst was outraged. He informed Chang-wei that he was deeply distressed, highly indignant and most surprised at the way the British had been treated and deceived. It was absurd to even contemplate seeing the emperor at this time. Besides, he did not have the king's letter and the state of his appearance would be not only disrespectful to the emperor but 'inconsistent with the dignity of the Embassy' (Staunton, 1824, p. 119). Amherst, Jeffrey added, told Chang-wei that the audience had always been arranged for the following day and he was 'not in the least prepared to appear in the emperor's presence until that time' (Jeffrey Amherst, n.d., n.p.).

Chang-wei informed Amherst that it had never been their intention to deceive the British. Instructions to conduct the embassy directly to Yuanmingyuan had been received only on the road as the embassy was proceeding to Peking. But the emperor had given his orders and it was too late to remonstrate.

Following Amherst's insistence that the emperor be informed that he was tired and ill from the journey and, accordingly, was totally unprepared for the honour of an audience, he also wished it to be made known that he had been 'distinctly informed that the Emperor had consented to postpone [his] audience to the following day' (Amherst to Canning, 8 March 1817, in BL IOR G/12/197 (Reel 2) F 288). For the moment, the British were told, the emperor only desired to meet the ambassador and had no intention of conducting any business (Ellis, 1817, p. 178).

Heshitai next invited the British to follow him to his apartment to discuss matters. Amherst replied that he was too unwell to leave his seat and wished to postpone any discussions until the following day. Heshitai, on being joined by Muketenge, urged Amherst in a 'very pressing and … indecorous manner for some minutes' to go with him to prepare for a meeting with the emperor. Heshitai, according to Staunton, said that '*your own ceremony* is all that will be required' (Staunton, 1824, p. 121, emphasis in original). Amherst was then asked if he had the Prince Regent's letter for the emperor in his possession (Morrison, 1820, p. 57).

Amherst pointed out his distress that the 'greater part of his suite had been separated from him' and that it was impossible to appear before the emperor at this time (Jeffrey Amherst, n.d., n.p.). Heshitai, according to Jeffrey, departed with Amherst's message but returned soon afterwards—the emperor was insisting on an immediate audience. There followed, Ellis (1817) wrote, 'a scene I believe, unparalleled in the history of diplomacy' (p. 177). Heshitai, described by Morrison (1820, p. 57) as anxious with 'perspiration' on his face, reached down and grabbed Amherst's arm 'with the seeming intention of raising him from his seat, and leading him away' (Staunton, 1824, p. 121). Amherst, Jeffrey wrote, immediately 'released himself from [Heshitai's] grasp by shaking him off' (Jeffrey Amherst, n.d., n.p.). This, according to Staunton, was not easy as Heshitai was a strong man of 36 years in contrast to the 'old and infirm' mandarins that the British normally dealt with. Amherst read the act as an attempt 'of transporting me thither [before the emperor] even without my consent' (Amherst to Canning, 8 March 1817, in BL IOR G/12/197 (Reel 2) F 289). He added, 'I therefore shook him off, and prepared, as far as I could, to resist force by force; but I was glad to find that he desisted from further violence' (Amherst to Canning, 8 March 1817, in BL IOR G/12/197 (Reel 2) F 289). Things became heated as the crowd of mandarins pushed forward and Lieutenant Cooke had to be cautioned by Amherst not to draw his sword (Staunton, 1824, p. 120). Staunton attributed the crowd's rude and uncivil behaviour to the fact that the mandarins and princes present were 'Tartars'. He added:

> I doubt whether any assembly of the superior class, or indeed any class, of Chinese, would have shown themselves so totally regardless, not merely of the considerations of courtesy, but even of the common feelings of humanity. (1824, p. 121)

The British interpreted Heshitai's invitation to adjourn to his apartment as a trick to remove Amherst to an isolated place inside the palace where further resistance over the kowtow would have been difficult. The query about the Prince Regent's letter suggested that this was no casual encounter. Once in the emperor's presence, it was felt, Amherst would have no alternative but to kowtow. Jeffrey recalled:

> This was a very critical moment for us. The Chinese from their numbers might have forced us to perform any ceremony they chose, and separated as we were from the greater part of the Embassy, might have inflicted any punishment on us, without our being able to offer any resistance. (Jeffrey Amherst, n.d., n.p.)

Other stressful incidents occurred while Heshitai was running back and forth to the emperor. Staunton was approached by an old prince who remembered him from the time of the Macartney Embassy, but Staunton 'very prudently avoided any intercourse with him' (Ellis, 1817, p. 180). Another prince, with a long silver beard, came up to the British and 'uttered the words *Fa-lang-ke*'. Morrison told him, 'We are not French but English' (Morrison, 1820, p. 58). Some princes, distinguishable by round embroidered cloth badges on their robes, came into the room to stare rudely at the British and then left (p. 58).

Heshitai soon returned with a message from the emperor informing the British that he would see them the next day. In the meantime, it was arranged for the emperor's physician to call on Amherst at his quarters. Heshitai's manner towards the British became more civil. Amherst wrote that he:

> not only acquiesced in my manifest determination to go … to my own residence, but even assisted me … by seizing a whip from one of the soldiers … dispersing a crowd of Mandarins in their court dress and with buttons of elevated rank, who received this chastisement as if it were a discipline to which they were not altogether unaccustomed. (Amherst to Canning, 8 March 1817, in BL IOR G/12/197 (Reel 2) F 290)

Heshitai's energetic actions, Morrison (1820) thought, were due to his 'showing off his anxiety and zeal' before the emperor who was most likely watching the scene from a palace window. Alternatively, Heshitai was venting his anger on the crowd (p. 58). Jeffrey agreed, describing Heshitai as being in a state of 'a great rage' (Jeffrey Amherst, n.d., n.p.). When Amherst and his party entered the barouche, Heshitai got into his chair and departed, never to be seen again by the British. The British were conducted immediately to their quarters, situated a mile and a half away, where they arrived at half past seven in the morning.

29 August 1816: The Day of Dismissal from the Qing Court

The villa assigned to the British consisted of several buildings situated around three courtyards decorated with shrubs and flowers. Staunton thought the accommodation was not as grand as that provided for the Macartney Embassy, but its aspect was more 'cheerful and airy' and the rooms were neat and clean (Staunton, 1824, p. 123). The house, in Jeffrey's view, was 'very spacious and [was] by far the most comfortable house we had seen in China' (Jeffrey Amherst, n.d., n.p.). The British looked forward to spending several days at the compound, recovering from their journey in the pleasant surroundings and unpacking their luggage, which had been delivered.

The British were joined by two Cantonese interpreters at the compound, newly arrived after their own very tiring overland journey from Canton. One was a linguist that the British called 'A-chow' whom Staunton had recognised in the crowd at Yuanmingyuan and who had followed the embassy back to Sungyun's compound where he offered his services to the British. The other was a Cantonese silk merchant. Staunton discovered that the Canton Government had sent four interpreters, two of whom had been dispatched to Zhoushan in case the embassy had landed there as had been the case with Macartney.[2] Staunton, noting that the need for

---

2 The Jiaqing emperor had memorialised in an edict dated 25 June 1816 notifying the viceroys and governors along the China coast that 'England wishes to present tribute by way of the sea route, landing at Tianjin to enter the Imperial capital, [which] has already been approved. However, the windy season makes sailing uncertain, so that we cannot tell exactly where the ambassador will land ... The ambassador is not allowed to change his route. Nor is he allowed to land secretly. Both civil and military officials near the seacoast are ordered to take good care of their defence' (Fu, 1966, vol. 1, p. 403).

Cantonese interpreters on this occasion was superfluous, believed they were spies sent by the Canton Government. But he thought that, as it was not in their interests to jeopardise their standing with the British, it was unlikely they 'would willingly take a part against them' (1824, p. 124).

Amherst was soon paid a visit by the emperor's physician who felt his pulse and diagnosed that his patient's illness was due to the climate and strange food. He told the emperor, however, that Amherst was not sick and had only been pretending. Meanwhile, a very 'handsome and plentiful Chinese breakfast' was served, but only four members of the embassy turned up to the table. Amherst had some food in his room and tried to get some sleep, but this was impossible as curious mandarins kept entering his room trying to catch a glimpse of him (Jeffrey Amherst, n.d., n.p.). Davis (1841) related that they 'peeped through the windows of [Amherst's] private apartment, making holes with their fingers in the coloured paper windows' (p. 154). Staunton (1824) also complained of mandarins 'prying and intruding into our very bed-chambers' (p. 124). Jeffrey managed 'a very comfortable nap' before being awakened by 'the sound of plates and dishes in the adjoining room'. He added, 'I found a capital Chinese breakfast prepared to which we all did ample justice' (Jeffrey Amherst, n.d., n.p.).

Chang-wei's arrival at the compound at around 11 o'clock in the morning further interrupted British rest. He came with the devastating news that because of the emperor's anger over Amherst's supposed feigned illness, the embassy was dismissed and was ordered immediately to leave for Tongzhou. A distraught Yin woke up Morrison: 'All has gone wrong! Kuang [Guanghui] wishes to see you; you are to go away directly' (as quoted in Morrison, 1820, p. 59). Yin and Guanghui were joined by Muketenge who was asked by Guanghui if it was true that the embassy had been ordered to leave. Muketenge, in a rare utterance, answered, 'They are to go' (p. 60).

Jeffrey had been informed by the servants soon after breakfast that the luggage carts were not allowed to be unpacked. His father's dismissal, according to him, was due to the emperor being offended that Amherst had failed to appear before him and had, therefore, determined that 'he should not see the light to the Sun's countenance' (Jeffrey Amherst, n.d., n.p.).

The British were astonished by this unexpected turn of events. They were denied access to their luggage, although some of the embassy managed to obtain a basin of water and a change of linen (Jeffrey Amherst, n.d., n.p.). The crowd, however, remained with several people persisting in 'rudely peering in the windows' and 'thrusting open the door to gaze on the foreigners' (Jeffrey Amherst, n.d., n.p.). Amherst deliberately took his time, hoping that the emperor would change his mind and permit the embassy to stay but was advised by Chang-wei to eat some lunch before embarking on the return journey to Tongzhou. Jeffrey wrote that it was his birthday and felt sure 'no one ever passed a birthday in so singular a manner' (Jeffrey Amherst, n.d., n.p.).

British preparations for departure were interrupted in the early afternoon by the arrival of a large blustering mandarin storming into the courtyard of the compound and demanding to speak to an interpreter (Morrison, 1820, p. 60). Received by Ellis and Morrison, as Amherst and Staunton were resting, the mandarin informed them that he had been sent by the greatest military mandarin in the empire, namely, the 'general of the nine gates' and one who 'commanded a million men', who insisted that the ambassador leave his domains at once. The King of England, the mandarin continued, was a respectful and obedient man, but Amherst was not. The emperor was writing to the king to complain about Amherst, especially over his use of disrespectful language. On being informed that the ambassador had not used 'disrespectful language' but had only requested a deferment of the audience, the mandarin replied that, 'The ceremonies of the Celestial Empire are unalterably binding' (as quoted in Morrison, 1820, p. 60). He added that there was still a chance of the embassy being received if the ambassador agreed to kowtow. Ellis, according to Staunton (1824, p. 128), 'very properly' declined any discussion on the subject. The embassy was ordered to leave immediately.

Return to Tongzhou

Several of the Chinese attendants accompanying the embassy were disappointed and sympathetic to the British. Yin, Abel (1818) wrote, 'walked from person to person, consoling with each as well he could, and attributing our difficulties to the will of heaven' (p. 109). The day was very hot and the British felt that the prospect of travelling at night was better than suffering the heat of the day. Abel described their departure from Sungyun's compound taking place as 'fast as possible' where the 'pomp of imperial favour no longer attended us' (p. 110). The British had an early dinner, served in the Chinese style, and set out on the return to Tongzhou. Amherst gave up the barouche for the sick and he, Jeffrey, Staunton and Ellis each travelled by separate palanquins.

The embassy was no longer accompanied by mandarins or Chinese soldiers and the crowds that had been present on the road from Peking to Yuanmingyuan had disappeared. Night was falling, but on arrival at the western city gate some Englishmen left their carts and picked up a piece of the city wall as a souvenir. Their route skirted the walls of the city again and passed the eastern gate where the embassy re-entered the road to Tongzhou (Staunton, 1824, p. 130). Curious crowds had now gathered to see the British as they travelled through Peking's outskirts. Jeffrey described his palanquin being surrounded by numbers of inquisitive Chinese who had:

> [come] out with their lanterns to have a look at me. Their lanterns were made of paper and thin Bamboo, and my amusement was to kick at them and break them when they thrust them into the Palanquin. (Jeffrey Amherst, n.d., n.p.)

Heavy rain began to fall, making progress exceedingly difficult with carts upturned and luggage scattered on the side of the road. At ten o'clock at night, Amherst's bearers abruptly stopped in the middle of the road and insisted that they needed to rest. The withdrawal of imperial favour had resulted in no dinner or rest stop being provided and the British were hungry. Some kind bearers offered Staunton tea and cakes procured from a nearby farmhouse, which touched him greatly (Staunton, 1824, p. 131). Hayne (n.d., vol. 2) wrote that this and similar acts of kindness shown by the bearers 'showed more humanity that the Courtiers of His Majesty' (p. 97). Jeffrey was very relieved when he made contact with the palanquins carrying his father and the other commissioners. He wrote that he could not leave his palanquin because he had his writing desk and his father's robes with him (Jeffrey Amherst, n.d., n.p.). This is an important reference as it confirms that, while Amherst did not have his credentials with him at Yuanmingyuan, his robes were at hand, which in part contradicts historians who account for their absence as a major reason for Amherst's refusal to appear before the Jiaqing emperor.[3]

---

3   For example, see Napier (1995, p. 80) and Kitson and Markley (2016). Kitson and Markley wrote that Amherst arrived at Yuanmingyuan, 'Fatigued, separated from his diplomatic credentials and ambassadorial robes' (2016, p. 1).

British relief at meeting up with other members of the party at this time was expressed by Staunton (1824): 'for to be entirely alone, in such a road at night, without the means of being understood, and in a strange country, would have been indeed desolate' (p. 132). Jeffrey described one of the English coachman stumbling onto his palanquin during his search to find Morrison or some other person who could speak Chinese 'in order to procure assistance as he had left the carriage sticking fast in the mud' (Jeffrey Amherst, n.d., n.p.). Amherst was also hungry, but Jeffrey had some biscuits that he handed over to his father when his palanquin stopped alongside. The bearers, in turn, also gave Jeffrey some of their breakfast. 'A consequence of the emperor's displeasure', Jeffrey wrote, was that 'none of the marks of attention with which we had formerly been treated' were present (Jeffrey Amherst, n.d., n.p.).

Davis (1841, p. 157) described the return to Tongzhou as the most wretched night of his life, 'except perhaps [for] the one immediately preceding'. Travelling in a Chinese cart without springs on the granite road was harder 'than the emperor's heart' and was equivalent to being 'pounded in a mortar'. Davis attempted to walk but found this exceedingly difficult due to torrential rain, puddles and the holes in the road.

Amherst's bearers, and those in charge of the palanquins carrying Staunton and Ellis, did not return to work until three o'clock in the morning. Staunton's arrival at Tongzhou three hours later surprised the boatmen who, nevertheless, received him 'joyfully and kindly' (Abel, 1818, p. 111). The barouche carrying the sick had arrived a little earlier as well as several carts whose occupants, according to Jeffrey, were 'almost jumbled to death' (Jeffrey Amherst, n.d., n.p.). Abel had arrived at four o'clock in the morning.

The British were dismayed to find that the houses where they had previously been quartered were boarded and shut up, while the triumphal arch that had been erected opposite Amherst's boat had been torn down. Jeffrey, no doubt reflecting his father's view, interpreted this behaviour as a calculated act 'by the Chinese to mark the difference of our present situation to what it had been before' (Jeffrey Amherst, n.d., n.p.). Some of the luggage did not reach the embassy for a couple of days, but its appearance without any loss drew praise from Staunton (1824, p. 131) who commented on the honesty and diligence of the Chinese porters.

A Partial Exchange of Presents

Guanghui and Sulenge paid a late visit to the British after their arrival at Tongzhou. Arriving at 10 o'clock at night, they were 'tired and forlorn' and were received by Ellis, with Toone and Davis acting as interpreters as Amherst, Staunton and Morrison were sleeping. Amherst was woken up and met the legates on his boat, but on this occasion made the point of refusing to offer his arm to Sulenge, which he had done on previous occasions out of respect for his age and 'supposed infirmities' (Staunton, 1824, p. 134). Imperial orders had been received, Amherst was informed, for a partial exchange of presents. The legates had three presents for the King of England, consisting of a white agate sceptre or *ruyi*, a string of sapphire beads referred to by Davis as 'court beads' and a box of embroidered purses. Three British presents had been chosen by the emperor: the portraits of the Prince Regent and his wife Caroline of Brunswick, a case of maps of the 'United Kingdoms', and a collection of prints and drawings (Minute of Conference between the Chairs and Mr. Barrow respecting Presents for China, in BL IOR G/12/196 (Reel 1) F 47). The British presents, according to Jeffrey, were more valuable, 'yet the Chinese with their usual impudence observed that the Emperor in this instance had followed his usual custom of "Giving much and receiving little"' (Jeffrey Amherst, n.d., n.p.).

Davis (1841) agreed. He thought the emperor's presents were of 'paltry' value, but nonetheless was pleased that the gesture of an exchange of presents had been made considering the fact that the British were facing a journey through the whole length of the empire to Canton. Amherst thought the legates seemed apprehensive that he might not agree to the exchange as they eagerly forced the presents into his hands before explaining 'the object of sending them' (Amherst to Canning, 3 March 1817, in BL IOR G/12/197 (Reel 2) F 296). An exchange of presents, the legates hoped, would ensure that the king would not be angry with the embassy on its return to England. The king, Amherst reassured them, would give him a favourable reception, well aware that he had done his duty. He took the opportunity at this time, however, to inform them of his indignation at the manner in which his embassy had been treated in contrast to Macartney's (Jeffrey Amherst, n.d., n.p.). Guanghui placed the blame on Heshitai. Deciding to pursue a conciliatory tone as one best suited to Company interests at Canton, Amherst told the legates that he consented to the exchange of presents and also had 'no objection …

to extend the delivery of any other articles which might have attracted His Imperial Majesty's notice' (Amherst to Canning, 3 March 1817, in BL IOR G/12/197 (Reel 2) F 297).

The British presents chosen by the emperor were laid out in a temporary enclosure and unpacked the following morning in the presence of Guanghui and Sulenge. Amherst made a deliberate show of bowing before the portrait of the Prince Regent as it was being unwrapped. He explained:

> I took care myself to be present; and having required that the rabble should be sent to a distance as unworthy to contemplate it, I approached the Picture, and in conjunction with those of my countrymen present, pulled off my hat, and made a low bow. This proceeding was evidently mortifying to the Legate, but it answered two good purposes. It shewed that the Emperor of China was not the only Sovereign in the world entitled to respect, and it was the best confirmation I could give of what I had all along proposed to be the European ceremony. I then enquired particularly as to the place where it was intended to hang the pictures of the King and Queen, and having received satisfactory information on that head ... I recommended them to Quong's [Guanghui's] care [and] took my leave. (Amherst to Canning, 3 March 1817, in BL IOR G/12/197 (Reel 2) F 298)

Davis (1841) wrote that Guanghui's face at this time looked as 'black as thunder' from Amherst's actions having 'so completely ... discomposed [Chinese] established notions of the universal supremacy of the great emperor' (p. 170). Davis added later, 'It might be well for Chinese assumption if lessons of this kind were more frequently taught it; and the increasing means of direct communications from the west seem calculated to multiply the opportunities' (p. 170).

The presents, once inspected by Guanghui and Sulenge, were repacked and placed in Sulenge's care who was leaving that afternoon for Yuanmingyuan. Staunton (1824) wrote, 'we finally separated from this old gentleman, who has obtained a dispensation on account of his age, from the duty of further attendance on the Embassy' (p. 135). Guanghui remained with the embassy until it left China, assisted for a short time by Chang-wei and Yin. The diplomatic part of the embassy, Davis (1841) noted, was now terminated.

Immediate British Reactions to their Reception at Yuanmingyuan

The stressful and confrontational nature of negotiations over the kowtow that took place on the journey of the embassy to Peking has been noted in the previous two chapters. The duplicitous conduct of the high-ranking mandarins appointed by the emperor at this time shocked the British and failed to measure up to British notions of civility and politeness. Events at Yuanmingyuan not only confirmed British perceptions of the imperial court as a site of rough, rude and uncouth 'Tartars', but firmly established the futility of any further British diplomatic overtures to the Qing court. British disappointment at being denied access to Peking, let alone making a grand entrance befitting the status and dignity of the British sovereign, helped reinforce notions of the impenetrable access to China's society at this time (Sample, 2008, p. 32).

While Staunton had serious doubts about a successful outcome of the Amherst Embassy, he was always certain that 'we shall be received as well at least as the former Embassy' (*Staunton Letters*, on board the *Discovery*, Ladrone Islands, 12 July 1816). The 'very favourable Edict' received by Amherst while the squadron watered at Hong Kong confirmed that the 'Emperor is very well placed to receive the Embassy' (*Staunton Letters*, on board the *Discovery*, Ladrone Islands, 12 July 1816). His Imperial Majesty, Staunton informed his mother when the British arrived at the Gulf of Bei Zhili, was 'particularly anxious to see us'. He added that the emperor:

> even expressed his superior [crossed out] and 'peculiar' esteem for the British nation—on the other hand, it is already hinted that His Majesty does not calculate our making a long stay … it is therefore probable that we shall quit Pekin as soon, or sooner than the former Embassy—on this subject however I shall feel no kind of regret, provided our Entertainment while we are there, is gracious and friendly. (*Staunton Letters*, on board HMS *Alceste*, Gulf of Pechelee, 7 August 1816)

Their reception, it has been seen, was neither gracious nor friendly. Amherst noted the striking difference with the manner in which his embassy was received at the Qing court compared to Macartney's reception. Hampton (2009) has written that an ambassador is first and foremost 'a reader of signs' who bases his interpretation largely on historical precedent where 'what has happened before is placed at the scene and service of political negotiation' (p. 5). The former embassy, Amherst noted, was marked by 'decency and regularity' (Amherst to Canning, 8 March 1817, in BL IOR G/12/197 (Reel 2) F 284). Time was allowed for 'decorous preparation' and the needs of individuals were considered. Above all, not only Macartney's honour, but also that of the king and the emperor, was maintained and appearances were upheld. Amherst's reception, on the other hand, consisted of 'hurry and confusion' with a 'total disregard' for the comfort and composure of the individuals (Amherst to Canning, 8 March 1817, in BL IOR G/12/197 (Reel 2) F 285).

Amherst was adamant, understandably, that his treatment at Yuanmingyuan was 'inhospitable and inhuman'. He made it clear that his view of the Qing court as 'little better than a Tartar camp' was formed not from the 'practices of the polished courts' of Europe, but rather from Macartney's reception at the time of the Qianlong emperor (Amherst to Canning, 8 March 1817, in BL IOR G/12/197 (Reel 2) F 293).

The Importance of Appearances

The British emphasis on Western diplomatic protocol, courtly appearances and the importance of making a dignified, elegant and grand entrance, befitting the status of Britain's place in the world before the Qing court, was of vital concern to Amherst and his party and had been given prominence during the embassy's preparations. But the lateness of the hour, weather conditions and travel arrangements ensured that a proposed grand entrance into Peking and Yuanmingyuan was impossible. Rather, Amherst complained that the Qing court acted on, 'A pervading wish to remove away from us every thing that constitutes the splendour or even respectable appearance of an Embassy' (Amherst to Canning, 8 March 1817, in BL IOR G/12/197 (Reel 2) F 294).

A specific insult was the manner in which Amherst arrived at Yuanmingyuan, separated from the rest of the embassy, including the marine guard, the band and attendants. While his credentials were missing, his ambassadorial robes, it has been noted, appear to have been at hand, but the circumstances of an exhausting and rushed arrival at the Summer Palace left no time to collect them (Jeffrey Amherst, n.d., n.p.). Adding to British judgements that the Qing court had an ulterior motive in the nature of their reception was the fact that only Amherst, Staunton, Ellis and Jeffrey were proposed to be received by the Jiaqing emperor at the time. Amherst was acutely aware that, owing to the absence of his credentials, packed away in the luggage that had yet to arrive, he was 'consequently unable to present [him]self in [his] public character' (Amherst to Canning, 8 March 1817, in BL IOR G/12/197 (Reel 2) F 294).

Amherst's most damning assessment of his reception concerned the insult to Great Britain and the British sovereign in which, 'The attempt to drag us before the Emperor in such a guise as would befit only his vassals from the meanest and most barbarous islands of the China seas' (Amherst to Canning, 8 March 1817, in BL IOR G/12/197 (Reel 2) F 295).

The change in British status following its dismissal was humiliating and evidenced after their return to Tongzhou when a beggar remained standing and did not bow as Amherst passed by. Ellis (1817) commented that the 'British Embassador' was no longer considered worthy of respect, 'even from the lowest class of society' (p. 191). The reason, of course, was that the embassy had dismally failed. Amherst's failure to formally appear before the Jiaqing emperor ensured that the ritual cycle surrounding such a reception was never commenced, let alone completed. Amherst's status, seen from the perspective of his rejection by the emperor at court, ensured that his position protocol-wise in China remained in a state of flux. His status as the representative of a powerful foreign sovereign required that he be placated and accommodated on the one hand, but he was not entitled to the respect normally accorded an anointed tributary ambassador. The British expected that they would be accorded the same respect as Macartney, achieved through his two receptions before the Qianlong emperor at Jehol, resulting in a further opportunity to build on the goodwill with the Chinese. However, it became clear following Amherst's arrival at Tianjin that the Qing court was not prepared to grant him any dispensation based on the Macartney precedent, and that he was required as a new arrival to adhere to all the protocols of the Qing court, which were ultimately enforced without any concessions.

Amherst's degrading treatment by the Qing court reinforced British group cohesion at this time and reaffirmed their belief that he had acted correctly in refusing to compromise British power to make an appearance before the Jiaqing emperor. Further clarification of Chinese actions came to light when the British received an account of the court's view on the matter from the judge of Bei Zhili province who was assigned as one of the early conductors of the embassy on its journey back to Tianjin. Staunton wrote (1824) that the judge was not a pleasant man; rather, he was:

> Vain, boastful, professing to know a great deal about foreign countries, but puffed up with the most extravagant notions of the grandeur and importance of his own, and especially of the Tartar family now on the throne. He affected to consider the Embassy from England as quite a trifling concern to China. (p. 141)

The judge's view of the 'trifling' importance of the embassy to China is understandable; the Qing court regularly received tributary missions and the Jiaqing emperor was in a hurry to proceed to Jehol and the Amherst Embassy was not invited. The British, of course, were specifically irritated on hearing the judge's assessment of Britain and the status of their sovereign. Morrison noted that the judge had read only French missionary reports on European countries, resulting in outdated and inaccurate views. England's importance, the judge informed them, was not as great as other European nations and it was absurd that her king was 'pretending to compete with the Emperor of China' (as quoted in Ellis, 1817, p. 196). The judge thought England was dependent entirely on commerce and, although it had a strong navy, the French were a far superior land force. He also thought England was divided into four parts and had four kings (Abel, 1818, p. 144). While Amherst and Ellis did not comment on this false assertion, it suggests that the judge thought Britain was divided into a number of petty principalities similar to those found in maritime Southeast Asia, which traditionally sent tribute to the Qing court. Nevertheless, Abel (1818, p. 144) thought the judge was the most informed Chinese on European geography and history encountered by the British in China.

The judge conceded that the embassy had certainly been rushed to Yuanmingyuan, but he thought the emperor was far too reasonable to have dismissed it if he had known the true state of affairs. The performance of the kowtow, however, was essential and non-negotiable. Moreover, the judge offered his opinion that the performance of the kowtow would not have altered Britain's status in Chinese eyes nor relegated the British to tributary status. Rather, it would have permitted the British the honour of sitting on cushions in the presence of the emperor, thus according them with a privilege reserved for the princes and the highest mandarins, and one that was never given to envoys from tributary states. Amherst made

9. TO YUANMINGYUAN, RECEPTION AND DISMISSAL

no comment on learning this except to remind the judge of the Kangxi emperor's dispensation given to the Russian envoy in 1721 where an alternative was suggested.

The British Learn of the Reception Intended for Them at Yuanmingyuan

A book published in 1865 written by the surgeon attached to the first British Legation at Peking, D. F. Rennie, contains a reference to Amherst's reception at Yuanmingyuan (p. 234). Rennie held a conversation with a 70-year-old assistant commissioner for foreign affairs, referred to as 'Tsoon-Luen', who remembered the morning in 1816 and said that the embassy 'miscarried through some unaccountable mismanagement'.[4] Of interest is Tsoon-Luen's assertion:

> The Emperor was actually sitting on the throne in the state apartment at Yuen-ming-yuen, waiting to receive the King of England's letter, when the announcement was brought to him that the Ambassador had departed. (Rennie, 1865, p. 235)

Rennie concludes that such 'mismanagement' refers to Amherst's refusal 'to appear before the Emperor immediately on his arrival at Yuen-ming-yuen, and also to perform the kow-tow in the presence' (p. 235).

Platt (2018) has also written that it had been the emperor's intention to have a successful meeting, even if it meant compromising on the protocol surrounding the kowtow, stating in an edict three days before Amherst's arrival at Yuanmingyuan that 'it is better to meet with them than to send them away' (p. 179). In a critical breakdown of communication, Heshitai did not relay this vital information to Amherst as apparently intended; rather, he tried in his own brusque way to 'deliver' Amherst before the Jiaqing emperor when the former was clearly in no condition to proceed. Given Heshitai's personality and reputation, it is not surprising that he misread or only gave lip service to the emperor's intentions and, by his own actions, missed what could have been a cordial meeting between Amherst and the emperor. It was only subsequently when the Jiaqing emperor found out the true circumstances under which Amherst and his

---

4   The present study has been unable to identify 'Tsoon-Luen'.

party had travelled overnight and been mishandled and mistreated on arrival at Yuanmingyuan that he issued a further edict severely punishing Heshitai and others involved (p. 178).

The members of the Amherst Embassy were given a different account at the time. Chang-wei told Morrison on 3 September that the emperor never intended to give the British an audience on the morning they arrived at Yuanmingyuan, but wanted only to pass by them seated in his palanquin to view their intended ceremony (Staunton, 1824, p. 139). If dissatisfied—in other words, if Amherst did not perform the kowtow—the emperor planned to expel them without any other reception. Heshitai had hoped that Amherst might have been persuaded 'by the lure of promises' to have then kowtowed the following day at a public reception (pp. 139–140). Staunton added that, if true, the British were particularly glad they had escaped such humiliation 'so unworthy' of Amherst's public character (p. 140). Hayne (n.d., vol. 2) summed up British feelings:

> It is a pleasant reflection to feel persuaded had LA [Amherst] given way in that fight at Yuangming yuan, it most probably would have led to more disagreeable scenes than which actually occurred—despite the Emperor's presence … a little persuasive violence might have been used to get those in His Majesty's presence [to fall] on both knees … So that all was for the best. (p. 115)

British relief at being spared a dishonourable reception was reinforced on 11 September when they learned of the intended program of three proposed receptions had they been formally received by the Jiaqing emperor.[5] Handed to Morrison for translation by Chang-wei, the document revealed that the embassy's reception was to have taken place in a hall with the emperor sitting at the upper end on a raised altar. Amherst was expected to enter and kneel by the altar while delivering the Prince Regent's letter to a high-ranking mandarin who, in turn, would hand it to another mandarin who ascended the steps and gave it to the emperor. This was in contrast to Macartney who had delivered the king's letter

---

5   For a full translation of the 'Outline of the Ceremonies to be observed on the English Embassador's (Tributary Envoys etc.) presenting the Peaou-wan, or official document from his Sovereign', see Morse (1926/1966, vol. 3. pp. 295–297). See Appendix F for a translation of the final ceremony, 'Ceremonies to be observed at the Audience of Leave', reproduced from Ellis (1817, pp. 499–500, Note No. 5).

directly into the hands of the Qianlong emperor.[6] Amherst was then to be conducted down to a lower level where he would receive a gift of a *ruyi* or jade sceptre for the Prince Regent. At this location, Amherst would address the customary questions presented in the name of the emperor by a mandarin and would next be conducted to further down the hall where, facing the throne on the distant altar, he would perform the kowtow with nine prostrations. Following this ceremony, Amherst was to be led outside the hall where he was to kowtow once more behind a row of mandarins. At this point Amherst would be permitted to sit down but would be required to prostrate himself again, along with the princes, while the emperor drank milk tea. Two other prostrations were required: one at the time when Amherst was presented with milk tea and the other when he finished drinking (Morse, 1926/1966, vol. 3, pp. 295–297).

Predictably, the British were astonished on reading this document, although Ellis (1817, p. 215) assumed that it reflected what the Chinese 'wished to have happened' and not, therefore, what they insisted on. Nevertheless, the sheer audacity of the intended program was breathtaking and represented a reception for the Amherst Embassy that, when measured by previous European embassies, was marked as the most humiliating and degrading. The issue was the number of prostrations expected. Ellis confessed that his earlier support for one kowtow in the actual presence of the emperor and at a reasonable distance from him was very different from the four prostrations expected on this occasion. This expectation, Ellis admitted, placed the performance of the kowtow in a considerably 'different character' (p. 215). The reception would have been even more degrading than that experienced by the Dutch in 1795, especially the expectation that Amherst would kowtow behind a row of people out of view of the emperor. The extra ceremonies, Ellis thought, were more indicative and expressive of inferiority and more objectionable than the kowtow itself, and it was inconceivable for a British ambassador to submit to a reception less honourable than those given previously to other European monarchs (p. 217). Staunton (1824) summed up the British view: Heshitai had done them a great favour in sparing them from a potentially embarrassing and humiliating experience where Amherst's status and character as a British ambassador would have been compromised leading to a 'more disparaging' scene than their actual dismissal (p. 140).

---

6   Macartney wrote that he delivered the king's letter 'into the Emperor's own hands, who, having received it, passed it to the Minister, by whom it was placed on the cushion' (Cranmer-Byng, 1962, p. 122).

On 14 September, Chang-wei called on Staunton to tell him that he was due to leave the embassy in a couple of days. He further informed Staunton of the latest news from Peking, published in the *Peking Gazette*, that the emperor had since learned the truth of the conditions under which Amherst had arrived at Yuanmingyuan. The emperor had noted in his letter to the viceroy of Canton at the time of the expected arrival of the embassy that Amherst would be received at his court within the context of bearing presents and tendering 'good-will with feelings and in a language respectful and complaisant'.[7] Arrangements were made to receive the embassy in a 'liberal, gracious, safe and suitable manner' where it would 'graciously be presented with gifts'. Problems started, according to the emperor, from the time of the banquet at Tianjin when Amherst did not return thanks for the feast or banquet by obeying the regulated form of three kneelings and nine knocks of the head on the ground (Imperial edict in the *Peking Gazette*, 4 September 1816, as quoted in Ellis, 1817, p. 501, Appendix 6). If he had, the Jiaqing emperor made clear, the embassy would have been brought to Yuanmingyuan the same day (Imperial edict in the *Peking Gazette*, 4 September 1816, as quoted in Ellis, 1817, p. 501, Appendix 6; Vermillion edict, 'Paper respecting the Embassy', drawn up by the Emperor, in Ellis, 1817, pp. 506–508, Appendix 11). Guanghui and Sulenge should not have permitted the embassy to proceed to Tongzhou and matters were exacerbated by their connivance in allowing the clandestine departure of the British ships. The deception became even more apparent once the embassy arrived at Tongzhou where Heshitai and Muketenge sent a 'confused and obscure' report that Amherst had practised the ceremony (Imperial edict in the *Peking Gazette*, 4 September 1816, as quoted in Ellis, 1817, p. 501, Appendix 6; Vermillion edict, 'Paper respecting the Embassy', drawn up by the Emperor, in Ellis, 1817, pp. 506–508, Appendix 11).

The Jiaqing emperor reported that he ascended the throne at half past five in the morning and called the ambassador to an audience. Heshitai made three reports on this occasion; in the first, he told the emperor that Amherst was not able 'to travel fast'; he next reported that Amherst was ill and a short delay was necessary; finally, he confirmed that Amherst was too ill to present himself for an interview before the emperor. While Amherst was being escorted to his lodgings where he was afterwards called

---

7   The Jiaqing emperor's reply to the viceroy of Canton, respecting the embassy sent from the Prince Regent, which reached the viceroy on or around 12 July 1816.

on by the emperor's physician, the assistant commissioners (Staunton and Ellis) were also ordered to appear in an audience before the emperor but they too refused, claiming they were also ill and needed to defer their audience until the ambassador was well.

Their response caused the Jiaqing emperor to expel the embassy and send the 'Embassadors back to their own country, without punishing the high crime they had committed' (Imperial edict in the *Peking Gazette*, 4 September 1816, as quoted in Ellis, 1817, p. 501, Appendix 6; Vermillion edict, 'Paper respecting the Embassy', drawn up by the Emperor, in Ellis, 1817, pp. 506–508, Appendix 11). The emperor added that China was 'the sovereign of the whole world'. For what reason, therefore, 'should contumely and arrogance like this be endured with quiet temper?'

The emperor only discovered some days later that Amherst and his party had travelled overnight to Yuanmingyuan and that their 'court-dresses' had yet to arrive; he added that Amherst thought, 'how can I in my ordinary garments lift up my eyes to the great Emperor' (Imperial edict in the *Peking Gazette*, 4 September 1816, as quoted in Ellis, 1817, p. 501, Appendix 6; Vermillion edict, 'Paper respecting the Embassy', drawn up by the Emperor, in Ellis, 1817, pp. 506–508, Appendix 11). The emperor also blamed his courtiers, present at the time of Amherst's arrival at the anteroom at Yuanmingyuan, for not informing him of the true state of affairs, which would have seen the audience moved to a later date. The mandarins and princes, it has been seen, were more intent at gaping at the British than reporting to their emperor. He complained, 'yet they sat immoveable while the affair was going on' (Imperial edict in *Peking Gazette*, 4 September 1816, in Ellis, 1817, p. 501, Appendix 6). Heshitai was immediately blamed and was dismissed from his position in the court and lost the honour of wearing his yellow riding jacket. He and Muketenge were blamed also for allowing Amherst to proceed to Tongzhou without first rehearsing the kowtow and for sending confused reports on the matter to the emperor. Chang-wei, on the other hand, was promoted because he had told the emperor the truth that Amherst had no intention of kowtowing. Yin, meanwhile, was relieved that he was sufficiently junior in rank that he 'happily fell below the emperor's notice' (Staunton, 1824, p. 147). Guanghui and Sulenge were not so fortunate. Both were censored for allowing the embassy to proceed beyond Tianjin after Amherst had refused to perform the kowtow ceremony. Sulenge lost his position as president of the Board of Works and was degraded to a blue button of third rank. He also lost the rank of general in the army and was ordered to pluck out his peacock's feather ('Substance of Imperial Edicts inflicting Punishments on Soo, Ho, and Kwang' in Ellis, 1817, p. 509, Appendix 12). Guanghui was reduced to a secretary of the eighth rank, dismissed from his position as salt commissioner and was posted to 'Man-chow Tartary' the following spring.

The emperor was 'much appeased' on learning the truth and decided to accept three presents from the British sovereign. To have accepted any more, Chang-wei said, would have been 'indecorous … unless he had also determined to receive the ambassador' ('Substance of Imperial Edicts inflicting Punishments on Soo, Ho, and Kwang' in Ellis, 1817, p. 509, Appendix 12). Further, as the emperor was due to leave for Jehol, it was too late to recall the embassy and it would have been too costly to invite the embassy to accompany him. All these details, Chang-wei said, were printed in the *Peking Gazette* and he promised to obtain a copy and hand it secretly to Staunton. He begged Staunton not to tell Guanghui or any of the others that the British had received this from him ('Substance of Imperial Edicts inflicting Punishments on Soo, Ho, and Kwang' in Ellis, 1817, p. 509, Appendix 12).

The diplomatic encounter between the British and the Qing court formally ended with the embassy's departure from Yuanmingyuan. As preparations were made for the journey to Canton, paid for by the Qing Government, customary within the context of even a failed tribute mission, the emperor issued orders for it to proceed on the shortest route via Nanjing and the Poyang Lake and for his officials to treat it with civility 'and silence' thereby causing 'gratitude and awe' ('Substance of Imperial Edicts inflicting Punishments on Soo, Ho, and Kwang' in Ellis, 1817, p. 509, Appendix 12). It must not be forgotten, the emperor emphasised, that the embassy had come to his court with 'the intention of offering tribute' and must accordingly be treated with respect and honour on its journey to Canton ('Translation of an Imperial Edict addressed to the Viceroy of Kiang-nan (Jiangnan), respecting Treatment of Embassy, received October 8, 1816' in Ellis, 1817, pp. 502–503, Appendix 8). Amherst later told Canning in his official report that:

> The precipitate and unwarranted rejection of the Embassy from the Palace Gates has left an injury to repair. Even in the eyes of the Chinese themselves the rules of hospitality have been violated. Possibly some apprehension may be entertained of the manner in which the transaction will be viewed in Great Britain. (Amherst to Canning, 21 April 1817, in BL IOR G/12/197 (Reel 2) F 379)

Chang-wei and Staunton thought there was now a need for conciliation between the British and the Chinese. The occasion of travelling together in a four-month journey to Canton appeared to offer a unique opportunity to repair relationships. Staunton (1824) wrote that he and Chang-wei 'agreed in sentiment, that the best thing now to be done, was to think as little as we could of the past, and to consult together from time to time, how matters might be placed on the most amicable footing for the future' (p. 168). The intended 'honourable treatment' of the embassy on its return to Canton was attributed by Amherst as 'a wish for reparation in the only way which the pride of the Emperor would allow' (Amherst to Canning, 21 April 1817, in BL IOR G/12/197 (Reel 2) F 379).

10

Overland to Canton: The British Cultural Encounter with China

The only worthwhile objective left for the embassy following its premature dismissal from Yuanmingyuan was the opportunity to expand British knowledge of China during its four-month journey from Tianjin to Canton. Representing only the second group of Englishmen to visit the interior of China, this aspect of the embassy has received little attention from historians apart from a 2014 article by Gao. However, Gao's arguments are contentious, especially his assertion that the men of the Amherst Embassy were permitted 'greater opportunities to explore the real state of Chinese society' than their compatriots in the Macartney Embassy (p. 570). While Gao appears to base his opinion on Amherst's statement that his embassy was permitted 'a greater degree of liberty than had been granted to any former Embassy', the evidence does not substantiate this claim (Amherst to Canning, 8 March 1817, in BL IOR G/12/197 (Reel 2) F 281). A closer reading of the accounts of the Amherst Embassy reveals that British freedom to explore towns and cities was prohibited by a series of imperial edicts whose strictness of implementation was determined on the whim of provincial officials and severely restricted by the presence of large crowds. While Staunton (1824) expressed the hope that the presence of Mandarin speakers would enable them to 'throw some new and interesting light on the moral character and condition of this singular people', he acknowledged the power of preconceived notions for strengthening, rather than correcting, existing prejudices regardless of the impact of direct experience (p. 206). Any exploration of the 'real state of Chinese society' remained impossible.

What follows is an exploration of the British encounter with China in this phase of the embassy with a focus on its members' reactions and judgements of the country and its people.

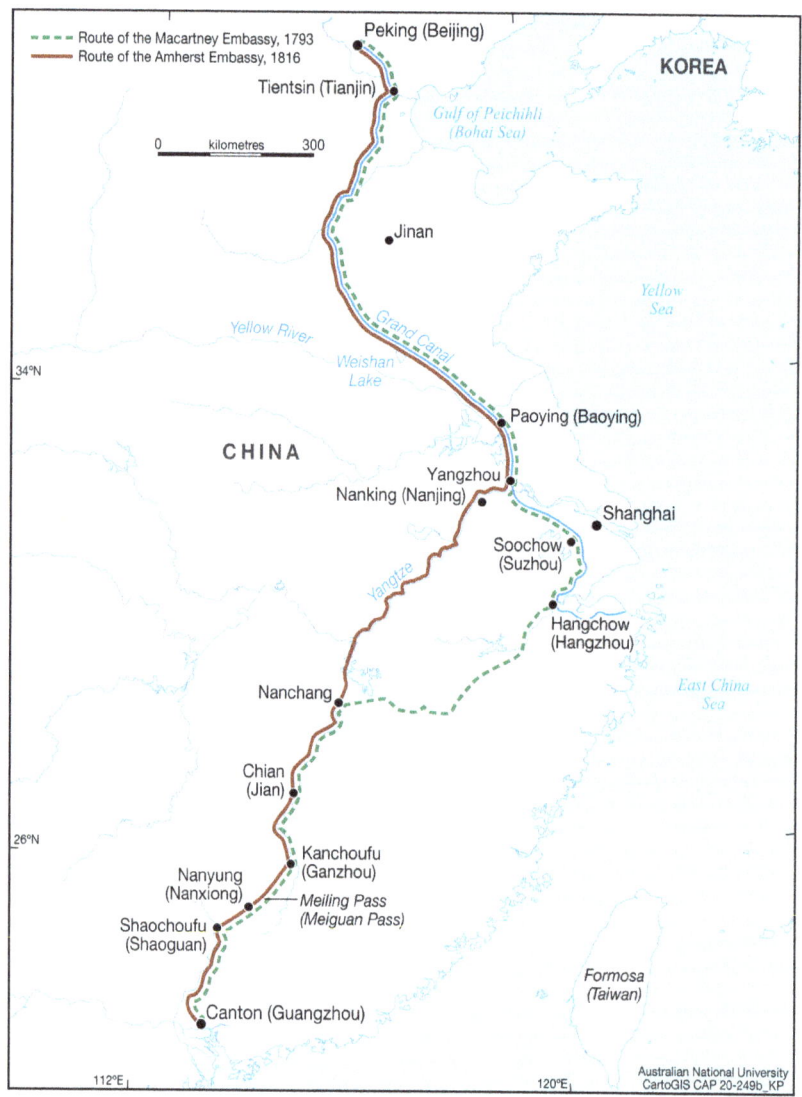

Figure 9: The routes of the Macartney Embassy (1793) and Amherst Embassy (1816).

Note: Amherst's route deviated from Macartney's by travelling down the Yangtze River to Nanking and through the Poyang Lake before rejoining Macartney's route at Nanchang and onto Canton.

Source: CartoGIS, College of Asia and the Pacific, ANU. Based on map in Cranmer-Byng (1962, p. 157).

British perceptions of Chinese society, of course, were formed inevitably within the context of the embassy's personal standards of civilised conduct founded on good manners, appropriate behaviour and appearances. British assessments of the Chinese countryside, towns and villages were measured not only in comparison with England, but also, and significantly, with the earlier accounts of the Macartney Embassy where evidence of economic decline since that time was widely noted. Barrow's main aim in his book *Travels in China* (1804) of ascertaining China's place on a scale of civilisation was not a major concern for any of the Amherst Embassy's commentators. Rather, their collective British response to China was overshadowed by the Chinese insult to British honour at Yuanmingyuan, which they attempted to counter by stressing the imperative of maintaining an impressive and dignified British appearance as the embassy travelled through China.

British accounts of their journey follow a timeline of daily occurrences and detailed descriptions of the countryside and towns passed on the way. The approach of this chapter is thematic rather than chronological, and an attempt is made to portray what a British embassy would have looked like to Chinese observers and how its personnel felt and responded to the alien environment in which they found themselves. Emphasis is placed on the cross-cultural encounter with the Chinese, rather than a simple travelogue of visits to specific cities or temples.

The chapter concludes with Amherst's arrival and reception in Canton in early January 1817 and his departure on the *Alceste* at the end of the month. The homeward voyage saw the shipwreck of the *Alceste* off the coast of Sumatra and Amherst's subsequent meeting with Napoleon on the island of St Helena. The former emperor's views on the outcome of the embassy provide an alternative 'imperial' perspective on Amherst's approach to his diplomatic mission.

The embassy left Tianjin on 8 September 1816, travelling to Canton in a series of straggling convoys and reached its destination on 1 January 1817. It followed Macartney's route down the Grand Canal as far as 'Kwa-choo' (Guazhou). From there, it made a detour following the Yangtze River and proceeding through the Poyang Lake, thus traversing 280 miles (over 450 kilometres) of country not visited by the Macartney Embassy. Arriving at Nanchang, the capital of Jiangxi province, the embassy rejoined Macartney's route into Canton. The last stage of the journey was a short overland hike across the Meiling Mountains on the boundary between the provinces of Jiangxi and Guangdong.

The cost of the embassy's journey to Canton, it has been noted, was borne by the Chinese Government. An initial fleet of 60 boats carried the 73 Englishmen and 400 Chinese boatmen, trackers and Chinese officials accompanying the embassy. Massive amounts of British luggage and stores, including crates of the bulky presents refused by the emperor (consisting of a fire engine, sedan chairs, delicate crystal chandeliers and fragile chinaware and glassware) were packed on board.

Guanghui was left in sole charge of the embassy after the early departure of Chang-wei and Yin.[1] Hayne (n.d., vol. 2) described Yin coming at breakfast time to say farewell along with his staff who had been handsomely rewarded by the British. To offer their gratitude, Yin's 'underlings' proceeded to prostrate themselves before Amherst. Hayne wrote, 'The very idea of prostration [was] so repugnant to Englishmen's feelings that L. A. [Lord Amherst] could not bear to see them and would not permit it' (p. 160). The conduct of the embassy was overseen by Manchu officials, either a judge, treasurer or general, who joined Guanghui as the embassy progressed through their respective provinces (Morrison, 1820, p. 65). Reactions towards the embassy, in particular the amount of freedom permitted to its members to visit towns and roam the countryside, varied according to the disposition of the various provincial officials. Official meetings with Amherst were rare, a fact that angered the British who read this as a further insult to his status as their sovereign's representative.

Referring to events at Yuanmingyuan, Amherst wrote that the Chinese had violated 'the rules of hospitality' and he was not looking forward to the long journey to Canton (Amherst to Canning, 21 April 1817, in BL IOR G/12/197 (Reel 2) F 378). Staunton (1824, p. 205) quoted Morrison who succinctly summed up the British feeling that they were now travelling to Canton 'under the *frown*' of the Chinese Government. He added that 'the unwarrantable and inhospitable treatment … the mission experienced' at Yuanmingyuan had disposed the British to 'look on surrounding objects, in some degree, with a jaundiced eye' (p. 206). Ellis (1817) thought the fact that Guanghui had been delegated to conduct the embassy to Canton

---

1   Both Chang-wei and Yin had left the embassy by 18 September 1817. Chang-wei was appointed the judge of Shandong Province. Morrison (1820) said he 'owed this promotion to the Duke [Heshitai] who was himself downgraded' (p. 64). Davis (1841) spoke highly of Yin, praising his frankness and kind treatment when Amherst and his party arrived at Haidian: 'when the rest deserted us. We had formed a pretty intimate acquaintance with both of them … and knew how to make allowances for the servants of such an autocrat as their emperor, whose single word was sufficient to consign them to death, in the event of any suspicion of a collusion with foreigners' (p. 168).

indicated 'an additional punishment' to his dismissal from the office of salt commissioner at Tianjin (pp. 193–194). Nevertheless, Ellis hoped that new experiences would change his view of China as an 'uninteresting nation' (p. 198).

The changed status of the embassy was apparent immediately with the removal of special honours traditionally accorded to a tribute embassy. Staunton (1824) complained on arrival back at Tianjin from Yuanmingyuan, 'No [mandarin] visited … or message of congratulations took place' (p. 145). Honours such as ornamental arches and columns of soldiers dropping to their knees in salute as the embassy flotilla passed through towns were evident, but this was in response to the presence of high-ranking mandarins accompanying the embassy rather than respect paid to the British ambassador. Abel (1818) appreciated the unique circumstances in which the embassy's journey was being conducted and how it coloured British reactions to China. He wrote:

> I apprehend … that any person travelling through a country in a hurried journey, under a suspicious surveillance, must always be unqualified to pronounce on a question that respects a whole nation. (p. 205)

Abel (1818) and Ellis (1817), who gave the fullest descriptions of China in their accounts of the embassy published in Britain, candidly acknowledged the limitations of their perceptions. Dangerously ill during the journey to Canton and largely bedridden, Abel's (1818) account 'on the progress of the Embassy, and the nature of the country through which it passed' (p. 142) was dependent largely on the reports of others, notably Morrison and Cooke. Ellis (1817) admitted also to short sightedness.[2] Staunton, whose account was printed privately for family and friends, complained petulantly that the Macartney accounts had left him nothing new to say about China. He wrote:

> The comparative novelty of a first discovery, are wanting on the present occasion; on which we are continuing, under circumstances which are certainly somewhat unsatisfactory and discouraging, to trace a route, which has of late been repeatedly and fully described by others. (1824, p. 205)

---

2   Ellis (1817) wrote, 'indeed my powers of observation of visible objects in general are very limited, partly from shortness of sight, but principally from negligence' (p. 222). Later in his journey, on 30 November, Ellis wrote, 'Orange groves have been seen this morning; the shortness of my sight has prevented me from remarking them' (p. 361).

Figure 10: 'Sunrise on the Grand Canal of China', painted by the official artist of the Amherst Embassy, William Havell (1782–1857), depicting the 'British' boats moored at anchor along the Grand Canal.
Source: Image courtesy of Bonhams, Sydney, and with acknowledgment of Sphinx Fine Art, London, original owners of the copyright.

Barrow (1817a) wrote later, somewhat facetiously, that the journey down the Grand Canal from Peking to Canton was 'now nearly as well known as the road from London to Edinburgh' (p. 465). Yet, Staunton hoped the detour through Nanjing and the Poyang Lake would prove not only 'one of the most pleasant and interesting circumstances' of the voyage, but would also present the opportunity of making new discoveries (1824, p. 207). While Staunton's account of the embassy was published in 1824 for private distribution only, it seems not unreasonable to suggest that he may have published his journal for a general readership had he discovered anything new or novel about China that had not been described in previous British accounts. To have done so would have enhanced his already considerable reputation and fame as Britain's foremost sinologist by bringing his name before the wider British public.

The Macartney Embassy accounts of China, specifically Alexander's impressive and broad pictorial representation of China based on 2,000 sketches and paintings and Barrow's *Travels in China* (1804), which was widely referenced on the journey, had effectively established a template for British perceptions of the country and its people (see Legouix, 1980). Staunton (1824) wrote in the context of the British anticipation of learning the true moral character of the Chinese people at this time:

> We may find that experience is not always profitable to knowledge—and that our ingenuity in adapting every thing to our preconceived notions is such, that our erroneous prejudices are often strengthened, instead of being corrected, by those facts and occurrences, which, had they been dispassionately considered, must have effected their removal. (p. 206)

Barrow's views on China, it has been noted, were scathing. The Chinese did not enjoy freedom or liberty, individualism was crushed by reverence and submission to a despotic ruler, and life was governed by ancient custom marked by filial piety of juniors to their seniors. Rationality and scientific enquiry based on experiment and observation was not only alien to the Chinese, but also the mass of the people lived under the yoke of superstition and idolatry. China's failure to interact with the wider world brought a lack of both social and commercial progress, leaving it backward and incapable of change. China, Barrow concluded, was worn out by 'old age and disease' (1804, p. 258). Henry Hayne, Amherst's private secretary, who made constant reference to Barrow's (1804) book, summed up the prevailing mood of his countrymen at the time of the Amherst Embassy. He agreed with Barrow and wrote in his diary: 'What a government to serve under—what a country to live in' (n.d., vol. 2, p. 125).

Of interest is the fact that markers of abhorrent Chinese customs described by Barrow (1804), such as female infanticide, foot binding and their habit of eating strange and unclean foods such as cats and dogs, received little attention in the accounts of the Amherst Embassy. This suggests either that they were so entrenched in the British imagination that there was no further interest in describing them, or that little evidence was available to substantiate them.[3] However, other earlier British perceptions of China were confirmed. China was a 'curious' but boring place. Ellis (1817) especially thought his journey to Canton was 'dreadfully dull'.[4] Havell, the embassy's draftsman, left only a handful of sketches and paintings of China, in contrast to the

---

3 On the subject of female infanticide, Abel (1818, p. 233) wrote that, in travelling through the country, there was not a 'sufficient number of facts for estimating the … credibility' of the earlier estimates of 2,000 infant deaths in Peking alone noted by Sir G. L. Staunton.
4 Ellis (1817) commented that 'taking a walk was the only amusement afforded in this dreadfully dull journey' (p. 199).

voluminous visual record left by Alexander at the time of the Macartney Embassy, thereby contributing little to enhance British knowledge of China and suggesting that he found little to inspire him.

General British impressions of China, however, changed as the embassy travelled south into more fertile, picturesque and prosperous areas of the country, and where they received more civil treatment from the Chinese authorities. Staunton learned in discussions with a military mandarin, who remembered him from the occasion of entertaining viceroy Sungyun on board the *Perseverance* at Whampoa in 1811, that the emperor had ordered that 'every kind of public attention and honor should be paid to the Embassy', evidenced by the rank of the great officers designated to escort the embassy (Staunton, 1824, p. 188).[5] Official confirmation arrived in the form of a copy of an imperial edict, received by the British on 8 October, that instructed the officers conducting the embassy to treat it 'with all the civilities due to an Embassador'. The edict read:

> The said Embassy came with the intention of offering tribute; still treat it with civility, and silently cause it to feel gratitude and awe; then the right principles of soothing and controlling will be acted on. ('Translation of an Imperial Edict addressed to the Viceroy of K'iang-nan (Jiangnan), respecting Treatment of Embassy, received October 8, 1816' in Ellis, 1817, pp. 502–503, Appendix 8)

British expectations of an open exploration of Chinese towns, however, were soon thwarted when another imperial order arrived prohibiting such excursions.

The visitors noted the vast and sophisticated network of internal commerce evidenced by the great number of grain junks returning from Peking and admired the physical beauty of the lakes and mountains while sailing down the Yangtze River, but visits to temples or 'joss houses' presented numerous examples of gross idols and Chinese superstition. The embassy read the number of dilapidated buildings and lack of new construction as evidence of economic decay, but the presence of some prosperous Chinese farmers in the southern provinces reminded them more of the dignity and industriousness of the British yeoman. Although Ellis (1817) noted some fine 'gentlemen's country-houses' on the banks of the Poyang Lake, he sought to qualify his observation: 'it being understood that gentlemen's applies only to the houses, and not to the owners' (p. 333).

---

5   The conversation took place on 26 September 1816.

Contact with local Chinese was random and communication restricted, even for the Mandarin speakers. Staunton and Havell 'rambled' together whenever possible: 'We met but few of the country people on the course of our walks, and those we did meet, appeared unusually indifferent and incurious' (Staunton, 1824, p. 297). Peasants stood respectfully aside as the British passed but rarely raised their eyes from the ground (p. 297). Other social encounters were with shopkeepers and monks during visits to various temples.

China was experienced overwhelmingly from the decks of the boats that represented a British space in much the same way as modern-day tourists encounter alien cultures from the air-conditioned comfort of luxury buses or Western-style hotels. Accommodation on board was comfortable with furniture brought from England and a kitchen at the stern where cooks prepared English-style food and footmen served European wines. In their alien surrounds, British camaraderie and attitudes persisted, reinforced by regular communal dinners and the odd cricket match played on Chinese riverbanks.

Sensory historians have explained the importance of the senses in people's perceptions of an alien culture. David Howes explained in his Introduction to *Empire of the senses* (2005) that sensory perception is primarily the product of culture and is the major medium through which people classify and understand different societies (p. 3). The 'senses', according to Mark Smith (2007), are a product of place and especially time. Historians have noted a change in the European hierarchy of the senses during the eighteenth century where the visual, or sense of sight, defined by objectivity, logic and reason, emerged as the most important sense for classifying alien cultures (Howes & Lalonde, 1991).

British perceptions of China experienced the country as a visual and objective encounter. Hence, notes were taken of the distant appearance of cultivated fields, housing, waterways, wildlife and farming practices. Closer to hand, the daily sight of the Chinese boat trackers pulling the boats through the Grand Canal informed the British about the condition of the lowest class of Chinese society. Ellis (1817) described these men, who were at once simultaneously 'objects of compassion and disgust', as 'deformed, diseased, emaciated, and covered with rags' (p. 251). Trackers observed later in the voyage were more presentable. Those of Jiangxi province, for example, were 'stout well looking men' who wore 'neat blue uniforms bordered with red braid'. The pleasing demeanour of the 'lower orders' as well as the neat and clean appearance of the general population seen at this stage of the journey reminded Staunton (1824, p. 186) of Europeans of the same class.

Chinese smells persistently caused the British great discomfort. Abel (1818) wrote on nearing Canton, 'A stranger in China rarely experiences a pleasing emotion without it being destroyed by some circumstance offensive to the senses' (p. 198). Moorings close to towns resulted in British complaints of smells and foul air, while Chinese noises were especially grating to English ears. Ellis (1817) complained that 'nothing is done in China without noise and rout' (p. 384).

Cultural curiosities constantly amused or irritated British sensibilities. The propitiation of the river spirits at local temples by the ritual slaughter of cocks by the Chinese boatmen who prostrated themselves 'before a table covered with yellow silk, ornamented with the figures of dragons' at local temples was noted (Abel, 1818, p. 147), and no doubt recalled comparisons with recent British experiences at Tianjin.

Chinese attitudes to the value of human life mortified the British. Ellis witnessed a man falling into the Grand Canal: 'The Chinese would not make the least effort to save [him] and seemed to regret … the perseverance of one of the ambassador's guard and of our servants [who] succeeded in recovering the body' (1817, p. 249). British reactions to the corpse amused the Chinese who laughed at their response (Journal of Sir William Fanshawe Martin, 1817, p. 50, in BL ADD MSS 41346-41475). The Chinese reluctance to help, Staunton (1824, p. 183) explained, was due to the absurdity of Chinese law where witnesses who interfered in life and death situations were in danger of being liable to either imprisonment or torture if a fatality occurred.[6]

British disembarkation from the boats onto alien Chinese soil replaced the visual sensorium with those of other senses. Immersion in Chinese crowds especially ensured an acute awareness of cultural differences through the senses of smell, sound and touch. British access and freedom to 'ramble' through the countryside and towns was constrained constantly by crowds of curious onlookers whose closeness distressed them. Sensory

---

6   On 23 September, during the first day of travelling on the Grand Canal, a Chinese boatman fell off Ellis's boat and, despite British attempts to rescue him, drowned. The mandarin who eventually arrived to inspect the coffin ordered Chinese witnesses to kneel before him and he interrogated them as culprits (Ellis, 1817, p. 249).

historians, such as Alain Corbin (1986), confirmed the discomforting touch of the 'alien other' in which the unease and annoyance of the 'putrid masses' make crowds dangerous. Walking through the crowded, narrow streets of Chinese towns assailed British senses affected by strange noises, smells, touches, and indecipherable dialects and signs. Volatile crowds presented a potential danger for unrest, conflict and a restriction on personal movement. The presence of Chinese soldiers, endeavouring to keep curious crowds at bay, often exacerbated the conditions in which the British found themselves. At other times, however, Chinese crowds were polite. Such behaviour, the British thought, was in marked contrast to the rudeness of the Qing court at Yuanmingyuan.

Although Amherst informed George Canning, President of the Board of Control, that his embassy was permitted greater freedom to travel around the countryside than the men of the Macartney Embassy (Amherst to Canning, 3 March 1817, in BL IOR G/12/197 (Reel 2) F 281), this view is contentious given that British access to Chinese towns was tightly controlled. Daily itineraries were planned on the basis of the flotilla arriving at its anchorage near a town late at night and departing early in the morning, thus leaving little or no time for visits. Additionally, imperial edicts were issued periodically during the journey to Canton that forbade the British from going ashore. The first was received on 10 October while the embassy was halfway through the Grand Canal.[7] Staunton (1824) wrote in response, 'the interior of towns, we are aware, [are] in some degree forbidden ground' (p. 244). Ellis (1817) added that the Chinese 'jealousy of the cities is equally ridiculous and inhospitable' (p. 250).

Nanjing

The embassy entered the Yangtze River in 50 boats on 19 October at the start of a month-long journey along a route not previously undertaken by Englishmen. The ancient capital of Nanjing was a highly anticipated stopover, especially as Macartney had not visited the city, and it was hoped that new discoveries would be made serving to inform and expand British knowledge of China. The city was currently under the rule of a viceroy who had been governor at Canton in 1809 and shown great hostility towards the British at that time (Davis, 1836/1851, vol. 2, p. 14).

7   See Appendix G.

Some members of the embassy, led by Amherst and Staunton and accompanied by a British marine, a military mandarin and a Chinese soldier, set out to explore the town. Stopping first at a couple of 'remarkable joss-houses' containing highly decorated representations of Buddha, referred to as *Fo* by the British, they continued walking towards the city when they were startled by a Chinese soldier on horseback who rushed past them 'and ordered the [city] gates to be shut' (Staunton, 1824, p. 264). On being told that foreigners were not permitted to enter Nanjing, Amherst refused to leave until the gates were opened and complained of the personal insult to the dignity of a British ambassador. Crowds of local Chinese, also denied access to the city at this time, gathered. The gates remained closed despite the embarrassed pleas from the Chinese mandarin accompanying Amherst as well as Staunton's 'strongest expression' of British indignation at the gates being slammed in the ambassador's face (p. 265). A stand-off ensued. Amherst and Staunton stood firm while Ellis and Davis were ordered to return to the boats to make a formal complaint to the legate Guanghui.

Fortunately, the matter was resolved quickly. Ellis and Davis returned within an hour with news that orders had been issued to throw open the gates. Guanghui apologised for the misconduct and ignorance of the officer issuing the order who turned out to be the district's civil governor and the soldier who had 'rushed' past the Englishmen. The gatekeeper, who had followed instructions to shut the gates, was in danger of being *bambooed* or punished by being struck by bamboo poles, but Amherst intervened and, with some difficulty, procured the man's pardon and release.[8] Amherst was invited to enter the city, but 'his Lordship refused and said he would not have stopped a day [at Nanjing] but for the wind' (Journal of Sir William Fanshawe Martin, 1817, p. 66, in BL ADD MSS 41346-41475). Guanghui intercepted the British on their return to the boats and issued a rare invitation to tea. He apologised to Amherst who reassured him that it was never his intention to contravene Chinese rules or regulations (Staunton, 1824, p. 266). Guanghui's diplomatic and cordial manner at this time impressed Staunton who thought him a man 'of sound sense and above common Chinese prejudices' and who, on the whole, 'was not

---

8 In contrast to the Macartney accounts, the Amherst Embassy references several occasions of 'bambooing'. Soldiers or guards who were lax in their duty and who failed to keep a proper eye on the British were punished in this way (see Ellis, 1817, p. 324). British disgust at the practice was countered by Staunton who pointed out that 'bambooing' was no more reprehensible than the cat-of-nine tails used in the Royal Navy (Staunton, 1824, p. 423).

unfavourably disposed toward us' (p. 267). Amherst's firm stand on this occasion was seen by Ellis (1817) as initiating 'our unrestrained liberty of excursion' (p. 300), at least at Nanjing. Only a week later, however, British movements were restricted by another imperial edict prohibiting them going ashore.

Earlier Jesuit accounts had described Nanjing's famous white porcelain tower, but Ellis noted that it was 'useless and unpleasant both to myself and to those who may chance to toil through these pages' to describe it further (p. 303). Nanjing was depicted as consisting of 'four principal streets … through one of the larger a narrow canal flows, crossed at intervals by bridges of a single arch' (p. 303). British attempts to climb a nearby hill to enjoy the view of the countryside were interrupted by a crowd that grew in number from a couple of hundred to thousands of people surrounding the sightseers. Plans to visit adjoining temples were shelved as Ellis and his party faced the challenge of forcing their way back to the boats. Once back in the secure and ordered space of 'home', Ellis reflected on the reasons for China failing to incite British interest, let alone admiration, despite its antiquity. Significantly, he made an important distinction between Chinese antiquity and the classical antiquity of Western Europe:

> In viewing this city, [Nanjing], striking from its situation and extent, and important from its having been the capital of an immense empire, I felt most forcibly the deficiency of interest in everything relating to China, from the whole being unconnected with classical or chivalrous recollections. Here are no temples, once decorated, and still bearing marks of the genius of Phidias and Praxiteles; no sites or forums once filled with the eloquence of Cicero or Demosthenes, no plains once stained with the scared blood of patriots, and heroes; no, it is antiquity without dignity or veneration, and continuous civilization without generosity or refinement. (p. 305)

Ellis's colleagues agreed with his assessment, which reflects both their ignorance of Chinese history and literature as well as the influence of a classical education in providing upper-class Englishmen with their historical and literary frame of reference for classifying culture. China, Davis (1841, p. 4) thought, had been civilised when Europe was still a barbaric society, but the country had never progressed due to its resistance to foreign commerce and technological improvement. Chinese submissiveness to one man, Davis thought, equated to a mechanical obedience best described as a 'control over animals' (p. 3).

Guanghui paid Amherst a long visit at this time that was notable for its informality. The legate, according to Ellis (1817, p. 307), was 'unusually communicative' and proceeded to tell the British about the public life of the emperor. This rare piece of intelligence on the Chinese court grabbed even Barrow's attention and he referred to it later in the *Quarterly Review* (Barrow, 1817a, p. 478). The 'Son of Heaven', Ellis (1817) reported:

> is [also] a victim of ceremony; he is not allowed to lean back in public, to smoke, to change his dress, or in fact to indulge in the least relaxation from the mere business of representation. It would seem, that while the great support of his authority is the despotism of manner, he himself is bound with the same chain that holds together the political machine; he knows freedom in his inner apartments, where probably he consoles himself for public privations by throwing aside the observance of decency and dignity. (p. 307)

Havell Goes Sketching

William Havell, the embassy's artist, left only a handful of sketches and paintings of China. His body of work did not contribute any new or unique representations of the country or its people in contrast to the impressive and broad pictorial representation of China produced by Alexander at the time of the Macartney Embassy. His work was not used to illustrate any of the accounts of the Amherst Embassy and Ellis's journal, published in 1817, was illustrated with aquatint plates based on drawings by Charles Abbot. While at Nanjing, however, Havell displayed an interest and appreciation of Chinese sculptures seen in a local temple that was not shared by his compatriots.

British preconceived assessments of Chinese art forms in general, and religious art forms in particular, were governed by images represented on Chinese porcelain and lacquerwares that flooded into Britain from Canton during the *chinoiserie* craze throughout the eighteenth century. Images of Chinese deities on these wares portrayed the Buddha as a portly, laughing character, whose depiction was geographically and representationally removed from its true context as sculptures made for the tomb or temple (see Rawson, 1992, p. 165). Havell was not concerned with the symbolism of the 'representations of the divinities' he found in the temple at Nanjing but focused instead on the form and composition of the images. These delighted him because they were 'very superior to any thing … he had imagined, Chinese art could have produced' (Staunton, 1824, p. 271). His astute, educated eye recognised artistic skill and represented a very different assessment of Chinese religious art from the usual British abhorrence of the gross forms of Chinese 'idols' and animal forms found in Chinese temples.[9] Chinese sculpture, perceived universally by Englishmen as an inferior and primitive art form compared to Western aesthetics founded on Greco-Roman classical traditions, had found an unexpected admirer. Unfortunately, Havell was unable to complete his assignment as large crowds of curious locals interrupted his view and impeded his sketching. Staunton's (1824) assessment of the crowd's behaviour on this occasion, however, was laudatory, and he drew an analogy with British crowds, where:

> A solitary Chinese, while surrounded by an English mob, would have been rather … hazardous … and if made by a foreigner, in Turkey or Persia, would probably have been expiated by his instant destruction. (p. 272)

Reflecting on the sculptures at the temple at Nanjing, Ellis (1817) wrote:

> On viewing the works of art of the Chinese, whether painting, drawing, engraving, sculpture, or architecture, I am surprised that they should have stopped where they have done; there were but a few steps to make, and they would have got into the high road of good taste; as it is, they are grotesque and uselessly laborious. (p. 310)

This conclusion reflected Barrow's stadial theory of civilisation expounded in *Travels in China* (1804) where he sought to ascertain China's status. China's natural progression in the arts, traced to antiquity, suddenly stalled. No further progress had taken place due to Chinese arrogance and belief in its superiority, which had prohibited embracing any foreign innovations that may have assisted its progress and improvement. This view also correlated nicely with Barrow's much-quoted assessment of Chinese innovation: 'they can be said to be great in trifles, whilst they are really trifling in everything that is great' (1804, p. 355). Ellis (1817)

---

9   Grotesque stone figures of animals guarded the piers along the Grand Canal, where highly decorated temples with ornamental roofs were noted by the British near the city of 'Tong-chang-foo' (Ellis, 1817, p. 249).

had the last word, not only on Chinese art, but, on China in general: 'It has been said, that there is nothing new under the sun, certainly there is nothing new in China; on the contrary, everything is old' (p. 310).[10]

Staunton and Amherst, meanwhile, climbed the summit of the hill in Nanjing and gazed on the view of the surrounding countryside where little evidence was seen either of a sizable population or the fact that Nanjing had once been a great imperial city. The men of the Amherst Embassy, however, had at least discovered 'the actual state of this celebrated city'. Staunton (1824) pointed out:

> Although the gates of Pekin had been shut against us, those of Nan-kin at least had yielded to our summons, and thus the original and most ancient capital of the empire, which had been visited, I believe, by no former Embassy, fairly laid open to our curiosity. (p. 271)

General British Views of China

British accounts of Chinese life were, inevitably, cursory. City streets were 'composed entirely of eating houses' and crowded with barbers who skilfully shampooed their customers on street corners (Abel, 1818, p. 134). At least six imperial edicts were imposed as the British travelled to Canton. These were posted on city walls and houses and throughout city streets. Staunton (1824) recorded on 30 October that there were three edicts regarding the embassy pasted on the walls of a house within sight of the English boats: 'One of them was written in characters so large, as to be legible from our boats by means of a telescope' (p. 285). The British were prohibited from entering city limits and, if they did, the local population was ordered not to talk or laugh with them and women were told to hide. Shopkeepers were not allowed to sell them goods and the sale of Chinese books was prohibited. Manning, on a visit to Datong in early November, set off on his own and visited a bookshop where he managed to select some volumes that were stacked up on the shop counter, but a stranger appeared and ordered the sale be stopped (Staunton, 1824, p. 316).

---

10 Ellis (1817) commented that the best Chinese art dated from the Ming period and that the 'tartar conquerors of China would seem to have communicated the barbarism without the energy of their ancestors' (p. 380).

The British did manage to purchase some local souvenirs during their travels. These consisted mainly of small pieces of chinaware, specifically tea cups with covers, destined, presumably, for an English mantelpiece.[11] Chinese shopkeepers showed a discerning ability to distinguish between the gentlemen of the embassy who were charged higher prices than the members of the band, while Chinese soldiers accompanying the British shoppers 'winked at the shop-keepers to increase their prices' (Hayne, n.d., vol. 2, p. 127). Service in some towns was excellent. The very civil and well-behaved shopkeepers of Guazhou were praised by Staunton (1824): 'They served us, and tied up and delivered the parcels just as a respectable grocer would do in England' (p. 249). Staunton purchased some tea on this occasion, while Havell bought a roll of paintings at a picture shop although these were 'indifferently executed' (p. 249). The shops of Wuhu in the province of Anhui, Ellis (1817, p. 314) noted, were excellent and would not disgrace those found in the Strand or Oxford Street. Some sold European knives and bales of woollens stamped with the Company logo. Porcelain shops were extensive, but the British were unable to purchase any pieces because of the large crowds following them and the fear of shopkeepers that their stock might be damaged (p. 190). Hayne (n.d., vol. 3) described one scene where some in a crowd were:

> noisy and frolicsome amongst themselves and mischievous, throwing over stalls, pulling down signs, and they pushed one of their comrades down on a pile of coarse crockery-ware and enjoyed the joke at the expense of the poor shop-keeper. These are the sedate Chinese! (p. 14)

The presence of the imperial edicts referred to earlier, however, operated to restrict any meaningful contact with Chinese locals and were interpreted by the British as evidence of the 'contemptuous and despotic indifference to our comforts, which animates the sovereign of these dominions' (Staunton, 1824, p. 287). Hayne (n.d., vol. 3) recorded that the general who officiated over the embassy while in Nanjing had informed the British that in the past some 'Tartars passing thro' the Country had grossly violated decorum with their women' (p. 7). Similar precautions were now taken with the British, but their lack of interest and good conduct, whereby they 'did not even notice the females', had resulted in a relaxation of some

---

11 Staunton earlier informed his mother of a gift from the Hong merchant Puankequa of some chinaware of 10 cups and covers of a 'very pretty light pattern which will do well enough upon [your] mantle piece' (*Staunton Letters*, 18 March 1811).

of the rules (p. 3). A more practical reason, in Hayne's view, was the need to secure city streets against the onslaught of the immense curious crowds that gathered and followed the Englishmen, although an edict posted in the city of Wuhu expressly forbade the British 'carrying away with us any women or children' (p. 13).

Despite the edicts, some worthwhile social encounters did take place. Staunton visited a Chinese school where a group of eight to nine year olds of the poorest class were reading aloud and learning by heart the *Shee-shoo* and *She-king*.[12] Staunton gave the teacher a black lead pencil and some English paper with the names of the children written in Chinese and English; graphite pencils were a European invention and would have been a novel gift for a Chinese child.[13] While unconvinced of the value of rote learning, Staunton was very impressed with Chinese attitudes towards the value of education. Discipline was not harsh and the children were described as enjoying their time at school (Staunton, 1824, p. 305). Davis (1836/1851, vol. 1) quoted Morrison regarding the Chinese regard for education: 'In China there is much to blame, but something to learn. Education is there made as general as possible, and moral instruction is ranked above the physical' (p. 240). Davis thought this state of affairs resulted from the 'industry, tranquillity, and content' of the Chinese people (p. 240).

Apart from walks in the countryside and visits to towns and temples, the British also spent time playing cricket, which, according to Hayne (n.d., vol. 3, p. 68), was undertaken without seeking official permission, which was unlikely to have been granted. Jeffrey wrote that the carpenter 'made us some bats from the Camphor wood and from this time whenever we came to a good piece of ground we had a game of cricket'. 'The Chinese', he added, 'thought we were all gone mad' (Jeffrey Amherst, n.d., n.p.). The sight of energetic English gentlemen running around the fields of China contrasted with the sedentary behaviour of the Chinese upper classes who 'seldom mount a horse' and on whom the 'benefits of walking' were lost (Davis, 1836/1851, vol. 2, p. 35). Davis concluded that, 'Nothing surprises … Chinese gentlemen more than the voluntary exertion which Europeans impose on themselves for the sake of health

---

12   The *Sishu* (The Four Books) and the *Shijing* (The Book of Poetry).
13   Graphite pencils were made by the Germans and English. During the Napoleonic Wars, the supply of British graphite to France was stopped. A French chemist created pencil leads by mixing powdered graphite with ground clay and firing it, a process still used today (see Blaxland, 2008, p. 6). Amherst used a graphite pencil for many of his notes.

as well as amusement' (p. 35). Cricket matches attracted large crowds of Chinese spectators who ringed the field. 'The Chinese', Staunton (1824) wrote, 'soon ascertained enough of the game, to be sensible of the necessity of keeping a respectable distance' (p. 368).

British Lack of Access to Chinese Society

Lack of contact or access to Chinese domestic life remained the greatest disappointment for the British. Chinese domestic architecture closed off any glimpse of family life as compounds were hidden from view and rendered the British passive observers of China. Davis (1841, p. 183) described the 'dead walls in front of dwelling-houses, which were always secluded within an inner court'. Ellis (1817) saw some scenes of home life portrayed on glass paintings at Nanchang, but the only other exposure to Chinese domestic rituals were street processions connected with weddings or funerals witnessed in the streets of Chinese towns (p. 352). Ellis lamented, 'I only regret that our situation precludes all hope of seeing any [other] domestic ceremonies' (p. 203). Opportunities for a deeper understanding of the Chinese national character were thus denied to the British. Abel (1818) wrote:

> Persons travelling in a country in which they are looked upon by the government as objects of jealousy, and by people as beings in all respects inferior to themselves, must have continually to contend with prejudices likely to defeat their attempts at forming a correct estimate of the inhabitants. (p. 232)

Any access to the higher ranks of Chinese general society, corresponding to the social status of the gentlemen of the embassy, was impossible. Abel affirmed:

> With the higher or better informed classes of society, for they are essentially the same in China, we had very little social intercourse that was not purely official or ceremonious; and on all these occasions found them so cased in the armour of form that it was impossible to reach their natural character, or to depend on their information as the simple statement of matters of fact. (p. 232)

British access to the 'middling class' was confined to shopkeepers, or those encountered as part of the crowds in towns and cities, and Abel lamented the fact that these occasions provided little opportunity for judgement on the state of Chinese society (p. 233). During an earlier walk in the countryside along the Baihe River, Abel had encountered a group of 'handsomely clothed' Chinese women who, with the arrival of some Chinese soldiers, 'hobble[d] off as fast as their crippled and stunted feet could carry them' (p. 88). A few women at Nanchang defied imperial orders and looked at the Englishmen (Ellis, 1817, p. 353). Ellis noted that their painted faces presented a 'carnation tinge to the complexion' and their fine eyes 'though angularly shaped were together tolerably attractive' (p. 353). Hayne (n.d., vol. 3) suspected that these were ladies of 'dubious virtue' (p. 29). British appearances, Abel noted (1818), also made an impact on the Chinese:

> We were to these people as the inhabitants of another world. Our features, dress, and habits were so opposed to theirs, as to induce them to infer that our country, in all its natural characters, must equally differ from their own. 'Have you a moon, and rain, and rivers in your country?' were their occasional questions. (p. 131)

Ordinary Chinese were sometimes very friendly to the British. Villagers helped Abel with the collection of plant specimens, while some members of the embassy established a strong rapport with their boatmen who were a great source of gossip on the embassy's progress. Thus, the British were told that Guanghui's reluctance to travel in rough weather was due to his 'small liver' that made him timid and afraid (Hayne, n.d., vol. 3, p. 24).[14] On a couple of occasions, military mandarins invited the Englishmen onto their boats for refreshments. Ellis (1817) related that he and the young midshipman Charles Abbot were invited on board a boat of a military mandarin 'for the usual purpose of looking at us':

> Abbot, as the youngest, was the principal object of his attention, and [our host] amused himself by dressing [Abbot] in Chinese clothes: he seemed to live in great familiarity with his servants, and put my hat on to excite their merriment; I, in return, took his cap, and the buffoonery was complete. (p. 211)

Abel's (1818) account included several occasions where he interacted with ordinary Chinese in the time before he fell ill. Removed from the pressures of official business, Abel spent time mingling with itinerant barbers and hawkers who set up stalls at the sites where the embassy docked to cater to the Chinese on the boats. He visited a food stall 'arranged with great neatness and order' whose cook was a 'plump and sleek old man, naked

---

14 Here the British are mistaken. Rather than the liver, the boatmen were probably referring to Guanghui's gallbladder. In traditional Chinese medicine, a small gallbladder makes one cowardly.

to the waist' and whose complexion suggested he had 'passed all his life within the influence of a furnace' (p. 90). The cook insisted on showing Abel all the secrets of his art and begged him to 'partake of its produce', but Abel found the hot sesame cakes too oily for his taste (p. 91).

Abel was also asked to join some Chinese soldiers camped on the riverbank who were sitting around red lamps suspended from three sticks, smoking pipes and playing dominos. Time was spent comparing the respective size of their hands with Abel, much to everyone's amusement, while Abel's gilt buttons and fine linen shirt were much admired. Abel declined some offerings of clothing but accepted some white cloth badges inscribed with Chinese characters worn by the soldiers around their necks.

Keeping up British Appearances: Dinner Time

Amherst maintained embassy morale during the long journey through China with formal dinners marking British ceremonial occasions held on shore whenever the terrain permitted the setting up of tables. Hayne (n.d., vol. 2, pp. 151–152) referred to Saturday night drinking sessions held in accordance with the 'old ship custom of drinking on Saturday night at sea to the wives, sweethearts and absent friends'. These were elaborate affairs governed by strict protocols of etiquette characterised by cordial conduct consisting of refined manners, politeness and fine conversation that defined rank and personal civility. A formally laid dining table complete with fine silverware, cutlery, crockery, crystal glassware and a countless range of serving dishes, all brought from England, added to the opulence and formality of the occasion. The strong social bonds resulting from shared experiences of China evinced at these times by the 20 'gentlemen' of the embassy reaffirmed British identity and values and endorsed the perceived superiority of British civilisation in the alien environment of China (see Elias, 1939/2000, pp. 5–6).

The sensory anthropologist Lisa Law has written on the power of food to 'articulate national identity' by evoking memories of the taste, aroma, and texture of home (2005, p. 236). Its potency derives from its classification as a category of 'cultural separateness' (Tannerhill, 1995, p. 230). A variety of fine produce was provided to the British by their Chinese hosts. In northern China, these consisted of sheep, bullocks, pigs, fowls and a variety of vegetables and fruits. On reaching the Yangtze River and

Poyang Lake, the British were supplied with vast quantities and varieties of vegetables, deer, game fowls, geese, ducks and fresh fish, as well as white grapes, apples and mandarins. Breakfasts, given information from British cookbooks of the time, consisted of rolls, cakes, eggs and fruits. Dinner, served at four o'clock in the afternoon, was the main meal of the day. Three cooks were in charge, namely, two British cooks and Staunton's Cantonese cook. Normal meals took place on individual boats among small groups of only two to four, attended by several staff.

English cookbooks of the period suggest the menus that may have been offered during the Amherst Embassy. Food historians have noted the change that took place in British cuisine at this time where the preference was for bland, honest food, cooked simply and without the embellishment of fancy sauces thought to disguise the integrity of original ingredients (Turner, 2004).[15] French cuisine, notable for sliced meats or fricassees smothered in sauces, was not to British taste. Southern European cooking, characterised by dishes of greasy food, reeking with garlic and swimming in olive oil, was considered most unpalatable (Margaret Visser as quoted in Howes & Lalonde, 1991, p. 127). The similarity of this continental style of cooking with Chinese cuisine familiar to the members of the Amherst Embassy was noted by Davis (1836/1851, vol. 2), who wrote that 'Chinese cookery has a much nearer resemblance to the French than the English' (p. 25). British preference for hearty soups such as a country-style vegetable broth with shredded cabbage was eminently suited to the ingredients supplied to the embassy. Soups were followed by meat dishes consisting of hams, braised goose and roast chicken. Accompanying the main dishes was a variety of entrees such as boned crumbed chicken breasts, sautéed fish, and boned game of pheasant and stuffed partridges in aspic.[16]

The sensory experience of the British meal enjoyed by the embassy members functioned momentarily to transform the Chinese environment into a part of Britain (Law, 2005, p. 226). Smells of food cooked in the British manner wafted across the landscape, while strange sounds of cutlery scraping plates would have puzzled Chinese witnesses. The accompanying music provided by the ambassador's band assisted the cultural transformation, as well as attracting large crowds of Chinese.

---

15   Turner (2004) wrote that British tastes by the nineteenth century had shifted to 'simpler and more local flavors … the new ideal was that food should taste of itself' (p. 301).
16   This menu is an adaptation of a formal dinner given for the Prince Regent at the Brighton Pavilion in January 1817. It is referred to as an indication of dishes that may have been prepared at the time of the Amherst Embassy (see Tannerhill, 1995, pp. 298–300).

People climbed up surrounding trees to see the table laid and hear the band more distinctly. Curious mandarins often visited the British at table where their presence caused an annoying, hot and stuffy atmosphere; an alien presence that might spoil the ambience of the occasion. The band, however, was culturally adaptable and took advantage on occasions to entertain both the British and Chinese. Staunton (1824) described its playing on shore at the time when the embassy was due to enter the Yangtze River:

> Our band played on the bank opposite Lord Amherst's boat, for some time during the afternoon, and drew together a considerable audience of mandarines as well as country people, who all appeared, by their manner and attention, much pleased with our music—The band played, among other pieces, the Chinese tune of *Moo-lee-wha*, which the natives readily recognised. (p. 249)[17]

A constant source of amusement for the British during their travels through China was the shabby military appearance of the Chinese soldier. The victors over Napoleon were unimpressed and critical of what they saw. Primitive weapons of bows and arrows, rusty flintlock rifles and effeminate uniforms resembling dresses attested to China being an unwarlike nation (Ellis, 1817, pp. 225, 267). The British passed some forts made up of temporary structures of matting and 'rudely painted, so as to have the appearance of brick or stone at a distance' that reminded the visitors of a production seen in country theatres and a 'good laugh' was had by all (pp. 225, 267). Davis, whose account of the embassy was published after the First Opium War, was a harsh critic of the primitive nature of Chinese weaponry and the childishness of its soldiers and officers. The Chinese commander of Amherst's boat, for example, was fond of a game where an Englishman was invited to blow in his face, after which he turned his face away, but then turned around and 'ran in and seized his antagonist by the leg to upset him' (Davis, 1841, p. 178). Davis believed this action indicated the importance of bodily strength and dexterity in the Chinese military, but thought it also proved 'the low state of the art of war among them' (p. 178).[18] Nonetheless, some Chinese

---

17 *Molihua* or 'Jasmine Flower'.
18 Davis's (1841) account contained his opinion on the strategic importance of Tianjin for any future British engagement: 'It must be viewed as the first object of attack to any force which should make an attempt in the neighbourhood of the capital, and try the strength of Chinese troops in that quarter. Its vicinity to the sea, and its vast importance as the depot for grain and salt, render it extremely obnoxious to foreign invasion' (p. 189).

military officers were singled out for acting with great civility. One lent John Griffith, the embassy's chaplain, his horse so that Griffith could ride back to the entrance of the junction of the Grand Canal, which he had missed (Staunton, 1824, p. 193).

Even Ellis admired a military parade seen on the beach at Anqing in Anhui province. Four hundred and fifty Chinese soldiers, decked out in 'full armour, drawn out on the beach with their officers in their stations, and their colours, music, tents, &c, duly arranged and displayed', saluted the British boats (Staunton, 1824, p. 317). Davis (1841), however, played down the occasion. The soldiers made a 'good theatrical show' and reminded him more of an opera chorus than 'men whose trade was slaughter' (p. 225). In his view, the small marine guard accompanying the Amherst Embassy could have taken Tianjin with ease (p. 89). This early assessment of the primitive state of the Chinese military was reinforced as the embassy travelled through China.

Insulting Chinese behaviour remained a constant source of irritation for the British. Morrison, acting on Amherst's orders, wrote a letter of complaint to Guanghui, notable for harbouring a veiled threat:

> This morning—when His Lordship went out of his boat, there were native soldiers who several times rudely stood and intercepted his path. [Further] as Mr. Ellis passed Chin-tazin's boat, his servants rudely began to laugh. It is seriously apprehended that to treat us who are visitors in a foreign country with such rudeness, may provoke some unpleasant occurrences, and therefore Your Excellency is now [requested] to take some means to prevent so unfortunate an affair. (Correspondence During the Embassy to China (September 1815 – September 1817), in BL IOR MSS EUR F 140/38 (a))

Although Morrison was aware that Chinese officials who acted civilly towards the British exposed themselves to the ill will of the mandarins, concern with external appearances befitting the status of the embassy drew complaints when their dignity was thought to be compromised (Correspondence During the Embassy to China (September 1815 – September 1817), in BL IOR MSS EUR F 140/38 (a)). Chinese officials acted most 'unhandsomely' when complaints were made about Guanghui being assigned a superior boat to Amherst. Morrison informed Amherst in a private letter that they 'deserved any trouble it may occasion them'

(Morrison to Amherst, n.d., in BL MSS EUR 140/38 (a)). He continued in a passage that succinctly summarises much of the British frame of mind during their journey to Canton:

> There was at first on the part of the Chinese who spoke to me a disposition to be rudely familiar and assuming. Having withstood the Emperor and the Duke at the door of the Court, it would perhaps be wrong to submit to the gross neglect of the Legate ... at the extremity of the Empire. (Morrison to Amherst, n.d., in BL MSS EUR 140/38 (a))

Troubles also arose over incidents involving quarrels between the members of the band and some Chinese. Morrison told Amherst, 'some of our people—the band it is supposed—have struck some Chinese, which gave occasion to … ill-natured [complaints]' (Morrison to Amherst, n.d., in BL IOR MSS EUR 140/38 (a)). Accordingly, Amherst imposed a curfew on the band and the British servants who were not allowed to leave their boats after dark without special permission (Staunton, 1824, p. 251). On the whole, however, the lower orders of the embassy acted with 'a very fair character' and there were only a few instances of drunkenness and quarrels among themselves (p. 360). The earliest Chinese complaint about bad British behaviour on the journey to Canton occurred as the boats were entering the Yangtze River. An investigation revealed, however, that this was 'a boyish piece of fun of Jeffrey Amherst's in pushing a boy into the water' (Hayne, n.d., vol. 2, p. 248).

British respect for Guanghui increased on the sad occasion of the death of a British marine who slipped on the deck of Morrison's boat and drowned. Morrison informed Amherst, whose boat was moored some distance away down river, that:

> The Chinese, by order of the Legate, afforded every assistance, & at my request, during the night, cut a grave-stone the following Epitaph: 'The Tomb of Millidge, one of the Body-guards of the British Embassador; Nov 11. 1816'. This is a translation. The words were in Chinese. (Morrison to Amherst, n.d., in BL IOR MSS EUR F 140/38 (a))[19]

---

19   Morrison also informed Amherst that a death certificate had been issued in order for it to be registered with the Qing court and the viceroy at Canton. It read, 'On the 11th Nov 1816, one of the British Embassador's Body-guard named Millidge, aged 31 years, in passing from the head to the stern of the boat, the plank being rendered slippery by rain, lost his footing; fell into the water & was drowned'. Staunton (1824, p. 320) incorrectly referred to the marine as 'Millage'.

Guanghui's response at this time was praised by Staunton (1824, p. 321) and described as 'very civil' and expressing 'great concern'.

Apart from observing the Chinese people in the towns and villages they visited, the British took the opportunity of mapping their route through the Yangtze River. Amherst informed Canning that because this was country 'hithertoo unexplored' by any Englishman:

> I was anxious to preserve the best memorial of it which our very limited means would allow: and this has been effected by the industry and accuracy of Mr. Charles Abbot, the eldest son of the Speaker of the House of Commons ... who accompanied me on my landing in China. He had prepared as detailed a map & memoir of the country as could be accomplished without the aid of some of the most essential instruments, and with occasionally, but little time for observation. (Amherst to Canning, written aboard the *Caesar* at sea, 21 April 1817, in BL IOR G/12/198 (Reel 2) F 256–257)

The Arrival of the *Alceste* at the Pearl River

The HMS *Alceste* arrived at Lingding Island, outside of Macao, on 2 November after a journey of almost three months exploring the Gulf of Bei Zhili, the eastern coast of Korea and the Ryukyu Islands.[20] Captain Maxwell, following the precedent of the HMS *Lion* at the time of the Macartney Embassy, was under orders from the Admiralty to proceed to Whampoa to refit in preparation for Amherst's arrival. Dispatches were received on board announcing the failure of the Amherst Embassy, followed soon after by an edict sent by the viceroy of Canton prohibiting the *Alceste* from entering the Pearl River to meet Amherst. Amherst, it seems, was expected to find his own way to the British ships anchored outside the Pearl River, travelling by a back passage 'without suffering to call, much less to stop, at Canton' (Barrow, 1817a, p. 479).

---

20 Restrictions of space prohibit discussion of the Ryukyu Islands in this study. For the account of these, see M'Leod (1818/1820) and Hall (1840/1865).

Maxwell received conflicting orders from the Canton Government. It was initially confirmed that a passport and pilot would be assigned to the *Alceste*, permitting the ship to proceed to Whampoa, but this order was countermanded three days later by a senior mandarin sent by the viceroy. Maxwell told the mandarin that an imperial edict had specified that the Amherst Embassy be treated with the same respect as that accorded to Macartney, and that consequently he was allowed to go to Whampoa. The mandarin offered no response. Maxwell remained calm in the face of the mandarin's 'rudeness' but responded in a tone and manner that, according to Basil Hall (1840/1865), 'made the Mandarin's button wag on top of his bonnet' (p. 69). On being asked by the mandarin if the *Alceste* was carrying any cargo that would have required the ship being registered as a trading vessel, Maxwell replied:

> Cargo, did you say!—Powder and shot, sir, are the cargo of a British man-of-war! Did you see his Majesty's pendant flying at the mast-head? If you did not, I desire you will take a good look at it on your way to Canton, where you may tell the Viceroy you have seen a flag that has never been dishonoured—and please God, while it waves over my head it never shall. (as quoted in Hall, 1840/1865, p. 69)

Several days passed with no resolution of the stand-off. Maxwell gave orders on 12 November for the *Alceste* to approach the mouth of the entrance to the Pearl River where she was surrounded by 17 Chinese war junks and the shore batteries were seen making full preparations to repel the ship. The junks 'beat their gongs, fired guns, and threw up sky-rockets, to give the alarm', but no damage ensued (M'Leod, 1818/1820, p. 104). Maxwell, deciding to take matters into his own hands, loaded one of the quarterdeck guns and personally fired it at the Annahoy fort, destroying an outside wall and invoking from the crew of the *Alceste* 'three roaring cheers' (p. 104).[21] The result, according to Hall (1840/1865, p. 71), was 'instantaneous and most ludicrous'. Maxwell told him that the Chinese 'fell flat on their faces … like Persians at sunrise'.

---

21   M'Leod (1818/1820) added that this was a deliberate action taken by Maxwell who was aware that, in the event of the Chinese 'demanding who fired, instead of those who ordered, or of seizing upon any innocent person, he might fully place himself in the situation of being individually responsible for all consequences'. Staunton (1822, p. 313) added later that by this act Maxwell placed the whole weight of responsibility on himself.

Figure 11: The engagement in 1816 of the HMS *Alceste* under Captain Sir Murray Maxwell with the Chinese fortresses on the Bocca Tigris, both of which he immediately silenced.

Note: Drawn by John M'Leod, surgeon on board the *Alceste*. Engraved by Dubourg and published and sold in 1818 by Edward Orme, Bond Street, London.

Source: Image from Wattis Fine Art, Hong Kong, and now in the author's collection.

The breeze sprung up soon after, and the *Alceste* sailed through the Bogue on its way to Whampoa. Captain Maxwell later received an official explanation that the junks did not fire at the *Alceste* in anger but were merely saluting the ship. The British read this as a flagrant lie but were afterwards gratified to learn that Maxwell's actions had resulted in 'a remarkable improvement in the condition of foreign residents' at Canton (Hall, 1840/1865, p. 75). The Indiaman *General Hewitt*, which had been involved in a serious altercation with the Canton authorities and prevented from loading teas for her return voyage to England on the grounds that she was a tribute ship, was now allowed to take on cargo.[22] The *Alceste*, anchored at Whampoa, also began taking on provisions and making preparations for Amherst's return expected in late December.

---

22   The *General Hewitt* had arrived at Lingding Island on 12 September 1816 but was refused permission to travel up-river to Whampoa to load tea. The Hong merchants refused to deliver the Select Committee's letter to the viceroy and the suggestion that Captain Campbell would go in person to deliver the letter was received with much alarm as he had not been granted permission to travel to Canton. Following the committee's suggestion that tea would be loaded at Lingding, the *General*

Amherst's Return to Canton and Reception

The local people grew ruder and the crowds became less interested in the British as the embassy procession approached Canton. Progress was slow and difficult through the rapids and shallow streams as the trackers struggled to keep the boats under control. The picturesque countryside was conducive for walking and Staunton (1824) was amused to see 'pinnacles of hills dotted with parties of Englishmen' from the embassy (p. 395). The mountains separating the British from Canton were seen on the morning of 16 December and, three days later, preparations involving 3,000 men were made to cart the baggage over the mountain pass. Amherst was transported in a 'glazed palanquin' carried by 12 soldiers and the commissioners travelled in palanquins borne by six soldiers. The servants, guards and band members were each carried in small open chairs by two bearers (p. 439). Nights were spent at rest houses where graffiti on the walls revealed the names of the Dutch embassy of 1795 and some of the Amherst party added their signatures (p. 445). Five days out from Canton, the flags on the British boats were changed to 'tribute flags' (Ellis, 1817, p. 399). Lines of handsome soldiers were drawn up as the British passed and Amherst was moved to a superior boat, while Guanghui was thought to be increasingly cordial and civil in his manner. A small white cottage, passed on 30 December, reminded Ellis of England 'to which indeed all our thoughts begin now to turn' (p. 404).

Some British Conclusions on China

While many of Barrow's (1804) earlier assessments of China were confirmed by the members of the Amherst Embassy, especially that the Chinese were a 'frowzy people', some new judgements were made at this time. Ellis (1817) commented on Chinese affection for their children and thought that 'their civil institutions' enforced the 'reciprocity of good

---

Hewitt was surrounded by Chinese war junks. An impasse lasted for several weeks. The ship eventually reached Whampoa on 23 October after a series of visits by some mandarins and the committee's letters not being received by the Hoppo resulted in the committee sending a naval officer to force his way into Canton to deliver a letter to the viceroy. A compradore from the British Factory was arrested for having been complicit in the officer's visit. The stand-off continued into November and was not resolved until the compradore was released and Captain Maxwell had forced his way up the river (Morse, 1926/1966, vol. 3, pp. 265–269).

conduct' (p. 204). Evidence of Chinese familial love was illustrated by Chang-wei's 18-year-old son having to return home to live with his mother 'as she could not endure being separated from him'. This, Ellis thought, showed that Chinese 'ladies', as distinct from women of the lower classes, had 'their full share of influence in Chinese families' (p. 204).

The reports of the Amherst Embassy confirmed Macartney's earlier views on the clear distinction between the Manchu or 'Tartars' and the Han Chinese. Macartney wrote that China consisted of:

> Two distinct nations ... the Chinese and the Tartars, whose characters essentially differ (notwithstanding their external appearance be nearly the same) and whose minds must naturally be differently bent by the circumstances which respectively govern them. They are both subject to the most absolute authority that can be vested in a prince, but with this distinction, that to the Chinese it is a foreign tyranny; to the Tartars a domestic despotism. (Cranmer-Byng, 1962, pp. 221–222)

Macartney thought that China's failure to progress higher on the scale of civilisation was due to the impact of the Manchu conquerors who had held China back while their European contemporaries were 'every day rising in arts and sciences' (pp. 221–222). In Davis's (1841) view, the 'Tartars' were too proud to learn from foreigners, in contrast to the progressive and inquisitive British who never missed an opportunity to study them (p. 109). 'Knowledge', for the British, was 'power', reflecting the value they placed on intelligence at a time of an expanding maritime-based empire that was global in nature. Davis further noted the coarse manners of the 'Tartar' military officers, who he thought were also 'illiterate' (p. 203). He added that, 'The very inferior consideration of the military, as compared with the civil mandarins, is purely Chinese, and appears under Tartar despotism, as a singular anomaly' (p. 203).

The British did have some positive experiences in their dealings with Qing officialdom. Thus, the 'gentlemanly behaviour' of an officer from Shandong province was found to be 'extremely pleasing' (Ellis, 1817, p. 264). Specific praise was accorded to the escort who accompanied the embassy through Jiangxi province due to his 'conversation [which] was full of expressions of the highest consideration' of England and with 'humble allusions' to China (Staunton, 1824, p. 391). Staunton praised the civility and attention shown by local officers on the Yangtze River for their efforts in overseeing the British boats (p. 239). Even Davis (1841) approved of Chang-wei, the Han Chinese junior legate, who had accompanied the embassy since it first arrived off Dagu:

> The ease and good breeding of the better sort of Chinese, when they are on friendly terms, is very striking, and by no means what might be expected from the rigid nature of their ceremonial observances. (p. 191)

Chang-wei's 'real politeness' and pleasant manner resulting from a daily familiarity with the British represented a state of mutual admiration between him and the senior members of the embassy. Chang-wei sat with the British at dinner, although he did not much 'relish' English cooking, and expressed his warm admiration of 'the blunt integrity and straight-forwardness of the English character' (p. 191). Such, however, were exceptional relationships. The other Manchu mandarins involved with the embassy displayed little or no interest with either Amherst or the commissioners. The British saw their arrogance and disinterest as indicative of a regime clinging to past glories and grounded in the belief that China was the centre of the universe. The presence of highly educated Mandarin-speaking Englishmen in the Amherst Embassy, eager to learn as much as they could about China, presented a unique opportunity for the senior mandarins of the Qing Government to learn more of the outside world in general and of Britain in particular. The opportunity, however, was not taken up. Instead, Amherst, the British complained, was treated by the senior mandarins with the most 'wilful neglect … of all the common courtesies and rights of hospitality' due to the envoy of a foreign state (Staunton, 1824, p. 408). Staunton, in particular, was scathing of the lack of honours accorded to Amherst in contrast to those paid to the Chinese conductors of the embassy. He concluded that the 'complimentary display' showed to the embassy was 'as worthless, as their military shew is contemptible' (p. 409). Amherst was insulted late in the journey when the conductors of the embassy were given a three-gun salute on passing a military post while he was ignored. Morrison was instructed to send a formal note of complaint regarding this 'piece of inattention' (p. 425).

Staunton sought to sum up the attitude of the ordinary Chinese people towards the British. Their predominant feeling, Staunton thought, was 'an overpowering curiosity, perfectly inoffensive and good-humoured', which contrasted with the 'contemptuous and malignant spirit' displayed to the

British by the Cantonese (p. 409). Ellis's (1817) assessment of China, on the other hand, reflected ambiguous British feelings of the country resulting, in part, from the failure of the embassy and the nature of its reception at Yuanmingyuan. He concluded:

> However absurd the pretensions of the Emperor of China may be to universal supremacy, it is impossible to travel through his dominions without feeling that he has the finest country within an imperial ring-fence in the world. (p. 323)

Return to Canton

On New Year's Day 1817, seven miles from Canton, the members of the Amherst Embassy noted the ambassador's barge from the *Alceste*, flying the royal standard and bearing Captain Maxwell and Metcalfe, approaching them at a rapid rate followed by 21 other boats of the British ships anchored at Whampoa (Jeffrey Amherst, n.d., n.p.). Two lines of barges belonging to the *Lyra* and the Indiamen were lying downstream waiting to escort Amherst to his lodgings prepared at 'the temple of Ho-nan' (Haizhuangsi), situated on the banks of the Pearl River opposite the British Factory, which had been 'splendidly fitted up' in a European fashion by the order and expense of the Chinese Government (Staunton, 1824, p. 479). Hayne (n.d., vol. 3) commented that the Chinese 'bishops' had been 'cajoled and bribed' to give up their own apartments (p. 115).[23] 'The paraphernalia of idol worship', Abel (1818) wrote, 'had given place to the commodious furniture of an English home' (p. 206). Jeffrey added that the Chinese had consented 'to the removal of their Josses from the part of the temple which we inhabited and they were stowed away in a lumber room' (Jeffrey Amherst, n.d., n.p.). Hayne (n.d., vol. 3) elaborated that the 'gods and goddesses were either out of doors or shut … up in cupboards' that were now replaced by 'stoves, and British furniture' (p. 115). The temple had been transformed into 'a palace fit for a British Embassador' (p. 115). Charles Abbot wrote a long letter to his father dated 2 January 1817:

---

23   Hayne (n.d., vol. 3) added that the gateway or 'portico' to the temple was guarded on each side by gigantic statues representing Chinese gods, or guardians of the temple. These were painted and gilded in the 'most gawdy colours and with hideous fierce countenances' (p. 117).

> Here I am comfortably settled in an arm-chair by the fire-side, in a Chinese temple, which has been appropriated to the Embassy during their stay here, and been made to look like an English house by the kindness of the gentlemen of the British Factory. (The Hon. C. Abbot to his father, Lord Colchester, Canton, 2 January 1817, in Colchester, 1861, vol. 2, pp. 13)

Amherst and the embassy dined that evening at the British Factory. The function was attended by over 100 people, all of whom were English apart from the American Consul. It was a splendid evening with toasts after dinner, complimentary speeches and songs (Hayne, n.d., vol. 3, p. 117). 'Every heart was glad' and the Englishmen 'experienced in the heartiness of the reception a pleasing contrast with the pretended hospitality of the Chinese' (Ellis, 1817, p. 407). Amherst took the opportunity to scrupulously maintain the appearance of His Majesty's ambassador and informed George Canning later in his official report that it was only now that he was able to do so (Amherst to Canning, 21 April 1817, in BL IOR G/12/197 (Reel 2) F 358).

Amherst had a final formal engagement to attend, namely, an imperial banquet held for the delivery of the letter from the Jiaqing emperor to the Prince Regent. Informed that he was expected to kowtow, he replied he would bow on receiving the letter. On 3 January, a letter from the mandarins notified the British that the ceremony had been downgraded to a reception for the delivery of the letter and that the prostration ceremony was dispensed with.

An unauthorised copy of an imperial edict dated 6 September addressed to the viceroy of Canton found its way into British hands the following day. Its wording differed from other edicts and blamed the failure of the embassy at Yuanmingyuan on the actions of the British ambassador and commissioners, specifically, for not observing 'the laws of politeness toward their own sovereign' who had sent presents at great cost and across great distance to indicate his respect and obedience to the emperor. A reception for the British was to be held where the viceroy was to instruct Amherst of his failure 'to lift [his] eyes to the face of Heaven' and to give thanks to the emperor for the benefits received while in China (see Ellis, 1817, pp. 505–506, Appendix 10). The British found themselves in a predicament. Decisive action was required to stop the viceroy from making an insulting address, but care also had to be taken not to reveal how a copy of the edict had come into their possession (p. 411).

The reception was held on 7 January in a large yellow tent constructed outside the temple. Preceded by the band and the marine guard, Amherst and his party, dressed in their ambassadorial robes and uniforms, made a splendid appearance. The emperor's letter, housed in a bamboo tube covered with yellow silk, was placed on a small sedan chair carried by 36 bearers. The viceroy handed the letter to Amherst who received it with a profound bow and handed it to his secretary, Henry Hayne. Jeffrey noted in his journal, 'The viceroy seemed astonished at the little respect with which the Imperial letter was handled, but said nothing' (Jeffrey Amherst, n.d., n.p.). Entering a side apartment, Amherst and the viceroy held a brief discussion during which the mandarin asserted in a haughty tone that the British had benefitted from Chinese trade for about 100 years (Amherst to Canning, 21 April 1817, in BL IOR G/12/197 (Reel 2) F 362). He claimed that Britain could not 'dispense with the commodities of China', whereupon Amherst replied that these were not indispensable and that both Britain and China mutually benefited from the trade, which was equal and reciprocal (Amherst to Canning, 21 April 1817, in BL IOR G/12/197 (Reel 2) F 363). Both men then adjourned to the tent for fruits and refreshments. Jeffrey described a 'most ridiculous scene' that took place as the viceroy and Amherst walked to the tent:

> The Viceroy and ambassador walked together at the head of the Party, but the former wishing it to appear that he was of the highest rank endeavoured to get a little ahead of my father, but my father perceiving his object stepped out also, until our arrival at the tent put an end to the race. (Jeffrey Amherst, n.d., n.p.)

The British read Amherst's performance in front of the viceroy as a moral victory. Abel (1818) described the mandarin as a 'character of cunning' who endeavoured to adopt an overbearing attitude but who soon 'grew pale, and his eyes sunk under the stern and steady gaze of the English Ambassador' (p. 210).[24]

Father Lamiot, the only French missionary still at Peking, had sent a Latin translation of the emperor's letter (Amherst to Canning, 21 April 1817, in BL IOR G/12/197 (Reel 2) F 364). Its contents were the same as noted in the earlier copy where the encounter at Yuanmingyuan was attributed to 'the pertinacious and successful refusal of the ambassador

---

24 Barrow, in his review of Abel's book in the *Quarterly Review* in 1819, commented: 'We did not think that Lord Amherst could assume so formidable a look—at all events we are inclined to think that the presence of Captain Maxwell and the recollection of the guns of the Alceste … were not without their due share in "blanking the once bold visage" of the viceroy' (p. 83).

and Commissioners to attend the emperor, under the absurd pretext of sickness' (Ellis, 1817, p. 413). It also contained some assertions, referred to as 'falsehoods' by Abel (1818), that Macartney had kowtowed and that Amherst had at first promised to do so, but afterwards refused. Abel concluded, 'We felt no regret in learning that with a government so faithless, the delivery of the letter had terminated the Ambassador's official intercourse' (p. 211).

Amherst had a busy social calendar at Canton. He paid a visit to Guanghui who was 'cheerful and chatty' and who sent a communique suggesting that some of the British presents might still be accepted by the emperor. The British believed that this indicated that 'the Imperial court is not without apprehension of the possible consequences of the abrupt dismissal of the Embassy' (Ellis, 1817, p. 414). A decision was taken to decline all such suggestions as conciliating the emperor would add to British humiliation. Amherst was also invited to a dinner held in his honour by Chun-qua, one of the principal Hong merchants. Ellis hated it. He complained of the infernal noise of the 'sing-song' and instruments and noted the mandarin buttons worn by the Hong merchants were purchased at a high price to provide immunity from government punishments (p. 419). Guanghui, in contrast, enjoyed a breakfast held at the British Factory where 'his manner and conduct was perfectly unembarrassed, easy, affable, and cheerful: he seemed to feel himself among friends, and lost no opportunity of shewing attention to those within his reach' (p. 414).

Amherst's Departure from China

Amherst prepared to leave Canton on 20 January 1817. Guanghui paid a call in the morning 'and seemed quite sorry to leave us' (Jeffrey Amherst, n.d., n.p.). Amherst, accompanied by all the boats of the Company's ships, was given three cheers as he left the pier. Ellis (1817) wrote:

> It was impossible to hear [these] without strong emotions. There was an awful manliness in the sound so opposite to the discordant salutations and ridiculous ceremonies of the nation we were quitting. (p. 421)

The viceroy, who was watching the departure from a distant boat moored in the river, sent Amherst his card, but Amherst chose to ignore it. The viceroy's action, the British thought, was not meant as a point of civility but, rather, as concern to witness the departure of the embassy. The *Alceste*, moored at Whampoa, was reached at three o'clock in the afternoon. The man-of-war was decorated with her colours and her yards were manned (Jeffrey Amherst, n.d., n.p.). Amherst informed George Canning that, on boarding the *Alceste*, 'I considered my intercourse with the Chinese Authorities as at an end' (Amherst to Canning, 21 April 1817, in BL IOR G/12/197 (Reel 2) F 374).[25] A parting dinner was held in the evening for Staunton who was travelling to England separately on the Indiaman *Scaleby Castle*. Three days later, the *Alceste* arrived at Macao after passing the forts whose personnel paid the 'utmost respect' with the guard turned out and saluting as the ship passed (Amherst to Canning, 21 April 1817, in BL IOR G/12/197 (Reel 2) F 374).[26] The governor of Macao sent his apologies for not receiving Amherst as all appointments had been suspended because a state of mourning was declared for the late queen of Portugal. Metcalfe suspected that this was deliberately timed to coincide with Amherst's arrival so that the Portuguese 'may boast to the Chinese' that the British ambassador had received 'no mark of attention from them' (Metcalfe to Amherst, Macao, 21 January 1817, in BL IOR MSS EUR F 140/38 (a)). Amherst was also informed that several Chinese troops had entered the settlement and had set up camp opposite the intended landing place of the embassy at Macao, ostensibly as a mark of respect. On 28 January 1817, Amherst left Macao and 'finally took leave of the Coast of China' (Amherst to Canning, 21 April 1817, in BL IOR G/12/197 (Reel 2) F 374).

Postscript

The *Alceste* and *Lyra* left Macao together, but separated at Manila from where the *Lyra* sailed for India. A little after seven o'clock in the morning of 10 February 1817, the *Alceste* hit a reef in the Gaspar Straits off the coast of Sumatra. Jeffrey wrote to his sister:

> The shock which it gave was tremendous; I was walking up & down in my father's Cabin & could hardly keep my legs … there was a large hole in her [the *Alceste*'s] bottom … water had already filled one store room … the bumping was dreadful, as whenever

---

25 Amherst's notes and letters, and subsequent career, reveal that he chose not to pursue any further interest in China.
26 The *Asiatic Review* (August 1818, p. 192) quoted the *Madras Courier* for 9 February 1818: 'In China all was quiet. The Chinese were busily employed about rebuilding the fort that the Alceste bombarded with such effect. They are also building new ones in different parts of the river'.

the ship rolled, she struck again against one of the rocks … all the
pumping was useless. (Jeffrey Amherst to his sister, 2 March 1817,
in BL IOR MSS EUR F 140/230)

The boats were hoisted out and loaded with 'such provisions as were not wet' and set off with the members of the embassy to a small uninhabited island situated three miles away (Jeffrey Amherst to his sister, 2 March 1817, in BL IOR MSS EUR F 140/230).[27] Jeffrey wrote that Captain Maxwell joined the group the following day, where it was decided:

That the barge with my father & the gentlemen of the Embassy
should start at three o'clock for Batavia; each gentleman was
allowed to take a change of linen … We did not start till six
o'clock, & had some difficulty in clearing the rocks. We were
thirty three persons in the barge, & fifteen in the cutter which
came with us. We had the good luck the second day to have some
rain by which we got some water to drink. We arrived on the
fourth day at Batavia, and the first sight of the [British] ships was
the most cheering sight we ever saw. (Jeffrey Amherst to his sister,
2 March 1817, in BL IOR MSS EUR F 140/230)[28]

The 200 Englishmen, and the boatswain's wife, who remained on the island were in constant danger of attack by large numbers of Malay pirates who had already burnt the wreck of the *Alceste* and threatened an assault on the island. Help reached the besieged group 12 days later with the arrival of an Indiamen, *Ternate*, that scared off the Malays. Maxwell's conduct throughout the calamity was widely praised in England and Ellis (1817) commended him for his 'firmness and commanding character … [which ensured] sufficient security for the maintenance of discipline' (p. 452). Maxwell was later called before a court martial for the loss of the *Alceste* but was completely exonerated.

A Meeting with Napoleon on St Helena

The members of the embassy set sail for England from Batavia in the Indiaman *Caesar*. Returning via South Africa, the *Caesar* arrived at St Helena on 27 June 1817 where Amherst met Napoleon. Napoleon's views on the fate of the Amherst Embassy are not mentioned in Ellis's

---

27 The island was situated 240 miles (386 kilometres) from Batavia.
28 Abel's plant specimens, collected under the orders of Sir Joseph Banks and destined for Kew, were mistakenly discarded at this time for a change of linen for one of the members of the embassy.

(1817) account, but are instead recorded in a book written by his English surgeon, Barry O'Meara, published in 1822. Napoleon was very knowledgeable on the impasse of the kowtow and displayed a most pragmatic attitude to the issue. Amherst, he thought, should have bribed the mandarins: 'If a million of francs had been given to the first mandarin, everything would have been settled' (as quoted in O'Meara, 1822, vol. 2, p. 69).[29] The embassy, in Napoleon's view, had not been sent on behalf of British national honour; rather, it was 'as an affair of merchandize' sent on behalf of 'the tea-merchants in England' (p. 44). Therefore:

> Advantages might with great honour be purchased. Besides, when you send ambassadors to those barbarians, you must humour them and comply with their customs. They do not seek you. They never have sent ambassadors in return for yours, nor asked you to send any. (p. 44)

Napoleon told Amherst that the consequence for his embassy, in which £100,000 pounds had been 'thrown away' and ill blood between the British and Chinese had resulted, was caused 'by a ridiculous misunderstanding' (p. 178). Amherst had been informed 'by bad advisors' and had proceeded to act under the misguided apprehension that an 'ambassador represented' his sovereign. Napoleon, as a former emperor himself, made it clear that he believed Amherst's rank equated to that of the princes or the 'grandees' of the court, who, in China, were expected to perform the kowtow before the emperor. The emperor, therefore, 'had a right to require it' (p. 176). Further, Amherst was chastised on his presumption whereby he attempted 'to regulate the etiquette of the palace of Pekin by that of St. James's'. England and Russia, according to Napoleon, should:

> instruct their ambassadors to submit to the *ko-tou*, upon the sole condition that the Chinese ambassador should submit in London and Petersburg to such forms of etiquette as are practised by the princes and grandees. (p. 178)

Napoleon did not consider the kowtow a humiliating act, but thought that in respecting the customs of another country, 'you make those of your own more sacred' (p. 178). He had, of course, missed the fundamental point of Chinese tributary diplomacy. The kowtow for Napoleon, it appears, was

---

29 Gabriel de Magalhaes, in his account of the Dutch embassy sent to China in 1655, acknowledged that the Dutch bribed the viceroys of Canton and a number of Chinese officials, especially the Manchu president of the Board of Rites, which almost secured Dutch success in their objectives (see Kops, 2002, pp. 568–569).

just theatre or mere ceremonial, and it meant nothing beyond an act to please the emperor. In this respect, the British had more in common with the Chinese than they did with Napoleon. Both knew the kowtow was an act of profound political significance, changing forever the basis of the relationship between the actor and the recipient. They did differ, however, in the role of the ambassador. For the Chinese, the role of an ambassador was not simply to pay respect or deliver messages, but to portray the submission of his sovereign. In any event, the victors over Napoleon were in no mood to be lectured. The *Literary Gazette* commented in its November 1817 issue:

> The conversations with the Ex-emperor are rather hacknied, and we shall only offer one remark on the dicta ascribed to him, - that if he had sent an Embassy to China, he would have taken care to dispatch a person who would have observed all the prostrations required. We trust the difference between the Prince Regent of England and a Corsican adventurer will always be held a sufficient answer, at least in this country, for our not being prone to pursue exactly the same course; and it may be further added, that what would have been a disgrace to a British nobleman, might have been unobjectionable in one of the revolutionary dignitaries of the new order.

Staunton had the last word on Napoleon's views. He wrote to Amherst from St Helena after a conversation with the governor, Sir Hudson Lowe, on the issue of the kowtow: 'I shall only say that it will not be the first time that England and Bonaparte have differed upon matters of State policy' (Staunton to Amherst, St Helena, n.d., in BL MSS EUR F 140/38 (a)).

11

Aftermath: Britain's Reaction to the Failure of the Amherst Embassy

The Amherst Embassy's fate was announced to the British public by *The Times* on 10 May 1817. The Company ship *Prince Regent*, newly arrived from India, had met the *General Hewitt* at St Helena and brought the news that 'The Embassy has wholly failed, and the presents which were to have been the pledge of amity and intercourse have been returned so we have not lost all' (*The Times*, 10 May 1817). Some of the presents had been sold at Canton, but the bulk of them were returning to England on board the *General Hewitt*. Reasons for the embassy's failure were not yet known, but it was hoped that trade at Canton had not been affected. The *General Hewitt*'s arrival in England was 'hourly expected' (*The Times*, 10 May 1817). *The Times* published an extract of a letter written by a junior member of Amherst's retinue five days later on 15 May that described the honourable treatment the embassy received on its travels through China to Canton. The English had enjoyed walks in the countryside due to 'a liberty rather *taken* than a liberty *given*' (emphasis in original); had travelled over 'a considerable portion of new ground, or more properly speaking water', and had received a 'very sulky' reception at Canton where the embassy was not saluted (*The Times*, 15 May 1817). An article published on 26 August 1817 contained some more details of the embassy, but a full account was not available until Ellis's (1817) journal appeared in British bookshops in late October.

The importance of the Amherst Embassy in shaping British views of China in the crucial period leading to the First Opium War (1839–1842) is the subject of this chapter. While Staunton informed Morrison in a letter dated April 1818 that 'the whole question of this Embassy [in England] is now passing fast into oblivion', Amherst's hostile reception by the Qing court was important for providing new intelligence on Chinese officialdom and contributing to a reassessment of China that informed later British policy (see Hampton, 2009, p. 4).[1] Henceforth, British reviewers in popular journals portrayed the Chinese emperor and his court as a barbaric Tartar horde and praised Amherst's firm actions in upholding British honour and the status of the British sovereign. Although the embassy failed in the short term in achieving its goals, its long-term significance remained and is traced here through references to it in the period leading to the First Opium War. Ellis's and Staunton's opinions were canvassed both at the time of debate over the review of the Company's charter in 1833 and also in the House of Commons in 1840 on the eve of British military intervention in China. The true legacy of Amherst's reception at Yuanmingyuan was to confirm the futility of further diplomatic initiatives to achieve British commercial goals in China and to promote the expediency of using force, if necessary, to achieve these aims. Such sentiments were shared by some American traders at Canton and stated bluntly by one trader, Isaac Bull, who commented later in 1840, 'The English may talk reason with the Chinese until the day of judgment, [but] the latter will not give them what they want without force' (as quoted in Miller, 1974, p. 98).

Amherst arrived back in England on 16 August 1817. Captain Maxwell sent a letter expressing 'the honour, the heartfelt pride, and gratification of being ship mates with Your Lordship for eighteen months' (Maxwell to Amherst, Ship *Caesar*, Isle of Wight, 16 August 1817, in BL IOR MSS EUR F 140/39).[2] The Dowager Amherst wrote, 'Welcome! Thrice Welcome! To thy native land My Dearest, Dear Lord Amherst, & your Dear Boy. How thankful I am' (Dowager Amherst to Amherst, 20 August 1817, in BL IOR MSS EUR F 140/39). The Archduke of Austria summed up the delight and relief of Amherst's friends: 'The joy I have felt in your safe escape outweighed by far that which the most successful

---

1   Hampton (2009) referred to the diplomatic space 'where knowledge of the Other is produced, where interest is weighed and gauged'.
2   Maxwell informed Amherst that his luggage was boarded on wagons and was on its way to his house in Grosvenor Street. Customs had mistakenly opened and inspected his bags, but they were due to be severely reprimanded by the collector, who had been attending church at the time.

result of your Embassy or scientific enquiry would have given me' (John, Archduke of Austria, to Amherst, Vienna, 1 October 1817, in BL IOR MSS EUR F 140/39). Lord Morley was the only one of Amherst's friends who expressed doubt over his decision not to kowtow before the emperor, but these thoughts were accompanied by qualifications. His 'uninformed feeling' was that he would have 'complied with any ceremonial [and] … would have gone in any state of fatigue or in any dress … into the presence of the Emperor', especially when accompanied by Mandarin speakers able to explain the truth of the ambassador's appearance (Lord Morley to Amherst, Paris, 21 September 1817, in BL IOR MSS EUR F 140/31). But if Amherst had evidence of a 'generally hostile feeling', then he was 'right to refuse' (Lord Morley to Amherst, Paris, 21 September 1817, in BL IOR MSS EUR F 140/31).

Amherst's chief grievance was the contrast in his reception with that of Macartney's. Macartney had maintained that there were 'a considerable number of great people at Court who [had] expressed their being much pleased with us, and who wished that we had continued here longer' (Cranmer-Byng, 1962, p. 155). Rather than being received in an orderly and regular manner where the dignity of the Chinese emperor and the King of England had been maintained, Amherst's reception was marked instead by 'hurry and precipitation' (Amherst to Canning, 8 March 1817, in BL IOR G/12/197 (Reel 2) F 285). Amherst was offended especially with the removal of every mark of splendour and 'respectable appearance' of his embassy, serving to reduce it to the degrading appearance of one of China's meanest tributary vassals. His uncompromising stance in China, on the other hand, was praised in the highest circles of the British Government. The governor-general of Bengal, the Earl of Moira, wrote:

> I am perfectly persuaded, and it seems the universal opinion here, that Your Lordship has gained more by your firmness than you could have done by any compliances with the arrogant proposition made to you. I do not speak merely as to the impression of the British character so worthily upheld by you. We are all convinced that for the Company's trade more advantage will flow from the anxiety of the Chinese to repair an affront which they apprehend may be seriously resented than could have arisen out of any Disposition infused into that Government by conciliatory submissions. (Earl of Moira, Calcutta, to Amherst, 13 April 1817, in BL IOR MSS EUR F 140/39)

Staunton agreed with Lord Moira. He pointed out later in his privately printed memoirs in 1856 that, although the Amherst Embassy had been 'stigmatised as a failure':

> It was practically, perhaps, the most successful of any that had ever been sent to Pekin by any European power; for it was followed by a longer interval of commercial tranquillity, and of freedom from annoyance, than had ever been experienced before. (p. 68)

This view was repeated by Davis in his later study *The Chinese* (1836/1851), where he stated that from 1816–1829 there was not a single stoppage of British trade at Canton apart from the incident involving the *Topaze* frigate in 1822, in which the Canton authorities made the first advance to a resumption of trade (vol. 1, p. 81).

Staunton's belief in the value of the moral example left in China by the Macartney Embassy applied also to the Amherst Embassy. Amherst's defiant stand and firm assertion of British values and honour in his dealings with the mandarins had achieved a more beneficial outcome for British interests than would have resulted from a mere ceremonial reception, 'had there been one', at the Qing court (p. 67). Davis was of the same opinion. Barrow, he pointed out, had observed that 'a tame and passive obedience to the degrading demands of this haughty court serves only to feed its pride, and … the absurd notions of its own vast importance' (as quoted in Davis, 1836/1851, vol. 1, p. 77). Amherst's strong stand based on his advice not to kowtow, Staunton argued, had a most positive effect on the Cantonese authorities resulting in a peaceful period of trade with few interruptions until the late 1820s. It seems ironic that the Amherst Embassy was judged by some as achieving a more successful outcome for British interests than its predecessor.

However, the reaction of one of the missionaries at Peking, presumably Lamiot, to the reception of the Amherst Embassy at Yuanmingyuan was one of concern. Amherst had in his possession an extract of a letter which read:

> Here [at Peking] it is much dreaded that the English will demand some satisfaction, for in truth, very unjustly have they been treated, and with great baseness. This may be attended with important consequences for us, and it will be well that we should be prepared beforehand. (Extract of a letter from one of the Missionaries at Pekin, n.d., in BL IOR MSS EUR F 140/38 (a))

Reactions of the British Media to the Amherst Embassy

In September 1817, the publisher John Murray wrote to Lord Byron informing him of his busy schedule:

> I have just come to town for a few days and have my hands quite full—I am preparing two accounts of the unfortunate China Expedition including one by John M'leod and one by Mr. Ellis (Ld Buckinghamshire's son). (Cochran, 1922, p. 78)[3]

Attention to the Amherst Embassy in England coincided with the publication of books on the embassy in 1817 and 1818. Further interest is not evident again until 1821 when reviews of Morrison's (1820) account of the embassy were published. Staunton's English translation of the Chinese account of a *Narrative of the Chinese embassy to the Khan of the Tourgouth Tartars in 1717* was also published in that year and reviewers made passing reference to the Amherst Embassy. The spotlight on the embassy resurfaced again in 1821 during the proceedings of an enquiry into trade with the East Indies and China before the Select Committee of the House of Lords.

The published accounts of the embassy, in particular Ellis's journal published in 1817 as intimated previously, confirmed Barrow's earlier views of China. Ellis's book was the first and acknowledged 'official' account of the embassy, and his views were significant in consolidating the first assessments of China to emerge from the Amherst Embassy. The American historian Stuart Creighton Miller (1974) has more recently summed up Ellis's contribution as one revealing:

> The alleged pretentions and arrogance of Chinese officials; Chinese propensity for filth, lying, cheating, and cruelty; the primitive state of Chinese science and medicine; and the slavish adherence to customs—all were present. (p. 52)

Ellis portrayed China as a stagnant and dull country whose people suffered from a lack of freedom and progress due mainly to the oppressive rule of the usurping Manchus. A letter to the editor of the *Asiatic Review* in January 1818, signed with the *nom de plume* 'Yen Kwang', not only repeated

---

3   The letter continues that he also had 'Two novels left by Miss Austen—the ingenious Author of Pride & Prejudice—who I am sorry to say died about six weeks ago'.

these judgements but added that Chinese pride and self-sufficiency only debased them among other nations due to their ignorance and misguided belief that the 'world is a plain with China in the middle surrounded by all other nations, kindreds, and tongues as tributaries'. While the experiences of both the Macartney and Amherst embassies had begun to 'open the eyes of the world at large' to China, much remained 'hidden from view'. The writer concluded, 'we plainly see that the inhabitants of the celestial empire are neither so great, so wise, or so powerful' as their eulogists have claimed (Yen Kwang to the editor, *The Asiatic Review*, January 1818, vol. 5, p. 4).

British readers were disappointed, however, that Ellis's (1817) book contained little new information or insight on China. The track from Peking to Canton, Barrow complained in his review in the *Quarterly Review*, was as earlier noted, 'nearly as well known as the road from London to Edinburgh' (1817a, p. 465). Although the Amherst Embassy had deviated from Macartney's route and travelled via Nanjing, 'the sameness, which is characteristic of China, seems everywhere to have occurred in the constant repetition of the same kind of objects' (p. 465). While the members of the Amherst Embassy took advantage of their opportunities to explore the Chinese countryside, these excursions had failed to produce any new knowledge of China. British rambles covered only a narrow range of terrain radiating from the boats where social contact was limited to peasant farmers, shopkeepers and temple priests. Crowds restricted any serious exploration of Chinese cities encountered en route and entry into Peking did not occur. Contact with Chinese women and insight into Chinese domestic life remained inaccessible. Barrow (1819) reminded his readers:

> We should always remember that we view the Chinese character only as drawn by foreigners, who, from the nature of the government, have at all times been the objects of suspicion, and who hold a very limited intercourse with the natives. (p. 76)

China's persistent refusal to communicate with the outside world was summed up by the *Eclectic Review* in 1821:

> We are completely shut out from personal communication with [the Chinese], being merely permitted to peep at them from Canton or Macao, as through a grate, where our Factory converse with them through the medium of a mercantile jargon, intelligible only to themselves and the individuals with whom they traffic. (vol. xvi, p. 37)

11. AFTERMATH

The most noteworthy outcome affecting British perceptions of China from the accounts of the embassy was a revised assessment of the Qing emperor and his ministers. Accounts of the Macartney Embassy had portrayed the Qianlong emperor as a venerable old gentleman-statesman who was healthy, vigorous, affable and pragmatic, and who had received the British with graciousness and politeness. The Qianlong emperor had, at least, engaged with the British personally, exemplified famously by his brief conversation with the young Staunton, which signified an interest in the outside world.[4] The Jiaqing emperor's reputation, on the other hand, based on his treatment of Amherst, whereby the ambassador was not even received, was judged by British popular journals in the most vitriolic of terms. At best, the emperor was 'a weak and capricious ruler, little acquainted with the affairs of government, or the condition of his people' (Barrow, 1819, p. 75).[5] At worst, he was 'a man of impetuous and capricious disposition, increased by a habit of constant inebriation' (*The Times*, 26 August 1817).[6] An official report on the state of China presented to the British Government in 1847 summed up the Jiaqing emperor's legacy: 'His life and reign is blank, as no just, noble, or generous action can be discovered' (Martin, 1847, p. 285). Modern historiography has revealed, on the contrary, that the Jiaqing emperor was pragmatic, sober, frugal, energetic and intent on instigating a series of new reforms in his reign (see Rowe, 2011; Wang, 2014). He was challenged not only with curbing the financial excesses of his father that had left the imperial coffers in a depleted state, but also by serious internal insurrections, assassination attempts and a serious pirate problem on the southern China coast (Wang, 2014, p. 128). His treatment of Amherst, however, served to define and denigrate the office of the Chinese emperor as a caricature of an oriental potentate in the British imagination. The emperor's ministers fared no better. China's despotic government was revealed to British readers as one characterised by 'childish vanity', insolence, meanness and 'unblushing falsehoods' (Barrow, 1817a, p. 465). Chinese mandarins, according to Ellis (1817), were arrogant, pretentious, rude, devious and liars. British reviewers were outraged by the Chinese suggestion at Tongzhou that Amherst perform the kowtow in private but was free to lie in making a false report to the king. Barrow, writing again in the *Quarterly Review*,

---

4   The interest or otherwise of Qing emperors in the 'outer world' was noted by Will (2008, p. 125).
5   Abel (1818) also described the Jiaqing emperor as 'a timid' man with a 'vacillating temper, sufficiently proved by his conduct to the British Embassy' (p. 118).
6   This comment was subsequently reprinted in the *Gentleman's Magazine* (July–December 1817, p. 231).

wrote that this proposition 'affords no bad illustration of the notions of the Chinese respecting the conduct of men in public situations' (1817a, p. 470).

Not surprisingly, British reviewers vilified Heshitai in particular who was portrayed as arrogant, rude and lacking in any sense of propriety. His suggestion to Amherst that he was prepared to 'be his friend' at Peking if Amherst agreed to kowtow was seen as an attempt to pressure, if not blackmail, the British into complying with the ceremony. Significantly, it was after this meeting that Amherst made his final decision not to perform the kowtow based on Staunton's advice, as well as his own judgement as to the best course of action available to him. Heshitai's subsequent report to the Jiaqing emperor, sent from Tongzhou confirming that the 'English tribute-bearer is daily practising the ceremony, and manifests the highest possible respect and veneration' ('Heshitai's Report from Tongzhou to the Emperor' in Ellis, 1817, p. 509, Appendix 13), exemplified for Barrow (1817a) 'the utter disregard of the Chinese for the truth, from the emperor on the throne to the lowest of his minsters' (p. 472). Heshitai's rude behaviour at Yuanmingyuan of grabbing Amherst's arm still angered the British many years after the event. A review in the *Asiatic Journal and Monthly Register for British India and Its Dependencies* of an account of the recent Russian embassy to Peking in 1820–1821 thought it relevant and appropriate to refer to the Amherst Embassy where Heshitai's act of:

> taking his Lordship [Amherst] by the arm in order to conduct him to another apartment, was nothing less than a brutal attempt to drag him into the presence chamber, where he would most probably have been compelled to undergo other humiliations. (Review of 'Travels of the Russian Mission through Mongolia to China, 1820-21' by George Timkowski, *Asiatic Journal and Monthly Register for British India and Its Dependencies*, 1827, p. 826)

Heshitai's behaviour, according to Peter Auber's account of China published in 1834, represented the 'most singular specimen of inhospitable and unmanly treatment' befitting the barbarity of a Tartar camp more than any 'which could have been expected even from the most uncivilised of crowned heads' (p. 263). The *Pocket Magazine*, which catered for a poorer educated clientele, was also scathing of Heshitai's insult to the representative of the British sovereign, describing it as a 'disgusting nonsense; insisting on the superior dignity of his Emperor over our King' (1818, vol. 1, p. 111). Amherst, the magazine concluded, would have been well within his rights to have thrown the insolent 'Ho [Heshitai] and Mu [Muketenge]' into the Baihe River (p. 110). The Chinese belief of there being 'only one sun in the firmament, so there was only one sovereign in the universe, the Emperor of the Heavenly Empire' was, in Auber's (1834, p. 261) opinion, absurd. The only interesting part of Ellis's (1817) account, *The Times* (8–9 October 1817) concluded, was that which:

> describes the Ambassador in some danger of being introduced into the presence of the Emperor of China in the same manner as an unwilling creditor would be introduced into a sponging-house by a couple of bailiffs.

Conversely, the *Edinburgh Review* presented a contrarian view of the Amherst Embassy's reception in its review of Ellis's (1817) book. The Chinese Government's right to deny entry into their country of restless, ambitious and intriguing European visitors 'who have played the game of war and ambition, for near three hundred years, in their immediate vicinity' of India was acknowledged (*Edinburgh Review*, 1818, vol. 29, p. 29). Amherst, described as a nobleman of the 'most amiable character', had in fact little diplomatic experience and was assisted by a man—namely, Staunton—who was 'considered by the Chinese as a dangerous person'. Amherst had been poorly briefed on his mission and many in England were 'prepared for the catastrophe of the Embassy', especially following the fate of the Golovkin Embassy. The kowtow, in the *Review*'s opinion, was no more humiliating than other court ceremony, and it was reasonable to expect that an ambassador visiting a foreign court should subscribe to local ceremonies and not 'attempt to prescribe a new one' (p. 29).

Although British public interest in the Amherst Embassy subsided after the appearance of the first accounts in 1817 and 1818, reference to it resurfaced throughout the following 20 years. Two books on China, it has been noted, were published in 1821. Reviews of Morrison's (1820) memoir of the embassy focused on the 'senseless state of idolatry' and superstition in China and the decay of its temples (see e.g. *The Eclectic Review*, 1821, vol. 16, pp. 569–571). The second book, mentioned previously, was Staunton's (1821) translation of *Narrative of the Chinese embassy to the Khan of the Tourgouth Tartars in 1717*. Its publication presented Barrow with yet another opportunity to voice his opinion on China through a review in the *Quarterly Review*. The Chinese, Barrow (1821) concluded, were a shrewd and ingenious people, excelling in the arts, manufacturing, agriculture, civil polity, literature and morals, and were indisputably far superior to other Asiatic peoples (pp. 414–415). But their condition suffered from a bad government and a terrible religion: 'the one, we think, renders them selfish and distrustful; the other superstitious and hypocritical' (p. 415). Chinese society had been made 'cold and repulsive' due to its exclusion of women shut behind family compound walls (p. 415). While Barrow thought a 'closer intimacy' with the Chinese people 'might incline us to entertain a somewhat more favourable opinion of them', this opportunity was prevented by government policy that was 'hostile to all international connections' and the difficult Chinese language prohibiting any communication with foreigners (p. 415). A final assessment of the emperor reflected the impact of the Amherst Embassy. The Qing emperor, in Barrow's opinion, was not a despot, but was little more 'than a puppet in the hands of a few great officers' (p. 415). Staunton's translation revealed further that the true status of a foreign mission 'in Chinese eyes' was one that was 'so little desirable' (p. 420).

The Legacy of the Amherst Embassy in the Period Leading to Free Trade

In 1821, an enquiry of the Select Committee of the House of Lords, initiated in part due to the current viceroy stopping trade at Canton, sought to investigate avenues for trade concessions in China. Reference was made to diplomacy's failure to secure positive outcomes:

> All the efforts of the Company since the splendid Embassy of Lord Macartney from the King of Great Britain, could not procure the liberty of a second port; and so things continue to this day. Another recent Embassy from the sovereign of this country, intended also to procure ameliorations in the trade, was not even admitted into the emperor's presence. (Charles Grant as quoted in *Report [relative to the trade with the East Indies and China] from the Select Committee of the House of Lords*, 11 April 1821, p. 165)

The insolvency of the Hong merchants, through whom the British conducted their trade, resulted in a serious dispute at Canton in 1829. The viceroy had refused to discuss the issue with the Select Committee, which threatened to withdraw the Company ships to Manila as well as sending in the Royal Navy in an attempt to secure a dialogue. The viceroy eventually backed down and agreed to new concessions at Canton, including the appointment of three new Hong merchants.

The Select Committee's firm and decisive action in the face of Chinese intimidation at this time was a direct legacy of Staunton's resolute stand both at Canton in 1814 and during the Amherst Embassy where British submission was thought only to aggravate and promote Chinese demands. A further legacy of the Amherst Embassy, and arguably the major one, was the British recognition of the value of military force in assisting the procurement of British concessions from the Chinese Government. Captain Maxwell's success in silencing the Bocca Tigris forts and forcing his way up the Pearl River had broken the serious stalemate over the loading of teas on board the *General Hewitt* in 1816, and had resulted in the viceroy ameliorating his hostile stance towards the British by insisting that the shots fired at the *Alceste* were intended as a salute rather than an aggressive act. British views on dealing with China arguably changed as a result of Maxwell's action, reflecting the efficiency of enlisting British power to achieve national objectives. The former president of the Select Committee, Charles Marjoribanks, informed the president of the Board of Control, Charles Grant,[7] in 1833 that diplomacy had failed in China and recommended:

> Commissioners be sent, accompanied by a part of the naval squadron in India; for to command the slightest attention or respect in China, you must appear with an appropriate force; let your requisitions be such as you are justified in making, and be prepared to insist upon them if refused. This may be readily done by occupying … one of the numerous islands in the Canton river, and, if necessary, seizing the forts which command its entrance. They have no force, either military or naval, to oppose to you, that is not contemptible. Under such circumstances I feel satisfied your demands would be granted in a very brief period. (Marjoribanks, 1833, p. 53)

Ellis and Staunton were also called on to give their views on the extension of the Company's charter in 1833. At issue was the question of maintaining the Company's tea monopoly in China in the face of growing pressure from British public opinion and manufacturers who

---

7   Charles Grant, later Lord Glenelg, was the son of the former chairman of the East India Company of the same name.

petitioned the government for opening up the China trade to all traders. Ellis presented a series of letters on the East India question to members of the two Houses of Parliament in 1830 in which he addressed the major question: 'In what manner can the trade with China be carried on with most advantage to the English nation?' (Ellis, 1830, p. 26). His answer reflected views consolidated at the time of the Amherst Embassy. The Chinese Government, he argued, had 'peculiar opinions' regarding any contact with foreigners who were considered a danger to national security and a threat to Chinese morals and political and domestic harmony. China's great internal trade, observed by him during his travels with the embassy, meant they had no need for commerce with other nations (p. 29).[8] Their trade with Britain was not founded on treaties between independent states but was solely in the hands of the Hong merchants who, in turn, were responsible for their dues to the Chinese Government. Ellis argued that, regardless of any change the British might make to the Company monopoly, the Hong merchants would retain their monopoly. Private traders, acting in an individual capacity in contrast to the powerful Select Committee, would be powerless to bargain with them, and control would soon fall into the hands of the more prosperous Hong merchants who would manipulate prices and the trade to their own advantage (p. 33). Diplomatic representation at Canton, in Ellis's view, was also useless. The presence of an American Consul had made no difference to the conduct of American private trade, whereas:

> The power possessed by the Company's supercargoes of stopping the whole British trade … has been found to be infinitely more calculated to prevent fresh exaction, than any diplomatic proceeding whatsoever, when addressed to a government so totally different, from the rest of the civilised world, in the laws and usages regulating international intercourse. (pp. 40–41)

Staunton held similar views.[9] He addressed the House of Commons on 13 June 1833 with a series of recommendations during the debate on the renewal of the Company's charter. The valuable tea trade still contributed almost £4 million annually into the British Treasury's coffers, he reminded

---

8   Davis also believed that free trade with China was 'fraught with great evil' that would result in the rise of tea prices and a degradation in tea quality (see East-India Committee, *The Times*, 24 February 1830, p. 3).

9   Staunton was elected first to the House of Commons as MP for the rotten boroughs of St Michael's in Cornwall and Heytesbury in Wiltshire between 1818 and 1833 (Staunton, 1856, p. 76). He was later elected as MP for Portsmouth. For a full examination of Staunton's career during this time, see Eastberg (2009, pp. 206–223).

the House, but was governed solely by the arbitrary control of Chinese local authorities at Canton and subject to severe and vexatious restrictions (Staunton, 1840, Appendix, p. i). Company agents, acting as a powerful united group, were able to oppose the arbitrary and oppressive acts of the local government, which was not possible by individuals acting alone. Such influence was the 'sole check operating to control and counteract the corrupt local administrators of the peculiarly arbitrary and despotic government'. Staunton, unlike Ellis, still believed that diplomacy had a role to play in gaining trade concessions:

> Notwithstanding the failure of all complimentary embassies to the court of Pekin, however otherwise beneficial in raising and procuring the due recognition of the national character, [Chinese] treaties with Russia prove there are no insurmountable obstacles to such an agreement. (p. ii)

The Charter for the East India Company was renewed in 1833 for another 20 years. The old title of governor-general of Bengal was changed to governor-general of India and the position of 'Chief Superintendent of Trade' in Canton replaced president of the Select Committee.[10] Significantly, the China trade was opened to all (Mersey, 1949, p. 53). Staunton's views on how to deal with the Qing Government changed in 1840, largely in response to the Chinese seizure and destruction of British property, consisting of opium valued at £2 million, at Canton (Eastberg, 2009, p. 221). Staunton asked the following question in an address to Parliament on the eve of the First Opium War: 'Is the contest in which we appear to be on the eve of embarking with the Emperor of China, a just and necessary war, or an act of cruel and iniquitous aggression?' (Staunton, 1840, p. 5). He still preferred a diplomatic solution for re-establishing British trade in China on a satisfactory and secure footing, but had reluctantly reached the conclusion:

> that the context in which we are about to engage with China is perfectly just … I rejoice to see that it has received this night the tacit approbation, at least, of the House. (p. 7)

While Staunton abhorred the opium trade and wished to see it abolished, he felt the current conflict was not about opium, but rather that the Chinese Government had breached international law in seizing British

---

10   Lord William Napier was the first appointed to this position, but his credentials were rejected by the viceroy of Canton when Napier arrived in 1834 (see Lovell, 2011, p. 6).

property and had broken their trust of safely protecting the trade and British citizens (Eastberg, 2009, p. 221). Asked how he would have responded to Commissioner Lin Zexu's actions at Canton in confiscating British opium, Staunton told Parliament:

> I must beg to tell … the House what I *did* do when I was in Pekin with Lord Amherst, and under somewhat similar circumstances. When threatened in a similar manner by the Commissioner's Imperial Master himself, because I refused to advise my noble colleague to perform the Chinese ceremony, I neither trembled nor obeyed; and all the world knows that that Embassy was not only allowed to return safety [sic], but traversed the whole Chinese Empire afterwards with greater convenience and equal honors to the preceding Embassy of Lord Macartney. (p. 20)

Eastberg (2009, p. 223) has argued, convincingly, that Staunton's views on China were largely outdated and overtaken by events by the time of the First Opium War. Western perceptions of China had consolidated. Pertinently, Miller wrote in the context of some American opinion, which is applicable also to British views, that China's defeat in the Opium War was hardly a surprise given earlier reports of its military backwardness. He added:

> The Amherst mission and the action of Captain Maxwell in Canton provoked one [American] editor in 1818 to declare that the country 'slumbers, like a drowsy and emasculate Mammoth … till invasion, from the East and West shall enter her realms, and with fire and sword, purge away the gross and stagnant humors that clog her distempered frame'. (*American Monthly Magazine and Critical Review*, 1818, vol. II, p. 443 as quoted in Miller, 1974, p. 92)

Western abhorrence of the kowtow had become inextricably linked with Chinese identity and cultural imperatives in the Western imagination. John Quincy Adams, a former United States president and diplomat, wrote at the time of the First Opium War that its cause was not opium but the kowtow, blaming:

> The arrogant and insupportable pretensions of China, that she would hold commercial intercourse with the rest of mankind, not upon terms of equal reciprocity, but upon the insulting and degrading form of relations between lord and vassal. (as quoted in Blusse, 2008, p. 88)

12

Retrospect: Reflections on the Amherst Embassy

Amherst and his embassy have not been judged kindly by history.[1] The causes and the goals of the embassy have been lost in the scholarly debate over Amherst's failure to appear before the Jiaqing emperor as a result of refusing to kowtow. Amherst's own performance has been viewed as lacklustre, even inept, indecisive and overly cautious, and captive to the uncompromising pro-Company views of Staunton.[2] The embassy has been described as not merely a failure but 'a fiasco' (Tuck, 2000, p. viii) and compared unfavourably with its predecessor the Macartney Embassy, although both failed to achieve their objectives (Platt, 2018, pp. 159–177). Both implicitly and explicitly, Amherst has been apportioned a substantial part of the blame for the mission's failure.

Amherst has been judged unfairly. The embassy did not fail because of his leadership or as a result of his final decision not to kowtow. Amherst was not a great leader by any measure, but he was a competent one

---

[1] Douglas Peers wrote in his entry on Amherst in *The Oxford Dictionary of National Biography*, 'Neither historians nor his contemporaries and successors have been kind to Amherst; John Malcolm wrote of him that he was being compared to "the person who brought the blue flies into the butcher's shop"'. This refers to his later appointment as governor-general of Bengal. The dictionary also referred to Amherst admitting to Lord Morley, 'I would not have you suppose that I deem myself a man of sufficient calibre to govern India in difficult times'. In both China and later in India, he faced very difficult situations not of his own making and coped admirably under extreme pressure, eventually being vindicated for his decisions in India and leadership choices.

[2] Gao (2016) wrote, for example, 'Amherst had to yield to Staunton's "experience-based" assessment of the situation' (p. 610).

whose style was low key but effective.[3] He was charming and his strong personal qualities of honesty and integrity stood him in good stead with his colleagues. He was focused on the major issues and engaged in their resolution at all the stages of the embassy. As the record shows, he kept up the morale of the party throughout a long and trying voyage and a very difficult journey through China, especially in the period before and immediately after Yuanmingyuan. He was clearly respected as a man and as a leader who was considerate, even tempered, good humoured and fair-minded, and who set an example to his men by his own behaviour.[4] He was very capable but not intellectually superior, wrote competently but without flair, and was considered a decent man. Under the most difficult of circumstances, the party never split into factions, nor was the leadership group marked by jealousy or rivalry.[5] Amherst's leadership style won him loyalty as he was consultative and inclusive, balanced in his judgements, hardworking and approachable. Despite criticism to the contrary, Amherst was calm under pressure and comfortable making decisions, usually having first canvassed the views of his colleagues. Ultimately, the record shows he took full responsibility for his decisions. Throughout the whole enterprise, Amherst was a very steady hand on the tiller.

Both the Chinese and British thought of themselves as exceptional—each being utterly convinced of their own superiority—and found little to admire or emulate in the other. A major difference was that the British, as an emerging maritime-based empire that was global in nature, were keen to learn as much as they could about the Chinese political and commercial systems and decision-making in order to better exploit the

---

3   Canning wrote of him on his appointment as governor-general of Bengal in 1822, 'the appointment … is not a very *strong* one; but … Amherst is at least blameless. He is in good political principles; a Government man without implicitness and a courtier without subserviency' (Canning to Huskisson as quoted in Philips, 1940, p. 239, emphasis in original).

4   Amherst's friends spoke highly of his character. Lord Sidmouth summed these up in a letter dated 31 December 1815: 'I have no doubt of the success of the Embassy, upon the judgment, temper and address of the Person, in whose hands this important entity is fortunately placed' (in BL IOR MSS EUR F 140/35).

5   Eastberg (2009, p. 217, fn. 560), in her chapter on British debate on China and Lord Napier's appointment as the chief superintendent of British trade to China in 1834, mistakenly ascribed Lord Napier's dislike of Staunton to Amherst. Eastberg wrote, 'No love was lost between Napier and Staunton. According to Priscilla Napier [1995, p. 82], Amherst recorded in his notes from his studies in preparation for his mission that Staunton "may be deeply versed in Chinese literature … but in politics his [sic] a Driveller"'. A review of Amherst's notes revealed no mention of Staunton, and a close reading of Priscilla Napier (1995, p. 82) showed that these were Lord Napier's words, not Amherst's. Further, Amherst's notes were written in 1815, before Staunton's subsequent political career.

trading opportunities that China offered. In contrast, the Qing court, in the British view, still saw itself as presiding over the centre of the universe. The court was ignorant of foreign nations, especially those of Europe, and was not interested in better understanding the British, continuing to ascribe to them the role of a traditional vassal who had travelled from afar to pay tribute.

The period following the Macartney Embassy of 1793 saw a substantial growth in British knowledge of China. The accounts of earlier embassies were augmented by the observations of men like Staunton, Morrison and Davis whose scholarship, knowledge of Mandarin and practical experience of dealing with the Canton authorities represented a fundamental shift from the Macartney Embassy in the depth of British understanding about China.

With the benefit of hindsight, it is not difficult to identify where the Amherst Embassy failed; indeed, it is difficult to see how it could have been successful in achieving its objectives. From its conception, it was hostage to the legacy of the Macartney Embassy. The widely held British belief in the positive impact on the Qing court made by the Macartney Embassy, which suggested that any future British mission would be treated as a special case and not within the narrow confines of the tribute system, turned out to be a myth. Rather, it has been seen, the Jiaqing emperor was determined to reassert Qing ceremonial protocol and insist on proper observances in order to not create an awkward and unacceptable precedent.

Nonetheless, the legacy of the Macartney Embassy had an indirect but important impact on the Amherst Embassy's reading of China. Barrow's book, *Travels in China*, published in 1804, was especially influential, as has been seen, in shaping and influencing the views of China held by the senior members of the Amherst Embassy. All of them had read Barrow's book and several carried copies with them to China. Ellis, in particular, whose first published account of the embassy was accepted as the official record of the embassy, makes no secret of his indebtedness to Barrow. Staunton (1824) complained in his private account that Barrow and others of the Macartney Embassy had left him with little new to report on China: 'The comparative success of the former mission, and the interest and novelty of first discovery, are wanting on the present occasion' (p. 205).

The remedies to the identified deficiencies of the Macartney Embassy, such as its lack of British linguists and local expertise on the inner workings of the Qing bureaucracy, were ironically to prove especially damaging. Although Staunton and Morrison were highly talented men and certainly had the required skills and attributes, they were both viewed with deep suspicion by the Qing court and the emperor, evidenced by the imperial edict received at Canton in January 1815 (Imperial edict, 8 January 1815).[6] This was on account of their linguistic skills in Mandarin and, in the case of Staunton, his tough stance during the course of several disputes with the local authorities at Canton. Morrison was also the subject of concern; he had come to the attention of authorities for illegally teaching Mandarin at the British Factory, for illegally setting up a Chinese printing press at Macao, and for illegally translating and publishing Christian and other texts from English into Chinese, all of which were strictly forbidden under the Canton trading system. Foreigners, long viewed as a potential threat to the fabric of Chinese society and a source of political insecurity, were of particular concern during the Jiaqing emperor's reign due to assassination attempts on the emperor's life, internal rebellions and piracy in southern Chinese waters throughout the first decade of the nineteenth century. Moreover, because of their Company status, the members of the Amherst Embassy were viewed by the imperial court and mandarins as mere traders and not worthy of inclusion in a mission sent in the name of the British monarch (Morrison, 1820, p. 52).

Cranmer-Byng (1962) has concluded that the Macartney Embassy was doomed to fail 'from the very beginning' and 'never stood the slightest chance of success' (p. 34). This judgement is even more applicable to the Amherst Embassy where the burden of the Macartney Embassy precedent inevitably doomed it to fail. The Amherst Embassy's fate was effectively sealed at the imperial banquet held in Tianjin on 13 August 1817, only three days after Amherst arrived in northern China. There the issue of the kowtow was raised formally, the Chinese asserting that Macartney had performed the ceremony before the Qianlong emperor and that Amherst was required to do the same. This claim became impossible to refute when the Jiaqing emperor asserted that he had personally witnessed Macartney kowtowing to his father in a large yellow yurt in the *Garden of the Ten Thousand Trees* (*Wanshuyuan*) (Fu, 1966, vol. 1, p. 326).[7] Ellis (1817),

---

6   Reference to Staunton as 'young and crafty' and as someone who was likely to 'make trouble' is made in Chapter 4 of this study.
7   This reception took place on 14 September 1793.

it has been seen, noted on 23 August: 'With this imperial assertion before us, however false or erroneous, it will be difficult, in the event of a renewed discussion, to press the precedent of Macartney' (p. 154). Amherst subsequently wrote in his report to George Canning that Guanghui and Sulenge informed him at the time of the imperial banquet at Tianjin that, 'the late Emperor, tho' he had accepted Lord Macartney's European homage, had in fact disapproved of it, and that therefore, could not be made a precedent on any future occasion' (Amherst to George Canning, 12 February 1817, in BL IOR G/12/197 (Reel 2) F 226). Either way, Amherst was left with no room to manoeuvre. He either had to kowtow, or refuse to kowtow and face the full wrath of the emperor's displeasure. He chose the latter after weighing up the options of what would cause the least damage to the Crown and British interests. This wedging of Amherst on the question of the kowtow in the context of the Macartney precedent was a central cause for the failure of his embassy. Ellis (1817) described it as 'the rock upon which the Embassy was wrecked' (p. 227).

Gao (2016) has suggested that there was an 'inner kowtow controversy' among the members of the Amherst Embassy. This characterisation is not borne out by a detailed examination of the embassy's negotiations with the Qing court. It needs to be stated that no member of the embassy was attracted to the prostration ceremony nor proposed kowtowing for its own sake simply to please the Chinese, not least because compliance was not reciprocal nor based on any notion of equality. Those who were prepared to consider kowtowing only did so reluctantly as an expediency to achieve a stated objective for the embassy. All agreed that unless there was a return in the form of Chinese concessions then it was not worth considering further. The latter view was certainly the position of Amherst who held out the possibility of kowtowing until the very end of negotiations. His pre-departure instructions had been ambiguous, even contradictory, but permitted him to use his 'own discretion' if the success of the mission warranted it. Amherst had tried to make sense of his instructions, first by asserting the Macartney precedent (and offering to enhance it by kneeling and bowing three times), and when this approach failed, he kept open the possibility of kowtowing up until it became apparent that further negotiation was fruitless. He offered, like Macartney, to perform the full ceremony if a court official of equal status would kowtow before a portrait of the Prince Regent, or, if the emperor would supply a written commitment undertaking that any Chinese official appointed to the Court of St James's would kowtow before the British monarch.

Ellis initially argued that refusal to comply with mere court ceremonial was not a sufficient reason to consign the embassy to certain failure, a position to which Amherst was prepared to give serious consideration.[8] However, by the time Amherst made his final decision, Ellis had conceded his earlier position and stated that he readily deferred to the weight of Staunton's local knowledge and arguments against kowtowing. Acknowledging this stance, Ellis (1817) wrote:

> Whatever may have been my private opinion … of compliance with the Chinese ceremonial, I am not disposed to maintain any substantial advantage would have resulted from the mere reception of the Embassy. (p. 437)

It appears that Ellis may have had a personal financial motive for advocating compliance with the kowtow. He wrote that while some members of 'our crew' may have rejoiced in Amherst's refusal to kowtow:

> [For] my part, as I undertook the voyage to these distant seas more for profit than reputation I cannot but regret that I have lost the opportunity of bringing my venture to the market. (p. 227)

Ellis's admission drew a sharp rebuke from Barrow (1817a), who wrote in the *Quarterly Review* that 'the value of his opinion [on the kowtow] is greatly diminished by a candid, though we think rather indiscreet, avowal' that he had private business interests riding on the outcome of the embassy (p. 477). Ellis did not elaborate on the nature of his 'venture', but it likely involved the importation into China of some form of British manufactures or other products.[9] Ellis did admit later on occasions throughout his subsequent career that he believed complying with court protocol might have given the embassy a better chance of success but made no attempt to substantiate this claim in any meaningful way ('Note' attached to Ellis, 1830, pp. 63–64).[10] Amherst's final decision against kowtowing came down to the fact that, in the end, he could not satisfy

---

8   This, as seen in Chapter 10, was also Napoleon's view.

9   Staunton had been involved in an unsuccessful business venture in 1811 importing 'Salisbury flannels' into Canton, but the Chinese merchants offered only half the cost (*Staunton Letters*, 9 February 1811).

10   Ellis wrote, 'I have never seen reason to change the opinion … that no success could attend the mission, without complying with the particular usages of the Chinese court'. He qualified his decision by emphasising that this view referred to the kowtow 'in the presence of the Emperor'.

himself that it would guarantee obtaining the principle objectives of the embassy or would open a dialogue with the emperor or his senior ministers on these objectives.

Tuck's (2000) account of the embassy, as has been noted, is the most comprehensive analysis of the mission, but his conclusions are ambiguous. He argued that Amherst was planning to perform the kowtow after receiving an assurance from Heshitai that he would be a friend and advocate of the British at the Qing court on the condition that he performed the ceremony. However, Amherst changed his mind after consulting with Staunton, leading to the embassy's failure and Tuck's assessment that Staunton was to blame for the outcome. Tuck argued that, had Amherst agreed to kowtow, an imperial reception or 'the formal encounter, would almost certainly have passed off successfully' (p. xxxv). But he never explained what he meant by 'successfully' and proceeded to contradict himself in his conclusion when he added:

> However, even if the audience had taken place, it is unlikely, despite … Ho's [Heshitai's] ambiguous promise to help, that Amherst's negotiating proposals would have received any more sympathetic hearing than the requests made by Lord Macartney, which had been summarily rejected twenty-two years before. (p. xxxv)

Staunton immediately understood the nature of Heshitai's 'ambiguous promises'. He recognised that the mere reception of the embassy before the emperor would not have resulted in any subsequent opportunity for negotiation of British goals, thereby rendering any such reception as meaningless in practical terms. His views were validated on receipt of the official *Outline of the Ceremonies* to be observed by the British ambassador where it was proposed that numerous kowtows be performed and that, at best, the emperor would be seen only from a distance.

While Amherst was swayed by Heshitai's promise, which formed the basis of his initial intention to kowtow, Staunton immediately saw through the mandarin's largesse. Staunton's judgement was based on a number of factors. The first arose from his ability to understand Mandarin and 'having heard, in the original language' Heshitai's 'utterances' (Staunton, 1824, p. 100). Staunton related that Heshitai's displeasure was never far from the surface. Second, Staunton's views were influenced heavily by the series of personal threats made towards him by the Qing court and his awareness of the Qing court's declared suspicion of him. Finally, the court's persistent assertion that Macartney had kowtowed in 1793, a proposition strenuously denied by the British, served to confirm to them that the Qing court was lying and could not be trusted. Staunton put forward his conclusions in a minute dated 18 January 1817 in which he declared that Heshitai's motives of assistance were 'easily disposed of':

> They were not voluntary given but elicited by our own remarks. They proceeded from a man, who was evidently extremely anxious as well as personally interested to gain his point, a point which he had previously tried to accomplish by intimidating and gross insults without effect—(for instance … asserting loudly that the Emperor was the Sovereign of *all* Nations, and threatening our immediate dismissal if we persevered in refusing to perform a ceremony, which the Emperor in *that character* required from us). [Heshitai's promises] were … in themselves vague, inconclusive, and unworthy of credit, being merely confined to assurance of a gracious reception, the ungracious nature of which we already could pretty well anticipate from information gained from other quarters, and to his promises of personal aid and friendship in the subsequent furtherance of our views, promises which it was easy to make and still more easy to violate. (Staunton Minute dated 18 January 1817 in Morse, 1926/1966, vol. 3, p. 303, emphasis in original)

Staunton opposed performing the kowtow for several reasons. The act of obeisance was not mere court ceremonial but, rather, an act of the utmost significance: an act of homage that, under the tribute system, relegated the practitioner to vassal status and his sovereign to an inferior status below the Chinese emperor. On this point, he was strongly supported subsequently by Morrison.[11] Equally, while performing the kowtow might secure an audience with the emperor, it did not guarantee that a positive outcome would follow, as Amherst learned after his expulsion.[12] Once relegated to vassal status, the holding of negotiations would be impossible; negotiations implied equal status and the Chinese did not negotiate with vassals.

---

11 'Those nations of Europe who consider themselves tributary and yielding homage to China, should perform the ceremony' (Morrison, 1820, p. 9). Morrison objected particularly to the lack of reciprocity in the ceremony and its 'interference with the idea of equality'.

12 See Appendix F for the proposed final court ceremony signifying the conclusion of Amherst's mission, after which he was to leave Peking.

In Staunton's view, a British ambassador's performance of the kowtow would adversely affect not only the hard-won status enjoyed by the Company representatives at Canton, but also would have profound implications for the future of British standing in China, as well as undermining the achievements of the Macartney Embassy 23 years earlier. The effects on British relations with China resulting from a 'submission to intimidation', Staunton felt, would be 'certain and permanent' (Staunton Minute dated 18 January 1817 in Morse, 1926/1966, vol. 3, p. 304, Appendix 5). Ultimately, Staunton (1822, p. 150) blamed the 'precipitate dismissal' of the embassy on the 'peculiarly untoward character' of the Jiaqing emperor. Amherst's sound judgement, thought Staunton (1822, p. 71), not only maintained British honour and promoted British commercial interests, but also ensured that 'Our character as the subjects of a free and independent state, has remained unsullied and entire'.

Amherst's record shows that he consulted with the senior members of his suite throughout the mission and formally sought their views both on arrival off Dagu and before making a final decision not to kowtow at Tongzhou. Some have criticised these consultations as weakness on Amherst's part, but it was clearly good leadership practice because, in the end, he was always going to be the one who had the responsibility for the final decision. It was only Amherst who had to perform the prostration ceremony, and it would be his name that would go down in infamy as the first British ambassador to kowtow before the Celestials. As a courtier at the Court of St James's for much of his earlier career, and as the bearer of a famous military name in Britain, these must have been considerations that weighed heavily on his reaching a final decision, knowing as he did that it would almost certainly lead to his expulsion from Peking.

Those who have sought to blame Staunton's influence for the decision not to kowtow have underestimated Amherst. Although Amherst was impressed initially by Ambassador Ismailof's compromise in which a single kowtow before the Kangxi emperor had led to a long stay and some concessions, he had come to realise by the time he made his final decision at Tongzhou that this option would not be entertained. Moreover, he had come to the conclusion that he could not trust his Chinese interlocutors and could not be reassured that kowtowing would lead to any positive outcomes for the embassy. Staunton's arguments and the example of the Dutch embassy of 1795, which had left empty handed despite kowtowing on every occasion when required, were no doubt considered and evaluated. Amherst acknowledged the importance of Staunton's views and opinions and thanked him in a letter five years later (Staunton, 1822, p. 68). Accordingly, in the end, Amherst followed the Prince Regent's instructions where he was to refer 'on all occasions to the supercargoes for the best information and advice' and decided on the option that he thought would do the least lasting damage to British long-term interests both in Canton and Peking (Amherst to Canning, 28 February 1817, in BL IOR G/12/197 (Reel 2) F 270).

Several other factors contributed to the rupture in the relationship between the British and Qing court arising out of the Amherst Embassy. The actions of a number of the mandarins contributed significantly to a breakdown of trust between themselves and the British, and with the Jiaqing emperor. Their duplicitous mishandling of the kowtow issue, which resulted in stressful and prolonged negotiations and false reports informing the emperor that Amherst had rehearsed the ceremony, incurred the emperor's anger when he learned the truth that Amherst was not prepared to kowtow. The mandarins' failure to keep the Jiaqing emperor accurately informed of the state of these negotiations as well as other matters, specifically the departure of the British ships after landing the ambassadorial party at Dagu and the conditions under which the embassy was suddenly transported to Yuanmingyuan, resulted in the demotion and punishment of several key mandarins. From the above, it is obvious that the mandarins were in an invidious position and were subject throughout the course of the negotiations to similar, if not greater, stresses and pressures to those faced by the British. This is illustrated by the succession of ever more senior mandarins consigned to take over the negotiations to ensure the recalcitrant British complied with the emperor's wishes. The instructions the mandarins had to follow allowed them little or no room to manoeuvre. Moreover, they were only too aware that failure to deliver acceptable outcomes would incur the emperor's displeasure, thus resulting in severe and humiliating punishments, which proved to be the case. The historians Backhouse and Bland (1914) concluded that the mandarins:

> therefore lied to the Emperor about the [Amherst] Mission's attitude, and to the Mission about the emperor's, until at last, in order to extricate themselves, they were compelled to get rid of the foreigners at all costs. (p. 386)

This assessment seems a fair summation. Once expelled, the embassy was a potent irritant and embarrassment to the Qing court as well as an unwelcome financial burden. The choice of the shortest route to Canton is evidence of the emperor's eagerness to rid his realm of the unwelcome visitors as soon as possible.

The British were guilty of a series of miscalculations both before and during the Amherst Embassy that, in retrospect, can be seen to have damaged their prospects of success on a range of issues.

First, the repeated assertion that the grandeur of the Macartney Embassy and deportment of its members had led the Chinese to view the British as an exceptional people and a special nation that would henceforth be handled outside the tributary system was flawed. This belief derived from Macartney's own reporting, whereby he sought to put the best possible gloss on his embassy's achievements despite its failure to achieve any of its goals. This view was kept alive and repeated by Barrow and Staunton to protect Macartney's legacy and their own involvement in the embassy, and in Staunton's case, the need to also guard his father's legacy.

Second, Macartney's success in negotiating an alternative ceremony and avoiding the kowtow in front of the Qianlong emperor led to the mistaken British assumption that this would also be acceptable to his son. This proved to be the final nail in the Amherst Embassy's coffin. Significantly, the further assumption that compromise resulting from negotiation was possible at the Qing court was born at the time of the Macartney Embassy and led to the erroneous belief that it would be possible for Amherst to enter into negotiations with the Qing court on British trade requests.

Third, after deferring a decision on another embassy to China for at least a decade, the decision to dispatch the Amherst Embassy was made in relative haste and based almost solely on Barrow's personal initiative. As the private correspondence over many years between Staunton and Barrow reveals, the real push behind Barrow's actions was his private objective to help enhance the career and reputation of Staunton with another embassy seen as the perfect vehicle. Barrow was deeply indebted to Staunton's father and Lord Macartney, and throughout his early career at the Admiralty was always on the lookout for ways to repay the debt by helping the young Staunton.[13] Moreover, Barrow had based his arguments for another embassy on Staunton's reports from Canton—information that by 1816 was either out of date or no longer relevant. In addition, the British deliberately withheld notifying the Chinese of the impending embassy in order to limit the prospects of rejection and to present the Qing court with a fait accompli. The Chinese Government learned on 25 May 1816 of the expected arrival of the embassy, only 45 days before Amherst reached Chinese waters off Macao. Its arrival, shrouded in secrecy, aroused suspicion and concern for the Cantonese authorities. That the immediate pretext for the embassy, namely, the breakdown of trade relations in Canton between the Select Committee and the local authorities in 1814, had been resolved by the time Amherst arrived in China in July 1816 only complicated the issue.

Fourth, the belief that it was possible to negotiate with the Jiaqing emperor or his senior ministers on the attainment of British objectives proved false. Those dispatching the embassy knew that formidable obstacles lay in Amherst's path but thought that his personal charm, conciliatory manners and high aristocratic rank would facilitate a rapport with the Jiaqing emperor, ably assisted by Staunton's linguistic abilities and in-country knowledge. Access to the emperor based on an ability to communicate with him reflected Staunton's early belief that a knowledge of Manchu would assist him to converse with the Jiaqing emperor. Unfortunately, a diplomatic encounter conducive to negotiation on the basis of equality, or any negotiation for that matter, was always most unlikely if not, to the Chinese at least, inconceivable. The British received proof of this realisation after their expulsion from Yuanmingyuan when a copy of an imperial edict came to their attention (Morse, 1926/1966, vol. 3, pp. 295–297, Appendix 4). This edict set out the program planned in the event that the embassy had been received. It made clear that Amherst would not have had any opportunity to engage personally with the emperor during the three planned receptions. He was required to perform numerous kowtows; most of which were to take place out of the emperor's sight, at the far end of the reception hall and behind rows of other princes and mandarins (Morse, 1926/1966, vol. 3, pp. 295–297, Appendix 4). Moreover, the

---

13   In a letter dated 30 December 1805, Staunton requested his mother to thank 'Mr. Barrow' for his long letters and 'his endeavours to promote my interests' (*Staunton Letters*, Canton, 30 December 1805).

emperor was scheduled to leave for Jehol less than two weeks later without any invitation extended to Amherst and his party to join him there, unlike the invitation offered to Macartney and his immediate retinue in 1793.

In attempting to establish a more stable trade relationship, the British were not offering the Qing court anything that it wanted or needed and, therefore, possessed no bargaining power from which to negotiate. From the Qing perspective, the 'Canton trade system' was working satisfactorily and no Chinese entity was seeking closer or expanded trading relations with the British. Of specific importance to the political context in which the Amherst Embassy was received by the Qing court was the deterioration in Anglo–Chinese relations at the time. The Jiaqing emperor regarded the British and their motives with a high degree of mistrust as a result of their two attempted occupations of Macao in 1802 and 1808, and the aggressive British naval actions in intercepting foreign shipping in Chinese territorial waters in 1814. Staunton wrote later:

> The Chinese had … seen our troops more than once landed on their shores; and our naval forces had, during successive years, hovered about their coasts, with no hostile intention it is true, but in a way, which even the most unsuspicious nation might have considered in some degree questionable. (1822, p. 238)

Reflecting the emperor's concern, an imperial edict dated 11 January 1815 called for a strengthening of Chinese naval defence in the waters around Macao and the Pearl River Delta ('Imperial Edict, New Regulations to Control Foreign Merchants in Kwantung', 11 January 1815, in Fu, 1966, vol. 1, p. 395). The British occupations of Macao, Wang (2014) has argued, resulted in their being 'regarded as the most troublesome of Westerners' and raised serious alarm about Britain's imperial ambitions and expanding naval power (p. 248). The hardening of Qing attitudes at this time, Wang concluded, 'partly explains the emperor's rejection of the Amherst mission of 1816' (p. 248).

Davis, the 20-year-old interpreter in the embassy, destined to be the second governor of Hong Kong from 1844 to 1848, attributed the failure of the mission to the intrigues of the provincial Canton Government that had bribed the mandarins at Peking to prevent 'our obtaining any effectual access to the emperor' (Davis, 1841, p. 162). Citing their alarm at the 'sudden appearance' of the embassy only a year after Staunton had succeeded in getting his way with the local viceroy, Davis added:

> There could be no doubt whatever that every exertion had been made by that officer, through his connexions at Peking, to frustrate the success of the Embassy; and to this must be attributed the fruitless results of the mission, fully as much as to the difficulties of the ceremony. (p. 123)

Lamiot had written earlier in October 1807 of the obstacles facing any prospective European embassy to the Qing court. Amherst's pre-departure 'Notes' referred, somewhat prophetically, to Lamiot's conclusions on the role played by the mandarins:

> If the Chinese admitted the injustice of their proceedings a necessary consequence would be the punishment in various degrees of a considerable number of persons, all of whom are therefore united against you and use any means of intrigue, deception and bribery to circumvent you. (Amherst's 'Notes' in BL IOR MSS EUR F 140/36)

The Chinese mandarins, in Davis's (1841) opinion, were susceptible to bribery due to their meagre salaries and the fact that, unlike their British equivalents, they did not possess hereditary titles or enjoy substantial private incomes (p. 162). He thought that the best way to gain Chinese respect was to act in 'a manner dramatically opposed to themselves' (p. 191).

Qing distrust of the British also included the Jiaqing emperor's concerns about both Staunton and Morrison in Canton and their subsequent inclusion in the Amherst Embassy as the second commissioner and senior interpreter, respectively. Moreover, the Qing court considered their linguistic abilities as dangerous, allowing them to communicate directly with native Chinese in those provinces that had recently experienced uprisings against the government.[14] Amherst referred to Staunton's knowledge of the language in his official dispatch to George Canning, which 'was brought forward as furnishing the means of holding improper communications with traitorously disposed Chinese' (Amherst to Canning, 28 February 1817, in BL IOR G/12/197 (Reel 2) F 266). He added that the 'Chinese guard round the British quarters was ordered to be doubled' to prevent any 'traitorous correspondence between the Emperor's subjects, and the persons in the Embassy who were familiar

---

14 See Wang (2014, pp. 72–73) for the rise of the White Lotus movement in Shandong and Anhui province in the late Qianlong period.

with the Chinese language' (Amherst to Canning, 28 February 1817, in BL IOR G/12/197 (Reel 2) F 266). These concerns would certainly have helped stiffen the resolve to ensure that Amherst complied fully with court ritual if he were to be granted an audience with the Jiaqing emperor. While the emperor was criticised by Amherst in his reporting, it was in fairly low key and measured terms. The real vilification of the emperor followed Amherst's return to England when the British press took up the cudgels.

Throughout their respective embassies, both Macartney and Amherst stayed within the boundaries and rules of European Westphalian diplomatic practice, even when it was obvious that it was proving totally ineffective in securing their official aims. Neither appeared to have an alternative plan to fall back on and neither gave any serious thought to the use of threats of coercion, although both Macartney and Amherst noted privately that British power could assist in the achievement of British goals. Macartney wrote:

> If, indeed, the Chinese were provoked to interdict us their commerce, or do us any material injury, we certainly have the means easy enough of revenging ourselves, for a few frigates could in a few weeks destroy all their coast navigation and intercourse from the island of Hainan to the Gulf of Pei-chihli. (Cranmer-Byng, 1962, p. 211)

He added:

> The forts of the Bocca Tigris might be demolished by half a dozen broadsides, the river would be impassable without our permission, and the whole trade of Canton and its correspondencies annihilated in a season. The millions of people who subsist by it would be almost instantly reduced to hunger and insurrection. (p. 211)

Amherst stressed in his pre-departure notes that Britain acted as a responsible international citizen despite its power. If confronted by threats at the Qing court to either stop the British tea trade at Canton or, alternatively, to place it into the hands of the Americans, he was prepared to remind the court that:

> A proof of our moderation is the restoration of Java and the Moluccas, while the conquest and the expulsion by our navy of every other European flag from the Eastern seas is proof of our power. The consequence of the Chinese breaking with England would be our immediate occupation of their valuable islands

to the Eastward, particularly Formosa and Lieukieu, and the interruption of their Asiatic maritime trade. (Amherst, pencil notes on 'The objects of the Embassy' in BL IOR MSS EUR F 140/36)

Nevertheless, Amherst was guided in his actions by Barrow's advice that the diplomatic encounter should be conducted in a spirit of cordiality and equality but backed up with firmness, dignity and patience. Ultimately, the Amherst Embassy's reception proved the futility of engaging in any future diplomatic negotiation with the Qing Government to achieve British commercial aims in China. Morrison had expressed a view in early 1815 that the Chinese Government would never acquiesce to the demands of a few foreign merchants until forced to do so by an enemy 'nearer [to] their gates' (Morrison to Staunton, 10 January 1815, in Morrison, 1839, p. 425). Barrow (1819) commented that it was clear that the emperor, or 'Supreme Sovereign of the earth', had little regard for the truth and that he wished to decline any further diplomatic intercourse with Britain (p. 86). He added that, although trading conditions at Canton had improved since the embassy, the Chinese were nevertheless:

> busily engaged in building forts on every accessible part of the coast from the Bocca Tigris to the Pei-ho, His Imperial Majesty's ministers being under great apprehension that their treatment of Lord Amherst may be yet visited upon them by a less pacific mission than the last. (p. 86)

A revised British assessment of China, framed by the failure of the Amherst mission, arose from the diplomatic ashes. The publisher John Murray wrote to Lord Byron with his view on the reception of the Amherst Embassy at Yuanmingyuan:

> I wish I could shew you extracts from the Peking Gazette in which the Chinese speak of our Embassy—such contempt—we have got near to them by means of Nepaul [sic] and before I die I hope we shall have a war with them. (Nicholson, 2007, p. 207)[15]

It was clear that the Chinese Government would never voluntarily receive an ambassador as a means of redressing British grievances. China and its culture had nothing to offer the West apart from tea and a potentially large commercial market for British goods based on the fact that 'the Chinese are important because they are numerous' (Slade, 1830, p. iii). The final

---

15 I thank Professor Tim Barrett for bringing this reference to my attention.

12. RETROSPECT

word on the Anglo–Chinese diplomatic encounter was proclaimed by the Jiaqing emperor who informed the Prince Regent in a letter dated 11 September 1816:

> There will be no occasion hereafter for you to send an ambassador from so great a distance, and to give him the trouble of passing over mountains and crossing the ocean. If you do but pour out the heart in dutiful obedience, it is by no means necessary, at any stated time, to come to the celestial presence, ere it be pronounced that you turn towards the transforming influences which emanate from this empire. (Jiaqing emperor to the Prince Regent in *Asiatic Journal*, 1819, vol. 8, p. 342)

Amherst told Canning:

> Judging from what has occurred in the instance of the present Embassy, and of the Embassy from Russia in 1805, I conceive that no foreign Embassador is likely to be admitted into the presence of the Emperor Kia-King, unless he agrees to perform, to its full extent, the Tartar Ceremony of the Ko-tou. Perhaps the present emperor, whose reign has been frequently and very lately disturbed by insurrections of his subjects, may less readily dispense with outward forms of respect than his Father, whose reign was long and victorious, and who, being firm in the possession of real power and authority, might attach less consequence to any show of external homage. (Amherst to Canning, 21 April 1817, in BL IOR G/12/197 (Reel 2) F 377)

Amherst thought that 'the precipitate and unwarranted rejection of the Embassy from the Palace Gates has left an injury to repair' (Amherst to Canning, 21 April 1817, in BL IOR G/12/197 (Reel 2) F 378). He described his reception at the court as one of:

> hurry and confusion, of irregularity and disorder, of insult, inhumanity, and almost of personal violence, sufficient to give to the court of the emperor Kia-King the manners, character, and appearance of the roving-camp of a Tartar Horde. (Amherst to Canning, 8 March 1817, in BL IOR G/12/197 (Reel 2) F 285)

The Chinese were aware that the rules of diplomatic hospitality had been violated and were possibly apprehensive of 'the manner in which the transaction will be viewed in Great Britain' (Amherst to Canning, 21 April 1817, in BL IOR G/12/197 (Reel 2) F 379). Evidence of this, Amherst thought, was found in the 'honourable treatment of the Embassy on its' [sic] return' to Canton, and for the emperor's proposal for a partial exchange of presents as 'a wish for reparation in the only way which the pride of the Emperor would allow' (Amherst to Canning, 21 April 1817, in BL IOR G/12/197 (Reel 2) F 379). He requested that it be made known to the Prince Regent and his government, and to the Company:

> whose interests have been committed principally to my care, that I have executed my trust with fidelity, and that my want of success is not to be attributed to want either of zeal or discretion in the performance of my duty, [and] I shall be amply rewarded for the vexation and disappointment, for the difficulty and danger, without which it has not been my lot to execute this service. (Amherst to Canning, 21 April 1817, in BL IOR G/12/197 (Reel 2) F 380)

Amherst arrived back in England on 16 August 1817. The final line in his diary noted with happiness that he 'once more [had] the satisfaction of setting foot in old England' (as quoted in Ritchie, 1894, p. 20).[16] Having signed off his commission in late 1817, Amherst, unlike Staunton and Ellis, chose to avoid any public comment on China or Anglo–Chinese trade relations. Rather, he retired to his estate, 'Montreal', where he pursued a busy life commuting between Sevenoaks and London until called on to replace Lord Moira as governor-general of Bengal in 1823.

---

16   Ritchie's (1894) book includes several references to Amherst's handwritten diary at the time of his embassy to China. Peyrefitte (1992, pp. 513, 598) also refers to a 'handwritten journal' held in the private collection of Mr Michael Galvin of Santa Barbara, California. Attempts by the author to locate his diary have been unsuccessful.

Bibliography

Unpublished Primary Sources

Sources from the British Library, London, accessed at the National Library of Australia, Canberra

Adam Matthew Publications. (2006): East India Company Factory Records. Part 2: China, 1817–1832 [Microfilm].

Reel 1: IOR G/12/196: Copies of Correspondence, Lord Amherst's Embassy to China Feb 1815–Nov 1817.

Reel 2: IOR G/12/197: Correspondence, Lord Amherst's Embassy to China, Feb 1815–Apr 1817.

Reel 2: IOR G/12/198: Letters from Lord Amherst, Lord Amherst's Embassy to China, Jan 1816–Apr 1817.

British Library, London

MSS EUR F 140: Papers of 1st Earl Amherst, Governor-General of Bengal 1823–28 (1789–1835).

MSS EUR C 604: William Pitt Amherst Papers: 1816 Letters to his wife dated 10 and 17 June 1816 describing his visit to Batavia incl. comments on the Dutch administration and the return of Java to the Dutch.

MSS EUR B 363: 1815 Letter from Lord Amherst to Lady Amherst.

MSS EUR F 140/37: Journal of Jeffrey Amherst, son of Lord Amherst, on his father's mission to China.

RP 8351: Series of letters from Amherst to his wife, Sarah Countess Dowager of Plymouth, over 18 years of married life.

Box 130 946c: Letters to Sarah Amherst.

ADD MSS 41346-41475: Martin, William Fanshawe. Journal of Sir William Fanshawe Martin, as a 1st Class Volunteer on board H.M.S. *Alceste* during her voyage with Lord Amherst's abortive Mission to China 3 February 1816–17 August 1817. Martin Family Papers, 1793–1860.

Ref. # 8022.B.90. *A delicate inquiry into the embassies to China and a legitimate conclusion from the premises* (William Clowes, 1818).

Scenes in China: Exhibiting the manners, customs, diversions, and singular peculiarities of the Chinese, together with the mode of travelling, navigation, &c. in that vast empire. Taken from the latest authorities, and including the most interesting particulars in Lord Amherst's recent embassy (E. Wallis, 1820).

The National Archives, Public Records Office, Kew, United Kingdom

FO 97/95: Foreign Office Records: British Mission to China, 1816, Notes.

FO 60/9: Sir Gore Ouseley, James Morier, Henry Ellis, and domestic various, 1814.

Royal Asiatic Society, London

Manning, Thomas TM/9/1/1; TM/9/1/9.

Devon Heritage Centre (South West Heritage Trust), Exeter, United Kingdom

Addington Family: Viscounts Sidmouth political and personal papers of Henry Addington, 1st Viscount Sidmouth, 1816: 152M/C1816/OF1-OF4.

Duke University (Electronic Resources)

Hayne, Henry. (1966). Diaries of Henry Hayne. In *China through Western eyes: Manuscript records of traders, travellers, missionaries, and diplomats, 1792–1842* (Vols. 1–4). London, England: Adam Matthew Microform Publications. (William R. Perkins Library, Duke University, Reel 19)

Staunton, Sir George Thomas. *Diary 1792–1793: Journey to China, 1792–1793*. London, England: Adam Matthew Microform Publications (China Trade, Politics & Culture, 1793–1980 database). Retrieved from www.china.amdigital.co.uk.

Letters from the Papers of George Thomas Staunton to his mother during his time working for the East India Company in Canton. Rare Book, Manuscript and Special Collections Library, Duke University. Retrieved from www.china.amdigital.co.uk.

Kent History and Library Centre, United Kingdom

U1350-E16: Amherst Manuscripts: 'Family Papers'.

Yale Collection of American Literature, Beinecke Rare Book and Manuscript Library

Letters, Earl Amherst of Arracan to Sarah, Countess of Arracan, 1806–1822.

Published Primary Sources

Abel, Clarke. (1818). *Narrative of a journey in the interior of China in the years 1816–1817*. London, England: Longman Hurst, Rees, Orme, and Brown.

Anderson, Æneas. (1796). *A narrative of the British embassy to China in the years 1792, 1793, and 1794*. London, England: J. Debrett.

Anderson, Gertrude A. (Ed.). (1925). *The letters of Thomas Manning to Charles Lamb*. London, England: Martin Secker.

Anson, George, Esq. (1790). *A voyage round the world in the years 1740–1744* (Vols. 1–2). London, England: John and Paul Knapton.

Aspinall, A. (Ed.). (1938). *The letters of King George IV: 1812–1830* (vols. 1–3). Cambridge, England: Cambridge University Press.

Assay, Charles. (1819). *On the trade to China, and the Indian archipelago: With observations on the insecurity of the British interests in that quarter*. London, England: Printed for Rodwell and Martin.

Auber, Peter. (1834). *China. An outline of the government, laws, and policy: and of the British and foreign embassies to, and intercourse with, that empire*. London, England: Parbury, Allen, and Co.

Bagot, Josceline. (1909). *George Canning and his friends*. London, England: John Murray.

Baikov, Feodaor Iskowitz. (1732). *The travels of Feodor Iskowitz Backhoff from Muscow into China* (1st English ed.). London, England: Printed by assignment from Messrs, Churchill, for H. Lintot.

Barrow, John. (1804). *Travels in China, containing descriptions, observations, and comparisons, made and collected in the course of a short residence at the Imperial Palace of Yuen-min-yuen, and on a subsequent journey through the country from Pekin to Canton. In which it is attempted to appreciate the rank that this extraordinary empire may be considered to hold in the scale of civilized nations*. London, England: A. Straham, or T. Cadell and W. Davies.

Barrow, John. (1807). *Some account of the public life, and a selection from the unpublished writings, of the Earl of Macartney: The latter consisting of extracts from an account of the Russian Empire: A sketch of the political history of Ireland: and a journal of an embassy from the King of Great Britain to the Emperor of China: With an Appendix to each volume* (Vols. 1–2). London, England: Cadell and Davis.

Barrow, John. (1810, May). Review of 'Ta Tsing Leu Lee: Being the fundamental laws, and a selection from the supplementary statutes of the Penal Code of China. Translated by George Thomas Staunton'. *Quarterly Review, 3*, 263–319.

Barrow, John. (1817a, April and July). Review of 'Narrative of a voyage in His Majesty's late ship *Alceste* to the Yellow Sea, along the coast of Corea and through its numerous hitherto undiscovered islands to the island of Lewchew, with an account of her shipwreck in the Straits of Gaspar'. By John M'Leod, Surgeon of the Alceste. *Quarterly Review, 17*, 464–506.

Barrow, John. (1817b, January). Review of '*Laou-sing-urh*', or 'An Heir in his Old Age', by J.F. Davis. *Quarterly Review, 16*, 396–416.

Barrow, John. (1819, January and April). Review of a 'Narrative of a journey in the interior of China, and of a voyage to and from that country, in the years 1816 and 1817: Containing an account to the most interesting transactions of Lord Amherst's Embassy to the Court of Pekin, and observations of the countries which it visited', By Clarke Abel. *Quarterly Review, 21*, 67–91.

Barrow, John. (1821). Review of 'Narrative of the Chinese embassy to the Khan of the Tourgouth Tartars, in the years 1712, 13, 14, and 15; by the Chinese ambassador, and published by the emperor's authority at Pekin. Translated from the Chinese, and accompanied by an appendix of miscellaneous translations'. By Sir George Thomas Staunton. *Quarterly Review, 25*, 414–426.

Barrow, John. (1847). *An auto-biographical memoir of Sir John Barrow, Bart., late of the Admiralty; including reflections, observations, and reminiscences at home and abroad, from early life to advanced age.* London, England: John Murray.

Barrow, John. (1975). *A voyage to Cochinchina* (Milton Osborne, Ed.). Kuala Lumpur, Malaysia: Oxford in Asia Historical Reprints. (Original work published 1806)

Bell, John. (1763). *A journey from St. Petersburg in Russia, to diverse parts of Asia* (Vols. 1–2). Glasgow, Scotland: Robert and Andrew Foulis.

Bird, Isabella. (1899). *The Yangtze Valley and beyond: An account of journeys in China.* London, England: John Murray.

Cochran, Peter (Ed.). (1922). *Byron's correspondence with John Murray* (Vol. 2). London, England: John Murray.

Colchester, Charles (Ed.). (1861). *The diary and correspondence of Charles Abbot, Lord Colchester Speaker of the House of Commons 1802–1817* (Vols. 1–2). London, England: John Murray.

Cranmer-Byng, J. L. (Ed.). (1962). *An embassy to China: Being the journal kept by Lord Macartney during his embassy to the Emperor Ch'ien-lung, 1793–94.* London, England: Longmans, Green and Co.

Crawfurd, John. (1830). *Journal of an embassy from the Governor General of India to the Court of Ava in the year 1827.* London, England: Henry Colburn and Richard Bentley.

Cummings, J. S. (Ed.). (1962). *The travels and controversies of Friar Domingo Navarrete 1618–1686* (Vols. 1–2). Cambridge, England: Hayluyt Society.

Davis, John Francis. (1841). *Sketches of China: Partly during an inland journey of four months, between Peking, Nanking, and Canton; with notices and observations relative to the present war* (Vols. 1–2). London, England: Charles Knight & Co.

Davis, John Francis. (1851). *The Chinese: A general description of China and its inhabitants* (Vols. 1–2). London, England: C. Cox. (Original work published 1836)

De Gray, Earl. (1860). Obituary of Sir George Thomas Staunton. *The Journal of the Royal Geographical Society of London, 30*, cxxiv.

De La Loubère, Simon. (1969). *A new historical relation of the Kingdom of Siam.* Kuala Lumpur, Malaysia: Oxford in Asia Historical Reprints.

Du Halde, J. B. (1741). *A description of the Empire of China. Containing a geographical historical, chronological, political and physical description of the Empire of China, and Chinese-Tartary, Corea and Thibet* (3rd ed., Vols. 1–4). London, England: T. Gardner in Bartholomew Close for Edward Cave.

Eames, J. B. (1974). *The English in China: Being an account of the intercourse and relations between England and China from the year 1600 to the year 1843 and a summary of later developments.* London, England: Curzon Press. (Original work published 1909)

Ellis, Henry. (1817). *Journal of the proceedings of the late embassy to China.* London, England: T. Davison.

Ellis, Henry. (1830). *A series of letters on the East India Question. Addressed to the Members of the Two Houses of Parliament by Henry Ellis, Third Commissioner of the late embassy to China, Letter I* (2nd ed.). London, England: John Murray.

Forster, John Reinhold (Trans.). (1771). *A voyage to China and the East Indies, by Peter Osbeck. Together with a voyage to Suratte, by Olof Torren, and an account of Chinese husbandry, by Captain Charles Gustavus Eckeberg.* London, England: Benjamin White. (Translated from 1765 German ed.)

Fu, Lo-Shu (Ed.). (1966). *A documentary chronicle of Sino-Western relations (1644–1820)* (Vols. 1–2). Tucson, AZ: University of Arizona Press.

Great Britain, *Resolutions to be proposed by Sir George Thomas Staunton. China Trade*, House of Commons, 16 April 1833, 25, 467.

Hall, Basil. (1865). *Narrative of a voyage to Java, China and the Great Loo-Choo Island: With an account of Sir Murray Maxwell's attack on the Chinese Batteries and of an interview with Napoleon Buonaparte at St. Helena.* London, England: William Tegg & Co. (Original work published 1840)

Hall, R. & Shelton, S. W. (Eds). (2002). *'The rising country': The Hale-Amherst correspondence, 1799–1825.* Toronto, Canada: The Champlain Society.

Holland, Elizabeth Vassall Fox. (1909). *The journal of Elizabeth Lady Holland (1791–1811)* (Vol. 1). London, England: Longmans, Green and Co.

Johnson, James. (1806). *An account of a Voyage to India, China, &c. in His Majesty's Ship Caroline, performed in the years 1803–4–5 interspersed with descriptive sketches and cursory remarks, by an officer of the Caroline.* London, England: Richard Phillips.

Li, Dun J. (Ed.). (1969). *China in transition: 1517–1911.* New York, NY: Van Nostrand Reinhold Company.

Marjoribanks, Charles. (1833). *Letter to the Right Hon. Charles Grant, President of the Board of Control, on the present state of British intercourse with China.* London, England: J. Hatchard and Son.

Markham, C. R. (Ed.). (1876). *Narratives of the mission of George Bogle to Tibet, and of the journey of Thomas Manning to Lhasa.* London, England: Trubner & Co.

Martin, Montgomery R. (1847). *China: Political, commercial, social; in an official report to Her Majesty's Government* (Vols. 1–2). London, England: James Madden.

Memorials addressed to H.M. Government by British Merchants Interested in Trade with China. (1840, August). Presented to both Houses of Parliament, August 1840, No. 7.

M'Leod, John. (1820). *Voyage of His Majesty's Ship Alceste, to China, Corea, and the Island of Lewchew: With an account of her shipwreck* (3rd ed.). London, England: John Murray. (Original work published 1818)

Morrison, Eliza (Ed.). (1839). *Memoirs of the life and labours of Robert Morrison* (Vols. 1–2). London, England: Longman, Orme, Brown, Green, and Longmans.

Morrison, Robert. (1817). *A view of China for philological purposes; containing a sketch of Chinese chronology, geography, government, religion & customs.* Macao, China: Hon. East India Company's Press.

Morrison, Robert. (1820). *A memoir of the principal occurrences during an embassy from the British Government to the Court of China in the year 1816.* London, England: Hatchard & Son.

Morse, Hosea Ballou. (1966). *The chronicles of the East India Company trading to China, 1635–1834* (Vols. 1–5). Taipei, Taiwan: Ch'eng-wen Publishing Co. (Original work published 1926)

Nieuhof, Johan. (1669). *An embassy from the East-India Company of the United Provinces, to the Grand Tartar Cham, Emperor of China* (1st English ed.). London, England: John Ogilby.

Noble, Charles Frederick. (1762). *A voyage to the East Indies in 1747 and 1748.* London, England: T. Becket and P. A. Dehondt.

O'Meara, Barry E. (1822). *Napoleon in exile, or, a voice from St. Helena* (Vols. 1–2). London, England: W. Simpkin and R. Marshall.

Osbeck, Peter. (1771). *A voyage to China and the East Indies* (John Reinhold Forster, Trans., Vol. 1). London, England: Benjamin White.

Report [relative to the trade with the East Indies and China] from the Select Committee of the House of Lords, appointed to inquire into the means of extending and securing the foreign trade of the country, and to report to the House: together with the minutes of evidence taken in sessions 1820 and 1821, before the said Committee. (1821, 11 April). Retrieved from National Library of Australia database.

Roe, Sir Thomas. (1899). *The embassy of Sir Thomas Roe to the Court of the Great Mogul 1615–1619, as narrated in his journal and correspondence.* London, England: The Hakluyt Society.

Rose, George. (1860). *The diaries and correspondence of the Right Hon. George Rose: Containing original letters of the most distinguished statesmen of his day* (Reverend Leveson Vernon Harcourt, Ed., Vols. 1–2). London, England: Richard Bentley.

Spencer, Alfred (Ed.). (1921). *Memoirs of William Hickey (1749–1775)*. New York, NY: Alfred A. Knopf.

Staunton, George Leonard. (1797a). *An authentic account of an embassy from the King of Great Britain to the Emperor of China; including cursory observations made, and information obtained, in travelling through that ancient empire and a small part of Chinese Tartary*. London, England: G. Nichol.

Staunton, George Leonard. (1797b). *An historical account of the embassy from the King of Great Britain to the Emperor of China, abridged principally from the papers of Earl Macartney* (Vols. 1–2). London, England: W. Bulmer & Co.

Staunton, George Thomas. (1810). *Ta Tsing Leu Lee: Being the fundamental laws and a selection from the supplementary statutes of the Penal Code of China; originally printed and published in Pekin, in various successive editions, under the sanction, and by the authority, of the several emperors of the Ta Tsing, or present dynasty* (George Thomas Staunton, Trans. and Ed.). London, England: T. Cadell and W. Davies.

Staunton, George Thomas. (1821). *Narrative of the Chinese embassy to the Khan of the Tourgouth Tartars, in the years 1712, 13, 14, and 15: By the Chinese ambassador, and published by the Emperor's authority at Pekin. Translated from the Chinese, and accompanied by an appendix of miscellaneous translations*. London, England: John Murray.

Staunton, George Thomas. (1822). *Miscellaneous notices relating to China, and our commercial intercourse with that country*. London, England: John Murray.

Staunton, George Thomas. (1824). *Notes of proceedings and occurrences during the British embassy to Pekin in 1816*. London, England: Henry Skelton (for private circulation only).

Staunton, George Thomas. (1840). *Corrected report of the speech of Sir George Staunton, on Sir James Graham's motion on the China trade in the House of Commons, April 7, 1840: With an appendix containing resolutions on the China trade, moved in the House of Commons, June 13, 1833*. London, England: Edmund Lloyd.

Staunton, George Thomas. (1856). *Memoirs of the chief incidents of the public life of Sir George Thomas Staunton, Bart., hon. D.C.L. of Oxford one of the King's commissioners to the Court of Pekin, and afterwards for some time Member of Parliament for South Hampshire, and for the Borough.* London, England: L. Booth (for private circulation only).

Symes, Michael. (1800). *An account of an embassy to the Kingdom of Ava, sent by the Governor-General of India, in the year 1795.* London, England: W. Bulmer and Co.

The Chinese traveller. Containing a geographical, commercial, and political history of China. Collected from Du Halde, Le Compte, and other modern travellers. (1775). London, England: E. and C. Dilly.

Van Braam, Andre Everard. (1798). *An authentic account of the embassy of the Dutch East-India Company, to the Court of the Emperor of China, in the years 1794 and 1795.* London, England: R. Phillips.

Waln Jr, Robert. (1823). *China; comprehending a view of the origin, antiquity, history, religion, morals, government, laws, population, literature, drama, festivals, games, women, beggars, manners, customs, &c. of that empire, with remarks on the European embassies to China, and the policy of sending a mission from the United States to the Court of Pekin.* Philadelphia, PA: J. Maxwell.

Newspapers and Journals

American Monthly Magazine and Critical Review
Analectic Magazine
Analytic Review
Asiatic Journal and Monthly Register for British India and Its Dependencies
Asiatic Review
British Review and London Critical Journal
Chinese Repository
Eclectic Review
Edinburgh Review
Gentleman's Magazine
Journal of the Royal Asiatic Society
Journal of the Royal Geographical Society of London
Literary Gazette
London Review and Literary Journal
Quarterly Review

The Percy Anecdotes
The Pocket Magazine and Christian Miscellany
The Times (London)

Unpublished Theses

Eastberg, Jodi. (2009). *West meets East in British perceptions of China through the life and works of Sir George Thomas Staunton, 1781–1859* (Unpublished doctoral thesis). Marquette University, Milwaukee, Wisconsin.

Published Secondary Sources

Adas, Michael. (1989). *Machines as the measure of men: Science, technology and ideologies of Western dominance*. Ithaca, NY: Cornell University Press.

Allan-Ford, Susan. (2008). Fanny's 'great book': Macartney's Embassy to China and Mansfield Park. *Jane Austen Society of North America, 28*(2). Retrieved from jasna.org/persuasions/on-line/vol28no2/ford.htm.

Anderson, Benedict. (2006). *Imagined communities*. London, England: Verso.

Andornino, Giovanni. (2006). *The nature and linkages of China's tributary system under the Ming and Qing dynasties* (Working Paper No. 21). Global Economic History Network.

Anonymous. (1818). *A delicate enquiry into the embassies to China and a legitimate conclusion*. London, England: Thomas and George Underwood.

Anonymous. (1822). *The shipwreck of the Alceste an English frigate, in the Straits of Gaspar*. Dublin, Ireland: E Tute.

Anonymous. (1836). *Address to the people of Great Britain explanatory of our commercial relations with the Empire of China by a visitor to China*. London, England: Smith, Elder and Co.

Appleton, William W. (1951). *A cycle of Cathay: The Chinese vogue in England during the seventeenth and eighteenth centuries*. New York, NY: Columbia University Press.

Armitage, David. (2000). *The ideological origins of the British Empire*. Cambridge, England: Cambridge University Press.

Ashton, John. (1890). *Social England under the Regency*. London, England: Ward and Downey.

Backhouse, Edmund & Bland, John Otway Percy. (1914). *Annals and memoirs of the Court of Peking*. Boston, MA and New York, NY: Houghton Mifflin Company.

Bar, Moshe. (2004, August). Visual objects in context. *Nature Reviews: Neuroscience, 5*, 617–629.

Barrell, John. (2006). *The spirit of despotism: Invasions of privacy in the 1790's*. Oxford, England: Oxford University Press.

Bartlett, Beatrice S. (1991). *Monarchs and ministers: The Grand Council in Mid-Ch'ing China, 1723–1820*. Berkeley and Los Angeles, CA: University of California Press.

Bell, David Avrom. (2008). *The first total war: Napoleon's Europe and the birth of warfare as we know it*. New York, NY: Mariner Books.

Belting, Hans. (2005). Image, medium, body: A new approach to iconology. *Critical Inquiry, 31*(2), 302–319.

Berg, Maxine. (2006). Britain, industry and perceptions of China: Matthew Boulton, 'useful knowledge' and the Macartney Embassy to China 1792–94. *The Journal of Global History, 1*, 269–288.

Bickers, Robert. (1993). *Ritual and diplomacy: The Macartney Mission to China 1792–1794*. London, England: The British Association for Chinese Studies in association with Wellsweep Press.

Bjaaland Welch, Patricia. (2008). *Chinese art: A guide to motifs and visual imagery*. Singapore: Tuttle Publishing.

Blaxland, Wendy. (2008). *Pencils: How they are made*. London, England: Cavendish Square Publishing.

Blusse, Leonard. (2008). *Visible cities: Canton, Nagasaki, and Batavia and the coming of the Americans*. Cambridge, MA: Harvard University Press.

Borgen, Robert. (1982). The Japanese mission to China 801–06. *Monumenta Nipponica, 37*(1), 1–28.

Bowen, Huw V. (2006). *The business of empire: The East India Company and Imperial Britain, 1756–1833*. Cambridge, England: Cambridge University Press.

Brewer, John. (1997). *The pleasures of the imagination: English culture in the eighteenth century*. London, England: Harper Collins.

Briggs, Asa. (1962). *The age of improvement 1783–1867*. London, England: Longmans, Green and Co.

Brown, D Mackenzie. (Ed.). (1947). *China trade days in California*. Berkeley and Los Angeles, CA: University of California Press.

Carroll, John M. (2020). *Canton days: British life and death in China*. London, England: Rowman & Littlefield.

Chang, T'ien-tse. (1962). Malacca and the failure of the first Portuguese Embassy to Peking. *Journal of Southeast Asian History, 3*(2), 45–64.

Chiang, Connie Y. (2004). Monterey-by-the-smell: Odors and social conflict on the California coastline. P*acific Historical Review, 73*(2), 183–214.

Classen, Constance. (1997). Foundations for an anthropology of the senses. *International Social Science Journal, 153*, 1468–2451.

Classen, Constance, Howes, David & Synnott, Anthony. (1994). *Aroma: The cultural history of smell*. London, England: Routledge.

Clingham, Greg. (2015, April). Cultural difference in George Macartney's 'An embassy to China, 1792–94'. *Eighteenth-Century Life, 39*(2), 1–29.

Coates, Colin. (2000). *'A picturesque landscape': The metamorphoses of landscape and community in early Quebec*. Montreal, Canada: McGill-Queen's University Press.

Cockayne, Emily. (2007). *Hubbub: Filth, noise & stench in England 1600–1770*. New Haven, CT: Yale University Press.

Cohen, Paul. (1984). *Discovering history in China: American historical writing on the recent China past*. New York, NY: Columbia University Press.

Colley, Linda. (1984). The apotheosis of George III: Loyalty, royalty and the British nation 1760–1820. *Past & Present, 102*, 94–129.

Colley, Linda. (1986, November). Whose nation? Class and national consciousness in Britain 1750–1830. *Past & Present, 113*(1), 97–117.

Colley, Linda. (1992, October). Britishness and otherness: An argument. *The Journal of British Studies, 31*(4), 309–329.

Colley, Linda. (2005). *Briton's: Forging the nation, 1707–1837*. New Haven, CT: Yale University Press.

Collis, M. (1947). *Foreign mud: Being an account of the opium imbroglio at Canton in the 1830's & the Anglo-Chinese War that followed*. New York, NY: A.A. Knopf.

Conner, Patrick. (1997). *Chinese views – Western perspectives 1770–1870*. London, England: Asia House.

Conner, Patrick. (2009). *The Hongs of Canton. Western merchants in south China 1700–1900, as seen in Chinese export paintings*. London, England: English Art Books.

Corbin, Alain. (1986). *The foul and the fragrant: Odor and the French social imagination*. Cambridge, MA: Harvard University Press.

Cranmer-Byng, J. L. & Levere, T. H. (1981). A case study in cultural collision: Scientific apparatus in the Macartney embassy to China, 1793. *Annals of Science, 38*(5), 503–525.

Crossman, Carl L. (1991). *The China trade: Paintings, furnishings, and exotic curiosities*. Suffolk, England: Antique Collector's Club.

Cushman, Jennifer Wayne. (1993). *Fields from the sea: Chinese junk trade with Siam during the late eighteenth and early nineteenth centuries*. Ithaca, New York, NY: Cornell Southeast Asia Publications.

Dalrymple, William. (2019). *The anarchy: The relentless rise of the East India Company*. London, England: Bloomsbury Publishing.

Darwin, John. (2012). *Unfinished empire: The global expansion of Britain*. London, England: Allen Lane Penguin Group.

Davis, Jim. (2015). *Comic acting and portraiture in Late-Georgian and Regency England*. Cambridge, England: Cambridge University Press.

Debrett's New Peerage for 1822. (1822). London, England: Debrett's Peerage Ltd. and MacMillan.

Dening, Greg. (1992). *Mr Bligh's bad language: Passion, power and theatre on the Bounty*. Cambridge, England: Cambridge University Press.

Dickinson, H. T. (1999). 'Democracy'. In Iain McCalman (Ed.), *An Oxford companion to the Romantic Age: British culture 1776–1832* (pp. 34–42). Oxford, England: Oxford University Press.

Douglas, Mary. (1988). *Purity and danger: An analysis of the concepts of pollution and taboo*. London, England: Ark Paperbacks.

Douglas, Robert Kennaway. (1904). 'Amherst, William Pitt'. In *Dictionary of National Biography, 1885–1900* (Vol. 1). Retrieved from en.wikisource.org/wiki/Amherst,_William_Pitt_(DNB00).

Elias, Norbert. (2000). *The civilizing process*. Oxford, England: Blackwell Publishing. (Original work published 1939)

Elliott, Mark C. (2001). *The Manchu way: The Eight Banners and ethnic identity in Late Imperial China.* Stanford, CA: Stanford University Press.

Elliott, Mark C. (2009). *Emperor Qianlong: Son of Heaven, man of the world.* New York, NY: Longman.

Epstein, James. (1989, February). Understanding the cap of liberty: Symbolic practice and social conflict in early nineteenth century England. *Past & Present, 122*, 75–118.

Esherick, Joseph W. (1998, April). Cherishing sources from afar. *Modern China, 24*(2), 135–161.

Esherick, Joseph W. (1998, July). Tradutore, Traditore: A reply to James Hevia. *Modern China, 24*(3), 328–332.

Evans, H. (1879). *Our old nobility.* London, England: E. J. Kibblewhite.

Fairbank, John K. (1942, February). Tributary trade and China's relations with the West. *Far Eastern Quarterly, 1*(2), 129–149.

Fairbank, John K. (1943, February). The kowtow in the Macartney Embassy to China in 1793. *Far Eastern Quarterly, 2*(2), 163–203.

Fairbank, John K. (Ed.). (1968). *The Chinese world order: Traditional China's foreign relations.* Cambridge, MA: Harvard University Press.

Fairbank, J. K. & Teng, S. Y. (1941, June). On the Ch'ing tributary system. *Harvard Journal of Asiatic Studies, 6*, 135–246.

Fan, Fa-ti. (2004). *British Naturalists in Qing China: Science, empire, and cultural encounter.* Cambridge, MA: Harvard University Press.

Farrington, Anthony. (1999). *Catalogue of East India Company ships' journals and logs 1600–1834.* London, England: British Library.

Ferry, Bertholet & van der Aalsvoort, Lambert. (2014). *Among the Celestials: China in early photographs.* New Haven, CT: Yale University Press.

Figgis, Nicola & Rowney, Brendon. (2001). *Irish paintings in the National Gallery of Ireland* (Vol. 1). Dublin, Ireland: National Gallery of Ireland.

Forge, Anthony (Ed.). (1973). *Primitive art and society.* London, England: Oxford University Press.

Gao, Hao. (2014, October). The Amherst Embassy and British discoveries in China, 1816–1817. *History, 99*(337), 568–614.

Gao, Hao. (2016). The 'Inner kowtow controversy' during the Amherst Embassy to China, 1816–1817. *Diplomacy & Statecraft, 27*(4), 595–614.

Garrett, Valery M. (2002). *Heaven is high, the Emperor far away: Old Guangzhou and China trade*. Singapore: Marshall Cavendish.

Gelber, Harry. (2007). *The dragon and the foreign devils*. London, England: Bloomsbury.

Gluckman, Max. (1966). Les Rites de Passage. In Max Gluckman (Ed.), *Essays on the ritual of social relations* (pp. 1–54). Manchester, England: Manchester University Press.

Graham, G. S. (1967). *Great Britain in the Indian Ocean 1810–1850*. Oxford, England: Clarendon Press.

Grantham, A. E. (1934). *A Manchu monarch: An interpretation of Chia Ch'ing*. London, England: George Allen and Unwin.

Greenberg, M. (1969). *British trade and the opening of China 1800–42*. Cambridge, England: Cambridge University Press.

Hague, William. (2004). *William Pitt the Younger*. London, England: Harper Press.

Hall-Witt, Jennifer. (2007). *Fashionable acts: Opera and elite culture in London, 1780–1880*. Durham, NH: University of New Hampshire Press.

Hamashita, Takeshi. (1997). The intra-regional system in East Asia in modern times. In Peter J. Katzenstein & Takashi Shiraishi (Eds), *Network power: Japan and Asia* (pp. 113–135). Ithaca, NY: Cornell University Press.

Hampton, Timothy. (2009). *Fictions of embassy*. Ithaca, NY: Cornell University Press.

Henderson III, James. (1970). *The frigates: An account of the lighter warships of the Napoleonic Wars*. London, England: Leo Cooper.

Hertel, Ralf & Keevak, Michael (Eds). (2017). *Early encounters between East Asia and Europe: Telling failures*. London, England: Routledge.

Hevia, James. (1995). *Cherishing men from afar: Qing guest ritual and the Macartney Embassy of 1793*. Durham, England: Duke University Press.

Hevia, James. (1998, July). Postpolemical historiography: A response to Joseph W. Esherick. *Modern China, 24*(3), 319–327.

Hevia, James. (2009). 'The ultimate gesture of deference and debasement': Kowtowing in China. *Past & Present, 203*(Suppl. 4), 212–234.

Hillemann, Ulrike. (2009). *Asian empire and British knowledge: China and the networks of British Imperial expansion*. London, England: Palgrave Macmillan.

Honour, Hugh. (1962). *Chinoiserie: The vision of Cathay*. New York, NY: Dutton & Co.

Howard, David S. (1994). *The choice of the private trader. The private market in Chinese export porcelain illustrated from the Hodroff Collection*. London, England: Sotheby's Publications.

Howes, David. (Ed.). (2005). *Empire of the senses: The sensual cultural reader*. Oxford, England: Berg Press.

Howes, David. (2008, September). Can these dry bones live? An anthropological approach to the history of the senses. *The Journal of American History, 95*(2), 442–451.

Howes, David & Lalonde, Marc. (1991). The history of sensibilities: Of the standard of taste in mid-eighteenth century England and the circulation of smells in post-Revolutionary France. *Dialectical Anthropology, 16*, 125–135.

Hunter, W. C. (1965). *The 'Fan Kwae' at Canton: Before treaty days, 1825–1844*. Taiwan: Ch'eng-wen Publishing Company. (Original work published 1882)

Impey, Oliver. (1977). *Chinoiserie: The impact of oriental styles on Western art and decoration*. New York, NY: Charles Scribner's Sons.

Keay, John. (1991). *The honourable company: A history of the English East India Company*. New York, NY: Macmillan.

Kelly, J. B. (1968). *Britain and the Persian Gulf, 1795–1880*. Oxford, England: Clarendon Press.

Kitson, Peter J. (2013). *Forging Romantic China: Sino-British cultural encounters, 1760–1840*. Cambridge, England: Cambridge University Press.

Kitson, Peter J. (2016). The dark gift: Opium, John Francis Davis, Thomas De Quincey, and the Amherst Embassy to China of 1816. In Peter J. Kitson & Robert Markley (Eds), *Writing China: Essays of the Amherst Embassy (1816) and Sino-British cultural relations* (pp. 56–82). Cambridge, England: D.S. Brewer.

Kitson, Peter J. (2017). The 'catastrophe of this new Chinese mission': The Amherst Embassy to China in 1816. In Ralf Hertel & Michael Keevak (Eds), *Early encounters between East Asia and Europe: Telling failures* (pp. 67–83). London, England: Routledge.

Kitson, Peter J. & Markley, Robert (Eds). (2016). *Writing China: Essays on the Amherst Embassy (1816) and Sino-British cultural relations*. Cambridge, England: D.S. Brewer.

Klekar, Cynthia. (2006). 'Prisoners in silken bonds': Obligation, trade, and diplomacy in English Voyages to Japan and China. *Journal for Early Modern Cultural Studies, 6*(1), 84–105.

Kops, Henriette Ranhusen-de Bruyn. (2002, July). Not such an 'unpromising beginning': The first Dutch trade embassy to China, 1655–1657. *Modern Asian Studies, 36*(3), 535–578.

Law, Lisa. (2005). Home cooking: Filipino women and geographies of the senses in Hong Kong. In David Howes (Ed.), *Empire of the senses* (pp. 224–244). New York, NY: Berg Publishers.

Legouix, Susan. (1980). *Image of China: William Alexander*. London, England: Jupiter Books.

Lehmann, Gilly. (2003). *The British housewife: Cookery books, cooking and society in eighteenth-century Britain*. Devon, England: Cromwell Press.

Leys, Simon. (1997). *The analects of Confucius*. New York, NY: W.W. Norton and Co.

Liu, Lydia H. (2004). *The clash of empires: The invention of China in modern world making*. Cambridge, MA: Harvard University Press.

Lloyd, Christopher. (1970). *Mr. Barrow of the Admiralty: A life of Sir John Barrow, 1764–1848*. London, England: Collins.

Lovell, Julia. (2011). *The Opium War: Drugs, dreams and the making of China*. Sydney, NSW: Picardo Press.

Low, Setha M. & Lawrence-Zuniga, Denise (Eds). (2003). *The anthropology of space and place: Locating culture*. Devon, England: Prospect Books.

Luard, Evan. (1962). *Britain and China*. London, England: Chatto & Windus.

Maffeo, Steven E. (2012). *Most secret and confidential: Intelligence in the age of Nelson*. Annapolis, MD: Naval Institute Press.

Markley, Robert. (2006). *The Far East and the English imagination, 1600–1730*. Cambridge, England: Cambridge University Press.

Markley, Robert. (2016). The Amherst Embassy in the shadow of Tambora: Climate and culture, 1816. In Peter J. Kitson & Robert Markley (Eds), *Writing China: Essays on the Amherst Embassy (1816) and Sino-British cultural relations* (pp. 83–104). Cambridge, England: D.S. Brewer.

Marshall, Adrian G. (2016). *Nemesis: The first iron warship and her world*. Singapore: Ridge Books.

Marshall, P. J. & Williams, Glyndwr. (1982). *The great map of mankind: Perceptions of new worlds in the Age of the Enlightenment*. Cambridge, MA: Harvard University Press.

Mattingly, Garrett. (2010). *Renaissance diplomacy*. New York, NY: Cosimo Inc. (Original work published 1955)

Medick, Hans. (1989, January). 'Missionaries in the row boat'? Ethnological ways of knowing as a challenge to social history. *Comparative Studies in Society and History, 9*(1), 76–96.

Mersey, Viscount. (1949). *The viceroys and governor-generals of India 1757–1947*. London, England: John Murray.

Miller, Stuart Creighton. (1974). *The unwelcome immigrant: The American image of the Chinese, 1785–1882*. Berkeley and Los Angeles, CA: University of California Press.

Min, Eun Kyung. (2004). Narrating the Far East: Commerce, civility, and ceremony in the Amherst Embassy to China (1816–1817). In Bryan R. Wells & Philip Stewart (Eds), *Interpreting colonialism* (pp. 160–180). Oxford, England: Voltaire Foundation.

Morrison, Robert. (2019). *The Regency revolution*. London, England: Atlantic Books.

Mosca, Matthew W. (2010, June). Empire and the circulation of frontier intelligence: Qing conceptions of the Ottomans. *Harvard Journal of Asiatic Studies, 70*(1), 147–207.

Mosca, Matthew W. (2013). *From frontier policy to foreign policy: The question of India and the transformation of geopolitics in Qing China*. Stanford, CA: Stanford University Press.

Mungello, David E. (2005). *The great encounter of China and the West, 1500–1800*. Lanham, MD: Rowman & Littlefield Publishers.

Murray, Hugh. (1820). *Historical account of discoveries and travels in Asia* (Vols. 1–2). London, England: Longman, Hurst, Rees, Orme, and Brown.

Napier, Priscilla. (1995). *Barbarian eye: Lord Napier in China, 1834, the prelude to Hong Kong*. London, England: Brassy's.

Naquin, Susan & Rawski, Evelyn S. (1987). *Chinese society in the eighteenth century*. New Haven, CT: Yale University Press.

Nicholson, Andrew (Ed.). (2007). *The letters of John Murray to Lord Byron*. Liverpool, England: Liverpool University Press.

O'Brien, Patrick. (1998). Inseparable connections: Trade, economy, fiscal state, and the expansion of empire, 1668–1815. In Wm. Roger Louis (Ed.), *The Oxford history of the British Empire. Vol. 2: The eighteenth century* (P. J. Marshall, Ed., pp. 53–77). Oxford, England: Oxford University Press.

Ong, S. P. (2010, April). Jurisdictional politics in Canton and the first English translation of the Qing Penal Code (1810). *Journal of the Royal Asiatic Society of Great Britain & Ireland, 20*(2), 141–165.

Owen, Felicity. (1981). *William Havell, 1782–1857: Paintings, watercolours, drawing and prints* [Catalogue of an exhibition held at Sphinx & Son, Reading Museum and Art Gallery, 24 November – 18 December 1981].

Parkins, Wendy. (2009). Trust your senses? An introduction to the Victorian sensorium. *Sensory Studies, 14*(2). Retrieved from openjournals.library.sydney.edu.au/index.php/AJVS/article/view/9414.

Peers, Douglas M. Amherst. (n.d.). William Pitt, first Earl Amherst of Arracan (1773–1857). In *Oxford Dictionary of National Biography*. doi.org/10.1093/ref:odnb/445.

Perkins, Dorothy. (1999). *Encyclopaedia of China*. New York, NY: Checkmark Books.

Petech, Luciano. (1956). Some remarks on the Portuguese embassies to China in the K'ang-his Period. *T'oung Pao, 44*, 227–241.

Peyrefitte, Alain. (1992). *The immobile empire*. New York, NY: Knopf.

Philips, Charles H. (1940). *The East India Company, 1784–1834*. Manchester, England: Manchester University Press.

Platt, Stephen R. (2018). *Imperial twilight: The Opium War and the end of China's last golden age*. New York, NY: Alfred A. Knoff.

Plowright, John. (2002). *Regency England: Age of Liverpool*. New York, NY: Routledge. Retrieved from books.google.com.au/books/about/Regency_England.html?id=3oXnUf6sK9AC.

Porter, David. (2001). *Ideographia: The Chinese cipher in early modern Europe.* Stanford, CA: Stanford University Press.

Porter, David. (2010). *The Chinese taste in eighteenth-century England.* Cambridge, England: Cambridge University Press.

Pratt, Mary Louise. (1992). *The imperial eye: Travel writing and transculturation.* London, England: Routledge.

Pratt, Richard. (1994). *Imperial China: History of the posts to 1896.* London, England: Christie's Robson Lowe.

Pritchard, Earl H. (1936). *The crucial years of early Anglo-Chinese relations 1750–1800.* New York, NY: Octagon Books.

Pritchard, Earl H. (1938, July). The instructions of the East India Company to Lord Macartney on his embassy to China and his reports to the Company, 1792–4 Part II. *Journal of the Royal Asiatic Society of Great Britain and Ireland, 3,* 375–396.

Pritchard, Earl H. (1943, February). The kotow in the Macartney Embassy to China in 1793. *The Far Eastern Quarterly, 2*(2), 163–203.

Pritchard, Earl H. (1970). *Anglo-Chinese relations during the seventeenth and eighteenth centuries.* New York, NY: Octagon Books.

Rawski, Evelyn S. (1998). *The last emperors: A social history of Qing Imperial institutions.* Berkeley and Los Angeles, CA: University of California Press.

Rawski, Evelyn & Rawson, Jessica. (2005). *China: The Three Emperors, 1662–1795.* London, England: Royal Academy of Arts.

Rawson, Jessica. (Ed.). (1992). *The British Museum book of Chinese art.* London, England: British Museum Press.

Reddy, William M. (2001). *The navigation of feeling: A framework for the history of emotions.* Cambridge, England: Cambridge University Press.

Reid, A. (1994). Historiographical reflections on the period 1750–1870 in Southeast Asia and Korea. *Itinerario, 18*(1), 77–89.

Reid, Anthony (Ed.). (1996). *Sojourners and settlers: Histories of Southeast Asia and the Chinese.* St Leonards, NSW: Allen & Unwin.

Reid, Anthony & Yangwen, Zheng (Eds). (2009). *Negotiating asymmetry: China's place in Asia.* Singapore: National University of Singapore.

Rennie, D. F. (1865). *Peking and the Pekingnese during the first year of the British embassy at Peking* (Vol. 1). London, England: John Murray.

Ritchie, Anne Thackeray & Evans, Richard. (1894). *Lord Amherst and the British advance eastwards to Burmah*. Oxford, England: Clarendon Press.

Rockhill, William Woodville. (1897, July). Diplomatic missions to the Court of China: The kowtow question II. *The American Historical Review, 2*(4), 627–643.

Rockhill, William Woodville. (1905). *Diplomatic audiences at the Court of China*. London, England: Luzac and Co.

Rowe, William T. (2011, December). Introduction: The significance of the Qianlong-Jiaqing transition in Qing history. *Late Imperial China, 32*(2), 74–88.

Ruiz, Teofilo. (1985). Unsacred monarchy: The kings of Castile in the Late Middle Ages. In Sean Wilentz (Ed.), *Rites of power: symbolism, ritual & politics since the Middle Ages*. Philadelphia, PA: University of Pennsylvania Press.

Russell, Gillian. (1995). *The theatres of war: Performance, politics, and society, 1793–1815*. Oxford, England: Oxford University Press.

Sample, Joe. (2008). 'The first appearance of this celebrated capital'; or, what Mr Barrow saw in the land of the Chinaman. In Steve Clark & Paul Smethurst (Eds), *Asian crossings: Travel writing on China, Japan and Southeast Asia* (pp. 31–46). Hong Kong, China: Hong Kong University Press.

Sargent, Arthur John. (1907). *Anglo-Chinese commerce and diplomacy*. London, England: Clarendon Press.

Seaton, Robert Cooper. (1898). *Sir Hudson Lowe and Napoleon*. London, England: David Nutt.

Semmel, Bernard. (1970). *The rise of free trade imperialism: Classical political economy, the empire and imperialism, 1750–1850*. Cambridge, England: Cambridge University Press.

Sennett, Richard. (1994). *Flesh and stone: The body and the city in Western civilization*. New York, NY: W.W. Norton & Company.

Sherry, Norman. (1966). *Conrad's Eastern world*. Cambridge, England: Cambridge University Press.

Singer, Aubrey. (1992). *The lion and the dragon: The story of the first British embassy to the Court of the Emperor Qianlong in Peking, 1792–94*. London, England: Barrie & Jenkins.

Slade, John. (1830). *Notices on the British trade to the port of Canton*. London, England: Smith, Elder, and Co.

Smith, Mark M. (2007). Producing sense, consuming sense, making sense: Perils and prospects for sensory history. *Journal of Social History, 40*(4), 841–858.

Smith, Mark M. (2008, September). Still coming to 'our' senses: An introduction. *Journal of American History, 95*(2), 378–380.

Smith, Richard J. (2013). *Mapping China and managing the world: Culture, cartography and cosmology in late imperial times*. Oxford, England: Routledge.

South China Morning Post Ltd. & New China News Ltd. (1984). *Zhongguo Da Yunhe* [The Grand Canal of China]. Hong Kong, China: New China News Ltd.

Spence, Jonathan. (1998). *The Chan's great continent: China in Western minds*. New York, NY: W.W. Norton & Co.

Tambiah, S. J. (1977). *World conqueror and world renouncer: A study of Buddhism and polity in Thailand against a historical background*. Cambridge, England: Cambridge University Press.

Tannerhill, Reay. (1995). *Food in history*. New York, NY: Broadway Books.

Thorne, R. (1986). *The history of Parliament. The House of Commons, 1790–1820*. London, England: Secker & Warburg.

Trevelyan, G. M. (1978). *English social history*. London, England: Longman.

Tuck, Patrick. (2000). Introduction. In George Thomas Staunton, *Notes of proceedings and occurrences, during the British embassy to Pekin, in 1816* (Reprint, pp. vii–xlii). London, England: Routledge. (Original work published 1824)

Turner, Jack. (2004). *Spice: The history of temptation*. New York, NY: Vintage Books.

Van Dyke, Paul A. (2007). *The Canton trade: Life and enterprise on the China coast, 1700–1845*. Hong Kong, China: Hong Kong University Press.

Van Dyke, Paul A. (2011). *Merchants of Canton and Macao: Politics and strategies in eighteenth century Chinese trade*. Hong Kong, China: Hong Kong University Press.

Van Dyke, Paul & Mok, Maria Kar-Wing. (2015). *Images of the Canton Factories 1760–1822: Reading history in art*. Hong Kong, China: Hong Kong University Press.

Viraphol, Sarasin. (1977). *Tribute and profit: Sino-Siamese trade, 1652–1853*. Cambridge, MA: Harvard University Press.

Wade, John. (1835). *The black book: An exposition of abuses in church and state*. London, England: John Fairburn.

Wakeman Jr, Frederic E. (1978). The Canton trade and the Opium War. In Denis Twitchett & John K. Fairbank (Eds), *The Cambridge history of China* (Vol. 10, pp. 163–212). Cambridge, England: Cambridge University Press.

Wakeman Jr, Frederic E. (2009). Drury's occupation of Macao and China's response to early modern imperialism. In Frederic E. Wakeman Jr (Ed.), *Telling Chinese history: A selection of essays* (pp. 359–369). Berkeley and Los Angeles, CA: University of California Press.

Waley-Cohen, Joanna. (1993, December). China and Western technology in the late eighteenth century. *The American Historical Review, 98*(5), 1525–1544.

Waley-Cohen, Joanna. (2004). The new Qing history. *Radical History Review, 88*, 193–206.

Walker, Richard. (1985). *Regency portraits* (Vol. 1). London, England: National Portrait Gallery.

Walvin, James. (1997). *Fruits of empire: Exotic produce and British taste, 1600–1800*. New York, NY: New York University Press.

Wang, Gungwu. (2003). *Anglo-Chinese encounters since 1800: War, trade, science and governance*. Cambridge, England: Cambridge University Press.

Wang, Wengsheng. (2014). *White Lotus rebels and South China pirates: Crisis and reform in the Qing Empire*. Cambridge, MA: Harvard University Press.

Webster, C. K. (1938). Introduction. In A. Aspinall (Ed.), *The letters of King George IV, 1812–1830* (Vol. 1, p. lxiv). Cambridge, England: Cambridge University Press.

Western, J. R. (1956, October). The Volunteer movement as an anti-Revolutionary force, 1793–1801. *The English Historical Review, 71*(281), 603–614.

Wickberg, Daniel. (2007, June). What is the history of sensibilities? On cultural histories, old and new. *American Historical Review, 112*(3), 661–684.

Wilentz, Sean (Ed.). (1985). *Rites of power: Symbolism, ritual & politics since the Middle Ages*. Philadelphia, PA: University of Pennsylvania Press.

Wilkinson, Endymion. (2000). *Chinese history: A manual*. Cambridge, MA: Harvard-Yenching Institute.

Will, Pierre-Étienne. (2008, June). Views of the realm in crisis: Testimonies on imperial audiences in the nineteenth century. *Late Imperial China, 29*(1), 125–159.

Wills, John E. (1993, February). Maritime Asia, 1500–1800: The interactive emergence of European domination. *The American Historical Review, 98*(1), 83–105.

Wills, John E. (2009). *Embassies and illusions: Dutch and Portuguese envoys to K'ang-hsi, 1666–1687*. Los Angeles, CA: Figueroa Press.

Wilson, Ben. (2008). *Decency & disorder: The Age of Cant 1789–1837*. London, England: Faber & Faber.

Wilson, Kathleen. (1998). *The sense of the people: Politics, culture and imperialism in England, 1715–1785*. Cambridge, England: Cambridge University Press.

Wilson, Kathleen. (2015). Empire, trade and popular politics in mid-Hanoverian Britain: The case of Admiral Vernon. *Past & Present, 121*, 74–109.

Wolters, O. W. (1970). *The fall of Śrivijaya in Malay history*. Kuala Lumpur, Malaysia: Oxford University Press.

Wong, Bin R. (1997). *China transformed: Historical change and the limits of European experience*. Ithaca, NY: Cornell University Press.

Wood, Frances. (1994). Britain's first view of China: The Macartney Embassy 1792–1794. *RSA Journal, 142*(5447), 59–68.

Wood, Frances. (1998). *No dogs and not many Chinese: Treaty port life in China 1843–1943*. London, England: John Murray.

Wood, Herbert J. (1940). England, China and the Napoleonic Wars. *Pacific Historical Review, 9*, 139–156.

Woodside, Alexander Barton. (1971). *Vietnam and the Chinese model: A comparative study of Nguyen and Ch'ing Civil Government in the first half of the nineteenth century*. Cambridge, MA: Harvard University Press.

Zhang, Shunhong. (2013). *British views on China at a special time (1790–1820)*. Reading, England: Paths International Ltd.

Zhao, Gang. (2013). *The Qing opening to the ocean: Chinese maritime policies, 1684–175*. Honolulu, HI: University of Hawaii Press.

Appendix A: List of Persons and Their Salaries

This document is a copy of the original handwritten text found in the British Library, but reformatted for ease of clarity.

Proceeding in the Embassy under the charge of the Right Honourable Lord Amherst on board His Majesty's Ship *Alceste*, and the Company's Ship *General Hewitt* (in BL IOR MSS EUR F 140/36)

Name	Position	Salary (£)
His Excellency the Right Honourable Lord Amherst	Ambassador	12,000
Henry Ellis Esq	Secretary to the Embassy	3,000
Mr Henry Hayne	Private Secretary	750
Reverend Mr Griffith	Chaplain	300
Lieutenant Cook	In Command of the Guard	300
Mr Abel	Surgeon	300
Dr Lyn (proceeds without salary)	Surgeon	–
Mr Havell	Draftsman	300
Mr Marriage	Accountant, in charge of presents	200
Edward Vaughan	Butler	73.10
Thomas Mosely	Valet de Chambre	63
V. S. La Roche	1st Cook	105
Haynes Harrison	2nd Cook	52.10
Isaac Head Behennal	To take care of Lustres & Act as Footman	63
James Metcalf	Carpenter & Joiner & Act as Footman	63
Thomas Lindsey	Tailor, to act as Footman if required	63
Thomas Ives	Footman	26.5
George Norman	Footman	26.5
William Joiner	Footman	26.5

Name	Position	Salary (£)
John Pritchard	Footman	26.5
James Dennison	Coachman	31.10
Thomas Heath	Postilion	15.15
Thomas Hancock	Gilder in charge of the Frames & for glasses and mirrors	63
Thomas Hooper	Gardener	100
A. Clarke	Master of the Band	88.4
Daniel Price	Musician	50.8
William Godso	Musician	50.8
Thomas Wray	Musician	50.8
Joseph Garbett	Musician	50.8
Thomas Patterson	Musician	50.8
William Gooch	Musician	50.8
Thomas Clarke	Musician	50.8
James Pybus	Musician	50.8
Geo Thompson	Musician	50.8
Lewis Vincent	Bass Drum	50.8

Of the above Musicians the following have absence Money allowed to their Families &c:

A. Clarke Master	10/6 per week to be paid to his Father-in-law for the support to his son
Daniel Vice	half of his wages every three Months to be paid to his father
Thomas Wray	to pay his Father one guinea every Month
Thomas Patterson	to pay his wife two guineas every Month
William Gooch	to pay his wife one Pound every Month
Geo Thompson	to pay his wife two guineas every Month

People included in the Amherst Embassy not mentioned above:

Right Honourable Jeffrey Amherst	Page to the ambassador
Charles Abbot	Midshipman
T. B. Martin	Midshipman
Zachariah Poole	Assistant to Clark Abel
Lieutenant Charles Somerset	Attached to the Guard

APPENDIX A

Company people who joined the Amherst Embassy off Macao:

Sir George Thomas Staunton	Second Commissioner
Rev. Dr. Robert Morrison	Senior Interpreter
F. Hastings Toone	Chinese Secretary
J. F. Davis	Chinese Secretary
Thomas Manning	Chinese Secretary

Appendix B: Presents and Cost of the Amherst Embassy

This document is a copy of the original handwritten text found in the British Library, but reformatted for ease of reference.

Articles Ordered for the Embassy to China (in BL IOR MSS EUR F 140/38a)

Presents ordered for the emperor:	
From Rundell & Bridge	
1 Gold Box with the Prince Regent's Portrait Set with Jewels	£1,575
1 Gold Salver & Vase	£840
	£2,415
From Green & Ward	
1 Silver Waiter	£210
1 Silver Epergne	£187
4 Silver Dishes	£240
4 Silver Baskets	£200
4 Silver Stands	£240
1 Silver Plateau	£100
2 Pair Silver Cups & Saucers	£100
1 Pair Silver Candelabra	£250
1 Additional Set Glass Covers	£33
	£1,560
From the Plate Glass Company	
1 Looking Glass (134 inch by 70 inch)	£20
1 Looking Glass (132 inch by 67 inch)	£1,200
2 Convex Mirrors each 36 inch in diameter	£50

Presents ordered for the emperor:	
	£1,270
From Parkers & Perry	
1 Large Glass Chandelier	£945
Sundry Articles, Cut Glass	£150
	£1,095
From Blades	
2 Superb Candelabra	£530
Sundry Articles, Cut Glass	£150
	£680
Total	**Carried over £7,020**

Other presents:

- Broad cloths of the finest kinds made of soft Spanish wool—blue, plumb and yellow—the softer and finer the better
- Ermine and other superfine furs
- Portraits of their Majesties in their Coronation robes, to be housed in a gold box set with diamonds
- Another gold box set with stones to carry the Prince Regent's letter to the emperor
- Ornamental clocks—two for the Hall of audience
- Perfumes
- Liqueurs
- Porcelain sent to the emperor: a dessert service—white and gold scroll border with paintings of landscapes in colours consisting of 24 dessert plates, four shell dishes, four oval dishes, four square dishes, one centre dish and two cream bowls (£84.00)
- A large centre vase in French grey with white scrolls in relief with embossed gold and superb painting (£73.10.0)
- Large vases (Warwick form) rich white and gold design with borders of flowers richly painted in a straw colour (£42.00)
- A centre vase handles and gold designs with groups of flowers (£18.18) and a case (£6.5.0)
- Sedan chairs—two superb and elegantly finished and most richly ornamented packed in four cases (£802.12.6)

APPENDIX B

- Glassware/bottles/liqueurs including brandy and dried fruits (£399.12.6)
- Painting of Doncaster races packed in a case (£712.00)
- Engravings of the coast of England and Wales
- Presents for the ministers
- Lustres and chandeliers
- Hanging lamps
- Paintings of buildings and flowers, and views of the Thames including bridges and shipping
- Prints of distinguished persons
- Maps of Russia, England, Scotland and Ireland
- Charts of navigation from Europe to China
- Broadcloths, damasks, cutlery, razors, scissors and pen knives
- Porcelain, glass, cut glass, watches and clocks

Presents actually sent to the ministers included:

- Mirrors and frames
- Shades, glass and dessert services
- Decanters, centre bowls and cups
- Linens including 24 damask table cloths, superfine cloths, six reams of superfine and milled blue and gilt edge paper

Presents actually sent to the mandarins:

- Two silver liqueur frames with cut bottles and large oval dish
- Snuffs including Brazil snuff and Red Havana snuff
- Eight dozen glass bottles
- 12 Morocco Pocket books with gold locks
- 12 military telescopes

Presents	Cost (£)
Presents ordered for the emperor	16,416.6.01
Other presents	668.1.08
Presents actually sent to the ministers	4,887.19.11
Presents actually sent to the mandarins	10,555.1.0
Total	**22,005.13.7**

Appendix C: The Total Cost of the Amherst Embassy

This document is a copy of the original handwritten text found in the British Library, but reformatted for ease of reference. Source: BL IOR MSS EUR F 140/38a.

Item	Cost (£)
Cost of presents per invoice	22,005.13.7
Presents to be made personally by the ambassador	305.9.0
Presents sent to the viceroy of Canton previously to the sailing of the embassy	311.8.3
Dollars for use on the voyage	4,556.14.0
Bones for ditto	10.8.0
Maps of China, not sent as presents	45.17.6
Articles for the use of Mr Abel	558.14.6
Ambassador's carriage	814.17.3
Articles provided by Captain Maxwell*	14,295.18.7
Articles provided by Lord Amherst	1,316.14.2
Outfit of band exclusive of salaries	574.17.9
Advances of salaries, etc.	5,594.16.7
	50,391.9.5
Add balance in Lord Amherst's hands of his last account	163.19.4
Total	**50,555.8.9**

Note: * It is not clear what this amount covered; it could possibly refer to the refitting of the HMS *Alceste* or supplies for the embassy.

Appendix D: Ball's Secret Report (Commissioner of Teas at Canton)

A Secret Report on the Expediency of Opening a Second Port in China: 2 July 1816

Staunton's doubts of a successful mission in 1816 were not reflected by the author of a secret report written for Amherst and dated 2 July 1816 to coincide with the Amherst Embassy's arrival off Macao. Samuel Ball, Chief Inspector of Teas at Canton, was commissioned by the Select Committee to report on the *Expediency of opening a second port to British trade in China*. Reference to the document has not been made in any previous historical account of the Amherst Embassy and only a brief abstract is given here. The detailed report, printed at Macao, presumably on Morrison's press 'for private circulation only', is important for revealing Britain's ulterior motive for the embassy if negotiations had been permitted as well as making clear the very limited intelligence they had on the state of China's internal trade. Ball's sources were confined to the publications of Du Halde, Father Amiot, Sir George Leonard Staunton and John Barrow. The *Chinese Repository* refers to the report in an article published in July 1834 and a full copy was printed in the *Journal of the Royal Asiatic Society* in 1845 at a time when the question of access to new ports in China was of paramount British importance.[1]

---

1   The preamble to its publication written in 1845 reads, 'The time is now come when we are called upon to decide what new privileges we have to demand of the Chinese: and since a more unrestricted intercourse with that country is looked for, it becomes an object of the first importance to ascertain at what Ports these privileges may be best obtained' (Observations on the Expediency of Opening a Second Port in China, *Journal of the Royal Asiatic Society of Great Britain and Ireland*, 1845, vol. 6, p. 182).

Ball's report focused on the Chinese port thought to be the most favourable for the tea trade. Canton, it was pointed out, was unsuited due to its distance from the tea-growing districts and its role as an emporium useful only for the consumption of foreign imports. Further, 'the Canton people are neither the carriers of the imports to the distant provinces, nor of the exports to Canton', while black tea had to be transported overland to Canton, which cost the Company an additional charge of £150,000 per annum (Observations on the Expediency of Opening a Second Port in China, *Journal of the Royal Asiatic Society of Great Britain and Ireland*, 1845, vol. 6, p. 214). Other teas were transported by sea, suggesting that it was far more economical for the British to be allowed direct access to the ports of the tea-growing areas of Fukien. The report advocated that the port of 'Fu-chew in Fo-kien' (Fuzhou) province was ideally situated to advance British trade in China, enabling the easy access of British woollens, lead and other products into the markets of the Chinese interior. Ball had a further vision, namely, a British monopoly of the lucrative Chinese coastal trade. To date, Ball argued, the coastal trade was in the hands of the numerous 'Fokien junks' that daily passed 'to and fro at Macao, and along every part of the coast of China' (p. 196). He thought:

> Doubtless in a free and open intercourse with this country, the superior construction and security of European vessels, and knowledge of insurance, would enable foreigners not only to participate in, but perhaps monopolize, this branch of commerce, and even attract to the coast much of that still more valuable trade, which, from the risks and fears of a sea voyage, is at present conducted by inland carriage. (p. 196)

Ball concluded that the advantages of moving the bulk of British trade from Canton to Fuzhou were not remote and speculative but 'immediate and real' (p. 200). He considered this aim achievable:

> Perhaps it might not be difficult to show [the Chinese Government] that a change would be mutually beneficial; and whatever may have been said of the jealousy and suspicion of these people, it may be doubted whether they are so bigoted to forms as to sacrifice even their smallest interests where a change seems to involve no radical injury to their institutions. They have no objection to trade, if it can be carried on peacefully; and nothing can appear more reasonable on our part, or more intelligible to them, than our wishing to carry it on where we can purchase the articles we require the cheapest. (p. 201)

Ball's misguided assessment of a likely Chinese response to such a plan reveals a significant British misunderstanding of Chinese attitudes and policy towards the British and other Western traders. The British belief in the mutual benefits of international trade as the engine for driving greater prosperity and progress for both sides was not shared by the Chinese. Ball's report reveals that there was no British appreciation of the rationale behind the Canton trading system initiated as a mechanism for controlling and restricting foreign contact with the Chinese people. The expectation that China would open a second port to British trade in anticipation of mutual benefit was certainly a British illusion, and one that lies at the core of the issues that Amherst was expected to be able to negotiate with the Chinese Government.

It is worth noting that the *Chinese Repository* in 1834 reported Staunton's opinion that British trade be withdrawn from Canton altogether and be re-established 'in some insular position on the coast, beyond the reach of acts of oppression and molestation; where it may be carried on securely and honourably' (*Chinese Repository*, July 1834, vol. 3, p. 132). British frustration at the absence of defined regulations embodied in a formal treaty governing the important trade, thereby leaving it vulnerable to sudden interruptions from the conduct of the Chinese Government, persisted.

Appendix E: List of Chinese Officials Responsible for the Conduct of the Amherst Embassy

The two junior provincial officers sent to conduct the Amherst Embassy after it arrived in the Gulf of Bei Zhili were:

- Chang-wei (referred to by the British as 'Chang')
    - a Chinese and a civil officer, wore a blue button
    - came on board the HMS *Lyra* on 29 July 1816 and the HMS *Alceste* on 31 July 1816
    - left the embassy on 12 September
    - promoted to a judicial commissioner at Shandong at the conclusion of his role in the embassy.
- Yin
    - a Manchu and a military officer wearing a red button
    - came on board the HMS *Lyra* on 29 July 1816 and the HMS *Alceste* on 31 July 1816
    - left the embassy on 17 September.

The two senior mandarins in charge of the embassy, referred to by the British as the 'legates', were:

- Guanghui (referred to by the British as 'Kwang' or 'Quong')
    - a Manchu, age 58
    - Changlu Salt Commissioner stationed at Tianjin
    - remained with the embassy throughout its stay in China

- duties concluded at Canton on 19 January 1817
  - demoted at the time of the embassy's conclusion to a gold button and to a secretaryship of the eighth rank and posted to Manchuria.

  (See Appendix I for Morrison's letter to Amherst dated 26 November 1821 on the death of Guanghui.)

- Sulenge (referred to by the British as 'Soo')
  - a Manchu, aged in his seventies or eighties and infirm
  - president of the Board of Public Works
  - wore a red button
  - Hoppo at Canton in 1793 and received Lord Macartney on his return from the Qianlong court
  - left the embassy at Tongzhou in early September 1816
  - demoted at the time of the embassy's conclusion
  - lost his position as president of the Board of Works and rank as a general in the army
  - ordered to pluck out his peacock feather and reduced to a button of the third rank (Tuck, 2000, p. xxviii).

  (Not to be confused with Sungyun, Staunton's friend at Canton in 1811. Sungyun had accompanied Macartney as far as Hangzhou, during his journey from Peking to Canton [Cranmer-Byng, 1962, p. 369, fn. 38].)

The highest ranking mandarins sent to Tongzhou to oversee Amherst rehearsing the kowtow were:

- Heshitai (referred to by the British as 'Duke Ho')
  - a Manchu of the Bordered Yellow Banner and the emperor's brother-in-law
  - promoted and rewarded in 1813 after helping to repel a rebel attack on the Imperial Palace and foiling an assassination attempt on the Jiaqing emperor
  - had two meetings with Amherst prior to proceeding to Yuanmingyuan. The first was held on 22 August 1816 and the second on 27 August 1816
  - conducted affairs at Yuanmingyuan where he unsuccessfully endeavoured to deliver Amherst before the Jiaqing emperor

- last contact with the embassy was on the early morning of its reception at Yuanmingyuan
  - lost emoluments as a '*kung-yeh*' or 'Duke' for five years and forfeitied the honour of wearing the 'yellow riding jacket' following the failure of Amherst to appear before the Jiaqing emperor
  - allowed to retain his title and his private duties at the palace (Tuck, 2000, p. xxix).
- Muketenge (referred to by the British as 'Moo' or the 'Silent Moo')
  - a Manchu of the Bordered Yellow Banner and President of the Board of Rites
  - stripped of his presidency of the Board of Rites and retired following the dismissal of the embassy
  - died in 1829.

(See Appendix I for Morrison's news on the above sent in 1821.)

Appendix F: Imperial Edict: 'Ceremonies to Be Observed at the Audience of Leave'

This is a British translation of one of two imperial edicts handed to the British on 11 September 1816 of the ceremonies to be observed at the public audience of Amherst, quoted in Ellis (1817, pp. 499–500, Note No. 5).

On the day that the English Embassador takes leave, music and cushions shall be placed in the Hall of Light and Splendour (as on the two proceeding occasions).

About five o'clock in the morning his Majesty shall be most respectfully requested to put on the Imperial dragon-robes, and to ascend the Hall of Light and Splendour. The Princes, the Royal Personages, the Dukes, &c. shall be arranged in two wings withinside the hall, in the same manner as at the presentation. Whilst the band plays 'a glorious subjugation', his Majesty shall ascend the throne.

Soo [Sulenge] and Kwang [Guanghui] shall conduct the Embassador and suite, as on the first occasion, to the west side of the passage by the altar of the Moon, where, at this word given, they shall arrange themselves in order, It shall then be proclaimed 'Kneel!' the Embassador and his suite shall kneel, and wish his Majesty repose. Soo and the others shall then lead the Embassador through the western folding partition door to the level area within the hall, where he shall kneel down and wait till his Majesty himself confers upon the King of his country court beads and a purse. Meen-gan shall receive them, and deliver them to the Embassador, and also communicate, authoritatively, such orders as his Majesty may be pleased to direct on dismissing the Embassador.

This being ended, Soo, &c. shall conduct the Embassador out of the western folding door to withoutside the hall, where Soo shall take in charge for the Embassador the beads and purse, and then conduct him as before to the west side of the altar of the Moon. On the word 'Be arranged' being proclaimed, the Embassador and suite shall arrange themselves standing; the crier shall proclaim, 'Advance and kneel!' the Embassador and suite shall advance and kneel. It shall be proclaimed, 'Bow the head to the ground and arise!' The Embassador and suite shall then, toward the upper part of the hall, perform the ceremony of san-kwei-kew-kow (thrice kneeling and nine times bowing the head to the ground), and the music shall stop. The Princes, &c. shall next conduct the Embassador and suite to behind the western row of persons, where they shall perform the ceremony once and sit down.

Whilst his Majesty takes tea, the Princes, &c. with the Embassador and suite, shall arise from their seats, kneel and perform the ceremony once. After his Majesty has drank tea, they shall again approach their places and sit down. The attendants shall then confer tea upon the Princes, the Embassador, and the rest, for which, before and after drinking, they shall perform an act of reverence. They shall then stand up, and the music shall play 'subjugation manifested'. Whilst his Majesty retires to the interior of the palace the music shall stop, and the Princes, Embassador, and suite shall go out.

Appendix G: Substance of an Edict Seen on the Walls of a Building in the 8th Moon of the 21st Year of Kia King

This is a British translation of the imperial edict from Secret Consultations, East India Company, 1 January 1817, in BL IOR G/12/197 (Reel 2) F 367.

Whereas the English Envoy & Suite are returning to their Country, and their Language and Dresses are totally different from those of this Country, His Imperial Majesty has been pleased to order, that they should not anchor any where on their route, nor any one of them be permitted to go on shore; and whereas their Excellences the Viceroy and Fooyuen have ordered in conformity therewith, that no persons attempt to gather about them for the purpose of looking at them, or conversing with them; that none to trade with them in Books & Furniture or other Articles; that no women do come out to shew themselves to them, but that all persons pursue and attend their respective occupations as usual. This Edict is therefore issued to enforce the same, and to warn all persons against the consequences of disobedience.

Appendix H: Itinerary of the Amherst Embassy

August 1815

10　The British Government approves an embassy to the Qing court to be sent on behalf of the Prince Regent, paid for by the British East India Company (the Company). 'Its main purpose was—not to propose any innovation, but merely to secure and consolidate' commercial trade between China and Britain at Canton (Staunton, 1822, p. 239).

October 1815

2　Lord William Pitt Amherst's appointment as British Ambassador of the Special Mission to the Chinese Empire announced officially by the Prince Regent.

February 1816

8　The HMS *Alceste*, HMS *Lyra* and Company Ship *General Hewitt* depart Portsmouth.

18　One-day stopover at Madeira.

March 1816

10　Ships separate; the *Alceste* heads for Brazil, and the *Lyra* and *General Hewitt* for Cape Town.

21　The *Alceste* arrives at Rio de Janeiro.

31　The *Alceste* departs Rio de Janeiro.

April 1816

13　The *General Hewitt* arrives at Cape Town.

14　The *Lyra* arrives Cape Town.

18　The *Alceste* arrives Cape Town.

June 1816

7   The *Lyra* arrives Anjere Roads, Batavia.

9   The *Alceste* arrives Anjere Roads, Batavia, with the *General Hewitt* in sight.

10 Amherst sends a letter to Canton with an American ship.

12 The *Lyra* dispatched to China to announce the approach of the embassy to George Staunton at Canton with instructions for a secret rendezvous off Macao to be arranged.

18 Amherst attends a ball in Batavia held by the Dutch in honour of the anniversary of the Battle of Waterloo.

21 The *Alceste* and *General Hewitt* depart Batavia for China.

July 1816

9   The embassy meets up with the HMS *Orlando* whose commander, Captain Clavell, informs Amherst that Staunton and other members of the Company had embarked on the Company ships *Discovery* and *Investigator* for the Lemma Islands off Macao where they and the *Lyra* were waiting for the *Alceste*.

10 Amherst arrives at the Lemma Islands and meets with the waiting ships and the Company men from Canton.

11 Squadron weighs anchor at Hong Kong Island. Staunton comes on board the *Alceste*.

13 Imperial permission received to proceed to the Yellow Sea. Embassy is informed that mandarins have been dispatched to Zhoushan and Tianjin to await Amherst's arrival and conduct him to the Court at Peking.

27 The *Lyra* arrives at the mouth of the Baihe River and anchors closer to shore because of her shallow draft.

    Toone and Campbell visit some fishermen at sea and request that they take a note to inform the authorities of the arrival of the embassy. The fishermen refuse.

28 The rest of the squadron anchors off the Baihe River, further out to sea.

31 Two mandarins, Chang-wei and Yin, come on board the *Lyra* and take charge of Lord Amherst's letter to the viceroy. They comprise two of the four mandarins designated to escort the embassy after arrival at Dagu. Arrangements made for Morrison and Cooke to go ashore at Dagu to meet with the mandarins in charge of the embassy.

APPENDIX H

Morrison learns that the embassy would not remain long at Peking and that it was not invited to accompany the emperor to Jehol.

August 1816

4   Chang-wei and Yin visit the *Alceste*. The embassy was to receive high honours. First mention of the intended ceremony—the kowtow—that the British were required to perform before the emperor and that Amherst was to rehearse beforehand.

8   Preparations made for disembarking the embassy and landing on Chinese soil. Discussion among the British on the expediency of performing the kowtow. Staunton informs Amherst in a letter that to comply with the ceremony was inadvisable, even though its refusal might result in the total rejection of the embassy.

9   The embassy lands at Dagu. Amherst is informed that a higher ranked mandarin, Sulenge (President of the Tribunal of Works), was waiting at Tianjin to receive him. Twenty-three boats are provided to carry the ambassadorial party.

12 The embassy arrives at Tianjin. Amherst is informed that an imperial banquet is being given in his honour the following day.

13 The embassy attends an imperial banquet hosted by Guanghui and Sulenge. Long drawn out discussion on the ceremony the Chinese intend Amherst to perform before the emperor. Legates insist that Macartney had kowtowed before the Qianlong emperor and that Amherst should do the same. Amherst refuses to kowtow and performs the British ceremony of respect before an altar table, representative of the emperor, following the precedent of Macartney. The issue of compliance with the prostration ceremony is left unresolved.

14 The embassy proceeds up-river towards Tongzhou. Staunton pressured to use his influence to get Amherst to agree to kowtow. Sulenge and Chang-wei admit that Macartney had performed the British ceremony on the first reception but afterwards performed the kowtow.

15 The legates, Guanghui and Sulenge, arrive late in the evening in an agitated state. They ask, 'What has become of the British ships?'

16 The legates demand a 'yes or no' answer on the kowtow. The embassy boats are turned back towards Tianjin after Amherst refuses to commit to the prostration ceremony.

18 The embassy boats permitted to proceed towards Tongzhou after Amherst agrees to present a written declaration of the ceremony he proposes to perform in the presence of the emperor. Amherst informed that two mandarins of very high rank will receive him at Tongzhou.

20 The embassy arrives at Tongzhou.

21 Heshitai, called 'Duke Ho' by the British, and Muketenge (President of the Tribunal of Ceremonies) arrive at Tongzhou to observe Amherst rehearsing the kowtow.

Later that day, six high-ranking mandarins call on Amherst. Their rude manner is commented on by the British who refer to them as 'the Lads of Mougden'.

22 Conference with Heshitai—Amherst is informed that the kowtow could not be dispensed with. If complied with, the British would be conducted to the Qing court. Amherst hands Heshitai his letter for the emperor informing him of the proposed ceremony he plans to perform. The letter also contains a respectful and conciliatory approach to a solution on the ceremonial impasse.

23 Little official business takes place. Three Europeans dressed in Chinese costume from the Russian College at Peking visited the British boats but were treated with suspicion and ignored.

24 The emperor asserts he witnessed Macartney performing the kowtow. News received that Staunton is under suspicion by the Qing authorities.

25 News received that a letter is being prepared by the emperor for the king should the embassy be rejected, and that the emperor was particularly angry at the unauthorised departure of the British ships.

26 Affairs critical: Staunton fearing arrest, Amherst and Ellis still reluctant to close the door on negotiations regarding the reception of the embassy, and Amherst yet to make his final decision on the kowtow.

27 Meeting with Heshitai and Muketenge. Amherst stands firm—he is following his sovereign's orders to follow Macartney's precedent and will not kowtow. The British put forward their objectives for the embassy; these are not dismissed by Heshitai who offers his support on the condition that Amherst performs the kowtow.

On return from the meeting, Amherst and Ellis, following Heshitai's more agreeable and accommodating attitude, tend towards agreeing to kowtow. Staunton stands firm, concerned that recent intimidation might lead to a direct attack on him personally or Company interests at Canton. Staunton consults his Company colleagues—Toone, Pearson and Davis—who remain strongly against performing the kowtow. Morrison and Manning are prepared to consider kowtowing but only if concessions are made to the British. After weighing up the arguments, Amherst finally decides not to perform the ceremony.

That afternoon, the embassy receives a directive to proceed to Peking. The British confirm that their decision not to comply with the ceremony was understood. They are reassured by the mandarins that they will not be required to kowtow.

28 The embassy leaves Tongzhou for Yuanmingyuan at four o'clock in the afternoon.

29 The embassy arrives at Yuanmingyuan at daybreak after a very tiring overnight journey. Amherst, Staunton, Ellis, Jeffrey and Morrison, are separated from the rest of the embassy and conducted straight to the imperial compound. Requested to enter directly into the emperor's presence, Amherst refuses, pleading fatigue and the absence of his ambassadorial robes and credentials. Amherst is manhandled by Heshitai in an attempt to drag him into the emperor's presence where he will have no option but to kowtow. Amherst strongly resists.

Amherst retires to his quarters at the estate of Sungyun, considered a friend of the British from his time as the viceroy of Canton in 1811 and earlier from his role in the Macartney Embassy.

The emperor's physician arrives between 8 and 9 o'clock in the morning to examine Amherst. By noon, reports are received of the embassy's dismissal due to the emperor's anger over Amherst's 'feigned illness'. Orders arrive for the embassy to return to Tongzhou.

A mandarin wearing a red button visits the embassy and hints that assent to kowtow might still save the embassy, but this is dismissed by the British.

The embassy leaves the compound at four o'clock in the afternoon.

30 After a tedious night journey, the embassy arrives back at their Tongzhou base. Everything is shut, and indications make clear that the embassy is no longer being treated as a tribute mission.

At 10 o'clock at night, arrangements for a partial exchange of presents take place. Guanghui and Sulenge are dejected over events at Yuanmingyuan.

31 The formal exchange of presents from the King of England to the Jiaqing emperor, and from the emperor to the king takes place. Amherst performs the same ceremony as the Lords before the vacant throne of the king in the House of Lords, in front of a portrait of the Prince Regent.

Sulenge leaves the embassy. Guanghui, Chang-wei and Yin remain as its legates and conductors.

September 1816

2 The embassy sets out for Tianjin. The British are concerned over reduced provisions.

3 Chang-wei tells Morrison that the emperor had no intention of receiving the British on the early morning of 29 August; he only wished to view them from his palanquin to witness the ceremony the English proposed to perform before him. If he did not approve, the embassy was to be dismissed.

The British learn that the request for the embassy to proceed to Yuanmingyuan was a plot devised by Heshitai who hoped that Amherst, lured by his promises of support, would perform the kowtow at a public audience.

5 The British are informed that the emperor is now aware of the circumstances in which they had travelled overnight to Yuanmingyuan and is very angry with Heshitai who is deprived of his great offices at court. Muketenge and Sulenge are removed from their positions and Guanghui is reduced to the rank of a gold button.

6 The embassy reaches Tianjin but is not greeted with any ceremony.

8 News received that Chang-wei had been promoted to judge of Shandong province.

The embassy leaves the Baihe River and proceeds down a subsidiary stream towards the Grand Canal.

12 Several members of the embassy are very ill, including Abel and Toone.

13 The embassy is forced to leave ports of call at midnight or early daybreak to avoid access to towns.

14 Staunton notes a decline in prosperity compared to the time of the Macartney Embassy. Chang-wei informs Staunton that he is due to leave the embassy. News is received that the emperor is not cross with the British but with his own officers conducting the embassy.

15 The embassy arrives at Dongguan with its pleasing scenery of willows and poplars. Chang-wei (secretly) sends Staunton a copy of the *Peking Gazette* with an account of the embassy's dismissal.

16 Staunton meets the judge of Bei Zhili who provides him with an unflattering account of England and fears that the rejection of the embassy might cause the interruption of trade at Canton which would bring ruin to England. The judge asserts that the kowtow is indispensable and that the Chinese emperor is the sovereign of the world and the supreme head of all nations.

The treasurer of Shandong replaces the judge as the official overseeing the embassy.

17 The embassy enters Shandong province. There is a change in the officers attending the embassy. Guanghui visits the British for the first time since Tongzhou and blames Heshitai for the failure of the embassy. The British are informed that their route to Canton is to deviate from Macartney's and will go via Nanjing.

22 The embassy arrives at Linqing to an amiable reception. There is competition among provincial conductors of the embassy to provide the best supplies. The British squadron is made up of 50–60 boats of different descriptions.

23 The embassy enters the Grand Canal. The Chinese temporary forts are derided by the British.

25 The embassy journeys through well-cultivated open country; pleasant farm cottages surrounded by trees and distant mountains to eastward seen for the first time. Staunton notes that the lower orders are cleaner and more presentable than those of Europe.

26 Staunton informed that the emperor has instructed that every kind of public attention and honour be paid to the embassy as it travels to Canton.

30 The embassy enters Jiangsu province but deviates back into the Shandong countryside as Jiangsu is devastated by floods.

October 1816

1. Great numbers of grain junks (20,000) are observed by the British as evidence of a vast inland commerce.
2. Guanghui is noted as an infrequent visitor and not open in his communications with the embassy (in contrast to Sungyun and Macartney).
3. The judge of Jiangsu province joins the embassy.
4. Abel reported to be very sick—there is concern as to whether he will survive.
6. The embassy approaches the Yellow River. Huge number of boats observed, but nowhere near the amount observed in the Pearl River at Canton.
7. A sojourn ashore is undertaken due to danger of the boats' passage into the Yellow River. A rare meeting of Amherst, Guanghui and the other mandarins. There are problems of precedence in seating arrangements as both sides stand on their dignity.
8. The embassy makes good progress due to travelling under imperial orders that keep the channel cleared—innumerable boats detained under a temporary embargo while the embassy squadron passes. An increasing Chinese disposition of civility towards the British is noted.
9. An improvement in the appearance and habits of the people are noted by the British since crossing the Yellow River. Blue-brick houses and white-washed military barracks are seen and rice fields are noted for the first time.
10. The British received civil treatment by the local Chinese when out walking and are served tea. The British observe that they are restricted from landing at cities during the day due to an imperial order.
11. The most striking temple yet seen, the Temple of Gaomingsi. The British gain access to the temple through the obliging and civil kindness of two mandarins. Amherst given a conducted tour. Evidence of neglect noted. British go to the top level of the temple.

    Change of boats carried out with good humour. From now on communal meals are not possible.
12. Guanghui visits Amherst; very affable, but no official talks.

13 Toone and Martin (a midshipman on the *Alceste*) take a walk to visit a temple four miles away. They cause much alarm among the Chinese, even though the pair are accompanied by Chinese soldiers.

Morrison learns that the British ships had passed Zhejiang on their way to Canton and that the emperor had issued an edict to treat the embassy with civility and attention on their journey. One of the local officers said it was their duty to provide everything in their power and an honour to accommodate those 'who have travelled from so vast a distance to honour our country. China is indeed a great empire, but yours ranks in the world next to it' (Staunton, 1824, p. 230).

14 Amherst escorted around an imperial compound and garden (Garden of Wuyuan, last visited by the Qianlong emperor in 1780). Garden noted as very run down. Amherst is notified of the Jiaqing emperor's birthday celebrations are due to be held at Nanchang and is asked if he was willing to participate in proposed ceremony. The British make it clear there will be no kowtow. The British were prevented from visiting the islands where the 'Golden Mountain' is located.

15 A long walk in the fields. Still prevented from visiting the island.

16 Ellis crossed a bridge and entered the streets of Guazhou—a bustling city with shops and attractive women 'approaching our notions of beauty', but only a hasty glimpse as the soldiers were most active in enforcing the imperial edict that Chinese women not look on the strangers.

The mandarins in conversation with Morrison mention a favourable edict concerning the embassy's treatment and suggest that Amherst renew a direct intercourse with the Chinese Government, which was regarded as suspicious by Ellis. The British believed the emperor was obviously feeling dismayed by the treatment of the embassy, but none of these overtures were official. The British remained silent, which operated to keep Chinese apprehension alive of the possible effects of British resentment. The consent to exchange the few presents at Tongzhou was 'enough for conciliation' in Ellis's (1817) view: 'anything further, with ungenerous minds, might be mistaken for abject submission, if not positive alarm' (p. 290). Should the proposed acceptance of presents be rejected, 'the ground of dignified silence under provoked injury would have been lost, the regret of the Emperor for his conduct would have been removed' (p. 290).

18 The British walk around the town of Guazhou, but soldiers prevent their entry.
19 The embassy enters the Yangtze River.
20 Morrison receives a private copy of an imperial edict addressed to the viceroy of Jiangnan regarding the treatment of the embassy. The edict made clear the emperor's position:

- It was discovered that the ambassador had travelled overnight from Tongzhou and did not have his robes; because he dared not perform the ceremony in his ordinary clothes, he affirmed sickness.
- Heshitai did not report this correctly—his mistake—and the embassy was sent back.
- The emperor could not bear to reject the embassy, considering Britain had 'sent tribute of a sincere and devoted kind from so far in an expression of veneration and obedience' (as quoted in Ellis, 1817, p. 503).
- The emperor decided to accept the most trifling articles of tribute and bestow the kindness of receiving them.
- The emperor accepted maps, paintings and prints and conferred on the British sovereign a Jo-ee, purses and court beads to manifest the idea of giving much and receiving little.
- The ambassador received these with extreme joy and gratitude as showed by his manner, contrition and fear.
- The emperor instructed his officials to treat the ambassador civilly and appoint soldiers to conduct the safety of the embassy.
- The members of the embassy were not permitted to land or make disturbances throughout the whole route.
- The emperor instructed the military to have their armour fresh and shining, and weapons disposed in a commanding manner to maintain a formidable and dignified appearance.
- The emperor concluded that the embassy had come to China with the intention of offering tribute and ordered that it be treated with civility 'and silently cause it to feel gratitude and awe' (Ellis, 1817, pp. 502–503).

APPENDIX H

21 The viceroy of Jiangsu province paid a visit to Guanghui. Ellis observes the ceremonial formalities of their meeting. While no notice was taken of the embassy, Amherst ordered the guard and band to be drawn up for inspection. The embassy proceeded on its way. The city of Nanjing is seen in the distance.

Ellis says we 'may date our unrestrained liberty of excursion from this day'. It was promoted by Amherst's resistance at the gate.

Nanjing is rapidly decaying and the British express disgust at the filthy communal baths.

The viceroy was called away on a visit to an outlying district in the province and did not meet Amherst.

25 Amherst has a conversation with Guanghui on the public life of the emperor.

27 The embassy anchors at a small island, 'probably to render our intercourse with the inhabitants less easy' (Ellis, 1817, p. 309). The treasurer leaves the embassy without paying Amherst a farewell visit. The military officers are friendly in contrast to the civilian mandarins. Two are aware of the Duke of Wellington; Amherst gives one a medal containing a series of drawings representing the duke's battles.

30 Ellis (1817, p. 314) comments on the womanish appearance of the mandarins or total absence of manliness.

Another edict prohibiting the British from going ashore is issued.

November 1816

1 The British observe the beautiful variety of the banks of the Yangtze—mountains, hills, valleys, streams and woods—most picturesque combinations and delightful climate, 'but this only pleases the eye for a moment, and leaves the mind unsatisfied' (Ellis, 1817, p. 317).

3 The embassy arrives at Datong and stays for four days. Delightful walks noted.

4 Ellis much struck by the presence of the Chinese middling classes.

5 The embassy personnel see the tea plant for the first time. The local peasants civilly offer tea, although their exclamations at seeing the British are at first mistaken for insolence.

6 Another edict preventing the movement of the British is issued.

7   The embassy leaves Datong.

9   Despite the imperial edict, the shopkeepers of Anqing show no hesitation in selling the British any article they wish to purchase. There are lots of things to buy—necklaces, old china, agate cups, vases, etc.—but the British had neither money nor time to make purchases.

11 Heavy rain and boats leaking. A marine, Millidge, on duty at Morrison's boat, slips between the boats and drowns. Every assistance is afforded by the Chinese.

12 Funeral held for Millidge. Freshwater porpoises later seen.

14 Embassy leaves the Yangtze River and enters the Poyang Lake. The embassy reaches Dagu and stays for two days due to bad weather.

15 Rain delays. Purchases made at fine porcelain shops at very reasonable prices. British visit first halls or temples of Confucius and remark on their being no idols, but instead tablets bearing the names of 'deceased worthies'.

20 Embassy leaves Poyang Lake.

21 Guanghui sends Amherst a message requesting that no one enter the city of Nanchang because it is the emperor's birthday as well as the day of public examinations (the crowds would be disruptive).

22 Guanghui replies to Amherst's offer to fire a salute for the emperor's birthday: please decline because it is not the Chinese custom.

23 The embassy reaches Nanchang and resumes Macartney's route.

In shops it is observed that furs, porcelain, silks and glass paintings are not ill executed 'and interesting from the subjects being chosen in the scenes of domestic life' (Ellis, 1817, p. 352).

24 Guanghui expresses concern due to the presence of a military mandarin, second in command at Canton, who was passing through the city on his way to Peking and would report on what he had observed.

25 Guanghui, accompanied by the treasurer and judge of the district of Anhui, calls on Amherst. He voices regret at having to leave his friends in due course. Staunton expresses a hope that, like Sungyun, he would dine on board the British ships at Whampoa. He replied that although he was inferior to that distinguished mandarin, his feelings towards us were the same.

APPENDIX H

26 The embassy holds a cricket match.
27 The embassy leaves Nanchang.

   New boats noted as inferior (mat coverings). Constant rain. The Fuyuan at Nanchang had taken no notice of the embassy and Amherst sends a message regarding such rudeness with Morrison to Guanghui. The embassy enters a picturesque part of China—camellias noted.

December 1816

1   The embassy holds a cricket match. The British are prevented from visiting the town.
2   Reference made to the personal character of the governor preventing the British from visiting the town.
3   Over the last few days, the British anchorage has been enclosed by a railing to keep the local inhabitants out.
5   Very difficult and dangerous conditions for the boatmen—submerged rocks and strong currents. Boatmen navigate freezing water with a diet of only rice and a small quantity of meat.
7   Beautiful scenery described—river flowing between mountain ranges, highly picturesque wooded views, terraced valleys, pine trees and orange trees.
8   Abel reported as feeling better and collects tea plant samples.
11 The embassy visits the city of Ganzhou. The British note recent repairs to the city wall, presumably in anticipation of their visit. The 'commercial halls' of the Fukien merchants trading with Canton are mentioned.
13 The Chinese 'water-wheel' is admired as an outstanding piece of technology.
14 Staunton refers to the fact that the embassy has seen 27 pagodas during its journey.
15 The British learn that the five ships of the embassy have arrived at the port of Canton.
17 Amherst has a rare meeting with Guanghui, but as there were no British interpreters present, only 'A-chow' the Canton linguist, Amherst refused to hold any conversation conducted through 'that channel'.

18 The British leave the boats at Nankang for the land journey over the Meiling Mountains.

19 Noted in the town of 'Kong-quan' are several store houses through which all goods must pass into the Chinese interior. The 'invigorating influence' of European commerce is noted on the town and its people.

   The British luggage and articles are in the process of being packed up for the journey over the mountain into Guangdong province.

20 Some of the British hear the term 'fan-quei' as well as other forms of rudeness directed at them, as witnessed at Canton.

   Evidence of graffiti left by the Dutch embassy of 1795 seen engraved on the doors of a house.

25 The embassy reaches Shaoguan.

   The British are outraged that the legate is assigned a much superior boat to that of the ambassador. Appearances are important as the British draw closer to Canton.

January 1817

1 The embassy arrives at Canton.

2 Guanghui pays a call.

3 Amherst holds a function attended by all the gentlemen of the Factory and the American Consul.

7 A formal ceremony with the viceroy is held where a letter from the Jiaqing emperor to the Prince Regent is handed to Amherst.

9 Amherst and the commissioners pay a formal call on Guanghui.

   Afterwards, Amherst holds a function for the Hong merchants who attend wearing their 'state dresses'.

13 Staunton hosts a public breakfast for Guanghui at the British Factory.

19 Guanghui pays a final call on Amherst.

20 The ambassador, commissioners and suite embark at Whampoa, on board the HMS *Alceste*, to depart China.

Appendix I: Morrison's Letters to Amherst (1821)

Copy of Morrison's first letter to Amherst (date unknown, but written prior to November 1821) (in BL IOR MSS EUR F 140/50 (b))

My Lord,

I had the honour to receive the Letter you sent me in reply to my request concerning the Anglo-Chinese College; & beg to [give] … sincere thanks for your kindness.

The Monarch who in anger drove us from his Court, died in Tartary, suddenly on Sep 2 1820. His eldest son living has ascended the throne, and adopted the Title Taou-kwang [Daoguang] which means 'Season's glory'.

There remains a good deal of mystery in this part of the Empire respecting the demise of His late Majesty - the prevailing report is that he died a violent death, & that his successor has usurped the throne, Kia King [Jiaqing] having intended it for his fourth son.

My family Mrs Morrison & two children returned to China this year, & by divine goodness we all enjoy tolerable health.

I observe in the Peking Gazette that the Nobleman we called Duke Ho, is much employed by the new Monarch. He was restored & degraded more than once since his degradation on account of his behaviour to us.

The venerable Soo remained in high offices till the late Emperor's death - I have not seen his name mentioned since.

The Legate Kwang [Guanghui] has been a salt Commissioner at a place near the Po-yang Lake ever since his restoration; he is expected here as Commissioner of import & export duties, an Officer here called the Hoppo.

I beg my remembrance to my old acquaintance the Hon. Mr. Amherst [Jeffrey]. I pray God to keep him from the many temptations to which his rank & circumstances expose him.

I remain with respect,
My Lord,
Your Hon. Servant
(signed) R. Morrison

Copy of Morrison's second letter to Amherst, Canton, China, 26 November 1821 (in BL IOR MSS EUR F 140/50 (b))

My Lord,

Kwang Tajin [Guanghui] concerning whom you wrote to me, departed this life before I received your Letter. Instead of coming to Canton he was appointed Judge of the Province of Chih-le, and died in his boat just as he reached the borders of the region over which he was to preside: it was at the place where we were together about this time of the year in 1816. The officer who attended the Embassy whilst at the Joss-house in Canton is also dead. Duke Ho is still Commissioner of the Troops in Fo-kien Province.

Death, my Lord has also visited my family since I parted with you: Mrs Morrison fell a sacrifice to Cholera Morbus at Macao in June last. She was ill only 14 hours. I hope she "fell asleep in Jesus" - & that her immortal spirit is happy in heaven.

I had a good Letter from Hayne; he was well, but did not seem to like his situation.

Canton has been a good deal agitated this season by a case of homicide, or accidental death. A Chinese boat woman was drowned and an American seaman was charged … The Americans resisted the man's being delivered to the Chinese after which they relinquished the poor man, who protested his innocence; & the Chinese strangled him two days after they got him into their possession.

The present Emperor is deemed more decided in his conduct than his Father. During the 8th moon an epidemic prevailed in Peking which appears to have been a sort of Cholera… His Majesty gave considerable sums to buy medicines for the sick, & coffins for the dead. And according to the usage of the Imperial Family, he has sent to prepare his own tomb in the Mountains of Tartary.

I remain
Your Lordship's
Most Obedient Servant
(signed) R. Morrison

Index

Note: Page numbers in italics indicate illustrations or maps. Page numbers with 'n' indicate footnotes.

Abel, Clarke
    description of kowtow, 178–179
    perceptions of British, 155–156
    published account of Amherst Embassy, 10
    responses to Hong Kong, 139–140
ambassadors
    appearance, 108–109, 277
    characteristics, 67
    kowtow, 93–95, 102–103
    role, 23, 233–234, 282, 283, 314
    selection, 70–72
    status, 114, 185, 215, 235, 239
America
    perceptions of China, 298
    trade, 64–65, 65n5
Amherst Embassy. *see also* overland travel by Amherst Embassy
    analysis, 14
    assumptions, 2, 44, 50
    band, 89, 154, 166, 266–267, 269
    British East India Company role, 70–74
    in British media, 286, 289–294
    camaraderie, 124, 138, 163–164, 262–263, 265–267, 300
    comparison with Macartney Embassy, 233–234, 255, 287
    cost, 345–347, 349
    dismissal, 235
    dismissal from Qing court, 233–234
    errors, 309–310
    gifts, 111–112, 248
    historical research, 6–9
    intelligence basis, 68–69
    itinerary, 363–376
    journals, 11
    legacy, 287–288, 294–298
    membership, 89–90, 341–343
    motivations for, 54–56, 65–67, 92
    negotiations to enter China, 147–161
    objectives, 69–70, 117, 120–121, 132, 133, 157
    official approval of, 70
    official records of, 11–12
    preparation, 87–88, 91–93, 114–115
    prospects of success, 136–137, 301
    provisions, 114–115, 165
    published accounts, 10–11
    return to Britain, 279–283, 286–287
    salaries, 341–343
    secrecy, 74, 135, 144, 310
    selection of ambassador, 70–72
    status, 249
    summary, 363–376
    timing, 73–74, 122, 131, 153, 310

and trade, 66–67, 146, 287–288, 294–297
transport, 216–218, 229–230, 273 (*see also* sea travel; ships)
ulterior motives, 67, 351
Amherst, Jeffrey (son of William Pitt), 158, 167, 210
account of dismissal, 227
account of journey to Tongzhou, 229–230
to join Amherst Embassy, 87
journal, 11
voyage to China, 125
Amherst, Sarah (wife of William Pitt), 77–78, 79n25, 83, 84–85
Amherst, William Pitt
appointment to Embassy, 72–74, 83–85
background, 75–77
court experience, 80–82, 215
diplomatic experience, 30–31, 81–82
finances, 80, 84
first meeting with Chinese authorities, 151–153
home life, 79
kowtow, 208, 210–212, 304–305
leadership, 3, 124, 146, 299–300, 307
Lord of the Bedchamber, 80
loyalty, 63
marriage, 77–78, 83, 84, 122
military service, 79–80
personality, 30, 82–83, 300
preparation for Embassy, 91–93, 102–107, 120–122
Prince Regent, perceptions of, 81, 81n29, 81n30
privy counsellor, 116
responses to appointment, 86–88
Rio de Janeiro, 129
salary as ambassador, 70, 84, 87, 341

Anglo–Persian Definitive Treaty, 73n12
appearances in diplomacy. *see also* attire
importance of, 108–109, 183–184, 223, 234–237, 277
Macartney Embassy, 44, 100
role of display, 106
attire
Amherst Embassy members, 45, 151, 156, 175
Chinese military, 267–268
Chinese people, 147–148, 182
differences in, 148, 264
in diplomacy, 151–152, 156, 174–175
Macartney Embassy members, 100
mandarins, 149, 158, 183–184, 196

Baikov Embassy, 94
Ball, Samuel, 351–353
Banks, Joseph, 89
Barrow, John, 4
attitudes towards France, 65–66
biography of Macartney, 92, 96, 107
friendship with Staunton, 34–35, 36, 309–310
praise for Staunton, 66
support for British Embassy, 50, 61, 64, 309–310
Travels in China, 12, 48, 143, 247, 259, 301
views on China, 110–112, 113, 251, 293–294, 314
Batavia, 130–131
Britain
British navy, 55–56, 57
cuisine, 266
diplomatic missions, 93
HMS *Doris*, 55–56, 57
identity, 32

income from tea, 1n1, 24, 296
manufacturing, 110, 112–113, 121, 153
monarchy, 30–32
nationalism, 30–32, 81, 265–267
occupation of East Indies, 131
occupation of Macao, 28–30, 49, 311
perceptions of Canton, 27
porcelain, 113, 153
response to Amherst Embassy dismissal, 235–236, 289–294
reverence for monarchy, 81
sensory tastes, 113, 128–130, 182–183
as world power, 64
British East India Company. *see also* tea; trade
background, 24–25
Board of Control, 24–25
charter, 295–297
conflicts with local Chinese people, 25, 39–40
governance of India, 24
management, 24–25
monopoly on tea, 20, 24, 53, 295–297
official records, 11–12
perceptions of kowtow, 8–9
relationship with Chinese trade authorities, 20–21, 29, 53, 54–56, 59–60
role in diplomacy, 45, 46–47, 49–50, 67–70, 74, 302
role in selecting ambassador, 71
Secret Committee, 25
secret report, 351–353
Select Committee, 25, 54–56, 132, 296
selection of Amherst Embassy members, 67, 71
tea income, 1n1, 24, 296
threatened withdrawal of, 57
trade disputes, 1, 54–55

British perceptions of China, 90, 245
art, 258–259
Canton, 27
children, 169, 262
cuisine, 160, 168, 180, 218–219, 251
emperor, 9, 14, 189, 291
landscape, 168–169, 252
military, 167
people, 156, 158, 161, 247, 251–252, 257, 273–276
role of senses, 253–255
Tartar people, 14, 224, 233, 274
British worldview, 247
exceptionalism, 44, 69, 93, 104–105, 132–133, 162, 300
impact of Amherst Embassy dismissal, 249
travelling, 127–130, 139, 182–183, 257
British–Chinese diplomacy, 56, 293. *see also* imperial banquet; kowtow; mandarins; royal letters
bowing, 176, 232
British expectations, 69, 104–105, 107, 186, 233, 310
British presence in Peking, 43
conflict, 196–198, 209, 223–226, 256, 271–272
consular representation, 210
futility, 314–315
hospitality, 221–226, 228, 248, 256, 276–279, 315–316
impact of Amherst Embassy failure, 286
lack of trust, 59–60, 137, 298, 307–308, 310
reciprocity, 115, 121, 303
reconciliation, 242–243, 315–316
restrictions on cross-cultural communication, 20, 54–55, 58–59, 253, 260–262, 302
timing of Amherst Embassy announcement, 73–74

383

British–Chinese trade relationship, 18
  conflicting beliefs, 32
  inequality in, 311, 314
Buckinghamshire, Lord, 24, 64n4
  Board of Control of British East India Company, 24, 53, 66–67, 68
  choice of ambassador, 71–72
  correspondence with Amherst, 72, 119–120
  death, 120

Campbell, Walter, 123
Canning, George, 24, 76
Canton
  Amherst Embassy stay, 276–279
  authorities, 140–141
  Government interpreters, 226–227
  viceroy, 47, 48, 50–51
Canton trade system, 19–21, 311
  advantages, 21
  Factories (trading establishments), 20n10
  Hong merchants (official Chinese merchants), 20n10, 21, 133–134, 294–295, 296
  Hoppo (Chinese superintendent of customs), 20–21, 54–55, 133
  impact of Amherst Embassy, 294–295
  impact of international conflicts, 27–30
  trade authorities, 68–69
Cape Town, 130
ceremony in diplomacy
  importance of, 97–98, 107–108, 178–179, 181
  in tribute system of diplomacy, 17
  in Westphalian system of diplomacy, 185
Chang-wei, 149–151, 154, 155, 157, 159–160, 275, 355
  departure, 248
  kowtow discussions, 190–191, 192, 202–205
  promotion, 241
China. *see also* British–Chinese diplomacy; British–Chinese trade relationship; Jiaqing emperor; Qianlong emperor; Qing court
  Bocca Tigris ('the Bogue'), 26
  Chinese Embassies, 95
  Chinese exceptionalism, 300
  Confucian order, 17, 215
  domestic life, 290
  emperor, 16–17
  military force, 29–30, 267–268, 271–272
  and Nepal, 67n7
  Pearl River, 25–27, *26*
  perceptions of Britain, 236
  porcelain, 113, 153
  private trading, 18
  regulation of language (*see* cross-cultural communication)
  regulation of trade, 19–21, 54, 353
  suspicion of Britain, 28, 29–30, 58–60, 137
  Tartar people, 14, 224, 233, 274
  tribute system of diplomacy, 16–18
  worldview, 15
Chinese diplomacy. *see also* imperial banquet
  British expectations of, 197
  Chinese–Russian treaties, 94
  legates, 186, 191
  protocols, 51–52, 118
  symbolism, 101, 175, 178–179, 184–185, 193, 213
Chinese emperor. *see also* Jiaqing emperor; Kangxi court; kowtow; Qianlong emperor
  Son of Heaven, 16–17
  sovereignty, 187–188, 241
chinoiserie trend, 19, 258

Company. *see* British East India Company
Confucius, 17, 215
Cooke, Lieutenant, 154–155
cross-cultural communication, 148
  advantages of, 39
  ambassadors, 22
  Canton Government interpreters, 226–227
  fears of, 312
  in Macartney Embassy, 98, 99
  misunderstanding, 6
  restrictions on, 20, 54–55, 58–59, 253, 260–262, 302
  role in diplomacy, 44, 49, 106, 117, 167, 226–227
  in trade, 39–40, 69
crossing-the-line ceremony, 127

Dagu, 166–167
Davis, John Francis, 211
  account of journey to Tongzhou, 230
  on Amherst Embassy failure, 311–312
  discussion with Cantonese mandarin, 194
  proficiency in Mandarin, 74
  published account of Amherst Embassy, 10, 267
  views on China, 257
diplomacy. *see also* ambassadors; appearances in diplomacy; attire; royal letters
  ceremony (*see* ceremony in diplomacy)
  conflict, 190
  dishonesty, 233, 279, 291–292, 308
  equality, 105, 108, 185, 215, 314
  gifts (*see* gifts in diplomacy)
  hospitality, 221–226, 228, 248, 256, 276–279, 315–316
  interpreters (*see* cross-cultural communication)
  merchants' involvement in, 132–135
  reception of visitors, 169
  relationship with trade, 15, 31–32, 110, 181, 194, 287–288, 294–297
  role of dining, 171, 179–180, 184–185, 218–219, 229, 302
  role of letters, 132, 147, 148, 150–151, 157, 201–204
  secrecy, 310
  Treaty of Amiens, 28
  Treaty of Kyakhta, 94
  Treaty of Nanjing, 19
  Treaty of Nerchinsk, 94
  Treaty of Westphalia, 22
  trust, 59–60, 137, 279, 298, 306, 307–308, 310
  Western diplomacy, 185, 215, 234, 314
Drury, William, 28–29
Dutch East Indies, 130–131
Dutch Embassy, 93, 94, 100–101

Ellis, Henry
  account of Nanjing, 257
  advice on kowtow, 163, 198, 208, 210, 239, 304
  appointment to Amherst Embassy, 73
  published account of Amherst Embassy, 10, 285, 289–290
  responses to Rio de Janeiro, 128–129
  view on trade in China, 296
Elphinstone, John, 70, 73, 136n16

first European woman to visit northern China, 14
First Opium War, 297–298
France. *see also* Napoleon
  allegiance with Portugal, 27–28

diplomatic relationship with China, 65
French Revolution, 30 (*see also* international conflicts)
at war with Britain, 27, 30
Fuyuan meeting with Metcalfe, 132–133

General Hewitt, 123, 127, 136, 165–166, 272. *see also* sea travel; ships
tea trade, 285, 295
George III (King of England), 30
gifts in diplomacy
   choice of, 110–112
   formal acceptance, 46, 206
   Macartney Embassy, 100
   partial acceptance, 231–232, 242
   return of, 102
   transport of, 248
   tribute system of diplomacy, 16–17
Golovkin Embassy, 92, 100–102
   imperial breakfast, 101–102, 171
   refusal to kowtow, 48
Guangdong. *see* Fuyuan meeting with Metcalfe
Guanghui, 167, 190, 355–356
   Amherst Embassy escort, 152, 279
   exchange of presents, 231–232
   initial meeting, 154–155
   as intermediary to ministers, 170, 187–188
   kowtow negotiations, 177–178, 191–192, 194–195
   punishment, 213, 241–242
   role in Amherst Embassy dismissal, 227, 240
   role in overland voyage, 248, 256–257, 258

Hale, Elizabeth (sister to William Pitt), 11, 75n16, 77–78
Hall, Basil, 123, 129, 143–144, 158
   interactions with local Chinese, 147–149, 160
   perceptions of Amherst Embassy, 136–137
   published accounts of travels, 10–11
Havell, William, 125, 140, *250,* 251–252, 258–260
Hayne, Henry, 186–187
   journal, 11
   responses to Rio de Janeiro, 128
Heshitai, 356–357
   Amherst Embassy handler, 193
   British perceptions of, 292–293
   communications with Chinese emperor, 212
   discussions with, 199–202, 209–210, 305
   punishment of, 237–238, 241
   role in Amherst Embassy's dismissal, 223–226, 240–241
HMS *Alceste,* 165–166, *271. see also* sea travel; ships
   arrival in South China Sea, 136
   conflict at Pearl River, 270–272
   crossing-the-line ceremony, 127
   Maxwell, Murray, 89–90, 122, 270–272
   passengers, 123
   preparation, 114–115, 122
   visit from mandarins, 155–160
   voyage to China, 123–125
   wreck, 280–281
HMS *Doris,* 55–56, 57
HMS *Lyra,* 123, 127, 136, 147, 165–166. *see also* sea travel; ships
Hong Kong, 137
   Amherst Embassy stay, 136, 139–141
   first reference in British sources, 13
Howqua, 133–134

imperial banquet
   analysis of, 182–186
   impact on Amherst Embassy, 173, 302
   overview, 174–181

imperial edicts, 188, 242, 245, 252, 255, 270, 361
international conflicts, 27–30
    Anglo–American War, 55–56, 60
    French–British wars, 27, 30
Ismailof Embassy, 92, 94–95, 99

Jahangir emperor, 93
Jesuit missionaries
    blame, 98, 103
    perceptions of, 65
    support for British Embassy to China, 43
    views on Macartney Embassy, 99–100
Jiaqing emperor, 28, 29–30, 103–104. *see also* kowtow; Qing court
    Amherst Embassy edicts, 188, 242, 245, 252, 255, 270, 361
    Amherst Embassy planned reception, 237–240, 305, 359–360
    Amherst Embassy reception, 221–228, 234–235, 240–242
    attitude towards Europeans, 40, 60, 311
    British perceptions of, 291
    communication with, 191, 194, 199
    gifts from, 158
    imperial permission, 140–141, 186, 189–190
    kowtow, 44, 48, 95
    physician, 227, 241
    rebukes from, 57–58, 227
    reign, 291
    suspicion of Morrison, 58–59, 302
    suspicion of Staunton, 57–59, 66, 133–134, 204–206, 207–208, 302, 312

Kangxi court, 94, 99, 110n19
kowtow. *see also* British–Chinese diplomacy; diplomacy
    as act of submission, 31–32
    Amherst Embassy decision, 210–212, 304–305
    Amherst's instructions, 117–120, 161, 303, 308
    approach of Jiaqing emperor, 44
    Baikov Embassy, 94
    British understanding of, 44
    compromise, 95, 98, 176, 177, 192
    and diplomatic failure, 99, 101–102, 236, 302–303
    discussions of, 157, 161–166, 190–192, 193–194, 302–305
    Dutch Embassy, 93, 94, 100–101
    expected by Qing court, 47, 161
    Golovkin Embassy, 48, 92, 100–102, 171
    impact on trade, 211–212, 288, 294–295, 307
    implications for British sovereignty, 7, 107, 163, 185, 208, 283, 306–307
    Ismailof Embassy, 92, 94–95, 99
    negotiations, 157, 175–178, 181, 213–214
    perceptions of, 8–9, 99, 239, 298
    planned Amherst Embassy reception, 238–240
    portraits, 98, 153, 191, 195, 232
    Portuguese Embassy, 99, 107n16
    refusal, 94, 107, 185–186, 200–201
    role, 16, 203, 282–283
    similarity to Mughal court ceremony, 93

Lamiot, Louis, 41, 98–99, 102–107, 278, 312

M'Leod, John, 10, 159
Macao, 28–30, 49, 311
Macartney Embassy
    comparison with Amherst Embassy, 233–234, 255, 287

journal of Macartney, 92, 96–98
kowtow, 97–98, 176–177, 176n6, 209
legacy, 2, 43–44, 68, 106, 116–117, 301, 309
official account, 12, 117–118
overland travel, *246,* 250–251
precedent, 98, 102, 107, 161–163, 204, 302, 309
reception at Qing court, 43
role of mandarins, 96, 97
Macartney kowtow debate, 52
agreeing to kowtow, 176–177, 188, 279, 305
Chinese imperial records, 204
Jiaqing emperor's recollection, 302–303
Macartney's biography, 107–108
refusal to kowtow, 6, 98, 99, 102, 116–117
Staunton's recollection, 176–177, 192
unlikeliness of kowtow, 176n6, 195n17
Madeira, 126–127
Manchu language, 44
Mandarin language
in diplomacy, 49, 50, 68, 101, 106
restrictions on, 58, 302
role in Amherst Embassy, 70
mandarins, 355–357
access to Chinese emperor, 102–103, 141, 308
Amherst Embassy negotiations, 147, 193–202, 209–210, 212–213, 308
British perceptions of, 275
contact with Amherst Embassy, 149–151
in diplomacy, 215, 277–278
gifts, 111–112
role in Amherst Embassy dismissal, 228, 233, 241
Manning, Thomas, 66n6, 211
appearance, 138

membership in Amherst Embassy, 138–139
proficiency in Mandarin, 138–139
Martin, William Fanshawe, 11
Maxwell, Murray, 89–90, 122. *see also* HMS *Alceste*
conflict at Pearl River, 270–272
Metcalfe, Thomas
advice on kowtow, 163
meeting with Fuyuan, 132–136
Ming dynasty, 18
missionaries
in Canton, 58, 58n36
in Imperial court, 98–100
in Peking, 41, 65, 288
Morrison, Robert, 211
letters to Amherst, 377–379
negotiations with officials, 154–155, 170, 190, 203, 209
omission in interpretation, 209
proficiency in Mandarin, 58–59, 74, 138–139, 302
published account of Amherst Embassy, 10
translations, 13, 302
Mughal court embassies, 93
Muketenge, 357
appointment as Amherst Embassy handler, 193
discussions with, 199–202
role in Amherst Embassy dismissal, 227, 241

Nanjing, 255–258
Napoleon, 281–283. *see also* France
abdication, 64
exile, 126
views on kowtow, 282–283

opium trade, 7–8, 24, 205n23, 297–298. *see also* First Opium War
overland travel by Amherst Embassy, 165, 189, 242, *246*
accounts by members, 249–250

cost, 248
cricket, 262–263
crowds, 254–255, 257, 259, 261
cultural opportunity, 255–256, 260–262, 270, 275
dining, 265–267
imperial edicts, 242, 245, 252, 255, 270, 361
morale, 265–270
perceptions of Chinese people, 251–252, 260–262, 273–276
restrictions on, 245, 253, 263–265
route, 247, 270
sensory experiences, 253–255
treatment by Chinese, 268–269

pace of communications, 25, 56, 68, 73–74, 92, 310
impact on Amherst Embassy, 64
Peking Gazette, 41–42, 240
Portugal, 27–28
anti-British propaganda, 137
missionaries, 41
Portuguese Embassy, 99, 107n16
Portuguese royal family, 127, 128, 280
presence in Macao, 28, 137, 280
Puankhequa, 133

Qianlong emperor, 44. *see also* kowtow; Qing court
British perceptions of, 291
dismissal of gifts, 110
and Macartney Embassy, 116, 177
Qing court. *see also* Chinese emperor; Jiaqing emperor; Qianlong emperor; Yuanmingyuan
Amherst Embassy planned reception, 238–240, 310–311
Amherst Embassy reception, 154–155, 221–228
British expectations, 137, 186, 212, 233, 301, 309, 310
codes of behaviour, 215

dismissal from, 93–94, 187, 190, 226–230, 242–243
exceptions made for British Embassy, 44
interests, 110
officials, 14
protocols, 6, 152, 235, 293, 301
treaties, 94
variations to tribute system, 18
worldview, 300–301

Rio de Janeiro, 127–130
Roe, Thomas, 93
royal letters
in diplomacy, 42–44, 49, 104, 206, 225, 315
presentation of, 223, 238–239, 277–278
reception of, 170
wording of, 188
Russian–Chinese diplomacy
Baikov Embassy, 94
Golovkin Embassy, 48, 92, 100–102, 171
Ismailof Embassy, 92, 94–95, 99
Russian–Chinese treaties, 94

scale of civilisation, 247, 259, 274
sea travel
crossing-the-line ceremony, 127
imperial permission, 140–141, 189–190
navigation, 143–144, *145*
typhoon season, 122, 128
voyage to China, 123–131, 136–141, 143–146
ships
authority over, 189
departure, 189–190
hospitality, 147–153, 155–161, 196–198
movements, 205, 206, 214
wreckage, 280–281

Staunton, G. L. (George Leonard, father to George Thomas), 3n4
    death, 45n15
    education of son, 35–37
Staunton, George Thomas, *34*
    advice on kowtow, 3, 162–163, 208–209, 211–212, 305–307, 308
    ambitions for British Embassy, 40, 42–44, 49–50
    ambivalence towards British Embassy, 60–61
    appointment to Amherst Embassy, 70, 73, 135–136, 137–138, 302
    background, 35–37
    conversation with Qianlong emperor at age twelve, 3, 36, 161, 171
    employment with British East India Company, 37, 38
    in England, 45–46
    friendship with Sungyun, 50–53, 131–132, 171, 252
    income, 46
    intelligence on Qing court, 40–42
    leading British sinologist, 34–35
    letters of, 12–13, 33
    on Napoleon, 283
    personality, 33
    proficiency in Mandarin, 37–38, 66, 302
    Providence affair, 39–40, 42
    published account of Amherst Embassy, 10
    role in trade negotiations, 57–58
    school visit in China, 262
    translations, 13, 35, 42
    understanding of Chinese customs, 51–52
    views on trade in China, 296–297
Sulenge, 167, 356
    appointment of, 164
    attitude towards British, 152–153
    description, 170
    exchange of presents, 231–232
    as intermediary to ministers, 170, 187–188
    kowtow negotiations, 176–178, 191–192, 194–195
    punishment, 213, 241–242
    reception of Amherst Embassy, 160
    role in Amherst Embassy dismissal, 240
Sungyun, 50–53, 131–132, 171, 252

Tartar ceremony. *see* kowtow
Tartar court. *see* Qing court
Tartar people, 14, 224, 233, 274
tea. *see also* British East India Company
    British income from, 1n1, 24, 296
    Chief Inspector of Teas at Canton, 351–353
    international trade, 65n5
    monopoly on, 20, 24, 53, 295–297
    secret report on tea trade, 351–353
    trade disputes, 1
    value of, 296–297
Tianjin, 169–171
Tongzhou
    Amherst Embassy arrival, 194–195
    return voyage to, 228–230
Toone, Robert, 74, 211
    interactions with local Chinese, 147–149
trade. *see also* British East India Company; Canton trade system
    benefits, 22
    Chinese regulation, 19–21, 54, 353
    free trade, 53, 297
    impact of peace, 65
    local trade authorities, 68–69
    military force, 28–30, 46–47, 57–58, 295, 297, 313–314

INDEX

permits, 25
private trade, 18
Regency-era approach, 30
role in diplomacy, 15, 31–32, 110, 181, 194, 287–288, 294–297
secret report, 351–353
secured by tribute system, 16
supercargoes (Western traders), 19, 21, 25
Travels in China, 12, 48, 143, 247, 259, 301
Treaty of Amiens, 28
Treaty of Kyakhta, 94
Treaty of Nanjing, 19
Treaty of Nerchinsk, 94
Treaty of Westphalia, 22
tribute system of diplomacy, 16–18
   advantages of, 17–18
   British assumptions regarding, 50, 104
   conflict with Westphalian system, 105, 107, 185, 215
   right to trade, 16
   role of ambassador, 283
   role in Amherst's treatment by Chinese court, 9
   variations by Qing dynasty, 18
   vassal states, 31

Westphalian system of diplomacy, 22–23, 108, 313
   conflict with tribute system, 105, 107, 185, 215
   role of ambassador, 23, 282
   Treaty of Westphalia, 22
Whampoa, 270–272

Yellow Sea, 146
Yin, 149, 154, 155, 158, 160, 355
   departure, 248
   kowtow discussions, 190–191, 192
   role in Amherst Embassy dismissal, 227
Yuan dynasty, 13
Yuanmingyuan
   Amherst Embassy dismissal from, 227–228
   Amherst Embassy reception, 221–226
   voyage to, 215–221

www.ingramcontent.com/pod-product-compliance
Lightning Source LLC
Chambersburg PA
CBHW040209020526
44112CB00040B/2859